via Border ☑ S0-AGI-227

08th–15th Oct, 2009 (mailed)

CAPTAIN AMERICA AND
THE CRUSADE AGAINST EVIL

CAPTAIN AMERICA AND THE CRUSADE AGAINST EVIL

The Dilemma of Zealous Nationalism

Robert Jewett

and

John Shelton Lawrence

William B. Eerdmans Publishing Company
Grand Rapids, Michigan / Cambridge, U.K.

Wm. B. Eerdmans Publishing Co.
255 Jefferson Ave. S.E., Grand Rapids, Michigan 49503 /
P.O. Box 163, Cambridge CB3 9PU U.K.

Printed in the United States of America

08 07 06 05 04 03   7 6 5 4 3 2 1

Library of Congress Cataloging-in-Publication Data

Jewett, Robert.
    Captain America and the crusade against evil: the dilemma of zealous nationalism /
    Robert Jewett and John Shelton Lawrence.
        p.   cm.
    Includes bibliographical references and indexes.
    ISBN 0-8028-6083-4 (pbk.: alk. paper)
        1. United States — Foreign relations — 2001-   2. United States — Foreign
    relations — 20th century.   3. United States — Politics and government — 2001-
    4. Messianism, Political — United States.   5. Millennialism — United States.
    6. Jihad.   7. War on Terrorism, 2001 — Causes.   8. Civil religion — United States.
    9. Islam — Relations — Christianity.   10. Christianity and other religions — Islam.
    I. Lawrence, John Shelton.   II. Title.

E902.J49   2003
303.48′273017671 — dc21

                                     2002073880

www.eerdmans.com

To the memory of R. Franklin Terry,
   generous spirit and faithful critic

Contents

Preface

The title of our book comes from a comic-book character who combines explosive strength with perfect moral intuitions. In his public life Captain America serves as Private Rogers in the uniformed armed service, but when the level of danger becomes unbearable, he takes on a masked identity and rids the world of evil. Having grown up with Captain America during World War II, we met him again as our students helped us untangle America's sense of mission — and its affinity for violent crusading. This book explains the religious roots and historical development of this crusading tendency.

The "Captain America complex" that we describe in the following pages is the uneasy fusion of two kinds of roles. Should America be the "city set upon a hill" that promotes the rule of law even when faced with difficult adversaries? Or should it crusade on the military plane of battle, allowing no law or institution to impede its efforts to destroy evil?

As we completed the text of this manuscript in the winter of 2001-2002, while the World Trade Center's wreckage was still being trucked away from "Ground Zero," we were concerned about the United States' tendency toward military crusading. Sadly, our premonitions concerning zealotry's seductive call are being confirmed. As we write this preface in the autumn of 2002, events suggest that the increasingly strident crusade has undermined the global consensus that formed so quickly after the crimes of September 11, 2001. But we also find new signs of hope. Whether the signs are ominous or hopeful, we suggest that an understanding of the Captain America complex as a contradictory form of civil religion casts light on current developments and suggests a more promising path for the future.

In the international arena, we were heartened by the expressions of unity and sympathy in the aftermath of the tragedies of September 11. The Bush administration's prompt and eloquent appearance at the United Nations rapidly secured resolutions expressing world unity against terrorism that temporarily stirred a sense that new forces for world peace might prevail. In particular, we hoped that America might follow through on an earlier commitment to the International Criminal Court, a legal venue that seemed promising for the likes of Osama bin Laden and Saddam Hussein. But those hopes were quickly dashed, and this book's analysis of the links between American civil religion and popular entertainments explains their sudden eclipse. As the United States leaders contemplated their crusade in the post-9/11 world, they decided not to risk accountability to any form of international law. In July 2002, the United States wrangled a one-year exemption from any criminal prosecution by the ICC. Then, looking beyond its year of immunity, the Bush administration began to secure permanent exemptions through bilateral agreements — with Israel, Romania, and several other small nations as the first trophies. It coupled these initiatives with threats to withhold military aid from any country that would become a member of the ICC.

The world was puzzled. Why would a nation engaged in a global campaign against terrorism seem so obsessively opposed to an institution so well suited to its prosecution — and thus risk alienating most of its allies? Why would it opt out of shaping ICC statutes and procedures in directions that meet its sense of justice? Why abandon the commitment to international law that had transformed the second half of the twentieth century? Foreign commentators complained of unilateralism and hegemony, but such charges seem insufficient to account for the self-righteous passions of American policymakers.

We suggest that this seemingly illogical behavior points to a national fascination with stories of selfless crusaders who, like Captain America, must take on a secret identity and circumvent the law to rescue the innocent. Translated as an impulse for the world stage, the mythic imperative requires shielding American warriors in the war against terrorism, no matter how many rules they break or how unpopular they may become. That President Bush relished his depiction as Rambo by the German press (an incident discussed in chapter 3) seems consistent with the notion that crusading above the law has emotional resonance for a leader sworn to uphold the Constitution.

This book also sheds light on the idea of an "axis of evil" and the doctrine of preventive military strikes. Echoing conspiracy theories that have justified so many hostilities in earlier times, these doctrines warrant attacks based on suspicions rather than overt acts; they are typical expressions of the crusading mentality that this book seeks to explain; and they have spread fears about the unpredictability and potential illegality of future American actions. Compounding the anger over civilian casualties in Afghanistan, the United States isolated itself further by expressing irritation at appeals for lawful cooperation in dealing with terrorist threats and by advocating military actions that violate international law. Even that cooperation, which has been significant to date, has been redefined by the spirit of zealous command: If you are not for us, you are against us; anyone who fails to support our world-wide crusade is giving aid and comfort to the terrorists, and so forth. Though the world has much to fear from Saddam Hussein, Captain America's crusade has evoked fears among our closest allies. Almost every country that initially showed solidarity after September 11 now gives evidence of serious alienation.

In Israel, the setting for much of what we have to say about the collision of Christian, Islamic, and Jewish crusading, the scene has sadly degenerated beyond our pessimism at the time we wrote about the rebirth of millennial zealotry (chapter 8) and the globalization of zeal and militant jihad (chapter 9). Israel is the country whose ancient spiritual legacies of redemptive wrath and redemptive love energize both strands of America's divided consciousness. Now it is an arena of intensified conflict that conveys more and more the rhetoric and deadly flavor of holy war. Nevertheless, there are a few hopeful voices among Muslim leaders denouncing suicidal jihad and among Israeli and American activist organizations, such as Tikkun, who are determined to find fairness in dealing with the occupied territories.

One of our book's most important goals is to sustain the ideals of constitutional democracy that always suffer strain during crisis. The USA Patriot Act of 2001 has authorized intrusive restrictions of democratic rights that are taken for granted during normal times, and its long-term consequences could be extremely serious. Although the country went through the immediate trauma of 9/11 without the equivalent of World War II's internment of Japanese-Americans, we have seen executive initiatives for broad powers of secret, legally unsupervised detention. Since 9/11, the United States has imprisoned over a thousand people without releasing their names. A large number of prisoners arrested in Afghanistan remain at the Guantanamo base in Cuba, where they have no standing under U.S. law and no recognized status as prisoners of war governed by the Geneva Convention.

Another trend that concerns us is the rise of a zealous cult of the nation. In the Ninth Circuit Court in California, an atheist father challenged the "under God" component of the Pledge of Allegiance as a violation of his daughter's rights. When the court ruled in his favor on the basis of the "establishment clause" of the First Amendment, a national firestorm of piety followed. Senate majority leader Tom Daschle urged his colleagues to publicly affirm the full pledge as their expression of contempt for the court's decision, and there were many calls for new legislation — even a constitutional amendment — to place "under God" beyond any kind of judicial review. Such sentiments are coalescing with other efforts to sacralize the flag that would establish a theocratic foundation for the American nation. As we argue in chapter 14, the success of such measures would turn the United States into a mirror image of the theocratic Islam it now opposes.

In view of these dangerous developments, we take comfort in the fact that a debate about the crusade against evil is beginning to emerge within American religious organizations. As we show in the pages that follow, the tradition of zealous warfare has religious roots shared by Christians, Jews, and Muslims. It will not suffice merely to complain about the folly of our present course, for the sources of idealistic crusading must be exposed to light and replaced by healthier strands of faith and ethics that lie at the heart of every great religion. In the chapters that follow we invite the reader to join us in this soul-searching task.

October 2002

ROBERT JEWETT,
Heidelberg, Germany
JOHN SHELTON LAWRENCE,
Berkeley, California

1 The Challenge of a Contradictory Civil Religion

*And we Americans are the peculiar, chosen people — the Israel of our time;
we bear the ark of the liberties of the world. . . . Long enough have we been
skeptics with regard to ourselves, and doubted whether, indeed, the political
Messiah had come. But he has come in us, if we would but give utterance to
his promptings.*

Herman Melville, *White-Jacket* (1850)[1]

[T]o every sailor, soldier, airman, and marine who is involved in this mission, let me say, you're doing God's work. We will not fail.

President George H. W. Bush to armed services personnel
being sent to Somalia in December 1992[2]

The Strange Persistence of Biblical Language

One of the puzzles about the American civil religion is that biblical images of
peacemaking through holy war reappear during times of crisis.[3] This form of
peacemaking stands in tension with a constitutional system — also related to
certain biblical themes — that envisions conflict resolutions in voting booths
and courtrooms. Confronting the terrorist attacks of September 11, 2001,
President George W. Bush often framed the conflict with Osama bin Laden

1

and al Qaeda and the pursuit of peace in religious terms: "We're fighting evil" (or "the evil ones"), he pronounced on several occasions.[4] Initially drawing on the rhetoric of theological absolutes, Bush presided over "Operation Infinite Justice" as a "crusade against terrorism." In his remarks at the Washington National Cathedral service on September 14, he stood in the pulpit to announce a world-scale purgation of evil, maintaining that America was called "to answer these attacks and rid the world of evil."[5] When it became clear that the historical and theological overtones of this language undermined his aims to form a coalition that would include Muslim nations, he muted the biblical and religious language.

Yet the scope of the crusade has expanded. In his State of the Union address on January 29, 2002, President Bush identified the nations of Iran, Iraq, and North Korea as an "axis of evil" and renewed his commitment to purge from the world any states who grant terrorists "the means to match their hatred." Despite the virtually boundless scope of this crusade, he portrayed its purpose as benign because "we seek a just and peaceful world beyond the war on terror."[6]

It may seem strange that America's political rhetoric, especially in the crises that cry urgently to restore peace, continues to bear a distinctly biblical stamp. Presidential speech-making during several international conflicts in recent decades makes this point with stark clarity. For example, it seemed natural for Ronald Reagan, a secularized president from Hollywood, to conclude a speech supporting military efforts at peacemaking with the phrase "God bless you and God bless America."[7] Speaking about warlike situations in Grenada and Lebanon, Reagan casually mixed references to being "faithful to the cause of freedom and the pursuit of peace" with a definition of military casualties as "sacrifices" that we should not dishonor. When America stood at the threshold of a major ground war in the Persian Gulf, President George H. W. Bush told a convention of the National Religious Broadcasters that "America has always been a religious nation — perhaps never more than now." Citing words from Ecclesiastes that there is "a time for peace, a time for war," he described the Gulf War action as a cause defined by religious absolutes — "good versus evil, right versus wrong, human dignity and freedom versus tyranny and oppression." He audaciously proclaimed that the United States sought "nothing for ourselves," and that all the Gulf War coalition partners were "on the side of God." The Reverend Billy Graham stood with him to echo the sentiment that "there comes a time when we must fight for peace."[8]

The perspectives of those opposing America's military actions — from the Vietnam War, through the Nuclear Freeze movement, to the Afghanistan bombing campaign of 2001 — have often displayed similar biblical roots.

Speaking of the U.S. retaliation for the attacks of September 11, Jim Wallis, editor-in-chief of *Sojourners,* invokes Scripture in defining "two paths" as he tries to steer the public away from vengeful actions. In his editorial entitled "Overcome Evil with Good," he quotes from Romans: "Beloved, never avenge yourselves, but leave room for the wrath of God; for it is written, 'Vengeance is mine, I will repay, says the Lord.' . . . Do not be overcome by evil, but overcome evil with good" (12:19-21). In this spirit of St. Paul, Wallis calls for "discipline, patience, and perseverance in vanquishing the networks, assets and capabilities of violent terrorists" and "to honestly face the grievances and the injustices that breed rage and vengeance."[9] Echoing Wallis's sense of what was religiously appropriate during this national crisis, citizens across the country — many of them otherwise utterly secular in outlook — placed posters in their windows and bumper stickers on their cars that read JUSTICE NOT VENGEANCE. To recall the rhetoric of Abraham Lincoln's second inaugural address, both sides read the same Bible and seem to pray to the same God for world redemption.

The Steady Theme of Redeeming the World

An early and eloquent symptom of the world-redemptive impulse in American civil religion came in Herman Melville's novel *White-Jacket.* In the quotation at the head of this chapter we can see the union of religious and secular terminology to convey the sense of mission that continues to surface long after many people have lost touch with their religious roots. Americans are "the peculiar, chosen people — the Israel of our time," he wrote.[10] While the language of "chosen people" and "political Messiah" is no longer used by sophisticated Americans, the values and emotions associated with such ideas continue to exercise their power. A sense of mission "was present from the beginning of American history, and is present, clearly, today," as Frederick Merk could still write in his book on Manifest Destiny more than a century after Melville's florid expression.[11]

In its most expansive form, this sense of mission called the nation to nothing less than redeeming the entire world. Albert J. Beveridge, Pulitzer Prize-winning historian and senator, claimed precisely this at the beginning of the twentieth century as he spoke to the U.S. Senate: "Almighty God . . . has marked the American people as the chosen nation to finally lead in the regeneration of the world. This is the divine mission of America. . . . We are the trustees of the world's progress, guardians of the righteous peace." Adding a biblical gloss to his declaration, Beveridge quoted from Matthew 25:21: "Ye have been faithful over a few things; I will make you ruler over many things."[12] Frequently allied with President Theodore Roosevelt, Beveridge was celebrating the imperialist aspects of the Spanish-American War.

President Woodrow Wilson revived this tradition when he assured the citizens of Cheyenne, Wyoming, that "America had the infinite privilege of fulfilling her destiny and saving the world."[13] Despite secular tendencies, this sense of mission has continued to assert itself in presidential speeches in the second half of the twentieth century. Writing before he became president, Richard Nixon insisted that "our beliefs must be combined with a crusading zeal, not just to hold our own but to change the world . . . and to win the battle for freedom."[14] The most recent echo of such sentiments came when President George W. Bush made his remarkable declaration of the national will to purge terrorism from the world: "This will be a monumental struggle of good versus evil. But good will prevail."[15] Because he acted vigorously and brought dignity to the presidency at a time when the nation was clearly under grave threat, President Bush received unprecedented support from the public. However, we are concerned about the wisdom of setting the nation off once more on a mission of world redemption through a military crusade. We do not disagree that the deliberate destruction of civilian lives on American soil is an evil unmitigated by any excuse. That the nation must respond in creating a greater level of security for its citizens is unquestionable. The dilemmas of action here lie in *how* rather than *whether*.

The most vigorous kind of law enforcement is required, including innovative forms of international cooperation. But the language of war is profoundly misleading in a situation that is actually more analogous to a threat of piracy than an attack by an enemy nation — in contrast to a situation of war, which warrants holding a nation's government responsible for evil actions, with the result that their soldiers become fair targets on the field of battle. Moreover, no nation directly sponsors the al Qaeda terrorist organization, and the U.S. Congress has issued no declaration of war. In view of the American tendency to turn wars into holy crusades, the widely employed martial language is not only inappropriate but is likely to lead to excessive retaliatory campaigns of violence that augment the appeal of terrorism itself.[16]

Skepticism is the easy — but ultimately inadequate — response to apocalyptic calls for world cleansing. When Ronald Reagan urged a cosmic struggle "between right and wrong and good and evil," in which the nation is "enjoined by Scripture and the Lord Jesus to oppose it [the Soviet Union] with all our might,"[17] the opinion editor of the *New York Times* reminded us that the president also "commands awesome power that can be tragically misapplied." He leads a "fallible people, not a moral crusade."[18] In this book we would like to go beyond the limits of such cool skepticism by tracking the historical development of America's split personality, paying special attention to the spirit of zealous warfare that has so often seized the upper hand in policy and public opinion. Yet the power of the tradition we describe here is manifest even in the thinking of those who oppose military action against terrorism. This invisible influence on the partisans of peace-through-war and those of peace-without-war deserves to be brought to a much clearer awareness.

Our analysis seeks to explain why America, in the wake of September 11, seems so proudly resolute about repeating the errors of the Cold War. In their analysis of the campaign against terrorism, Ivo H. Daalder and James M. Lindsay warn against repeating the "militarization of containment" that undermined trust in constitutional government and caused the alienation of potential allies during the Cold War period.[19] They contend that "force of arms alone cannot defeat terrorism"; yet the gigantic increase in military spending after September 11 indicates that this lesson has been forgotten. The second Cold War tendency was to create "new threats even as [the nation] seeks to defeat the current ones,"[20] which seems to be repeated in the American reluctance to accept peace-keeping and nation-building tasks in Afghanistan. Finally, Daalder and Lindsay warn that the country should not repeat the Cold War tendency to "needlessly sacrifice its civil liberties" in the struggle against a foe.[21] Yet a number of steps the government has taken after September 11 appear to repeat this all-encompassing search for the enemy within, inviting a new era of McCarthyism. It is puzzling not only that the government readily repeats such self-defeating mistakes but that they receive the support of influential columnists and the vast majority of the American people. The prominent analyst Thomas L. Friedman of the *New York Times* spoke enthusiastically about the "crazy man theory" he saw behind President Bush's threats against "the axis of evil," while other commentators have spoken with enthusiasm about "winning World War IV."[22] Our study of the contradictory civil religion of the United States offers not simply an explanation of this peculiar and gleeful "forgetfulness" but also suggests a more realistic path to follow during the time of militant jihad.

We trace this contradictory tradition back to its origins in certain strands of biblical thought that were popular in colonial times. The ideas of holy war have been combined with a distinctively American sense of mission in language that fuses secular and religious images. In major developments of American life — the Civil War, the settling of the western frontier, the World Wars, the Cold War, the Vietnam War, the Gulf War, and the so-called war on terrorism — these ideas have continued to surface. But even more crucial for understanding the current dilemma is the fact that these ideas were embodied in popular stories of secular entertainment that gradually became the most pervasive expressions of the national complex. In order to grasp the current dilemmas of war and peace, and thus to develop coping strategies, we need to pay attention to the evolution of these popular narratives and their indebtedness to the religious heritage from the Bible.

The world-redemptive view of America's destiny prevails especially in such products of popular culture as comic books. In the form of simplified mythic storytelling, they often depict ideals that are widely felt but are no longer explicitly articulated in more sophisticated circles. As a point of reference in our exposition, we have chosen to identify *Captain America* comics as a kind of iconic shorthand for this tendency of popular entertainments to carry the zealous mainstream of political sentiment. Born in the frustrating year 1941, *Captain America* leapt beyond the then U.S. policy of neutrality toward the developing European war scene by creating a superhero who punched Hitler in the jaw — an image featured on the cover of its first issue. Since that time, Captain America has allied himself with many causes, always adding a selfless muscular component, whether in battling against Cold War enemies, post-Watergate presidential villains, or industrial magnates who pollute the air and water. In the eerily prescient issue of April 1999, Captain America had to confront his nemesis, the Red Skull, in New York City. Skull had raised the temperature of the city to a lethal level in January and then induced a ravenous hunger in the dying New Yorkers. This was his opening gambit in a campaign to gain control of the earth. The cover of that issue featured the good Captain and the Skull in vicious hand-to-hand combat — "for the fate of the world!"[23]

The creators of *Captain America* sometimes speak of carrying a heavy freight in upholding principles. In a typical editorial comment in a 1970 issue, an editor wrote: "Captain America is not a representative of America itself, but of the American ideal — individual freedom, individual responsibility, moral sensitivity, integrity, and a willingness to fight for right."[24] A letter to the editor from a medical student in the same issue refers to the problem of living up to this ideal and concludes with sentiments that many seem to share: "The fact that we retain such a high national standard is the best of signs, and I hope that we can maintain our zeal to try to bring reality closer to the ideal."

A Contradictory Civil Religion in the Time of Jihad

The effort "to bring reality closer to the ideal" has led us straight into the dilemma we face today. Shall we continue to mount crusades that will likely end

For decades, Captain America has brought star-spangled, muscular salvation. In this 1999 issue, Cap saves the entire world from an attack that begins in New York City.

Credit: Copyright © Marvel Comics, 1999

as badly as did the futile campaign in Indochina? Can global political realities be pummeled into a desired shape by increasingly accurate bombs? Why is there so automatic an acceptance of drastic alterations in public policy in the wake of September 11, including curtailments of civil liberties and huge increases in military expenditures? In contrast to earlier periods of vigorous debate,[25] how can we account for opinion polls that indicate 80-90 percent of the public supports policies that contradict previously dominant American values?

What is there about American nationalism that encourages such contradictory impulses, leading the nation to repeat the mistakes of the past? The answer lies partly in the biblical origins of American civil religion. Even though separated by centuries in time and by disparities in terminology, these older concepts — with their inherent contradictions — match, to an amazing degree, their current mythic counterparts. There are, in fact, two tributaries that run from the pages of the Bible down through American history, each bearing a distinctive approach to the mission of world redemption. We wish to demonstrate that the contradictions within our civil religion derive in large part from these competing tributaries.

The first tradition is what we call *zealous nationalism*. It seeks to redeem the world by destroying enemies. In the chapters that follow, we shall trace the development of this tradition from its biblical origins to recent expressions in American behavior and ideology. The phenomenon of zeal itself provides a fascinating access to the inner workings of our national psyche: the term itself, as we shall see, is the biblical and cultural counterpart of the Islamic term *jihad*. After analyzing zeal in chapter 10, we turn in subsequent chapters to the conspiracy theory of evil, to the problem of stereotyping enemies, to the mystique of violence, to the obsession with victory, and to the worship of national symbols such as flags.

Alongside *zealous nationalism* runs the tradition of *prophetic realism*. It avoids taking the stances of complete innocence and selflessness. It seeks to redeem the world for coexistence by impartial justice that claims no favored status for individual nations. It also derives from the Bible, though in passages that are quite different from those popular with zealots. It can be traced through the American experience in movements and writings that sometimes criticize aspects of the dominant consensus. But, more frequently, one encounters prophetic realism uneasily joined to its opposite.

Although we often speak abstractly of zealous nationalism and prophetic realism in the following pages, readers should understand this as our shorthand for coherent clusters of premises, emotions, images, and imperatives to action that are observable in the lives of nations.

Our conviction is that these two strands so long interwoven in the American mind have always been incompatible, and that the strain has now reached the breaking point. The crusading impulse of zealous nationalism and the constitutional legacy of prophetic realism could remain in uneasy wedlock in earlier times but not in a time of militant jihad, when other world cultures begin to exhibit similar crusading tendencies that inspire lethal conflict. Our conclusions are that prophetic realism alone should guide an effective response to terrorism and lead us to resolve zealous nationalist conflicts through submission to international law; and that the crusades inspired by zealous nationalism are inherently destructive, not only of the American prospect but of the world itself.

Captain America is now in his sixties and has faced humiliating fluctuations in the market for masked superheroes. Although he has been recently summoned one more time to protect the nation from danger, we suggest that the time has come for a dignified retirement.[26]

2 The Endangered Towers and the Crusade against Jihad

I am confident that Muslims will be able to end the legend of the so-called superpower that is America.

Osama bin Laden in a *Time* interview with Rahimullah Yusufzai, 1999[1]

We calculated in advance the number of casualties from the enemy, who would be killed based on the position of the tower. We calculated that the floors that would be hit would be three or four floors. I was the most optimistic of them all. . . .

Osama bin Laden in the videotape found at Jalalabad (November 9, 2001)[2]

However heady the appeal of a call to arms, however just the cause, we should still shed a tear for all that will be lost when war claims its wages from us. Shed a tear, and then get on with the business of killing our enemies as quickly as we can, and as ruthlessly as we must. . . . We did not cause this war. Our enemies did, and they are to blame for the deprivations and difficulties it occasions. They are to blame for the loss of innocent life. They are to blame for the geopolitical problems confronting our friends and us. We can help repair the damage of war. But to do so, we must destroy the people who started it.

U.S. Senator John McCain (October 26, 2001)[3]

The shock of September 11, echoing the audacious taunt of Osama bin Laden, will resound for years. Its message of vulnerability has been seared into national consciousness, cauterized by the flames of New York, Washington, D.C., and United Airlines Flight 93 that crashed in Pennsylvania. In the days immediately following the attack, it became clear that the world will forever turn on a different axis. America's singular role as a power with a superheroic invulnerability that protects the "free world" was suddenly shown to be hollow. Military power, despite sophistication in weaponry and extension of reach, could not guarantee the security of the homeland. The "intelligence" of the CIA could only refer us to its past generic warnings of danger — some amounting to nothing more than reminders of bin Laden's own publicly stated threats. For example, George Tenet, who headed the CIA during the Clinton administration, informed the press that bin Laden, months after declaring himself the scourge of the United States in the *Time* interview, was targeting "further attacks" on U.S. facilities and symbols of power.[4] However, no intelligence agency could possibly have predicted a suicide attack on skyscrapers with commercial airliners flown by hijackers armed only with box cutters. Yet the country embarked on a "war on terrorism" with a gigantic increase in military spending aimed at eliminating the threat for all time.

Contradictory Responses

The government response to the new challenges of stateless terrorism expressed the peculiar contradictory elements typical of the American civil religion. On the one hand, there is a retaliatory rage, fed by a reborn feeling of national innocence and violation. This impulse toward a crusade against the jihad leads in the direction of ruthless military action — defying world opinion, if that be the price. Ann Coulter, a writer who had lost a friend in the Pentagon crash, urged the following in a prominent publication:

> This is no time to be precious about locating the exact individuals directly involved in this particular terrorist attack. . . . We should invade their countries, kill their leaders and convert them to Christianity. We weren't punctilious about locating and punishing only Hitler and his top officers. We carpet-bombed German cities; we killed civilians. That's war. This is war.[5]

Similar sentiments came from Senator John McCain (in the epigraph at the head of this chapter), one of America's few war heroes from the Vietnam era.

He enunciates the cold willingness to kill innocents on the other side of the world — and then to assign the blame to others. The call for pursuit without restraints or mercy is only the most extreme of viewpoints that would commit America to multiple theaters of conflict. Its premise seems to be, in the words of Moises Naim, "that the fight against terrorism is a 'war' and therefore can be 'won.'"[6]

At the other pole of the national civil religious psyche is the awareness that America still belongs to a network of nations. Dozens of countries, after all, were represented among the victims at the World Trade Center, and they regard the attacks as directed at themselves as well. Those countries also want security for their citizens, and they have pledged their support for common efforts. Moreover, the tactical realities of pursuing the al Qaeda group demanded that the United States cooperate with nations such as Pakistan or Russia — countries it formerly deemed pariahs or hostile adversaries. Such relationships are understood to entail pragmatic compromise, resolution of past animosities, and the building of new, nonmilitary regimes of law and regulation.

In contrast to George W. Bush's initial language of zealous nationalism, some policies of his administration have relied on forms of international cooperation favored by prophetic realism. This anomaly was observed by law professor Diane Marie Amann in an editorial published in October 2001.[7]

> Who could have predicted that President Bush would become the voice of a New Multilateralism? Yet there he stands, between Britain's Tony Blair and France's Jacques Chirac, Japan's Junichiro Koizumi and Russia's Vladimir Putin, in photos that illustrate the United States' efforts these last weeks to build a global coalition against terrorism. That coalition now has taken to the air, with sustained strikes against targets in Afghanistan. The success so far of this joint endeavor compels a closer look at another opportunity for justice through cooperation, the proposed International Criminal Court. Not long ago that suggestion would have drawn laughter. Bush had swaggered onto the foreign-policy scene like a latter-day Matt Dillon aiming to shoot down the supposed menace of international entanglement.

This contradiction was also noted by elements of the American religious community who had attempted to shape the national response toward restraint and cooperation. At the White House on September 20, more than twenty religious leaders offered advice: they were all against a lone crusade. As reported by Jean Bethke Elshtain, this confidential consultation involved representatives of the Christian, Jewish, Sikh, Hindu, Buddhist, and Muslim faiths. They argued that "to yield to hate is to give victory to the terrorists."[8]

Seeking to reinforce the cooperative strategies of President Bush's administration, they articulated their conviction that "because these terrorist attacks were global in their consequences, the president is correct in seeking a coordinated international response."[9] Within the United States, thousands of civic and religious leaders urged the country to temper any response by recognizing the common humanity of all who could be affected by our actions. Signing a statement, "Deny Them Their Victory," they urged that the United States avoid taking on the demeanor of the terrorists. "We can deny them their victory by refusing to submit to a world created in their image. . . . We must not allow this terror to drive us away from the people God has called us to be. We assert the vision of community, tolerance, compassion, justice, and the sacredness of human life, which lies at the heart of all our religious traditions."[10]

Consistent with such counsel, the United States had already cooperated with the United Nations Security Council on September 12 in passing Resolution 1368, which condemned the attacks in New York and Washington without any qualification. Working further with the Security Council, the United States was party to a comprehensive measure, Resolution 1373, issued on September 28, which urged member states of the U.N. "to deny safe haven to those who finance, plan, support or commit terrorist acts, or provide safe havens," and urged them "to prevent and suppress terrorist attacks and take action against perpetrators of such acts."[11] The stage was thus set to move in concert with other nations, following policy guidelines agreed to by most of the world's community. Yet the military action in Afghanistan, with subsequent involvement in the Philippines and threats to invade Somalia or Iraq, Iran, and North Korea, have brought dismay to many who had hoped to moderate the conflict with al Qaeda through international consensus.

The outcome of this clash between zealous, unilateral military impulses and the more cautious search for diplomatic relations and policy reforms will affect the prospect of peace for nearly every citizen on planet earth. In the following pages we trace a decade of circumstances that led America's civil religion to this fateful confrontation with jihad.

The Background of September 11

The collapse of the Soviet Union in 1991 coincided almost exactly with the U.S.-led coalition's conduct of the Persian Gulf War. Driving Iraq's forces from Kuwait while the Soviet Union distanced itself from the conflict gave

America an increasingly confident feeling about its emergence as the world's sole surviving superpower. The destruction of the Berlin Wall symbolized the irrelevance of treaty alliances organized around the Cold War's bipolarities: the Warsaw Pact and the Southeast Asia Treaty Organization (SEATO) no longer made sense. The meltdown of the Stalinist command economies in countries such as Russia and East Germany tarnished the reputation of socialism and seemed to concede the wisdom of free markets. Capitalism and its accelerating globalization of world economies were symbolized by the World Trade Center, with its 110-story twin towers occupied by multinational corporations.

The coalescence of these seemingly favorable events had a restorative effect for the spirit of zealous nationalism that had brought the nation to grief in Southeast Asia. The one-sided victory of quickly assembled coalition partners in the Persian Gulf War evoked a euphoric outburst from President George H. W. Bush in March 1991: "By God, we've kicked the Vietnam syndrome once and for all."[12] The implication was that the failures of Vietnam had destroyed our confidence about using military power in the international arena. The triumphant coalition had inflicted embarrassingly large casualties on Iraq's forces, while sustaining a mere 240 deaths on its own side. (And of that number, a significant portion had been caused by the mistakes of "friendly fire" or by accidents removed from the battlefield.)[13] In conflicts after the Gulf War, U.S. casualties were always minimal because air power and cruise missiles had become the weapons of choice for striking at enemies. Military losses in Somalia in 1993, in the Khobar Towers bombing in Saudi Arabia in 1996, and in the attack on the U.S.S. Cole in 2000 did not even rise to 100 lives. For a country that moved so many of its forces among so many hostile adversaries, these numbers suggested near invulnerability.

It seemed that the United States, when it wished, could be like Captain America himself: strong, capable of acting without consulting or seeking direction, and exercising destructive power with few immediate repercussions. After the 1998 bombings of the U.S. embassies in Kenya and Tanzania, President Clinton sent cruise missiles flying toward Sudan and Afghanistan. No boomerang suddenly returned in these situations. Military might, though deployed ineffectively in that retaliatory endeavor, seemed cost-free. Even when the United States mistakenly bombed the Chinese embassy in Belgrade during the conflict in Kosovo, the consequences were dampened by modest monetary payments, apologies, and explanations emphasizing the element of mistake in choosing urban targets.

The attacks of September 11 were thus a major tremor — compounding human, financial, and national psychic cost. The country had not faced such an attack by an external enemy on its symbols of national identity since the British troops burned down the White House in 1812. The resulting question that so many Americans raised — "How could it happen to us?" — resolved itself into a host of subsidiary questions relating to the moral dimensions of the tragedy, and to the failures of military, intelligence, and immigration policies. From President George W. Bush's perspective, the most powerful explanation focused on the moral psychology of the United States' quickly designated adversary, Osama bin Laden. In an early effort to explain why America had become a target, the president emphasized a list of national political values that bin Laden's movement appeared to deny: "They hate our freedoms — our freedom of religion, our freedom of speech, our freedom to vote and assemble and disagree with each other."[14] His most reassuring answer was that Americans are so good that they are intolerable to absolute evil. At his White House press conference on October 11, 2001, a plaintive, frustrated tone came into his voice:

> I'm amazed that there's such misunderstanding of what our country is about that people would hate us. I am, like most Americans — I just can't believe it because I know how good we are. And we've got to do a better job of making our case. We've got to do a better job of explaining to the people of the Middle East, for example, that we don't fight a war against Islam or Muslims. We don't hold any religion accountable. We're fighting evil.[15]

The ready acceptance of this framework of innocence, which has elicited broad and strong support from the American people, helps to account for our surprise at being attacked. Unfortunately, it bespeaks a straitened imagination that cannot envision the perspective of others in the world who are extremely critical of America's power.

American journalism, however, was not content with such a simplistic reduction of the national circumstance and soon made known a litany of other countries' complaints against the United States: resentments of America's role in Israel; the effects of U.S. policies on the people of Iraq; the U.S. alliances with autocratic governments of the Middle East; its export of cultural materials that are deemed degrading even by many in the United States. *Newsweek* magazine published an issue with a bold cover title: "Why They Hate Us: The Roots of Islamic Rage — and What We Can Do About It."[16] But none of the reasons, singly or in combination, could excuse or justify the attacks of September 11. Just as America did not pause in the wake of the Pearl Harbor attacks to consider how its power had become provocative to Japan in the Pacific, it wanted to move on quickly after September 11 to what became known as "the war against terrorism" or "the first war of the twenty-first century," expressions used by President George W. Bush. Public discourse seemed to fear that, in the realm of policy and response, maintaining the border between explaining terrorism and justifying it was too difficult. Given the reluctance to ponder causes and the urgency to respond to additional threats, the president could quickly mobilize public sentiment for a legislative authorization to conduct war wherever it might take American military power.

Thus, by September 19, Congress had given the president authorization "to use all necessary and appropriate force against those nationals, organizations, or persons he determines planned, authorized, committed or aided the terrorist attacks that occurred on September 11, 2001, or harbored such organizations or persons, in order to prevent any future acts of international terrorism against the United States by such nations, organizations, or persons." The resolution passed 98-0 in the Senate and 420-1 in the House.[17] Senator Joseph Biden (D-Del.), chairman of the Senate Foreign Relations Committee and one of the shapers of the resolution that passed the Senate, seemed proud of the open-ended character of the use-of-force resolution, which — to borrow the language of mathematics — used variables rather than constants, when he said, "There is zero need for a declaration of war," and "No one should think that what we did here was less than a declaration of war."[18]

Emboldened by such strong cross-party support, Bush spoke to Congress on the following day with the pledge that "our war on terror . . . will not end until every terrorist group of global reach has been found, stopped, defeated." Challenging the world to think of its allegiance in bipolar terms, he said, "Every nation, in every region, now has a decision to make. Either you are with us, or you are with the terrorists." Devoid of the caution that Abraham Lincoln would have shown in speaking of divine judgment on the nation's causes, Bush concluded with a statement of his certainty that God was taking the American side in this conflict: "Freedom and fear, justice and cruelty, have always been at war, and we know that God is not neutral between them. Fellow citizens, we will meet violence with patient justice assured of the rightness of our cause, and confident of the victories to come."[19]

Martial Response and Lost Opportunities

The "patient justice" of which the president spoke would quickly reveal itself to contain a substantial impatience to drop bombs and test new military technologies in Afghanistan. In the first few weeks of the war, opposition forces to the Taliban — substantially aided by American air power and ground-based targeting teams — rapidly took control of the cities in a way that defied conventional wisdom about the fate of empires in Afghanistan. Speaking to cadets at the Citadel, the military college in Charleston, South Carolina, after the last of the cities had fallen, President Bush praised the new face of warfare that was emerging with its precision ordnance, surveillance planes without pilots, and laser-equipped ground spotters to identify targets. "Afghanistan has been a proving ground for this new approach" to "asymmetrical" threats from terrorists. "The conflict in Afghanistan," he said, "has taught us more about the future of the military than a decade of blue-ribbon panels and think-tank symposiums." He also chose this moment of military exuberance to renounce the 1972 Anti-Ballistic Missile Treaty signed with the Soviet Union.[20]

These rapidly earned victories were accompanied by the scenes of liberation in which citizens of Afghan cities emerged from the oppressive reign of the Taliban's version of Islamic law *(shari'a)*. People who had not been allowed to fly kites or listen to music celebrated the return of small pleasures. But many civilians in Afghanistan, though not targeted by the U.S. military, suffered or died from the stray bombs that fell on them. Although the military took pride in the humane accuracy of its targeting practices, there were repeated reports of explosions at Red Cross facilities, broadcast studios, and in villages that could not comprehend why they had lost family members and their homes were destroyed. One exile from Afghanistan, Abdul Sattar, who worked on removing land mines in his country, saw a cruel indifference in the way the United States had chosen to pursue its military campaign: "When there is bombing in people's villages, of course we are not happy. We are the victims of Washington and New York's World Trade Center disasters just as we were the victims of the Cold War."[21]

There may be a rough utilitarian calculus that will eventually justify the new style of war to those affected by it. However, it is clear that much of the good will that the United States enjoyed in the immediate aftermath of September 11 quickly evaporated. The opportunities for international harmonization so evident in the early aftermath had been substantial. The attacks on the World Trade Center killed citizens from eighty-six nations. There were countless expressions of solidarity and sympathy from around the globe. As suggested in Germany's *Süddeutsche Zeitung*, the remarkable wave of sympathy over the innocent victims of this atrocious crime might have created an unanticipated opportunity to recognize our common humanity. The German newspaper also called for a common effort on the part of the "reasonable world" to move against the "demented minds behind these barbaric acts."[22]

Candles were lit all over the world, including in most of the Islamic nations. Prayers of intercession and grief were offered in temples, synagogues, mosques, and churches around the globe; and this began before the precise identification of victims from other nations, who now have their own grief to surmount. In Iran, a country that still stood on the U.S. State Department's list of countries that sponsor terrorism, 60,000 soccer fans and players observed a moment of silence. In Germany, 200,000 gathered at the site of the fallen Berlin Wall to express their grief.[23] Recalling President John F. Kennedy's "Ich bin ein Berliner," they shouted, "We are New Yorkers." The routine anti-Americanism in European circles became remarkably silent. It was a moment when America could have reached out to all the hands that were extended to it. Unfortunately, the jihadic zeal of the opponent gave more urgency to retaliation than to the strategies of prophetic realism. In a season when flags were proudly visible in most American homes and cars, and when victory over the Taliban came so quickly, there was little interest in seeking common ground with adversaries — an essential element of prophetic realism. If an easy victory implied that God was on our side, why should we quibble about a little "collateral damage"?

Militant Jihad's Rationale

Just as the American civil religion is pulled between its zealous and its prophetic poles, the religion of Islam is similarly pulled between the angry shouts of holy warfare and the softer voices of tolerant coexistence, between *jihad* as warfare against "the infidel" (the unfaithful) or "the revolutionary struggle to seize power for the good of all humanity"[24] and *jihad* as struggle for inner mastery of desire. Sometimes the "infidel" was found within Islam and became the occasion for terrorist struggle or assassination. As the historian Bernard Lewis explains, Islam confronted the terror issue among Muslims early (656 CE): "Muslim rebels who believed that they were carrying out the will of God" murdered the third caliph, Uthman. That led to "the first of a succession of civil wars . . . fought over the question of whether the rebels were fulfilling or defying God's commandments." The Muslim sect of Assassins in Iran and Syria from the eleventh to the thirteenth centuries were likewise focused on the deficient piety of their own leaders.[25] Osama bin Laden stands in this tradition of holy revolt against his own leaders, claiming that his native Saudi Arabia has desecrated the land of Islamic holy places Mecca and Medina by permitting U.S. troops to be stationed there during the Gulf War and afterwards. So harsh were his religious criticisms that Saudi Arabia saw him as a danger and sent him into exile.[26]

Bin Laden's severest denunciations have been directed at the United

States, which he sees as guilty of oppressive injustices directed at every person who shares the faith of Islam. In 1998, groups associated with his al Qaeda organization published a manifesto entitled "The International Islamic Front for Jihad against Jews and Crusaders." It accuses the United States of "occupying the lands of Islam in the holiest places . . . plundering its riches, dictating to its rulers, humiliating its people, terrorizing its neighbors, and turning its bases in the peninsula into a spearhead through which to fight the neighboring Muslim people." The assembled warriors issued a *fatwa* (religious decree) demanding that all "Americans and their allies" be indiscriminately killed wherever they be found: "The ruling to kill the Americans and their allies — civilian and military — is an individual duty for every Muslim who can do it in any country in which it is possible to do so."[27] Since that time, bin Laden has actively publicized through numerous interviews his mission to "drive the Americans away from all Muslim countries." He has said repeatedly that the attacks, of which he approves without admitting any responsibility, are part of a "declared *jihad* against the U.S. government, because the U.S. is unjust, criminal and tyrannical."[28]

The attacks on September 11 were perceived as divinely authorized vengeance against an alleged tyranny. Lee Griffith reports that a prayer leader in a mosque in Islamabad, Pakistan, proclaimed on September 14 that the towers had fallen "because 'Allah intensified the fire and destruction of those planes.' Osama bin Laden himself proclaimed that God was 'giving the Americans what they deserve.'"[29] The hot fury of this zeal to purify the world of American influence has found its counterpart in the religiously toned struggles of the Hamas organization in Israel. Nasra Hassan, who has interviewed Hamas members for several years, gave detailed reports of their sense of commitment to service for Palestine's suffering people. The volunteers of martyrdom have attached the theology of the sacred to their random attacks on buses, in marketplaces, and other public places where flying nails and other debris can inflict surprise, terror, and death. It is a fatalistic religion, and it believes that everything is in the hands of Allah. Sheikh Ahmed Hassan, a spiritual leader within Hamas, put it this way:

> Love of martyrdom is something deep inside the heart. . . . The only aim is to win Allah's satisfaction. That can be done in simplest and speediest manner by dying in the cause of Allah. And it is Allah who selects the martyrs.[30]

This martyrdom is not without benefits to the martyr. In the view of a bomber who accidentally survived, the violence is a certain ticket away from hell:

It's as if a very high, impenetrable wall separated you from Paradise or Hell. Allah has promised one or the other to his creatures. So, by pressing the detonator, you can immediately open the door to Paradise — it is the shortest route to heaven.[31]

The call of heaven to the young Palestinians has been increasingly frequent. According to Hassan, the first bombing took place on the West Bank in 1993; thirty-seven human bombs exploded during the following five years. "Since the . . . second intifada began in September, 2000, twenty-six human bombs have exploded." Hamas has claimed nineteen of these as its operations, and Islamic Jihad claims seven. By the autumn of 2000, the toll on Israelis was considerable: 215 killed and 800 injured.[32] In 2001-2002, Israeli casualties from the random explosions grew considerably, as did the Palestinian victims caught in the crossfire of retaliation.

Just as the jihad of al Qaeda has understandably awakened Captain America's instinct for world crusade, the Palestinians' "human bombs" have stiffened the will of the Israeli government against any concessions. They answer every explosion with rocket attacks, assassinations, the bulldozing of private homes, air strikes, and other military tactics that arouse moral indignation around the world when they are used in the close quarters of urban life. The Israelis are locked into the kind of struggle with Palestinians that Captain America now faces in dealing with the worldwide remnants of al Qaeda who have survived the destruction of the Taliban in Afghanistan. Jewish and Christian zeal appears locked in conflict with Islamic jihad, each displaying a similar potential for fanatical violence, and each denying the more realistic components of its related cultural traditions.

The Parallel Logic of Crusade and Jihad

The shape of the current dilemma was intimated by the first attempt of Islamic radicals to destroy the World Trade Center in 1993, and by the wave of suicide bombings in Israel after 1993. Similar conflicts between terrorist groups intent on the destruction of their adversaries have surfaced in many other parts of the world. Terrorism must be defined in such a way as to take account of a wide range of conflicts. In *The War on Terrorism and the Terror of God*, Lee Griffith adapts the definition from a Quaker study: "Terrorism is a tactic, whether used by an established government, a revolutionary group, or an individual. The characterization of an action as 'terrorism' depends on *what* is done, not on *who* does it."[33] Our contention is that one must also ask

Newsweek joined the spirit of zealous crusade for the hot pursuit of bin Laden, evoking the vision of a time "after the evil" following his destruction.

Credit: © 2001 Newsweek, Inc.

why terrorist acts are committed. We believe that the answer lies in zealous forms of civil religion whose origins can be traced back to biblical archetypes that are honored by zealous strands of Christianity, Judaism, and Islam — and now influence other movements throughout the world.

Since September 11 it is clear that the conflicts between militant zeal and jihad endanger the proud skyscrapers and market squares in every city of the world.[34] A protracted struggle between "civilization and its enemies," announced by many commentators since September, is really a conflict between closely related forms of religious and cultural fanaticism that arise in part out of genuine injustices and inequalities. The dilemma is that violence directed against such injustice so frequently brings even greater evils in its wake.

The crusading tendencies within Christianity, Judaism, and Islam continually evoke counterproductive responses to the current dilemma. How reasonable is it to believe that the destruction of America could bring justice to the Islamic world? Or that the killing of Osama bin Laden could eliminate the threat of terrorism? How logical is it to believe that Israeli occupation of Palestine, no matter how well equipped with American armaments, can be peacefully maintained? Or that Palestinian authorities can be threatened into possessing magical power to prevent the rise of idealistic suicide bombers from an enraged and dishonored populace? How can one explain that the U.S. government, having discovered the necessity of international cooperation after September 11, should thereupon reject participation in an International Criminal Court that would be the most effective means of dealing with captured terrorists? Or that they would cancel the ABM treaty and continue a Star Wars defense system costing uncounted billions at the very time it has become clear that the greatest threat now employs ordinary civilian means to dispatch and demoralize its opponents?

The support for the attack on Taliban and al Qaeda forces in Afghanistan soared to the highest approval levels ever recorded in Gallup Poll records, which go back to the Korean War. In November 2001, 89 percent of Americans confirmed their belief in the correctness of those attacks.[35] This is not so surprising, given the belief that this was the "war against terrorism" that had brought destruction to American shores. The most coherent explanation for this behavior and its significant public support must focus on the faith that, in the words of President George W. Bush, we are engaged "in a fundamental struggle between good and evil" and that "we will win."

The very language that has been used in the American response to September 11 is ill suited to the challenge of worldwide terrorism. A limited military campaign in Afghanistan made sense only to counter the Taliban regime's support for al Qaeda's terrorism. Conforming to the legal definition employed in both international law and American constitutional law, Congress refrained from declaring "war" on Afghanistan because it did not specify any particular place at all as the target for military action. The British military historian Sir Michael Howard expressed his dismay at both the rhetoric and the tactics of America's "war on terrorism" in a speech entitled "Stumbling into Battle":

> To declare that one is "at war" is immediately to create a war psychosis that is totally counterproductive to the objective that we seek. It will arouse an immediate expectation, and demand, for some spectacular military action against an easily identifiable adversary, preferably a hostile state; action leading to decisive results.
>
> The use of force is no longer seen as a last resort, to be avoided if humanly possible, but as the first, and the sooner it is used the better. The newspapers demand immediate stories of derring-do, filling their pages with pictures of weapons, ingenious graphics, and contributions from service officers long, and probably deservedly, retired. Any suggestion that the best strategy is not to use military force at all but more subtle if less heroic means of destroying the adversary is dismissed as "appeasement."[36]

True to the scenario Howard feared, the American press, impatient for victory, immediately began numbering the days of the military action in Afghanistan. It was quickly compelled to stop counting because, except for the zealous ideology, one cannot really speak of a war against terrorism itself. Terrorists and pirates do not make war; that term applies to military conflict conducted by nations. Terrorist predations need to be countered by vigorous law enforcement, sometimes with the assistance of limited military actions. Answers about how to address the network of terrorists responsible for September 11 do not come easy. But maintaining the "decent respect of the opinions of mankind" clearly requires innovative forms of international law enforcement. Yet the language of warfare, virtually tantamount to a holy war, continues to be used by government leaders and in the news media.

After the airing of the Osama bin Laden tape that revealed his complicity and joy in the September 11 attacks, *Newsweek* magazine's cover featured a blurred image of his head under the headline "After the Evil." Coming after several decisive weeks of fighting against Taliban and al Qaeda forces in Afghanistan, this popular magazine's cover played to the simplistic belief that a single military campaign, carried out in one place, would end the threat of terrorist attacks against the United States. The same issue of *Newsweek* carried an article entitled "Evil in the Cross Hairs,"[37] an exploration of reviving secret assassinations as a method of advancing national security. Although the article reviewed the "mixed results" of assassinations in the past, it offered no reference to or wisdom from international law or criminal jurisdictions. The enthusiasm such publicity engenders in the annihilation of evil enemies, obvious in Senator McCain's statement in the chapter epigraph, brings these two forms of warfare parallel to each other.

The crusading logic believed by each side encourages actions that achieve the very opposite of their intended result. Each laser-directed bomb can be answered by another suicide attack, and as long as the underlying ideologies remain intact, there appears to be little prospect of resolution. As Michael Howard describes the destruction of the World Trade Center, "In six months time, for much of the world, that atrocity will be if not forgotten then remembered only as a history, while every fresh picture on television of a hospital hit, or children crippled by land mines, or refugees driven from their homes . . . will strengthen the hatred of our adversaries, swell the ranks of the terrorists, and sow fresh doubts in the minds of our supporters."[38] It is obvious that each escalation produces a counter-escalation; yet each side remains convinced that its violence is not only innocent and justified but also redemptive.

In the period following the quick rout of the Taliban in Afghanistan, John F. Burns of the *New York Times* found in Pakistan angry adversaries who advertised their willingness to die in continued confrontations with the United States. Ijaz Khan Hussein, a Pakistani pharmacist who had fought alongside the Taliban with 42 other companions — 41 of whom were killed in battle with the Americans and the Northern Alliance — seemed confirmed in his hostility toward the United States: "We went to the jihad filled with joy, and I would go again tomorrow." A seminary student outside Peshawar was similarly resolute: "Jihad will continue until doomsday, or until America is defeated, either way."[39] Such statements illustrate the dynamic, symbiotic elements of zealous war's state of mind.

Within our framework we believe that there are six important elements of the Captain America complex, which it shares with Christian and Jewish zeal as well as with militant Islamic jihad:

- Each side views its anger as blessed by the deity, which thereby absolutizes zeal and jihad and eliminates normal restraint.
- Each side conceives of its opponents as members of a malevolent conspiracy, originating from the realm of absolute evil, and thus sees any compromise as immoral.
- The stereotypes of the actors in this conflict are stark and extreme, with all goodness on one side and absolute evil on the other. To mourn over

the deaths of such opponents thus appears to make as little sense as concern over the seasonal demise of locusts.

- As the quote by Ann Coulter reveals, such opponents must either be killed or converted. Each side believes that its own violence is redemptive, while it deplores the violence of the other side as senseless and unjust.
- To allow oneself to be defeated by the other side is to abandon faith itself, whether in the form of Christianity, Islam, or Judaism, and whether devoutly religious or explicitly secular.
- Every action of one's enemies is perceived to desecrate the holy, and overcoming such desecration is seen as a religious and political imperative whose fulfillment will usher in an era of peace.

These features of popular zealotry derive from the biblical heritage held in common by Islam, Judaism, and Christianity. Yet within the very same biblical tradition — and in the cultural strands that derive from it — lie sources of prophetic realism that could lead our crusading societies on a more promising course. We explore the roots of both sides of this biblical and cultural heritage, along with its current secular embodiments, in chapters 4-9.

In the pages that follow, we raise the question whether it can ever be feasible to crusade against jihad — or for jihad to crusade against zeal. We seek to account for the similarities between militant forms of zeal and jihad in their religious origins and their political implications. We want to explore why bin Laden's joy at the destruction of alleged evildoers seems so similar to the attitudes of Ann Coulter and John McCain. We hope that a critical examination of the origins and implications of these zealous ideologies, along with an analysis of more realistic counterforces within current civil religions, may provide guidance for the extended period that appears to lie ahead, the time of jihad. Most advocates of such zealotry remain unaware of the biblical foundations, however, because the Captain America complex is being conveyed primarily by superheroic adventures, which derive from biblical narratives and now constitute the most compelling entertainments of the modern world. We explore this critical matter in the next chapter.

3 Popular Culture as a Bearer of the National Complex

*BEHOLD! THE CROWNING ACHIEVEMENT OF ALL MY YEARS OF HARD WORK. THE FIRST OF A CORPS OF SUPER-AGENTS WHOSE MENTAL AND PHYSICAL ABILITY WILL MAKE THEM A TERROR TO SPIES AND SABOTEURS! WE SHALL CALL YOU **CAPTAIN AMERICA**, SON! BECAUSE, LIKE YOU — AMERICA SHALL GAIN THE STRENGTH AND THE WILL TO SAFEGUARD OUR SHORES.*

Professor Reinstein's comment from the genesis episode
of *Captain America* comics in 1941

Kids need to understand that the President (and his team) will keep them safe and that evil-doers will be punished. ENDURING FREEDOM PICTURE CARDS presents the New War on Terrorism in a format that children can understand. Not included are the disturbing images shown repeatedly on national newscasts.

Topps Entertainments ad, December 2001[1]

The Strategic Defense Initiative has been labeled Star Wars. But it isn't about war. It is about peace. If you will pardon my stealing a film line — the force is with us.

President Ronald Reagan's 1986 comment
about his projected space weapons program[2]

In trying to locate the center of American political consciousness, discussions of religion have devoted much attention to officially sanctioned cultic events and spaces: the speeches and parades associated with presidential inaugurations; Fourth of July or Memorial Day celebrations; the Capitol's monuments; and sermons delivered around Thanksgiving Day.[3] While the national ceremonial culture and its marble icons offer important avenues to Americans' self-understanding of their national identity, something is missing in accounting for American political behavior of recent decades. What are the wellsprings that feed the recurrent American tendency to deviate from the values we formally celebrate? Why has voter participation steadily declined? Why have Americans become less involved in their civic organizations? Why do we so often feel chafed by the limits of the Constitution? Why are we so ready to empower leaders who promise to transcend constitutional limitations to "solve problems" that are actually intractable? How can one explain the decreasing patience with a democratic system that was designed to be no more than a means of finding "proximate solutions to insoluble problems"?[4]

Superheroic Entertainments and Civil Religion

We believe that these problematic tendencies of American culture are significantly nourished by a post-civic popular culture that has become a new center for shaping political beliefs and impulses to action. When we examine comic books, television programs, films, video games, and other arenas of fantasy experience, we find a competing, powerful center for symbolic education. American children who play video games in which they repeatedly "deliver the world from evil" did not learn this role listening to Bible stories on their parents' laps. Unlike Americans of centuries ago, we are no longer "people of one book" whose main source of stories and moral teaching for children is the Bible. In the quotation above, President Ronald Reagan provides a peaceful rationale for weapons orbiting in space while he pays homage to a supremely popular American movie that joins redemptive violence and religious piety.

If the discussion of American civil religion is to help us grasp what present-day citizens think and do, it must move beyond official cultic events marked on the calendar and pay attention to the fantastic but credible narratives to which so many Americans feel a deep emotional attachment. With this new recognition comes the consideration that inaugurations, Fourth of July or Memorial Day ceremonies, and Thanksgiving sermons have moved to the periphery of formative cultural experiences. Chapter 7 will explore the ascendancy in American politics of themes for international behavior that seem to flow from the realm of mythically inspired entertainment.

The interpretation we develop here focuses on the American superhero tale, which developed in the 1930s and embodies the neurotic conflicts of the Captain America complex. The recurrent telling of such stories has lent emotional credibility to the task of ridding the world of supervillains, or of converting unhappy people into cooperative citizens. Viewed as part of our religious history, these stories reveal themselves as secularized dramas of redemption in which innocent communities are saved by Everyman figures possessing superpowers. The redemptive story lines evoke those in the Bible, but the media for their conveyance have been so entertainingly transformed that the sources and implications of the Captain America complex — employing nondemocratic means to achieve democratic ends — initially seem opaque. How can the films, comic books, and games of popular culture that are created for profit and are designed for amusement be taken seriously as artifacts of civil religion? Do the stories and the ideals they advocate really align themselves with the public rhetoric of presidential speech writers and the convictions of the presidents themselves?

We intend to show that the pervasive power of the current civil religion derives not only from its conformity to a tradition reaching back to colonial times — when the public did in fact read the Bible with voracious interest — but also from its exuberant expression in popular entertainments during the last three-quarters of a century. The *Captain America* comic books, in part because of their crudeness, provide a vivid emblem of this contradictory civil religion. When we look at the pulp literature, films, television, and video games that receive the steady attention of most American minds, we must also recognize that they are thereby forming a cultural matrix for action. The superhero tales amount to a kind of mythic induction into the cultural values of America. A citizen's brief interludes at church, synagogue, or mosque are far less likely to impart a significant vision of how to cope with the world's conflicts. But as the artistic creators of popular entertainments respond to current events with mythic scenarios, they help to shape the public sense of what is appropriate in confronting the crises of national and international life.

The Rise of the American Monomyth

The Captain America phenomenon within civil religion is best understood as part of a broad mythic stream that flows through superheroic comics, television programming, films, and video games. In our book-length treatment of these popular culture artifacts, *The Myth of the American Superhero*,[5] we identify this set of narrative formulas as the *American monomyth*. There we intentionally draw a contrast with the age-old heroic paradigm first articulated by Joseph Campbell as the *classical monomyth*. This older story, found in every culture, tells of young people who leave their homes in search of adventure; they encounter threatening forces, undergo personal tests, and finally rescue the maiden or save the city by the use of their wit and newfound strength, often aided by magical powers. These stories typically end with the equivalent of "the prince married the princess and they lived happily thereafter," which in the ancient context of the fairy tales conveyed reintegration into the home community and the life task of political service. Marriage and political responsibility are the arenas of adult behavior in which the newfound strength of the classic monomyth's heroes and heroines can be symbolically employed. Campbell sees these stories as the narrative counterparts of rites of passage, in which young people are symbolically inducted into societies that expect them to accept the responsibility for the community's welfare.

In the modern superhero story of the American monomyth, on the other hand, helpless communities are redeemed by lone savior figures who are never integrated into their societies and never marry at the story's end. In effect, like the gods, they are permanent outsiders to the human community. We suggest that this new myth system, which crystallized its conventions of plot and character in the axial decade of the 1930s, shows a democratic face in that the protagonist is an Everyman, yet has a pop-fascist dimension in that these unelected, law-transcending figures exercise superpowers to overcome foes. The tales of the American monomyth depicting threatened communities typically express frustration with the limitations of constitutional government and with its allied ideals of reconciliation and compromise. These stories show that, when confronted with genuine evil, democratic institutions and the due process of law always fail. In the face of such a threat, democracy can be saved only by someone with courage and strength enough to transcend the legal order so that the source of evil can be destroyed. Hence the superhero, who couples transcendent moral perfection with an extraordinary capability for effective acts, spends much of his time in hiding, because he cannot be an identified voice in the corrupt democratic process. Even when present to the public, the superheroes of the comics and movies wear a mask or uniform that hides their identity as citizens. The American monomyth thus embodies the vigilante tradition, in which redeemer figures who often wore the white robes of the Book of Revelation rid the community of its ostensible enemies.

Since the superheroic redeemers cannot fully reside in a community that wishes to maintain its system of constitutional law and order, they must depart in search of the next community in peril. In the "peaceful" Heidi form of the myth — typically represented by prepubescent girls or sexless women such as Maria in *The Sound of Music* — psychological manipulation produces redemption of hardened hearts and evil actions. In the violent, macho form of the monomyth, which addresses physical threats to civic order that stem from crime or war, the superhero always steps outside any formal institutions to save the community — often inflicting death on evildoers but never following due process of law. The story of the American monomyth typically ends where it began, with the community in paradisiacal harmony but without the superhero or superheroine. The emergence of this story type was obviously bound historically to the opportunities for serialized episodes. The logic of returning again and again dictated that heroes cannot marry or take normal responsibilities because their extraordinary abilities lead them in the next episode to another zone of the democratic society that cannot cope.

The classical monomyth, Campbell argued, projected messages of responsibility to developing adults. In a similar way, many of the superheroic stories carry an invitation for the audience members to emulate the zealous action. For example, in the video games of the late twentieth century, the player is urged to take an imagined weapon in hand and to participate in a form of jihad against evil. These games frequently offer the player a world salvation premise that closely parallels that of the contradictory American civil religion. Atari's *Missile Command* television ad in the early 1980s, for example, carried precisely this message. A boy on the living room floor fires missiles at alien invaders from his console and announces cheerfully to his mother: "My mission in life is to save all of mankind."[6] An ad for a *Star Wars* game in 2002 echoed the same appeal with a more explicit moral theology: "You can even choose which side you'll fight for in this epic galactic struggle. Just remember, whether good or evil, there is only one true commander . . . you."[7]

The story line of the *Captain America* comics derived from a narrative tradition that originated in colonial times, when colonists created the "Indian captivity narratives," which often contained elements from biblical captivities or episodes of holy war.[8] Early forms of the cowboy western developed out of these narratives and were widely popularized by Buffalo Bill's Wild West shows, which first acted out the conquest of the West. Wild Indians would attack an innocent frontier house and threaten the maiden within, whereupon the cowboys would thunder into the arena on their horses.[9] The six-gun in the hands of unelected outsiders became the means of redeeming the innocent. These stories popularized Manifest Destiny and the allegedly selfless imperialism of earlier American civil religion, when seizing other countries surfaced as the nation's mission during the Spanish-American War.

In Owen Wister's classic story *The Virginian* (1901), which became required reading in thousands of schools because it conveyed the ideals of America, the hero is a cool and reluctant killer willing to forsake love and law to rescue a decent life for the community.[10] Wister was a personal friend of President Theodore Roosevelt; in fact, he dedicated his book to Roosevelt. In the axial decade (1929-41), this heroic paradigm of the cool man who operates outside the law with his guns is extended into the superheroic with the creation of a serialized radio program, *The Lone Ranger*. Like the Virginian, whose identity remains unknown to the story's public, the Lone Ranger is actually a Texas Ranger who has taken off his uniform so that he can pursue a quest of unending vengeance against killers who took the life of his fellow Rangers. Assisted by Tonto and his white super-horse, Silver, who provides tireless speed to outrun any foe, the Lone Ranger redeems a different helpless democratic community in every episode. His use of violence is qualified by elaborate restraints: he never kills or even seriously hurts anybody, even though he often shoots them; and though he has left official law enforcement himself, he always hands the subdued evildoers over to the authorities. He never marries the girls who pine for him as he rides off at the end of each episode with the words, "Hiyo Silver, away!"[11]

The closest model for Captain America, however, is Superman, the comic-book hero whose redemptive stories follow the story line of *The Lone Ranger*. This character was created during the Great Depression of the 1930s as a savior figure from the planet Krypton who arrived on planet earth in a tiny spaceship.[12] As the infant departs from his exploding planet in the cinematic form of this story (*Superman The Movie*, 1978), his father, Jor El, says: "We shall explore various concepts of immortality. . . . Earthlings can be a great people, they only lack the light. For this reason, I have sent them you, my only son." Superman's behavior on earth is remarkable principally for his enormous strength and his speed. Like the Virginian and the Lone Ranger, he too hides his identity, working as a reporter on a newspaper, thus functioning within a democratic institution far less satisfying than his redemptive job — which often entails saving the whole world. Even though Superman's community is also incompetent at protecting itself against the evil predators who afflict it, Superman is conservative about challenging the community's failing institutions. Like the Lone Ranger, he always delivers the evildoers to the police rather than killing them or dishing out his own punishment. The man of steel is thus cool, incapable of showing the hot retaliatory anger that characterizes normal conflict situations.

Coming to the world of comic books in 1938, Superman would eventually fight the Nazis, thus earning the scorn of Joseph Goebbels, who reportedly excoriated Superman as "Jewish" in a meeting of the Reichstag.[13] Goebbels seemed correct in identifying a formidable symbolic enemy. One of the comic book's covers in 1944 showed Superman with both Hitler and Tojo by the neck at the same time. So identified was the fighting Superman with "truth, justice, and the American way" that the comic books were widely sold to GIs during World War II, surpassing in popularity more "adult" publications such as *Life, Reader's Digest,* and *The Saturday Evening Post.*[14]

Superman has "died" several times in his more than sixty-year history, but he always undergoes a resurrection. As the nation meditated on the crimes and threats of September 11, Warner Brothers revived him one more time for national television in a new series called "Smallville." In a *TV Guide* article entitled "A Superman for All Seasons," Kevin Smith says: "In these perilous times, we need him more than ever." Smith confronts the contradiction of America's civil religion, and asks whether Superman's appeal was "some kind of vulgar power lust — coveting the strength of Kal-El under earth's yellow sun." His answer is that Superman really had no desire for power, but that he was merely the hard-working "Ultimate Immigrant . . . who came here and made something of himself. He works hard, pays his bills and finds time to stop Brainiac from enslaving Earth."[15] Here Smith encapsulates the preferred persona of the civil religion: the power to save earth combined with an ego that seeks nothing for itself.

Within a year of Superman's success, a legion of superheroes appeared in comic books with the same character formula: Batman, Sandman, Hawkman, and the Spirit were all born in 1939; they would be joined in 1940 and 1941 by Flash, the Green Lantern, the Shield, Captain Marvel, Sub Mariner, Wonder Woman, Plastic Man, and Captain America. From his assignment in the U.S. Army to his star-spangled costume, Captain America had a tighter identification with the American nation than any other superhero. Above all others, he offers a key to the American civil religion as it came to be embedded in the country's popular entertainments.

Living within the dynamic, movie-like story frames of the great comic-book artist Jack Kirby, Captain America represented the transformation of the 4F draft reject Steve Rogers. Kirby's Jewish background made him especially sensitive to the depredations of Nazi Germany, and he projected a world in which the United States would have military conflict with Germany a year before this nation actually entered the war. In *Captain America's* first issue in 1941 — nine months before Hitler's declaration of war against the United States — the U.S. government's Professor Reinstein has created a "strange seething liquid" that will instantly transform both the mind and body of a sickly weakling. As he faces Steve Rogers in the laboratory, he says calmly, "Don't be afraid, son . . . you are about to become one of America's saviors." As Steve's body shudders and turns pink, Reinstein says, "Today he volunteered for army service and he was refused because of his unfit condition! His chance to serve his country seemed gone!" As Rogers' body turns into a magenta steroidal bulk, Professor Reinstein says that he is "the first of a corps of super-agents whose mental ability will make them a terror to spies and saboteurs." Then turning to Steve, who now looks like a heavyweight body builder, he says, "We shall call you **Captain America**, son! Because, like you, America shall gain the strength and the will to safeguard our shores."[16]

Like other comic-book superheroes, Captain America took on a disguised identity as Private Steve Rogers, assigned to duty at "Camp Lehigh" of the U.S. Army. The narrative offers no explanation for the need for secrecy, but the convention of superheroes was so firmly fixed by 1941 that none seemed necessary — particularly because the principal foes of the early *Captain America* episodes were spies and saboteurs within the United States. Like Clark Kent, whose plodding performance in his above-ground life evokes the scorn of his editor, Steve Rogers/Captain America is constantly abused by his sergeant, who calls him a "bumbling meathead" and a "clumsy knucklehead." Because Captain America and his sidekick Bucky so often disappear from Camp Lehigh to go about their "relentless battle against the foes of freedom," Private Rogers often is punished with KP duty ("kitchen patrol"), where he humbly peels potatoes. The redeemer figure in his normal identity thus remains a scorned, marginal figure in the democratic society he is called to redeem.

Taking on the role of civic instructor, *Captain America* issued an invitation to its young readers to become involved in the fight for freedom as "Captain America's Sentinels of Liberty." For ten cents, readers could receive a badge recognizing their role in the "war against the spies and enemies in our midst who threaten our very independence." Each member signed an oath: "I solemnly pledge to uphold the principles of the Sentinels of Liberty and assist Captain America in his war against spies in the U.S.A."[17] To emphasize the importance of bringing youth into the fight against fascism, Timely Comics, the publisher of *Captain America,* brought out *Young Allies Comics* in the summer of 1941, which still predated America's official entry into the war with Germany and Japan. In its first issue, the cover of this comic book shows little Bucky delivering a savage punch to Red Skull, knocking down Hitler himself in the process. Bucky's cohorts are Toro, Tubby, Knuckles, and Whitewash — apparently the first black superhero. As his character moved from one illustrator or publisher to another, Captain America had numerous incarnations and also migrated to other media. Republic Pictures serialized a Captain America in fifteen chapters: instead of his red-white-and-blue flaglike shield, he carried a gun as a district attorney. But the tension between official role and redemptive capacity remained. To confront the villains, he had to strip off his business suit and don his mask and tights.[18]

The aging of the character, interrupted by intermittent downturns of the Captain America franchise, has not dimmed Cap's redemptive aura. If anything, his godlike powers of salvation have been embraced even more flamboyantly by his current creators. In an August 2000 story entitled "Heart," an elderly veteran of the Battle of the Bulge, Stanley Klein, reminisces for his grandchildren about the time that Captain America saved his life.[19] Steve Rogers' company was pinned down by German attackers who moved in for the kill, tossing a deadly "potato masher" grenade toward Steve's company. "Then came the intervention I can only describe as *divine:* Spa-tannnng" goes Cap's star-spangled shield, deflecting the grenade back against the German attackers. "BADOOOOM," the grenade explodes and destroys the Germans. Klein says, "Glory be," because "salvation arrived" in the form of Captain America and Bucky smashing Germans right and left. After the excitement of telling the story of his salvation one more time, Stan has a heart attack and has to be wheeled away to the hospital. There Captain America miraculously appears to share his final moments. Stanley Klein confesses to Cap that since the day of that rescue in battle, he "has cherished every moment of life" and that "I owe my whole family to you. Without you they never would have been."

Captain America's redemptive aura is not restricted to saving individual lives. In a 1999 story entitled "Red Glare," the entire country is under attack again by the Red Skull.[20] Heroes are crucified on the White House lawn, and the Skull has placed his own visage on the Lincoln Memorial in Washington. His armies are marching in the streets of Washington, and a "Skull Platoon" has placed New York under siege. It is a vision of "America destroyed by tyranny and chaos." Despite being urged to use powerful weapons to kill the Skull, Cap refuses to "save the world through premeditated murder." He wants to "find another way," a way that is less aggressive. Yet at the moment he lacks even his supershield, which has been broken. The citizens of New York are dying in 160 degree heat; people in Oxford, Mississippi, are drowning; and Los Angeles freezes to death. Sharon Carter, who accompanies Cap, carries her own blaster weapon and is willing to use it. But Cap continues to insist on hand-to-hand combat as the only honorable way to save the world. Finally, when he is near death himself and the end of the world as we know it is near, he stabs the Red Skull and saves humanity. This elaborate effort at restraint in the use of force — suppressing his own aggressive instinct — places Captain

America in the heroic tradition of the American cowboy killer, the man of purely innocent intention who draws second in the gun battle but shoots more quickly and accurately than the dastardly foe.

As a typical embodiment of the American civil religion, offering regeneration of a helpless democratic society by selfless superheroism, Captain America stands squarely within the narrative tradition that can be traced back through earlier forms of American entertainment to the biblical paradigms employed in the Indian captivity narratives. Other biblical and theological paradigms are also evident in the details of these stories, often created by Jewish artists. Jack Kirby's Captain America also fits comfortably within the Jewish *golem* tradition as an artificial creation with magical powers for the service of its master.[21] In these and countless other examples, superheroes and -heroines exercise the powers otherwise reserved only for God in dealing with evil. They are the individuated embodiments of a civil religion that seeks to redeem the world for democracy, but by means that transcend democratic limits on the exercise of power.

The Popularization of Crusading Zeal

The story of superheroes who must bypass the restraints of law to redeem the nation and the world has become dominant in the past sixty years, and it should now be recognized as a major source of the crusading idealism that marks the American civil religion. *Star Trek,* the most durable series in television history, began its long career in the 1960s with struggles over the "prime directive," which forbade the *Enterprise* from interfering with the cultures they encountered in the galaxies — a prohibition they almost always ignored. In the more tolerant multicultural series that followed the original — *The Next Generation, Deep Space Nine, Voyager* — the crew's leaders continued to redeem the distressed worlds they encountered. In *The Next Generation's* concluding episode, a story of time-travel entitled "All Good Things,"[22] the retired Captain Picard defies common sense and lawful orders to redeem all of human existence, back to its very beginnings. The Paramount corporation, which controls the *Star Trek* franchise, has created "The *Star Trek* Experience" at the Las Vegas Hilton. It offers fans the opportunity to enter the *Star Trek* world by participating in a simulated flight that is under attack by a vicious Klingon leader. The objective is to blow up Klingon power sources and enemy fighters. This fantasy tour provides an experience of the innocent under siege, who eventually prevail by means of superior technology and firepower.

This same moral and technological pattern is repeated over and over again

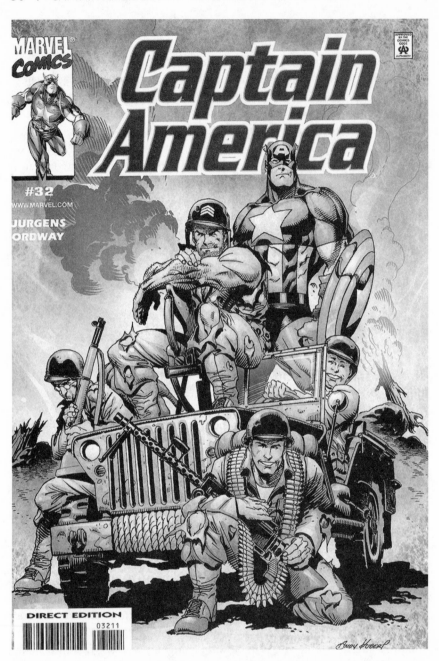

Since his birth shortly before World War II, Captain America has linked his zeal to the
U.S. Army — though he regularly defies his command to carry out secret missions.

Credit: © 2000, Marvel Comics

in the world of video games, from the above-mentioned Atari's *Missile Command* of the 1980s to the contemporary games such as *Duke Nukem* and *Doom*. The scenarios for *Doom* and *Quake*, the games that claimed so much of the time and attention of Eric Harris and Dylan Klebold, the Columbine High School murderers, embody plot elements familiar from the American monomyth. *Ultimate Doom*[23] presents a heroic character whose moral credentials are that he has defied the command of his Marine unit by protecting civilians: "You're a marine, one of the Earth's toughest, hardened in combat and trained for action. Three years ago, you assaulted a superior officer for ordering his soldiers to fire upon civilians. He and his body cast were shipped to Pearl Harbor while you were transferred to Mars, home of the Union Aerospace Corporation."[24] In a posthumously discovered videotape, Harris and Klebold paid tribute to *Doom's* inspirational role in their plans: Harris sits with his shotgun "Arlene" (a *Doom*-derived name) and says: "It's going to be like f — ing *Doom*. Tick, tick, tick. . . . Haa! That f — ing shotgun is straight out of *Doom*."[25] What they had assimilated from this game was its message that cleansing their world of the evil that afflicted them would require a radical defiance of law.

The disaster film genre is rife with stories of defiant heroes who have the wisdom to save the world. In the film *Armageddon,* the entire world is saved by a wildcat oildriller from Texas, Harry Stamper (played by Bruce Willis). Taking a crew of misfits with petty criminal records to drill and blow up the asteroid, Stamper discovers depravity in the highest ranks of government. When the drilling rig initially breaks down and the men cannot place their explosives at the proper depth, President Stanley Anderson and his advisors panic and decide to blow up the nuclear device on the surface. This futile gesture will obviously take the lives of the men aboard and, in turn, destroy any hope for human survival. When Colonel Sharp, who has piloted the shuttle, accepts this wicked and stupid order, Harry Stamper threatens to kill him. Finally, with just one second left, he coerces him to disobey; but Col. Sharp's disarming of the device by cutting its wires has disabled its capability for remote detonation. So Stamper eventually must accept the suicide mission that is required for deep emplacement of the nuclear explosive on the asteroid.

The final scenes of the film shuffle through villages, mosques, churches, and synagogues around the world. As in the sister disaster films *Deep Impact* and *Independence Day,* a grateful world lifts its eyes to the heavens and expresses relief at being saved by the heroes from the United States. The U.S. government gets national glory in *Armageddon;* but every viewer knows that the success must be credited to that singular man Harry Stamper, who courageously disobeyed an evil president willing to betray him and his men.

Even the Walt Disney stories bear messages about how benign power triumphs over aggressiveness to redeem disordered worlds. *The Lion King,* which has enjoyed great popularity as an animated film and as a Broadway musical, is a feudal restoration drama transposed to the African savannah. The film begins in a kind of peaceable kingdom. The lion King Mufasa rules a beautiful land, and the animals who are normally breakfast, lunch, and dinner for lions gather for a ceremonial blessing of the legitimate successor to Pride's Rock, the cub Prince Simba. As Simba grows toward adolescence, paradise is destroyed by an evil uncle, Scar, who has a plan to murder both Simba and his father, Mufasa. In his moment of supreme treachery, Scar triggers a wildebeest stampede and pushes Mufasa into it, thus succeeding in killing the King but missing his opportunity to kill little Prince Simba. However, he does psychically disable Simba by encouraging the cub to believe that his trek into the forbidden elephant graveyard was responsible for the tragedy. Simba accepts Scar's suggestion that he go into exile as his punishment. The suffering Pride Land yearns for a ruler of beneficent disposition, and Simba is eventually persuaded to return by the female Nala. He confronts Scar, then gently pushes him to his death among his disloyal hyenas. Simba marries his Nala, and they become the parents of a new cub — thus renewing "the circle of life." The assembled kingdom chants, "Simba, you must rule with peace, you must rule with love." Simba, the good lion who has established his lack of aggressiveness through an early experience of victimization and his benign disposal of Scar, has morally triumphed over the bad lion, who wanted to triumph through predation. Pride Land had become so corrupt that it could not generate its needed leaders. Only an outsider such as Simba, possessed of the purest motivations, could return and cleanse the suffering kingdom of its corrupt leaders and vicious hyenas.

Popular culture is dominated by these enthralling stories that depict impotent communities requiring an extraordinary outsider to cope with the evils in their midst. Many of the successful film careers of the twentieth century, such as those of John Wayne, Clint Eastwood, Charles Bronson, Sylvester Stallone, Mel Gibson, and Steven Seagal, have been built around the persona of the passive, strongly quiet person who explodes into righteous, purifying violence. The same is true of many successful mythic franchises such as the *Star Wars* film series.

Why haven't the great creators and performers succeeded in giving American society entertainments that reflect democratic premises — that institutions restrained by constitutions, responsive to voting constituencies, and staffed by persons of average means can provide effective government, even in the face of threats? Despite considerable imperfections, effective democratic government has been the reality of much of American life, both in routine daily life and in times of crisis.

We would like to believe in what might be called "the holiday effect." Since excessive work yields diminishing returns for tired workers, they often return from holidays with renewed zest and vigor for their tasks. It would be reassuring to discover that the fascist strand in the American monomyth has a similarly cathartic influence that invigorates the democratic life. Unfortunately, we find no evidence that this is the case in our civic experience. The American monomyth seems, in fact, to be the ritual life of zealous nationalism, giving it the emotional power that the more sober prophetic realism has trouble generating. We suspect that there is an American monomythic fantasy cycle here, in which the interplay between entertainments and political threats pulls us away from our democratic ideals.

The ad for the Topps "Enduring Freedom" picture cards cited at the beginning of this chapter illustrates how casually pop culture recasts our constitutional political system in its simplified, demonic terms — focusing on the power of the executive. Among the ninety cards in the full set, eleven depict President Bush, while one depicts National Security Adviser Condoleezza Rice. Topps Chairman Arthur Shorin tells the nation's children "that the President (and his team) will keep [them] safe and that evil doers will be punished." Also, the company sent one million of the cards free to American servicemen and -women, "as an immediate mini-morale booster."[26] In this fantasy world, which so much resembles comic books and adventure films, the presidency is in effect redefined as Captain America himself.[27]

American Superheroism as a Threat to Democracy

In thinking about the effects of the nation's mythic addiction to stories of community impotence and superhero redemption, one can understand why decades ago George Gerbner and Larry Gross believed that television violence, in addition to inspiring imitative behavior on the part of some, might have the predominant effect of encouraging passivity. "Fear may be a more critical concomitant of a show of violence than aggression. . . . Acceptance of violence and passivity in the face of injustice may be consequences of great social concern."[28] Given the requirements of the redeemer role — total selflessness, sexual renunciation, isolation from the community, and cool courage in the face of impossible odds — very few are audacious enough to respond directly to implicit invitations to imitate the hero. The rest of the audience may find their model of political behavior in applauding passively from the grandstand, convinced by the story that they are too impotent to cope with evil. Monomythic drama has the character of a tranquilizer, ex-

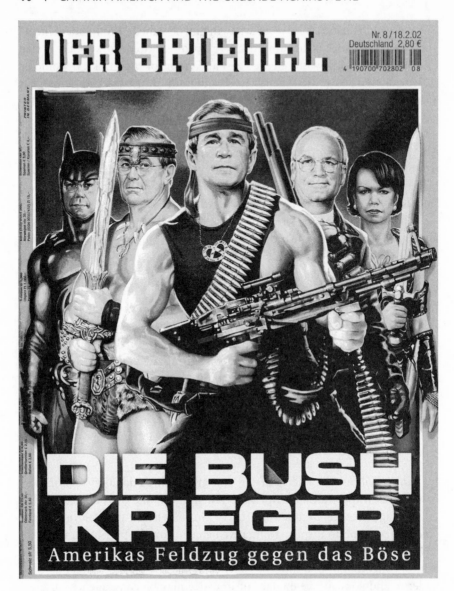

Germany's newsmagazine *Der Spiegel* suggested pop-culture heroism as the inspiration
for the Bush administration's war on terrorism. U.S. Ambassador Coats requested
poster-size reproductions for the White House.
Credit: © 2002, Spiegel, Gmbh.

changing the sense of communal alarm and obligation for the fantasy of an Eden-like resolution achievable only by superhumans.

The effect of this monomythic cop-out is to encourage the very central-ization of power that democratic theorists have considered to be the greatest potential danger to the political order. Superhuman leaders in monomythic dramas are granted unlimited powers to accomplish the impossible task of restoring paradise. They can make and enforce a personal sense of justice as they see fit, as did the 1941 Captain America, who was unleashed to attack Hit-ler before a formal declaration of war against Germany. Or Ronald Reagan's White House adviser Oliver North, Jr., who was determined to wage a war in Nicaragua despite an explicit congressional ban against it.

The question of who should be entrusted with such incredible power is answered by the monomythic conventions for the selfless superhero, but democratic theorists would pose decisive objections. As Karl Popper has sug-gested, democratic thinkers shun the traditional and authoritarian question "Who should rule?" because it presupposes we can identify the "good ones." Experience indicates the difficulty of finding persons in whom total power can be entrusted, and our most perceptive tradition about human nature informs us that power inevitably corrupts. Therefore, Popper argues, "we must ask whether . . . we should not prepare for the worst leaders, and hope for the best." He suggests that we replace the question "Who should rule?" with the question "How can we so organize political institutions that bad or incompetent rulers can be prevented from doing too much damage?"[29] The answer for American life and its civil religion lies in finding ways to check power rather than hoping that superheroic force will somehow redeem a "corrupt republic." Personal crusades against evil, so perfectly exemplified in the American monomyth, hardly qualify as standing within the tradition of democratic sentiment.

The results of surrendering personal responsibility to savior figures are evident in some of the greatest tragedies of the twentieth century. Ernest Becker has called such surrender "the Demonic" of our time. By this he refers to those tendencies of human action that defeat the possibility for survival and the equitable development of human potential.

> In the realm of human affairs, The Demonic *is* real. It is engendered by the acts of men, or better . . . by the *failure* of men to act. Specifically, it comes into being when men fail to act *individually* and *willfully*, on the basis of their own *personal, responsible* powers. The Demonic refers specifically to the creation of power by groups of men who blindly follow authority and convention, power which engulfs them and defeats them.

Democracy, Becker argues, attempts to cope with the demonic by envisioning each person as "an end in himself and a responsible, self-reliant point of authority to which power leaders and power institutions are beholden." In particular, democracy fears those entrusted with power: "It knew that the leader had to be controlled by responsible and willful masses of men, precisely because he will be corrupted by power into making decisions that are self-defeating. Whether he knows it or not, or admits it or not, the leader needs to be curbed, needs the broadest base of self-limiting decisions."[30]

Traditional democratic theory of limiting power expressed optimism about the wide diffusion of intelligence among the citizenry. Individuals acting on their own judgments could assert a collective responsibility superior in wisdom to the inspirations from individual saviors. Without denying that democracy often fails to live according to its own mythic heritage, one can clearly see that the American monomyth betrays deep antagonism toward the creative exercise of reason on the part of the public as well as the individual. Careful deliberation, knowledge of law, and mastery of book learning are usually presented in monomythic materials as indicators of impotence or corruption. In the exercise of redemptive power, purity of intention suffices. Heroes are either static, innately possessing all the wisdom they need, or they learn all they require from a single incident. The public and its representatives are pictured as too stupid to survive confrontations with evil.

The Challenge of Pop Fascism

During the twentieth century, American popular culture has woven a polyphonic mythos that echoes the presumption of Senator Beveridge that "the American people" are "the chosen people to lead in the regeneration of the world." These stories consistently place American-style heroes at the center of impossibly dangerous situations that seem to require geniuses possessing super powers of moral intuition, intellect, and physical force. The plots of these mythic tales typically include adulation from the impotent communities that benefit from the exercise of beneficent powers. Contradictory strands from civil religion are also usually apparent. And here we detect some thoroughly fascist notions:

- that super power held in the hands of one person can achieve more justice than the workings of democratic institutions;
- that democratic systems of law and order, of constitutional restraint, are fatally flawed when confronted with genuine evil;

- that the community will never suffer from the depredations of such a super leader, whose servanthood is allegedly selfless;
- that the world as a whole requires the services of American superheroism that destroys evildoers through selfless crusades.

A striking confirmation of the influence of these mythic images came in an incident at *Der Spiegel*, Germany's foremost news magazine. To accompany a feature article on the Bush administration's crusade against evil, the magazine created a satirical cover casting each national security player in the role of a zealous destroyer from American popular culture.[31] George W. Bush received a muscular Rambo body holding an automatic weapon and ammunition belts. Vice President Cheney became "The Terminator," while National Security Adviser Condoleezza Rice was dressed as Xena, Warrior Princess. Secretary of State Colin Powell was Batman, and Secretary of Defense Donald Rumsfeld was Conan the Barbarian, holding a sword dripping with blood.

Daniel Coats, the U.S. Ambassador to Germany, visited *Der Spiegel's* editorial offices, not to protest the caricature but to report that "the President was flattered," whereupon he ordered thirty-three poster-size renditions of the cover to be conveyed back to the White House.[32] Each of Bush's staff depicted on the cover reportedly wanted a copy. In this context it is difficult to forget that John Rambo, in *First Blood*, burns down the law enforcement headquarters of his hometown; and that in *First Blood, Part II*, he finally turns a shower of lead against the computers and radio equipment at the CIA control center. Or that in *Rambo III* he carries weapons to the mujaheddin in Afghanistan for their jihad against the Soviets, fighting furiously at their side. The fierce emotion and muscular power of Rambo obviously need a correspondingly larger brain to avoid such contradictory behavior. But the array of superheroic advisors ranked behind Rambo suggests that they support his crusade without grasping its divergence from the ethos of a constitutional democracy.

In the chapters that follow, we lay out the historical steps through which this contradictory miracle of faith became credible to the millions of people who enjoy such stories and consider them wholesome entertainment. That the ideas incorporated in these stories are indeed credible, not just to the fans of comic books, but even to political leaders, became evident in developments since the destruction of the World Trade Center and a portion of the Pentagon on September 11, 2001. We shall see that the fascist thinking lurking in the shadow side of the Captain America complex has roots in its religious foundations, and that these roots have always produced poisonous fruit.

4 A Rod of Iron or a Light to the Nations

Ask of me, and I will make the nations your heritage,
    and the ends of the earth your possession.
You shall break them with a rod of iron,
    and dash them to pieces like a potter's vessel.

Psalm 2:8-9[1]

I will give you as a light to the nations,
    that my salvation may reach to the end of the earth.

Isaiah 49:6

While Americans of earlier generations assumed they were the Israel of their time, we must recapture for our secular era what this meant. What sense of mission did the civil religion of writers such as Herman Melville, for example, derive from the pages of Holy Writ? To assist in this quest, we must pose this question from a double vantage point. First, using the tools of modern biblical research, we will ask: How did the ancient writers themselves answer the question of mission? Second, we will ask: How did early Americans, who read the Scriptures without the benefit of modern methods, understand this mission and apply it to themselves? Are there significant analogies to the adaptation of biblical themes in Judaism and Islam?

We begin with ancient Israel's traditions — to be a "rod of iron" or to be a "light to the nations."

The Birth of Israelite Zeal and Realism

A vivid sense of mission permeates the accounts of Israel's beginnings. The father of the people, Abram, was called to leave his home and set out for an unknown land where he would become a blessing for the entire world. "Go from your country . . . and I will make of you a great nation . . . and by you all the families of the earth shall bless themselves" (Gen. 12:1-3). The belief that God would battle to achieve this mission was solidified at the time of the exodus from Egypt. Moses proclaimed that Yahweh, the God of battle, would set his people free and give them the promised land.[2] God assured those who were being pursued by Pharaoh's chariots:

> Fear not, stand firm, and see the salvation of Yahweh, which we will work for you today. . . . Yahweh will fight for you, and you have only to be still. (Ex. 14:13f.)

> Sing to Yahweh, who has triumphed gloriously,
>   horse and chariot he has cast into the sea. . . .
> Yahweh is a warrior! (Ex. 15:1, 3)

They would be set free by violence to fulfill their mission of saving the world.

In actuality only one group of Israelites participated in this escape from Egypt, later becoming joined with other groups in the area of Palestine who accepted this founding myth.[3] It thereby became the "primary story of salvation for Israel. . . . The mythology of the story has powerful religious and social consequences," as shown by Thomas Dozeman: "The destruction of the Egyptian army . . . is a salvific event. . . . It is a celebration of the power of a national God, in which death for one group is salvation for another."[4] In contrast to other ancient traditions of holy war where the gods contended with each other,[5] Yahweh's battles served the cause of "Israel's deliverance" in order to achieve its national mission within the scope of world history.[6]

This incipient form of zealous nationalism developed a scheme of conquest a generation after the exodus.[7] Yahweh owned the land and would wrest it from the hands of the feudal rulers of Canaan whose overlord, Pharaoh, he had already defeated. God would give Canaan to his peasants in fulfillment of his promise to Abram.[8] Aided by the virtual power vacuum in the rugged and largely unoccupied hill country of western Palestine, this ideology provided the impetus for the infiltration, revolution, and coalitions that established Israel in Canaan.[9] Groups of varying racial and regional backgrounds formed a tribal confederation on the theocratic premise that Yahweh would be their king and defender. In contrast to the Exodus where Israel "only had to keep quiet and observe the great act which YHWH performed against the Egyptians," in the conquest narratives "the Israelites were involved in aggressive warfare led by Moses or Joshua."[10] Thereafter God would raise up charismatic leaders in times of emergency who would call out the volunteers for battle.[11] The response to such calls was "zeal," the passionate commitment to the national mission that matched the vehemence of the zealous God, Yahweh. He was called Yahweh Sabaoth, "the Lord of Hosts" that included both the army of Israel and the angelic warriors who contended mysteriously in their behalf.[12]

This ideology persisted in the dominant form of Israelite religion despite the emergence of the monarchy.[13] It was particularly prominent in the Northern Kingdom, where the passionate impulse toppled one dynasty after the other. With a tenacious willingness to "fight for right," popular prophets such as Elisha stirred up revolutions.[14] They called for total war against Yahweh's presumed enemies at home and abroad, which resulted in a disastrous series of purges and foreign campaigns.[15] Purges and reforms were motivated in part, according to Norman Gottwald, "by the desire to 'purify' religious practices in order to secure for the state the endangered blessing of Yahweh."[16] These prophets "were extremists in their insistence that Israel live wholly by the ancient rules of holy war. Yahweh's power to deliver his people must be trusted even in the face of seemingly hopeless odds."[17] Such extremism was a recipe for disaster in the Fertile Crescent where the great powers were constantly vying for dominance.

Despite the resurgence under Jeroboam II, in which military successes made possible by the nonintervention of the great empires were interpreted as Yahweh's blessings for an elect and righteous people, the Northern Kingdom could not survive. It repeatedly confronted Assyria, certain that Yahweh would guarantee victory for the righteous defenders of national independence.[18] As a result the Northern Kingdom was dismembered, its last remnant disappearing with the fall of Samaria in 721 BCE.[19] The reliance on a pure form of zealous nationalism proved suicidal.

A few years before this collapse a new type of religious impulse emerged — prophetic realism. A layman from a southern village traveled to the royal sanctuary at Bethel in Israel's Northern Kingdom, declaring there that Yahweh's justice worked impartially to thwart the excesses of believing and nonbelieving nations alike.[20] Amos sought to shatter illusions of superior virtue and inevitable victory, warning that the Day of Yahweh would be a shock rather than a comfort (Amos 5:18ff.).[21] He pointed out that Israel had indulged in the same sorts of war crimes for which other nations had been destroyed;[22] her callous disdain for the life of victims and her ruthless exploitation of the poor were destroying Israel from within (Amos 2:6-16).[23] As for the myth of superior chosenness, had not other nations also undergone exodus experiences (Amos 9:7f.)?[24] If the Northern Kingdom were not true to its mission of justice, what could keep it from suffering the fate of proud and brutal nations in the past?[25]

Amos was banned from Bethel as a subversive, but Hosea took up the critique from within the Northern Kingdom itself. He attacked the mystique of violence popularized during the purge of Jehu a hundred years earlier (Hos. 1:4-6).[26] He thus countered the tradition of Elijah and Elisha, which defined the nation as Yahweh's agency of wrath against heretics and foreigners. The matter of fighting for principle had developed, as Hosea saw it, into a blank check for assassinating one's rivals (Hos. 7:6f.). In the space of fourteen years, this violent mystique had resulted in the murder of four kings.[27] Atrocities came to be performed by troops and police against their fellow citizens of different political persuasion (2 Kings 15:16). The court system became corrupt and inefficient (Hos. 5:1; 7:1f.; 10:4), because a nation that believes it can rid the world of evil by killing its enemies no longer comprehends the need for the slow processes of law. Respect for authority disintegrated (Hos. 10:3), and the limits of self-restraint melted away: "They break all bounds and murder follows murder" (Hos. 4:2).[28] Because religion had degenerated into a means to guarantee success and power, the chosen people had lost touch with the vitality and stability of a living faith; they had crumbled from within, and destruction was inevitable (Hos. 5:11f.).[29] As Patrick Miller has shown, this divine judgment "is not capricious or irrational because it corresponds to the sin. . . . One observes here the consequential relationship between the deed (sin) and its result (punishment)."[30]

At first this new prophetic impulse stood on the periphery of Israel's religious consciousness, virtually drowned out by the voices of popular, nationalistic prophets in both North and South. However, with the fall of the Northern Kingdom, the self-critical, prophetic impulse came to the fore as a realistic appraisal of the national mission's failure. The simplistic claim that God would always favor the elect had led into the abyss and opened the way for a more realistic view. The critical impulse was picked up by Isaiah, who worked among the royal elite in Judah. He saw that Yahweh refused to play favorites, that God would shatter the vanity corrupting Israel's sense of mission. "I will put an end to the pride of the arrogant, and lay low the haughti-ness of the ruthless" (Isa. 13:11).[31] No nation was exempt from Yahweh's moral zeal, and the course of current events confirmed the fate of those who let themselves be driven by the arrogance of power.

When Hezekiah came to power in the South after a period of subjugation to Assyria and sought to revive fervent religious nationalism,[32] Isaiah argued for a realistic assessment of power factors.[33] Whereas Hezekiah's sense of mis-sion led him to assume that his crusade for independence would produce "peace and security" in his days (Isa. 39:8), the prophet sought to expose the myth that the chosen people would always prevail. He criticized the policies of creating an anti-Assyrian alliance with unreliable partners, and of relying on sophisticated arms systems: "Woe to those who go down to Egypt for help and who rely on horses, who trust in chariots because they are many and in horsemen because they are very strong, but do not look to the Holy One of Is-rael or consult the Lord!" (Isa. 31:1).[34] The devastating Assyrian invasion of 701 BCE confirmed Isaiah's realism and shattered the basis for militant nation-alism in Israel's Southern Kingdom. The defeat was interpreted by some as an indication that Israel had no distinctive mission, thus opening the doors to cynicism and the acceptance of foreign impulses. But for Isaiah, the defeat merely confirmed the bankruptcy of the uncritical strand of popular religion and the authenticity of the deeper prophetic vision first enunciated by Amos. Isaiah saw that the calamity could provide a catharsis that might destroy Is-rael's illusions of superiority in virtue and power (Isa. 1:25f.). In letting herself be purified by defeat, Israel might be able to take up her true national mission of bearing the word of God's impartial justice as the basis for world peace. The prophet envisioned that taking on such a role would make an era of gen-uine tranquility possible. Instead of a world empire ruled from Jerusalem with a rod of iron held above her prostrate enemies, a voluntary confedera-tion of nations could submit to adjudication of disputes by impartial law (Isa. 2:1-4).

The Critique of Zealous Warfare by Prophetic Realists

Israel's subsequent history reflects the dilemmas posed by these two conflict-ing versions of mission. By the seventh century BCE, zealous nationalism was on the upsurge once again. King Josiah declared independence from a declin-ing Assyria and created an effective military system with inspiration from the Book of Deuteronomy's ideology.[35] This influential work was published un-der Josiah's aegis to revive the zealous spirit of the ancient confederacy. It taught that Israel would always prevail in battle if it obeyed the cultic law. It neatly incorporated the prophetic impulse into its scheme with the dogma that the Northern Kingdom had fallen because it disobeyed the numerous strictures focused on ritual purity. The zealous energy released by this synthesis of cultic purity with imperial power permitted a reshaping of historical understanding in the books of Joshua, Judges, 1 and 2 Samuel, and 1 and 2 Kings. Prophetic realism's common sense was blunted by this absorption, producing massive illusions that could only lead to disaster. When the nation was confronted within a decade by the overwhelming power of Babylon, the nationalistic prophets influenced by Deuteronomy promised "peace" because Yahweh would never allow his obedient nation to be defeated (see Jer. 8:11, 19).[36]

The voice of realism in this confrontation with the Babylonian superpower was Jeremiah's. He opposed the popular synthesis of Deuteronomy as a dangerous and arrogant perversion of the national mission.[37] By gestures such as shattering pottery in the Temple and walking through Jerusalem wearing the yoke of a prisoner of war, he warned about the consequences of following the course of the fanatical nationalists.[38] They claimed, "No evil shall come upon us, nor will we see sword or famine," but Jeremiah hears Yahweh threaten to bring the Babylonians against them:

> Behold, I am bringing upon you
>   a nation from afar, O house of Israel, says the LORD.
> It is an enduring nation,
>   it is an ancient nation,
> a nation whose language you do not know,
>   nor can you understand what they say.
> Their quiver is like an open tomb,
>   they are all mighty men.
> They shall eat up your harvest and your food;
>   they shall eat up your sons and your daughters;
> they shall eat up your flocks and your herds;
>   they shall eat up your vines and your fig trees;
> your fortified cities in which you trust
>   they shall destroy with the sword. (Jer. 5:15-17)[39]

In response to such oracles, the populace rebuffed Jeremiah and imprisoned him for a time as a subversive. On the eve of the Babylonian siege, Jeremiah was summoned by King Zedekiah, who made a final attempt to enlist him in the zealous cause. "Inquire of Yahweh for us, for Nebuchadrezzar king of Babylon is making war against us; perhaps Yahweh will deal with us according to all his wonderful deeds, and will make him withdraw from us" (Jer. 21:2).[40] But it was too late for miracles. Jerusalem was sacked and its territory dismembered. When the fanatical fundamentalists revolted again ten years later, with the same mistaken image of national mission and grandeur, the capital was leveled and the remnants of its population deported into Babylon. The failure to accept prophetic realism in understanding its national mission had led to the annihilation of the Southern Kingdom just as it had earlier of the Northern.

During the captivity period, the two conflicting versions of mission continued to tug at the souls of the survivors. Isaiah's successors voiced the humane, tolerant viewpoint with their interpretation of Israel as a suffering servant for the redemption of the world and of a restored temple as "a house of prayer for all peoples" (Isa. 56:7). On the other hand, Ezra and Nehemiah developed a narrow, nationalistic perspective and reestablished a cult center in Jerusalem on the basis of a racist, legalistic exclusivism and a conviction that the great, terrible Yahweh was calling them into battle for the nationalistic ideals (Neh. 4:20). This effort to reestablish a zealous fervor came to a climax when Joel tauntingly reversed Isaiah's own words in a call to scuttle the heritage of prophetic realism through a renewal of zealous warfare: "Beat your plowshares into swords, and your pruning hooks into spears; let the weak say, 'I am a warrior'" (Joel 3:10).

This call to battle was heeded in a later generation by the Maccabees, who revolted against their Hellenistic overlords in the middle of the second century BCE. They were convinced that Yahweh was leading them in battle and providing the victories against the Greek mercenaries. They took considerable pains to follow the Deuteronomic instructions about massacring prisoners and burning cities; at first they even took the Sabbath regulations so seriously that they suffered some serious reverses. They directed their campaign as much against their own Greek-sympathizing fellow Jews as against the foreign troops. Judas Maccabeus "went through the cities of Judah; he destroyed the ungodly out of the land; thus he turned away wrath from Israel" (1 Macc. 3:8). The premise here is thoroughly Deuteronomic: misfortune for the chosen people is due to divine wrath provoked by traitors; if they are wiped out, wrath will be assuaged and victory will then be inevitable. Judas clearly enunciated the zealous ideology in these words: "It is easy for many to be hemmed in by few, for in the sight of Heaven there is no difference between saving by many or by few. It is not on the size of the army that victory in battle depends, but strength comes from Heaven" (1 Macc. 3:18f.).

The fierce ideology worked better against the Hellenistic mercenaries than it had against the Assyrians or Babylonians. The Maccabees won their war of independence. The author of Daniel, however, was realistic enough to maintain that the Maccabean warriors had contributed only "a little help" for God's cause and that elements of vainglory were present in their ideology and behavior (Dan. 11:34). In other regards, however, he agreed with the zealous nationalists that the enemy was beastly and ought to be annihilated. The empires are depicted as ferocious animals that devour one another in turn. The saints, on the other hand, remain human in their righteous obedience to the law of God.[41] The book envisioned a permanent period of world domination after Yahweh's triumph: "But the saints of the Most High shall receive the kingdom, and possess the kingdom for ever. . . . Their kingdom shall be an everlasting kingdom, and all dominions shall serve and obey them" (Dan. 7:18, 27). This empire would presumably be simple for the saints to administer because all of their potential enemies would have been destroyed.

Israel's Dilemma during the Roman Period

With the Roman invasion of Palestine in the next century, this vision of triumphant zealotry encountered the shock of reality. The struggle to redefine the national mission turned inward with the emergence of well-defined parties in Judaism, each offering its interpretation of the way to bring in God's kingdom.[42] The Pharisees contended that compliance with their updated version of the Deuteronomic law would bring the triumph of the saints. The movements of the Essenes and Zealots argued that courageous battle against Rome was required to destroy its demonic domination: if all Israel would rise up in arms, God's wrath would be assuaged and his angelic host would intervene to destroy Rome, leaving the saints to rule.[43] The Sadducees felt that their position of power through collaboration with the Roman authorities constituted the best of all possible kingdoms, so they rejected the prophetic tradition in its entirety. All of these groups, in fact, represented versions of the zealous tradition with its inflated sense of national virtue and its disdain for truly impartial justice.[44] Only in segments within the Pharisee party were there substantial elements of realism, but even these were mitigated by the spirit of Daniel that divided the world into stereotyped groups and yearned for the world domination by the saints. The synthesis of Deuteronomy, the Deuteronomistic history, and the apocalyptic triumphalism of Daniel appear to have drowned out the great prophetic version of Israel's national mission. What remained was the muddle of internecine warfare, with each faction seeing the devil in the others' camps, and with each devoutly bent on destruction. As the first century CE war on, this bitter ideological strife became more and more violent. It led to intermittent but bloody guerilla warfare against the Roman legions and to the dreadful sequence of assassinations and massacres described by Josephus in *The Jewish War*. It led in the end to the rebellions against Rome in CE 66-70 and again in 132-135, which decimated the population of Palestine. Israel proved unable to survive with its sense of mission so fragmented by zealotry.

The clear enunciation of prophetic realism during this final period was set forth by Jesus of Nazareth.[45] At the beginning of his ministry he rejected the dream of bringing the messianic kingdom through violence (Luke 4:5-8).[46] He located evil not in one's foreign or ideological enemy but in the heart of the chosen people itself, exposing the cruelty and callous disregard for life that legalistic self-righteousness had produced (Mark 3:1-6). He reversed the premise of divine favoritism for the chosen people, suggesting that sinners and foreigners would be the first to be welcomed into God's kingdom (Luke 4:16-30). As John Riches has shown, Jesus challenged the popular "belief that God's justice required that he destroy the wicked, notably the oppressors of Israel."[47] Jesus worked to alter the stereotypes that made zealous warfare seem necessary, picturing a hated Samaritan as humane[48] and welcoming into his circle disciples from various sides of the ideological struggle. He warned his fellow Jews about the dangers of subscribing to the zealous war aims, predicting that a revolt against Rome would bring destruction to Jerusalem (Luke 19:41-44; 23:26-31).[49]

While he expressed the willingness to support the Roman Empire by paying taxes (Mark 12:13-17), he condemned its propensity to substitute brute force for its vaunted world rule of law (Matt. 26:55). At the same time, he thrust a note of realism into the minds of the disciples when one of them began to use the sword against the authorities in Gethsemane: "Put your sword back into its place; for all who take the sword will perish by the sword. Do you think that I cannot appeal to my Father, and he will at once send me more than twelve legions of angels?" (Matt. 26:52f.). The background of zealous ideology is visible in this citation. Zealots had expected angelic intervention in the decisive battle with Rome, and as Josephus reports, this expectation remained vital until the final hours of the siege in Jerusalem some forty years after Jesus' death.[50] What Jesus seems to be arguing here is that an act of zealous rebellion will not guarantee the intervention of divine forces, as the nationalists assumed. And without such assistance, those who take up the sword will in all likelihood die by the sword. It is a supreme statement of prophetic realism.[51]

The Book of Revelation and the Dominance of Zealotry

The tragic dimension of Jesus' message concerning Israel's mission was not only that it was rejected and its promulgator put to death as a renegade; it was not only that it was misunderstood and distorted by those who preferred not to hear the truth about themselves; it was that the message itself came to be placed in a collection of writings that obscured its essential thrust. Jesus' message was interpreted by posterity in the light of Deuteronomy, of Daniel, and, worst of all, the Book of Revelation. This is a matter frequently overlooked by critical biblical scholarship, concerned as it is with the meaning of passages for their original audiences. For later generations, however, and throughout much of the course of the American experience in particular, it was the Book of Revelation that placed its stamp upon the whole Bible.[52]

Revelation stands triumphantly at the end of the canon, submerging the strand of prophetic realism — including the message of Jesus — under a grandiose flood of zealous images and ideas. It pictures the plot of world history as a battle between God and God's demonic enemies. Over and over again it promises total victory to the saints. It urges them to keep pure and undefiled while God annihilates their opponents, whom it stereotypes as bestial and irredeemable. Perhaps the most insidious impact on later generations lies in its coalescence of the humane tradition of the fatherhood of God and the zealous tradition of the annihilation of enemies. For example, the idea of God's word, defined in Isaiah 11:3ff. and in the early Christian tradition as the redemptive force that would replace warfare as a means of adjudicating conflicts, is transposed by Revelation 19 into an image of annihilation.[53] The fearsome rider on the white horse is called "The Word of God," in this vision:

> And the armies of heaven, arrayed in white linen, white and pure, followed him on white horses. From his mouth issues a sharp sword with which to smite the nations, and he will rule them with a rod of iron; he will tread the wine press of the fury of the wrath of God the Almighty. (Rev. 19:13-15)

The reader will recognize this passage as the inspiration for "The Battle Hymn of the Republic."[54] In following Revelation's use of this imagery, Julia Ward Howe failed to notice that the "sword" proper and the "sword of the word" indicate two diametrically opposed methods of redemption. The one originated in the tradition of zealous nationalism and the other in the tradition of prophetic realism.[55] Another instance of transposed ideas and images from Revelation is the use of "lamb" for Jesus, a term employed in Isaiah 53 and in early Christian tradition to depict redemptive self-sacrifice. In John's

Revelation the "lamb" is so ferocious an agent of war that people cry out to the towering mountains, "Fall on us and hide us from the face of him who is seated on the throne, and from the wrath of the Lamb" (Rev. 6:16).[56] The juxtaposition of tradition and image in the phrase "wrath of the lamb" would jar anyone not raised in the tradition of seeing the entire Bible through the lens of the Book of Revelation. But with this lens, the idea of redemptive love is simply subsumed under the category of redemptive wrath, and the stage is set for a long tradition of theological equivocation. Waging war out of "love" and destroying enemies in order "to save them" are the all-too-understandable results of such a perspective.

In summary, under the impact of the Book of Revelation, an appealing synthesis of apocalyptic, zealous nationalism became accessible to the uncritical mind. Its dominant feature was a dualistic premise about the participants in the battles that presumably drive history toward its predestined goal. On the one side was Satan, with his allies in multiple guises, acting through a grand, conspiratorial design to destroy the saints. To the zealot every rival became an agent of this satanic host and was thus stereotyped as inhuman and irredeemable. Standing on the other side were the saints, stereotyped as pure and entirely righteous, untouched by universal sin and maintaining a passive form of zeal while waiting for God's design of triumph to reveal itself. But with the attitudes engendered toward enemies and the precedent of the Deuteronomic tradition, it was a short step from passive to active zeal when the saints felt themselves called to participate in the final battle of Yahweh. The mythic perspective effectively undermined any pragmatic assessment of power factors and eliminated the possibility of compromise or coexistence. Revelation encouraged a foolhardy optimism concerning the outcome of history. No matter how destructive the battles become, it is the saints who will prevail both in this world and in the next.

Enclosed within this biblical synthesis are the completely antithetical motifs of disinterested love, individual freedom, coexistence of competitors under law, and realism about human responsibility for history. Two opposing images of God, two contradictory versions of national mission, and two different approaches to world redemption lie beside each other here in uneasy wedlock. To accept their coalescence today is to continue in the dangerous habit of "doublethink" and "double-talk." But for earlier generations of Americans, untouched by the realities that now drive this synthesis apart, the Book of Revelation provided the mythic framework for the mission of the nation. The materials were there ready and waiting for the development of the Captain America complex.

5 America's Zeal to Redeem the World

Hail Land of light and joy! Thy power shall grow
Far as the seas, which round thy regions flow;
Through earth's wide realms thy glory shall extend,
And savage nations at thy scepter bend. . . .
Then, then an heavenly kingdom shall descend,
And every region smile in endless peace;
Till the last trump the slumbering dead inspire,
Shake the wide heavens, and set the world on fire.

Timothy Dwight, "America" (1771)[1]

The Rise of a Millennial Mission

A distinctive sense of mission to redeem the entire world marked the first generation of immigrants in New England. The Puritans derived from the Book of Revelation their dualistic worldview and their belief that violence would inaugurate God's kingdom. They thought of themselves as standing in the succession of Christian warriors and martyrs that John Foxe had delineated from the Bible down to sixteenth-century England. As Winthrop Hudson explained, "The New England story was viewed as a continuation of John Foxe's narrative of the pitched battles between Christ and Antichrist that had marked the course of human history from the beginning."[2] Preachers such as John Davenport, John Cotton, Increase and Cotton Mather, and Thomas

Hooker worked on the task of building a holy commonwealth that would be invincible. Between 1629 and 1640, when their cause was in decline in England, more than 20,000 Puritans immigrated to America with this in mind. It was the call to battle that quickened their spirits, and they were fully convinced that such warfare had to be waged in the civil realm against the forms of corruption they felt were afflicting England. John Fiske said they were animated with "the desire to lead godly lives and to drive out sin from the community."[3] Their hope was that with the successful completion of such a war, the millennial kingdom promised in the Book of Revelation would surely arrive.

Michael Walzer has pointed out the decisive role of such ideas in the creation of the Puritan radicals:

> What finally made men revolutionaries, however, was . . . an increasingly secure feeling that the saints did know the purposes of God. . . . Beginning at some point before 1640, a group of writers, including Joseph Meade of Cambridge University, began the work of integrating the spiritual warfare of the preachers with the apocalyptic history of Daniel and Revelation. The religious wars on the continent and then the struggle against the English king were seen by these men as parts of the ancient warfare of Satan and the elect, which had begun with Jews and Philistines and would continue until Armageddon.[4]

The zealous leaders described by Walzer had shifted the thousand-year kingdom of Revelation 20 from the past to the immediate future and had reinterpreted the role of the saints in martial categories. So when the revolution came in England, preachers rose in Parliament to proclaim that the final battle with Satan was at hand. As one of them declared in 1643, "When the kings of the earth have given their power to the beast, these choice-soldiers . . . will be so faithful to the King of kings, as to oppose the beast, though armed with kinglike power."[5] Stephen Marshall exhorted the troops in Parliament in 1644: "Go now and fight the battles of the Lord. . . . Do now see that the question in England is whether Christ or Anti-Christ shall be lord or king." Henry Wilkenson wrote that Parliament's "business lies professedly against the apocalyptical beast and all his complices."[6] The battle was directed, of course, not only against the Cavaliers but also against moral corruption everywhere. The purge of heretics, worldlings, and the licentious was viewed as part of the same battle by which "the whore of Babylon shall be destroyed with fire and sword."[7] The terminology of this discourse derives almost exclusively from the Book of Revelation.

When the revolution was overthrown in England in 1660, there was a sense among the Puritans that the American colonies had become the new bearers of Protestant destiny. Increase Mather returned to Boston the following year with this in mind, "believing it was the last stronghold of Protestantism," as Perry Miller pointed out.[8] With such convictions, the New England colonists resisted the efforts of the Restoration regime to topple the rule of the saints. They evaded Charles II's letter of complaints in 1662, frustrated the royal commissioners in 1664, and evaded compliance with the Navigation Acts for the next ten years. Even after their charter was revoked in 1684, they resisted the efforts of Governor Andros and had the nerve to imprison him the moment they heard of the Glorious Revolution of 1688. Ernest Lee Tuveson has traced the development of this millennial nationalism in his book *Redeemer Nation*, noting the preachers' retention of the "fanatic notion" of overturning evil by the forceful rule of the saints.[9] He noted the impact of Jonathan Edwards' idea that with the conversion of the New World, the last corner of the globe, "divine providence is preparing the way for the future glorious times of the church, where Satan's kingdom shall be overthrown throughout the whole habitable globe."[10] As J. F. Maclear has shown, the idea that America was the millennial nation "gave to all succeeding American events a continuing cosmic importance. Thomas Prince saw the French and Indian War as 'opening the way to enlighten the utmost regions of America' preparatory to the millennial reign."[11] Frederic Baumgartner confirms that "for the Puritans, the French and Indian War in North America also served as a millennial event. . . . The French and their native allies served Antichrist by waging war on the people of God, and their early victories were signs that the great tribulation was beginning. The British victory in turn confirmed the deeply held belief among the English colonists that they were a chosen people building the New Kingdom in America."[12]

By the eve of the American Revolution, this sense of being the nation destined to usher in the millennial age was clearly developed. Timothy Dwight's 1771 poem "America" (quoted at the head of this chapter) describes the hopeless state of the world before the discovery of the new promised land and sets forth the promise of the millennial kingdom that would soon be administered by the saints in America. It would extend around the "earth's wide realms" and produce an "endless peace." Such a peace, of course, could only come through violence. In the poem's later stanzas, Dwight pictures the American warriors as joining with the heavenly host in the manner of the ancient Israelite ideology. Hugh Henry Brackenridge based his *Six Political Discourses Founded on the Scripture* (1778) on the same set of premises. He argued that King George was inspired by Satan and that Providence sided with the Americans in their revolution: "Heaven hath taken an active part, and waged war for us. . . . Heaven knows nothing of neutrality. . . . There is not one tory to be found amongst the order of the seraphim."[13] Perry Miller has described "how effective were generations of Protestant preaching in evoking patriotic enthusiasm" during the American Revolution.[14] In particular he traced the precedents and implications of the "day of publick humiliation, fasting, and prayer" called by the Continental Congress in 1775. All over the colonies the belief was that God would respond to such repentance, bless the impending revolution, and usher in an era of peace for the saints. This provided a powerful motivation for carrying out a rebellion against the greatest power on earth.

What made the American Revolution constructive was in part the creative interplay with the moderate traditions of Lockean liberalism, Enlightenment egalitarianism, and common-law definitions of political rights. Bernard Bailyn has shown how these traditions joined during the Revolutionary period "into a comprehensive theory of politics."[15] This provided the definition of political liberties that were thought to be endangered by the misuse of royal authority, the basis for the principle of separation of powers, the preference for resolving conflicts by lawful procedure, and the idea of federal union between existing states. These ideas reflect the impulse of prophetic realism, and in some instances it is possible to trace them back to the separatists and levelers in the earlier British Revolution who carved them out of their understanding of the biblical heritage.[16] Without this realistic leaven, the American Revolution might have been nothing more than a vicious crusade against the presumed sources of evil. The summary treatment of the unfortunate Royalists during the Revolution indicates that potential. So, while the zealous war ideology provided a powerful motivation for inaugurating and sustaining the revolutionary cause, it was the resources of prophetic realism that accounted for its relatively humane outcome. Its influence may be seen particularly in the Constitution, drafted and amended after the war, with its separation of powers, its defense of human rights, its federal approach to the powers retained by varied states, and its methods of conflict resolution through legislatures and courts.

In the decades after the Revolution, the sense of being the millennial nation expressed itself not only in the motto on the national seal, *Novus Ordo Seclorum* ("the New Order of the Ages"), but also in periodic religious revivals and reform movements. These religious activities were advanced in many instances with the conviction that, if the chosen people purified themselves further, they would be granted the promised dominion and peace. The evangelist Lyman Beecher wrote in 1835 that "the millennium would commence in

America" because with the success of the Second Great Awakening the conversion of the entire world was now in prospect.[17] William G. McLoughlin notes the widespread acceptance of these ideas that produced the "Evangelical pietism" of the nineteenth century:

> Congregationalists, Presbyterians, Baptists, Separatists and Methodists . . . believed that a Christian commonwealth could be achieved through the massing of votes of the regenerate to make "a Christian party in politics." These voters would elect only converted Christians to office and these legislators in turn would enact and enforce Christian morality throughout the nation. . . . They wanted to outlaw the Masons and the Mormons, to enact nativist laws [against Catholics], to enforce prohibition, to censor immorality, to prevent birth control, to maintain a Christian Sabbath, and eventually to restrict immigration and pass laws preventing the teaching of evolution.[18]

One may grant that some of these reform movements were in part responsible for the gradual improvement of the quality of justice during the nineteenth century.[19] At the same time, however, one should observe that the intolerant spirit in which evangelical movements advanced these causes produced much harm. The millennial hopes encouraged this harsh zealotry and led people to attach such cosmic significance to their reforms that inevitable disappointments followed their achievement. The golden Jerusalem appeared neither with the revivals nor with the most ambitious of the reforms. Moreover, the greatest evil in American society — slavery — was not amenable to pietistic solutions, as the abolitionist zealots discovered in the 1860s.[20]

Possibly the most ominous expression of this zealous nationalism was the sense of "Manifest Destiny" by which the unscrupulous wars against Mexico and the Native Americans were justified. The double sense of being the virtuous nation and being called to a millennial destiny is conveyed by Albert Weinberg in his study *Manifest Destiny.* He cites an editorialist from 1845 who touted the prevailing obsession with American virtue and destiny:

> It is a truth, which every man may see, if he will but look, — that all the channels of communication, — public and private, through the schoolroom, the pulpit, and the press, — are engrossed and occupied with this one idea, which all these forces are combined to disseminate: — that we the American people, are the most independent, intelligent, moral and happy people on the face of the earth.[21]

This sense of virtue served to confirm the validity of expansion. Providence was allegedly smiling because the moral requirements for millennial mission had been met. Weinberg says further:

> Even theological literature was scarcely more abundant in references to Providence than was the literature of expansionism. For it seemed that especially in expanding our territory, as a poet wrote upon the prospect of annexing Texas, "we do but follow out our destiny, as did the ancient Israelite." The expansionist conception of destiny was essentially ethical in its assumption that "Providence had given to the American people a great and important mission . . . to spread the blessings of Christian liberty."[22]

It was this mission of liberty that united reform movements and Manifest Destiny. Herman Melville appealed to it in urging the abolition of flogging in *White-Jacket:* "Since we bear the ark of the liberties of the world, it is clear that 'the political Messiah' . . . has come in us." The consequence, as Melville put it, was that deeds that ordinarily would be classified as "national selfishness" are acceptable, since they enhance the glory and power of the millennial cause: "We cannot do a good to America but we give alms to the world."[23] The task of prophetic ethics is herein absorbed into the redemptive mission, with the result that the grandiose ends justify any means. Even with so critical a thinker as Melville, the provisos of realism tend to be drowned out by the messianic chorus.

This millennial ideology had a potential for injustice that few could grasp at the time. If God had predestined the chosen nation to expand indefinitely, and if that expansion were for the sake of "Christian liberty," who was to demur? Yet it is a tribute to the power of prophetic realism that its impulse was not completely silenced. There were some who protested against paying the Mexican War taxes. A young congressman from Illinois by the name of Abraham Lincoln lost his seat in 1848 because he doubted the claim that Secretary of State Buchanan had formulated in classical terms, that "destiny beckons us to hold and civilize Mexico."[24] Hans Kohn lifted up the countervailing witness of the *McGuffey Readers,* which "strongly denounced wars and militarism" and "had their serious doubts about the wisdom and justice of the war against Mexico."[25] These popular textbooks also issued warnings about the dangers of partisan zealotry, particularly as posed by the radical democrats in the age of Jackson and afterward. Richard D. Mosier's study unearths such warnings as the following in one of the *McGuffey Readers:* "Let the American dread, as the archenemy of republican institutions, the shock of exasperated parties, and the implacable revenge of demagogues."[26]

These relatively realistic sentiments were combined with a doctrine of America's providential destiny to provide an example of equality and democracy to redeem the entire world. Like the sun itself, America should "shed its glorious influence backward on the states of Europe and forward on the empires of Asia." The *McGuffey Readers* were distributed by the millions, helping to shape the American sense of mission in relatively humane and responsible directions. They pictured this mission in terms of providing an example of equality and democracy to the world, though in typically grandiloquent terms. A similar approach was developed by George Bancroft, the nineteenth-century historian. He described the American Revolution as "most radical in its character, yet achieved with such benign tranquility that even conservatism hesitated to censure." He said that the Civil War was a clash of "armed men of the same ancestry against each other, yet for the advancement of the principles of everlasting peace and universal brotherhood."[27] Here is a framework similar to the Book of Revelation, with warfare bringing a peace that is nothing short of "everlasting." Yet the framework is intermixed with prophetic elements such as universal brotherhood and the preservation of life.

Clashes between Zealous Nationalism and Prophetic Realism

It was during the Civil War era that the tension between the two approaches to national mission snapped, leaving zeal against zeal to tear the nation apart. The issue behind this fateful crisis was the "peculiar and powerful interest" of slavery, to use Abraham Lincoln's words. Although the impulse of prophetic realism recognized from the beginning the inconsistency between slavery and democratic ideals, it acknowledged that the Union could not survive slavery's sudden abolition. The spread of slavery was limited by the Missouri Compromise and the Compromise of 1850, which in effect set slavery on the path to ultimate extinction. However, the long deadlock over the shape of western expansion, hindered for decades by Southern efforts to keep an equal number of states and votes in the Senate, was broken with the Kansas-Nebraska Act (1854) and the Dred Scott decision (1857). A plausible fear arose that slavery could now expand into the western and northern states.[28] The gradual resolution of slavery's threat thus gave way to a fatal erosion of the constitutional and legal limits, and an implicit scuttling of the democratic premise that all people were created equal. The Republican party arose to attempt to restore the limits against slavery's expansion, and when its candidate won the presidential election of 1860, the slave states seceded from the Union. The reforming zeal of the North clashed against the romantic zeal of the South, producing the bloodiest war in American history.

In the North, the crusade against slavery had long been buttressed by millennial premises and had directed its attack against the gradual processes of constitutional restraint. William Lloyd Garrison employed biblical metaphors to describe the American Constitution as a "covenant with death and an agreement with hell." In 1841 he printed a letter from an Ohio supporter that said, "My hope for the Millennium begins where Dr. Beecher's expires, viz., AT THE OVERTHROW OF THIS NATION."[29] Although Aileen Kraditor has shown that the majority of abolitionists rejected Garrison's extreme anti-institutional position, the fact remains that they sought to destroy the legal protections that slavery enjoyed and the political compromises that guaranteed its existence while hindering its expansion.[30] The apocalyptic language used by the abolitionists produced an expectation of violent upheaval. Harriet Beecher Stowe spoke of an imminent "last convulsion" that would remove the blight of slavery from the chosen people.[31] Hundreds of abolitionist preachers took up this line, until, with the opening of hostilities in 1861, Hollis Read could write *The Coming Crisis of the World: or, The Great Battle and the Golden Age,* which depicted the apocalyptic strife that would usher in the millennium. It was to be the battle of the North, "carrying the standard of Christ, against the South, ranged under that of the Beast," just as in the Book of Revelation.[32]

The most powerful embodiment of this zealous ideology was "The Battle Hymn of the Republic," written in 1862. Its terminology and imagery, as Tuveson shows, are derived almost exclusively from the apocalyptic portions of the Bible.[33] In the marching of the Union soldiers was "the glory of the coming of the Lord"; and with God marching on the side of the Northern armies, it saw victory as inevitable. The struggle would be strenuous and bloody, and many would die in the certainty that they would receive his "grace" for their faithfulness in battle. But they could fight to the last man with the certain knowledge that they were following the victorious signal:

> He has sounded forth the trumpet that shall never call retreat;
> He is sifting out the hearts of men before His judgment-seat:
> O, be swift, my soul, to answer Him! Be jubilant, my feet!
> Our God is marching on.

Who is this martial God who leads the Northern troops into battle? Who is the "Lord" who crushes the grapes of his wrathful wine by the feet of his troops? It is none other than the loving Christ seen through the lens of the Book of Revelation. The contradictory redemptive images of the peaceful suffering servant and the marching Lord of battle are joined in the final stanza. The redemptive task of the Northern soldiers is neatly shifted from annihilating the enemy to altruistically setting people free. The unselfish mission of the suffering, dying servant is incorporated into that of the warrior. The soldier dies — not killing others, but suffering for others. This sets the stage for the next 140 years of altruistic, martial zeal in America:

> In the beauty of the lilies Christ was born across the sea,
> With a glory in His bosom that transfigures you and me:
> As He died to make men holy, let us die to make men free,
> While God is marching on.

This ideology steeled the North for the long, bloody, and frustrating war. In time, such a war to "make men free" would not be able to halt its course until the entire world was involved. As the following citation from Rev. George S. Phillips reveals, such prospects were on the horizon even during the most discouraging hours of the war:

> Our mission . . . should only be accomplished when the last despot should be dethroned, the last chain of oppression broken, the dignity and equality of redeemed humanity everywhere acknowledged, republican government everywhere established, and the American flag . . . should wave over every land and encircle the world with its majestic folds. Then, and not till then, should the nation have accomplished the purpose for which it was established by the God of heaven.[34]

This vision of the national mission is clearly derived from chapter 20 of the Book of Revelation, wherein the saints rule the earth after the destruction of the Beast.

The North was not alone in developing a martial ideology with millennial overtones. John Hope Franklin has traced the emergence of a "militant South" in the decades prior to the war.[35] Along with a chivalrous martial tradition and a high level of regional pride, there was the conviction that "we need not fear the joust of arms — for the God of Israel will be on the side of his children," as a New Orleans newspaper proclaimed in 1855.[36] James Silver has shown how widespread such ideas were in the South and how decisive they were in sustaining the rebellion:

> Every Confederate victory proved that God had shielded his chosen people and every defeat became the merited punishment of the same people for

their sins. The war itself was a chastisement "inflicted by an Almighty arm. . . . If the people . . . were to turn with one heart and one mind to the Lord. . . . He would drive the invader from our territories. . . . He can turn them as he turns the rivers of water."[37]

In a similar manner, Rev. Benjamin W. Palmer described the South's millennial destiny prior to the opening of the war: "If she has the grace given her to know her hour she will save herself, the country, and the world."[38] When the Confederate states adopted a constitution, its preamble "invok[ed] the favor and guidance of the Almighty God." The fierce motto of the Confederacy declared, *Deo Vindice* ("God Will Avenge").[39]

With mutually exclusive forms of zealous nationalism pitted against each other, and the expectations of world redemption with the destruction of the other side, the stage was set for a war whose ferocity and duration challenged the illusions of both sides. The biblical expectation that the enemy would be cowardly was belied by those dreadful and "indecisive contests where overwhelming victory was impossible because neither side would run as they ought when beaten," in the words of Oliver Wendell Holmes, Jr.[40] It was a tragic cycle of destruction, with every prospect of increasing in brutality and injustice no matter which crusading army won the battle. Nothing short of the enemy's bloody annihilation could promise to appease the voracious appetite of such zeal.

The impulses characteristic of prophetic realism during this tragic conflict came to expression most prominently in the work of Abraham Lincoln, and especially in his second inaugural address. Reflecting his appreciation for military contingency and moral uncertainty, he said: "The progress of our arms, upon which all else chiefly depends, is as well known to the public as to myself, and it is, I trust, reasonably satisfactory and encouraging to all. With high hope for the future, no prediction in regard to it is ventured." Lincoln saw no connection between the justice of the Union's causes and the certainty of its victory. Mere hope was no warrant for confidence. Extending the theme of moral ambiguity, the speech refers to the expectations of both sides, noting not only the irony that "both read the same Bible, and pray to the same God" for opposite ends, but also that neither was completely justified in its assessment of the holiness of its cause. If the South should not "dare to ask a just God's assistance in wringing their bread from the sweat of other men's faces," the North must recall the admonition to "judge not that we be not judged." Lincoln thrust aside the sense of moral superiority that sustains zealous warfare in view of the fact that "the Almighty has His own purposes."[41] Divine judgment had fallen on "both North and South," and in some mysterious and tragic fashion the continued suffering of both may have its meaning in the impartial will of God. Lincoln continued:

> If we shall suppose that American Slavery is one of those offences which, in the providence of God, must needs come, but which having continued through His appointed time, He now wills to remove, and that He gives to both North and South, this terrible war, as the woe due to those by whom the offence came, shall we discern therein any departure from those divine attributes which the believers in a Living God always ascribe to Him? Fondly do we hope — fervently do we pray — that this mighty scourge of war may speedily pass away. Yet, if God wills that it continue, until all the wealth piled by the bond-man's two hundred and fifty years of unrequited toil shall be sunk, and until every drop of blood drawn with the lash, shall be paid by another drawn with the sword, as was said three thousand years ago, so still it must be said, "the judgments of the Lord are true and righteous altogether."

This is the heart of Lincoln's argument, for it shatters the simple identification of either side with God's justice. As Lincoln wrote in a note to Thurlow Weed shortly after delivering this address, such a message would not be "immediately popular. Men are not flattered by being shown that there has been a difference of purpose between the Almighty and them."[42] Yet until they would grow humble enough to acknowledge that "difference in purpose," they would be neither humane nor realistic.

The issue of a shared humanity receives emphasis at the end of the second inaugural. In it Lincoln juxtaposes a form of justice that recognizes the vulnerable complicity of each side with the issue of moral resolve in a manner that powerfully counters zealous ideologies. He depicts the zealot as so caught up in his moral crusade that persons cease to matter. He becomes implacable, cruel, and deadly. Mercy in such an ideology is a sign of weakness, a betrayal of the holy cause, a step toward compromise with evil. But for the same reason that charity is antithetical to zealotry, it is consistent with faithful resolve to carry out a task when no absolutes are available. Lincoln speaks of a "firmness in the right" in proportion as "God gives us to see the right," that is, in a mysterious and fragmentary fashion. Since every group's version of "the right" is subject to the provisos of prophetic realism, the group must never hold to it with fanaticism, showing disrespect for the value of life in the process. Yet Lincoln's kind of "firmness" involved a very high level of steadiness in face of the high cost required during the war to keep the democratic experiment from unraveling. He expresses this complex thought in a single sentence at the close of the address:

With malice toward none; with charity for all; with firmness in the right, as God gives us to see the right, let us strive on to finish the work we are in; to bind up the nation's wounds; to care for him who shall have borne the battle, and for his widow, and his orphan — to do all which may achieve and cherish a just, and a lasting peace, among ourselves, and with all nations.

Charity and realism are the consequences of Lincoln's stance. Since he was spared fanaticism by his conception of an impartial divine justice, he was set free not only to respond in charity to the needs of others but also to deal realistically with the tangle of historical responsibility. The realism is visible in the grasp of what truly makes for "a just, and a lasting peace" — not annihilation of the wicked but care for the victim. And who is to deny that Lincoln's plans for reconstructing the South, based on these principles of charity and the preservation of democratic institutions, would have accomplished a great deal more to "bind up the nation's wounds" than all the purges of the Radicals?

The second inaugural address exposed the living source of both charity and realism within the framework of God's mysterious purposes for those whom Lincoln had called the "almost chosen people." By repudiating zealous appropriations of that purpose, Lincoln opened the nation to its natural resources of mercy and common sense. He did so without scuttling the sense of national purpose and without leaving the nation adrift on a trackless, amoral sea.

Zeal's Frustration and the Claim of Manifest Destiny

When President Andrew Johnson sought to implement a kind of Lincolnesque reconstruction program, it was wrecked by the combination of Southern intransigence, Northern radicalism, and a lack of political skill. One is tempted to place the major share of blame on the Radicals, but the dilemma they faced so illuminates our current situation that it deserves a more judicious analysis. It is not enough to assert, as a prominent history textbook does, that Thaddeus Stevens and Charles Sumner were simply destructive zealots: "In the remorseless manner in which the Radicals drove through their program, we see evidences of a revolutionary spirit that would stop at nothing to attain its ends."[43] What, in fact, were the ends they so zealously sought? The irony is that they were the ideals of humane, prophetic realism: the enforcement of equal rights for former slaves, the dismantling of a social structure perceived to be undemocratic, and the reestablishment of democratic institutions. In the chaos of the

South after 1865, it appeared that none of these goals was being accomplished. Major General Carl Schurz reported after his extensive investigations that former rebels were rapidly returning to power in the new state and local governments. Blacks were being subjugated to the most barbaric pressures to force them back into their "places." Schurz reported that a "veritable reign of terror prevailed in many parts of the South."[44]

This situation posed a dilemma so deep and pervasive that it remains with us to this day. Protecting the rights of minorities required an unprecedented incursion of national power into the affairs of local governments. As the British historian W. R. Brock says, "The concept of Negro equality demanded interference with the processes of local government on a scale never before contemplated in America or in any other nation."[45] Yet to acquiesce in the continued violation of basic human rights was to deny the thrust of the American mission and to betray the hundreds of thousands of victims of the Civil War. The Radicals took the libertarian horn of this dilemma and carried it out until 1877 with remorseless zeal, enacting a series of unconstitutional measures in Congress and coming close to impeaching a president who thwarted their design.

Several factors intrinsic to zealous nationalism helped defeat radical Reconstruction. The chosen nation ideology had always emphasized that the Anglo-Saxon peoples are the bearers of the millennial destiny. When combined with the stereotyping that zealous nationalism encourages, it produced a widespread feeling in both the North and South that blacks were inferior and unsuited for full participation in the democratic process. At the same time, the North felt that it had emerged from the war as God's purified nation whose destiny had been confirmed by victory. Prominent preachers suggested that the bloodshed had burned out the "base alloy" of slavery and other sins so that the chosen nation could fulfill its millennial task. Horace Bushnell grieved that America's sins had brought her "to the point where only blood . . . can resanctify what we [North and South] have so loosely held and so badly desecrated." But now a new sense of unity had been produced, so that "the sense of nationality becomes even a kind of religion."[46] As early as 1864, Marvin R. Vincent preached the following:

> God has been striking, and trying to make us strike at elements unfavorable to the growth of a pure democracy . . . preparing in this broad land a fit stage for the last act of the mighty drama, the consummation of human civilization. . . . Who shall say that she shall not only secure lasting peace to herself, but be, under God, the instrument of a millennial reign to all the nations?[47]

Lasting peace was now assumed because evil had been cleansed by the blood of war. Following the logic of the books of Daniel and Revelation, the "saints" could now easily rule the cleansed world without having to deal with the works of Satan. As Robert Penn Warren observed, the victorious North felt "redeemed by history, automatically redeemed," but at the same time, the reforming impulse "burned itself out in the slavery controversy," not to reappear for another generation.[48] A seemingly contradictory set of attitudes resulted: complacency about the existence of evil among the saints and a petulant impatience with any resistance to their rule. The same philosophy produced both the zeal of the Radical Republicans and the complacency about the corruption of the nation as a whole.

The Religious Impulse in American Imperialism

In the decades after 1877, the millennial language was gradually infused with secular terms, and the nation became, as Maclear puts it, "preoccupied with progress of every kind — biological, technological, and cultural, as well as spiritual and moral."[49] The evolutionary terminology was grafted onto the redeemer nation concept; social Darwinism justified material progress and expansion. Success was readily identified as evidence of virtue. Horatio Alger became the new form of saint to rule over the world.

It was not long before these ideas combined to produce a new variety of imperialistic ideology. One of the most influential exponents of such imperial nationalism was Josiah Strong, who served as secretary of the American Home Missionary Society.[50] In 1885 he placed the evangelizing of the American West in the context of America's destiny to put the stamp of Christ on the entire world. He held that, since the Anglo-Saxon peoples represent the great ideas of civil liberty and "pure spiritual Christianity," God is preparing them with prosperity and power to be "the die with which to stamp the peoples of the earth." With the western expansion now at an end, America was ready to enter "the final competition of races . . . [as] the representative, let us hope, of the largest liberty, the purest Christianity, the highest civilization — having developed peculiarly aggressive traits calculated to impress its institutions upon mankind. . . . Can anyone doubt that the result of this competition of races will be the 'survival of the fittest'?"[51] Their calling, in other words, was to "Anglo-Saxonize mankind" for the sake of Christ, and when this was accomplished by missionary and imperial expansion, the "coming of Christ's kingdom in the world" would have been hastened. Although this task was pictured in martial terminology, with America as "God's right arm in his battle with the world's ignorance and oppression and sin,"[52] its role was to be a servant rather than the master of the world. This fragment of prophetic realism is absorbed into zealous nationalism in Josiah Strong's book *Expansion under New World Conditions:*

> This race has been honored not for its own sake but for the sake of the world. It has been made . . . powerful not to make subject, but to serve; . . . free not simply to exult in freedom, but to make free; exalted not to look down, but to lift up.[53]

This notion of unselfish mission is combined with a powerful sense of cultural and racial superiority that would inevitably lead to imperialistic warfare against the presumed enemies of progress. What other alternative would there be when lesser nations resisted the "stamp" of Anglo-Saxon civilization?

These ideas led directly to the Spanish-American War. It was clearly an unnecessary conflict, because the Spanish had acquiesced to American demands prior to the mysterious sinking of the battleship *Maine*. But an enormous groundswell of crusading spirit swept the country headlong into war. Henry Watterson editorialized in 1898:

> It is a war into which this nation will go with a fervor, with a power, with a unanimity that would make it invincible if it were repelling not only the encroachments of Spain but the assaults of every monarch in Europe. . . . It is not a war of conquest. It is not a war of envy or enmity. It is not a war of pillage or gain. . . . We find in it the law supreme . . . the law of man, the law of God. We find in it our own inspiration, our own destiny . . . [which] says that liberty and law shall no longer be trampled upon . . . by despotism and autocracy upon our threshold. That is the right of our might; that is the sign in which we conquer.[54]

It was, in short, a war to make men free, the natural consequence of the ideology expressed by "The Battle Hymn of the Republic." Its aims were altruistic and thus victory was allegedly inevitable, even if all the nations of the world were opposed. Henry van Dyke's sermon on Thanksgiving Day 1898 expressed this thought very succinctly: "Not for gain, not for territory, but for freedom and human brotherhood! That avowal alone made the war possible and successful."[55]

This "tidy little war" with Spain helped to consolidate the synthesis between prophetic ideals and zealous nationalism. As Walter Millis notes, it helped to generate "the notions of the national destiny and the national responsibility in the global context" that would guide American behavior in the new century.[56] That the war was so easily and cheaply won served to deepen illusions of America's virtue and destiny. The thesis that America won because of her virtuous aims was easily transposed to imply that since America had won so easily, her virtue was confirmed. The saints could gain ascendancy without even getting their hands dirty — proof that they were saints indeed! Only 460 Americans, after all, were killed in battle. However, the shock of it was not entirely absent, even in this triumphant scene. Some of the Filipinos refused to submit to American benevolence; they resisted the imperial design, so that brutal coercion had to be used, just as the supposedly degenerate Spaniards had done in Cuba. James Chace observes, "The insurrection went on for three years, and perhaps as many as 200,000 Filipino lives were lost."[57]

The election of 1900 saw America divided between the imperialists and the anti-imperialists, the latter representing with some precision the tradition of prophetic realism. But voices such as that of Albert J. Beveridge were to prevail. In his speech before the Union League Club in 1899, Beveridge concluded:

> Retreat from the Philippines . . . would be a betrayal of a trust as sacred as humanity. . . . And so, thank God, the Republic never retreats. . . . American manhood today contains the master administrators of the world, and they go forth for the healing of the nations. They go forth in the cause of civilization. They go forth for the betterment of man. They go forth, and the word on their lips is Christ and his peace, not conquest and its pillage. They go forth to prepare the peoples, through decades and maybe centuries of patient effort, for the great gift of American institutions. They go forth not for imperialism, but for the Greater Republic.[58]

To retreat — to accept defeat — would be to deny the millennial destiny to redeem the world. In a very real sense, the form such world redemption would take revealed itself in the reference to "the great gift of American institutions." Since these were to be Christ's means of bringing peace, in Beveridge's view, to advance them by force was not imperialism but the "betterment of man." The "healing of the nations," which Beveridge cites from the description of the heavenly Jerusalem in Revelation 22:2, would come when American democracy had swept over the world.

Was it really possible that the "Greater Republic" could be imposed by a zealous crusade? Were the attitudes and policies implicit in such an effort not antithetical to the very democracy America wished to advance? This was the dilemma that Beveridge's oft-cited speech before the Senate in 1900 tried to answer. It resembles the dilemma the United States faced in the latter phase of the Indochina war. Beveridge insisted that in response to Philippine resistance, "lasting peace can be secured only by overwhelming forces in ceaseless action until universal and absolutely final defeat is inflicted on the enemy." If some people charge "that our conduct of the war has been cruel," Beveridge reminded his fellow senators that "we are dealing with Orientals. . . . They mistake kindness for weakness, forbearance for fear." The "chief factor" in the delay of total victory was allegedly the "American opposition to the war." As for the complaint that the imperial crusade was antithetical to the Declaration of Independence, Beveridge insisted that it "applies only to people capable of self government," not to the "Malay children of barbarism." The crusade was grounded in something "deeper even than any question of constitutional power," so such matters should not stand in the way. For God "has marked the American people as His chosen nation to finally lead in the regeneration of the world."[59]

In retrospect, one can see that Beveridge's zealous ideology had to set aside the very democratic values it sought to advance. Here was the dilemma that would one day tear the myths asunder. The coalescence of zeal and realism might stand the pressure of the Spanish navy and the Philippine guerillas, but could it survive a massive shock? As we shall see, it would begin one day to break apart precisely at the fissures Beveridge tried so eloquently to fill.

World War I as a Millennial Crusade

With American participation in World War I, the price of such zealotry began to be paid, though in relatively small installments. The nation had entered the war, after much hesitation, because of Germany's violation of neutrality on the high seas. But the justification President Wilson developed had little to do with self-defense; it came straight out of the tradition of zealous nationalism. It was combined in so compelling a manner with motifs of prophetic realism that it achieved a modern synthesis. Part of the war's cost was the revelation of internal contradictions in this synthesis and their serious consequences.

Before the United States entered the war, Wilson led the country in the role of the righteous neutral, waiting for others to exhaust themselves before stepping in to enforce a lasting peace. The sense of saintly aloofness was visible in Wilson's refusal to ask for a declaration of war even after the sinking of the *Lusitania:* "There is such a thing as a nation being so right that it does not need to convince others by force that it is right."[60] In response to the immense bloodshed in Europe, Wilson made room for a realistic assessment of the need for an effective world government: "It will be absolutely necessary that a force be created as a guarantee of the permanency of the [peace] settlement so much greater than the force of any nation now engaged . . . that no nation . . . could face or withstand it." Wilson also saw that the hope for total victory was antithetical to genuine peace: "It must be a peace without victory. . . . Victory would mean peace forced upon the loser. . . . Only a peace between equals can last. Only a peace the very principle of which is equality and a common participation in a common benefit."[61]

Could such principles of coexistence drawn from the tradition of prophetic realism prevail when the saints themselves joined the battle? Wilson's war message to Congress in April 1917 reveals that they could not. The president was apparently conscious of the possible contradiction, since he took such pains to deny it: "My own thought has not been driven from its habitual and normal course by the unhappy events of the last two months. . . . I have exactly the same things in mind now that I had in mind when I addressed the Senate on the 22nd of January last."[62] Wilson then slipped into a zealous line of argument that contradicted his principles of coexistence and peace without victory. Since the German imperial government was driven by the lust for "selfish and autocratic power" and harbored "cunningly contrived plans of deception or aggression," it was impossible to coexist with it. "We are accepting this challenge of hostile purpose," Wilson said, "because we know that in such a government, following such methods, we can never have a friend; and that in the presence of its organized power, always lying in wait to accomplish we know not what purpose, there can be no assured security for the democratic governments of the world." Wilson then demanded that the country enter a crusade for millennial goals:

> The world must be made safe for democracy. Its peace must be planted upon the tested foundation of political liberty. We have no selfish ends to serve. We desire no conquest, no dominion. . . . We are but one of the champions of the right of mankind. We shall be satisfied when those rights have been made as secure as the faith and the freedom of nations can make them.[63]

As in "The Battle Hymn of the Republic," Americans would die unselfishly to set people free. The elements of prophetic realism had been blotted out by the ideology of zealous nationalism, and it was the the Book of Revelation's spirit that animated the whole.

A powerful surge of enthusiasm approaching hysteria swept over the country in the wake of Wilson's call to millennial battle. Theodore Roosevelt told the Harvard Club in 1917, "If ever there was a holy war, it is this war."[64] Jess Yoder's study of preaching during World War I shows the wide dispersion of this crusading ideology.[65] Randolph H. McKim proclaimed from his Washington pulpit:

> It is God who has summoned us to this war. It is his war we are fighting. . . . This conflict is indeed a crusade. The greatest in history — the holiest. It is in the profoundest and truest sense a Holy War. . . . Yes, it is Christ, the King of Righteousness, who calls us to grapple in deadly strife with this unholy and blasphemous power.[66]

An Episcopal minister wrote in the *Atlantic Monthly:*

> The complete representative of the American Church in France is the United States Army overseas. Yes, an army, with its cannon and rifles and machine-guns and its instruments of destruction. The Church militant, sent, morally equipped, strengthened and encouraged, approved and blessed, by the Church at home.[67]

We can see the apocalyptic battle of the saints against the beast in sermons such as these. Henry van Dyke, acting as a Navy chaplain, wrote an additional stanza for "The Battle Hymn of the Republic," which was widely used in training camps:

> We have heard the cry of anguish, from the victims of the Hun,
> And we know our country's peril if the war-lord's will is done.
> We will fight for worldwide freedom till the victory is won,
> For God is marching on.[68]

This theme of a redemptive war of the saints for the freedom of the world advanced by the clergy was precisely what President Wilson had proposed. And while it proved effective in stirring the country to enthusiastic mobilization, it bore within it the seeds of bitterness to come. Despite the grandiose promises, the democratic countries of Europe proved less virtuous than had been supposed, and the obsession with security led to postwar arrangements that fell short of improving the prospect for democracy. President Wilson sought to halt some of these tendencies, but the mixture of realism and zealous pretensions in himself and the country as a whole made it impossible.

A curious feature of the American character has come to the fore after each great war: a sudden indifference about the aftermath followed by a long period of disillusionment. Many causes for this pattern have been suggested, but we would submit that the millennial, zealous ideology itself has a great deal to do with it. The unquestioned premise was that a victorious crusade would truly make the world safe. This idea was derived from the books of Daniel and Revelation: that the destruction of the demonic Beast would automatically bring the world under the control of the saints. When this did not happen, a long and counterproductive withdrawal resulted.

The irony of the situation was that President Wilson's thought contained a wider amalgam of the two contradictory impulses than was the case with the population as a whole. His advocacy of the League of Nations stood in the tradition of prophetic realism, for it was the prophet Isaiah who first proposed a form of this idea. But while Wilson's advocacy for the League was fused with zealous premises in his own mind, that advocacy was peripheral to zealous nationalism for the country at large. The public was more consistent than was Wilson in one sense, because they reacted in the spirit of the zealous premises alone and thus felt terribly disillusioned when millennial peace did not follow the Armistice of 1918. Having been stirred by Wilson's rhetoric toward a "war to end all wars," Americans were unable to consider the need for complex institutions such as the League of Nations to adjudicate future conflicts. To admit the necessity for such institutions was to doubt the validity of the millennial crusade. It also meant coexisting with nations that seemed as degenerate as those the crusade had allegedly purged. The rhetoric about American unselfishness had encouraged such illusions of moral superiority that compromise with evil became repulsive. Refusal to participate in the League of Nations was thus perfectly consistent; isolationism was the logical consequence of the zealous crusade.

The tragic results of this reversion to the isolation of the "saints" were felt for the rest of the century, according to Hans Kohn. Since the United States refused to provide the League of Nations with the prestige and force it required, there was no effective way to sustain the small democracies in eastern Europe when Germany's military power revived. There was no international system to curtail Japan's aggression against its neighbors. As Wilson had warned in his speeches favoring American entrance into the League, such factors would produce another great war within twenty-five years.[69] The devastation of World War II and the corrosive spread of communism were made possible by the fateful decisions of 1919-1920. Yet the illusions shaped by the great crusade made the American public incapable of comprehending its own complicity in these tragic developments. As the inevitable disillusionment deepened, it brought a growing lack of faith in the democratic ideals with which zeal had been joined. It produced the moral cynicism and the hunger for alien ideologies that would serve to erode democracy itself.

World War II and the Disjunction between Zeal and Realism

World War II provided the circumstances under which the realistic and zealous elements in American nationalism would come increasingly into tension with each other. The country was seriously divided during the opening phases of the conflicts in Europe and Asia, with isolationist and pacifist sentiments setting the tone. The realists felt that intervention against Hitler was called for in the late 1930s; but by November 1941 they had convinced only 20 percent of the population that their cause was right.[70] Despite the horrors of fascism, America seemed to lack what Harry Scherman called for in 1941: a war philosophy "so basic that no wedging doubts can shake it."[71] President Franklin Roosevelt came to favor intervention much earlier than did the country as a whole, entering into cooperation with England on lend-lease and armed merchant ships, and placing embargoes on Japanese trade. A divided public and a hostile Congress would not support all these measures, so the administration carried them out covertly. By the time of the Atlantic Charter in August 1941, conflicting tendencies were clearly visible within Roosevelt's position. The Charter set forth the ideas of Wilsonian political realism, such as renunciation of territorial aggression, national self-determination, and "the establishment of a wider and permanent system of general security."[72] But these were joined with a zealous resolve concerning "the final destruction of the Nazi tyranny." Roosevelt repeated and strengthened these sentiments in his October 1941 message to the nation, in which he described the Nazi war aims in religious categories that were quite uncharacteristic of this secular president:

> In place of the churches of our civilization, there is to be set up an international Nazi church. In place of the Bible, the word of *Mein Kampf* will be imposed and enforced as Holy Writ. And in place of the cross of Christ will be put two symbols — the swastika and the naked sword. A god of blood and iron will take the place of the God of love and mercy.[73]

The issue before the nation was therefore one of cataclysmic significance, and it appeared as if irrevocable commitments had already been made to a crusade despite the lack of public support. The familiar tension between zeal and realism emerged in Roosevelt's rhetoric. Compared with Woodrow Wilson's rhetoric, the amalgam was less satisfactory. When Roosevelt resorted to zealous stereotypes, he approached a level of crudity never possible for Wilson.

After Pearl Harbor, the public was ready for another crusade to rid the world of evil and to make it safe for the saints. In his now famous December 8, 1941, address to Congress, Roosevelt proclaimed: "No matter how long it may take us to overcome this premeditated invasion, the American people, in their righteous might, will win through to absolute victory. . . . We will not only defend ourselves to the uttermost but will make very certain that this form of treachery shall never endanger us again."[74] His radio address the next day called for an unlimited crusade in a similar manner: "I repeat that the United States can accept no result save victory, final and complete. Not only must the shame of Japanese treachery be wiped out but the sources of international brutality, wherever they exist, must be absolutely and finally broken."[75] An uncompromising zeal manifested itself in such statements, and the tradition of religious warfare against the demonic Beast to usher in the era of peace gave shape to the secular terminology.

It was perfectly consistent for Roosevelt to propose the "unconditional surrender" formula at Casablanca and to accept the "Morgenthau Plan" for reducing Germany after the war to an agricultural province. These facets of total warfare were of immense help to enemy propagandists and may well have lengthened the war by eliminating any hope for negotiations with potential resistance elements in Germany and Japan.[76] Yet a form of total warfare was welcomed by the American public nurtured in the crusading tradition.

Religious terminology became prominent in popular renditions of the anti-fascist crusade. The first American casualty was buried in St. Paul's Cathedral in London, while other volunteers in his squadron sang "The Battle Hymn of the Republic."[77] The most popular war song after Pearl Harbor was "Praise the Lord and pass the ammunition . . . and we'll all stay free!" Vice President Henry Wallace used apocalyptic terminology to describe the war as a "fight between a free world and a slave world. . . . Through the leaders of the Nazi revolution Satan now is trying to lead the common man of the whole world back into slavery and darkness. . . . We shall cleanse the plague spot of Europe, which is Hitler's Germany, and with it the hell-hole of Asia — Japan. No compromise with Satan is possible."[78] Preachers echoing this line tended to emphasize moral requirements for victory. Peter Marshall, the chaplain of the U.S. Senate, suggested that victory for the chosen people would not be granted by God without the recovery of her holiness: "We are fighting for total victory, but we shall never achieve total victory unless we fight for total Christianity. . . . A nation obedient to the laws of God would lead the world."[79]

This moral emphasis reflects the Deuteronomic premise that only a righteous nation will triumph. It is reflected in the remarkable religious revival that took place within the armed services in the early years of the war. In the midst of the war, Stanley High described the "War Boom in Religion" and cited what a veteran chaplain said: "Compared to the last war, the religion in this army looks like a revival. . . . There is more religion per square mile in an army camp than in any civilian area of the country." This revival was motivated in part by the zealous explanation of the reverses in the early years of the war. As High observed, there was a "widespread feeling that the present state of the world is largely a result of the standards we've been trying to live by."[80] Even in an increasingly secularized populace, the zealous premises remained intact.

Sermons in some Protestant churches, however, did not offer the facile hope of victory through revival. Jess Yoder's study of such preaching concludes that the "prevailing theological emphasis which stressed the sinful nature of man was dramatized by the rise of fascism and the approaching war. Thus in contrast to World War I, World War II was considered holy; it was not ushering in the kingdom of righteousness, but a tragic manifestation of sin."[81] Influential ministers such as Halford E. Luccock warned against leading the public to be "so bespattered by the blood of the dragon Hatred that its mind could not be turned toward a magnanimous Christian peace."[82] And Reinhold Niebuhr developed realistic proposals about European reconstruction that were later taken up in the Marshall Plan; he was among the first to recognize the dangers of Russian domination of a prostrated Europe. Wendell Willkie popularized the idea of "One World" united in peace under international agreements. James Bryant Conant urged the students at Harvard to avoid "dogmatism and a holier than thou attitude" and to take responsibility for the postwar world without the illusion that American institutions could easily be extended to other countries.[83]

It is worth noting, however, that these impulses of prophetic realism did not come from leaders who simultaneously advocated zealous crusading. The impulses that seemed in tension within a man like Roosevelt came forth from separate groups and persons; it was no longer widely possible to hold both at the same time. Roosevelt himself became more and more dominated by the crusade ideology as the war progressed, losing much of his realism in relation to Russian allies and the situation that would result when their troops arrived in Berlin and Manchuria. He apparently believed that Russia's agreement to cooperate in founding the United Nations would guarantee the peace of the postwar world. He was elated by the "tremendous success" of the "Declaration of Four Nations on General Security" in 1943, which established the basis for the future world organization. Secretary of State Cordell Hull struck this note in his report to Congress: "As the provisions of the Four-Nation Declaration are carried into effect, there will no longer be need for spheres of influence, for alliances, for balance of power, or any other of the special arrangements through which, in the unhappy past, the nations strove to safeguard their security or to promote their interests."[84]

The subsequent willingness to bow to Soviet demands for a veto in the United Nations and for hegemony in eastern Europe and parts of Asia were consistent with such millennial premises. After all, was not Russia on the side of the saints, and was the crusade not being fought "so that we do not have to live in a totalitarian world"? If, as Roosevelt hoped, the "sources of international brutality, wherever they exist," were "absolutely and finally broken" by the war, why should one listen to dyspeptic realists? As William Henry Chamberlin observed, "Such realism was at a hopeless discount in a crusading atmosphere."[85]

In addition to raising the United States to superpower status, World War II produced a disjunction between the crusading and realistic impulses. Moreover, it presented the crusading impulse itself with severe credibility problems. No one could forget that it was really the attack on Pearl Harbor that forced America into the war, which meant that self-defense rather than crusading idealism played the major role. And the disappointing aftermath of the war confirmed the warnings of the realists: it exposed as an illusion the hope that, with the defeat of fascism, the threats to democracy in the modern world would be eliminated.

These insights, however, were slow to dawn on mainstream America, where the assumptions of zealous nationalism continued to dominate. After all, America had achieved its goal of "unconditional surrender." Its record of supremacy in war was impressive, especially when this victory was the third since 1898 to be achieved with minimal suffering on the part of the New World saints — at least compared with the millions of casualties suffered by others. The jocular faith that "God looks after children, drunks, and Americans" seemed confirmed.[86] American optimism was warranted: the difficult could be done immediately, and the impossible would take only a little longer. Americans now wanted to return to their traditional isolation, having so handily accomplished the job of cleansing the world. But even with the rapid demobilization of troops in 1945, threats were arising that would confirm the predictions of the realists and would stimulate a new phase of the Captain America complex.

6 The Frustration of American Zealous Nationalism

We must formulate and put forward for other nations a much more positive and constructive picture of the sort of world we would like to see than we have put forward in the past. . . . Finally, we must have courage and self-confidence to cling to our own methods and conceptions of human society. After all, the greatest danger that can befall us in coping with this problem of Soviet communism is that we shall allow ourselves to become like those with whom we are coping.

George F. Kennan, "The Long Telegram" from Moscow, 1946[1]

President John F. Kennedy [speaking to advisers]: *"The obvious argument for the blockade was [that] what we want to do is avoid, if we can, nuclear war by escalation or imbalance. . . ."*

Marine Commandant Gen. David Shoup [immediately after Kennedy's departure from the room]: *"He finally got around to the word 'escalation.' That's the only goddam thing that's in the whole trick. Go in [unclear] and get every goddam one. Somebody's got to keep them from doing the goddam thing piecemeal. That's our problem. Go in there and friggin' around with the missiles. Go in and frigging around with the [air] lift. You're screwed. You're screwed, screwed, screwed. Some goddam thing, some way, that they either do the son of a bitch and do it right, and quit friggin' around.*

excerpts from *The Kennedy Tapes: Inside the White House during the Cuban Missile Crisis*[2]

After the close of World War II, the impulses of zealous nationalism in America began to confront an unprecedented dilemma. For the first time in American history, a mortal threat followed immediately on the successful completion of a crusade; the very existence of the nation was jeopardized; and another great crusade did not seem feasible. The size of the adversaries and the threat of nuclear extinction marked limitations that all but the foolhardy had to admit. Marine Commandant Shoup's rabidly incoherent quotation above reveals military frustration in dealing with a nuclear threat to the American hemisphere. The Captain America complex had promised easy victory if superpower was properly used; yet its use threatened to blow up the world. Nevertheless, for most of this period the assumptions that had informed American thought and behavior for more than three centuries continued to be accepted. The incongruity between ideology and necessity was so great that a chronic state of frustration set in. The country gradually learned to live with it as a fiercely neurotic conflict carried out between its zealous and realist factions.

The Cold War's Thwarted Crusade

A natural beginning point for the story of this frustrated crusade begins with Winston Churchill's epochal "Iron Curtain" speech on March 5, 1946, at a small liberal arts college in Fulton, Missouri, where he held forth in the presence of an approving and applauding President Truman.[3] His words carried a zealous sound that echoed the Truman Doctrine:

> I do not believe that Soviet Russia desires war. What they desire is the fruits of war and the indefinite expansion of their power and doctrines. . . . From what I have seen of our Russian friends and allies during the war, I am convinced that there is nothing they admire so much as strength, and there is nothing for which they have less respect than for weakness, especially military weakness. . . . For that reason the old doctrine of a balance of power is unsound. We cannot afford, if we can help it, to work on narrow margins, offering temptations to a trial of strength.

As summarized by one observer, Churchill was warning, in effect, that to "check the expansion of the Communist block, the English-speaking peoples — a sort of latter-day 'master race' — must sooner or later form a union. They should immediately contract a military alliance and coordinate their military establishments. They must lead 'Christian' civilization in an anti-Communist crusade."[4]

But it was not quite so simple as that. While the above quotation indicates his gusto for zealous confrontations with evil, Churchill had a sense for the other, more realistic strands of civil religion that America had woven so uncomfortably with it. He wanted not merely to take a bellicose stance but to do so within the framework of "a good understanding on all points with Russia under the general authority of the United Nations Organization and by the maintenance of that good understanding through many peaceful years." He envisioned a new century of stability resting on a quiet combination of selfless intent, law, and military power:

> If we adhere faithfully to the Charter of the United Nations and walk forward in sedate and sober strength, seeking no one's land or treasure, seeking to lay no arbitrary control upon the thoughts of men, if all British moral and material forces and convictions are joined with your own in fraternal association, the high roads of the future will be clear, not only for us but for all, not only for our time but for a century to come.

But Stalin saw Churchill's statement as a "call to war." For a realist like Walter Lippmann, Truman's host role for the occasion was "an almost catastrophic blunder."[5] In the end, however, it was the American people, rather than Churchill's fellow citizens in Britain, who responded to his call.

A series of frustrating reverses overcame American illusions that the war had eliminated threats to freedom. Disagreements over the occupation of Germany, Austria, and Japan arose very quickly; Russian pressure on Iran, Greece, and Turkey mounted; the Chinese Communist armies continued their campaign to wrest control from the Nationalists. Although there were voices, such as General George Patton, who called for an immediate military crusade, it was a group of realists who set the tone for the initial American response. Among them were George Marshall and George Kennan in the state department, columnists such as Walter Lippmann and Dorothy Thompson, and theorists such as Hans Morgenthau and Reinhold Niebuhr. They had anticipated the power struggle with Russia and were prepared to suggest policies immediately.

Those voices were supported by a Senate leader, Arthur Vandenberg (R-MI), who underwent a remarkable conversion from isolationism to international realism after witnessing the rocket bombing of London. His 1945 speech to the Senate provides a glimpse of his shift in thinking: "I have always been frankly one of those who has believed in our own self-reliance. . . . But I do not believe that any nation hereafter can immunize itself by its own exclusive action. I want maximum American cooperation. . . . I want a new dignity and a new authority for international law. I think American self-interest requires it."[6] Modern weapons dispelled the illusion of the security of the chosen nation after the unconditional surrender of its enemies. It was time to take cooperation and international law seriously. Under Vandenberg's leadership, the Senate showed bipartisan support for realistic measures such as the refugee and rehabilitation acts, the support of Greece and Turkey, the lenient arrangements for the British loan, and, most importantly, the Marshall Plan.

A key figure in this productive but short-lived period was George F. Kennan. He conceptualized a strategy of "containment" with substantial non-military components; and he guided the policy-planning committee of the state department in developing the Marshall Plan, which had such a positive effect on European recovery. Kennan's view of the situation was that the United States would have to coexist with Russia for an indeterminate span of time. Given the size and aggressive orientation of this adversary, the best that one could hope for was to limit the scope of conflict and wait for more favorable circumstances. His long experience in Russia led him to understand the peculiar combination of insecurity and cynicism that shaped its foreign policy. The rhetoric of his assessment in the famous "Long Telegram" of 1946 had been quite harsh. For example, he wrote that "we have here a political force committed fanatically to the belief that with the U.S. there can be no permanent modus vivendi, that it is desirable and necessary that the internal harmony of our society be disrupted, our traditional way of life be destroyed, the international authority of our state be broken, if Soviet power is to be secure." He added that "world communism is like a malignant parasite which feeds only on diseased tissue."[7] However, he saw possibilities for calmly containing her belligerent tendencies, in the anticipation that the United States could hope to see a milder form of behavior after Stalin's death.

Kennan advanced these ideas while explicitly rejecting the idealistic, crusading, pretentious aspects of American foreign policy. He criticized the "American Dream" of being "innocent of every conscious evil intent" and the sort of "adolescent self-esteem" that it encouraged.[8] And he also emphasized, as conveyed in the quotation at the head of this chapter, America's need to more fully realize its own ideals. He exposed the illusions that had guided American policy through the twentieth century, which had produced the feeling that the world wars and the disorder thereafter were "monsters that had arisen from nowhere, as by some black magic. We deluded ourselves with the belief that if they could be in some way exorcised, like evil spirits, through the process of military defeat, then nothing would remain of them and our world would be restored to us as though they had never existed."[9]

In response to Russian threats in 1946, Kennan spoke against the "hysterical sort of anticommunism" that was replacing the earlier stereotype of the well-intentioned, cooperative Russia propagated by the Roosevelt administration. He pointed out repeatedly that Russian foreign policy advanced not through military conquest but through political pressures, subversion, and propaganda. The fears that Russia wanted to capture Western Europe by military means or to provoke an atomic war were "largely a creation of Western imagination."[10] In the face of calls for great anti-communist crusades, Kennan quietly insisted: "These peoples are not ogres; they are just badly misguided and twisted human beings, deeply involved in the predicaments that invariably attend the exercise of great power."[11] His choice of the word "invariably," which surely included the United States itself, indicates his appraisal of the perennial dilemma of power and the extent of his break with the zealous stereotypes.

However, the stereotypes persisted, leading to the military distortion of the containment policy, locking the United States into the military alliance system, and blocking potential negotiation. Kennan resigned from the state department in 1950 because he was unable to counter these tendencies. As he saw it, the difficulty lay not so much in the complex dilemmas of foreign policy as in the "deep inner crisis" that the postwar threat provoked within America itself.[12] One British interpreter of the Cold War, Fred Inglis, paid tribute to Kennan's large vision in these words: "He has striven for a transcendental understanding of world struggle, not just a rationalization for the American or the Western point of view."[13]

This crisis regarding the presence of communist power must be understood in the light of the zealous ideology that continued to shape the thinking of less sophisticated Americans. Unlike the handful of realists who stood close to centers of power for several years after the war, most Americans experienced a double frustration. They were baffled at the inexplicable emergence of the communist threat so soon after the successful crusade of World War II, and they were perplexed by the lack of a clear-cut crusading response on the part of their government. Tradition as well as recent experience had led them to yearn for a quick and total solution when a seemingly demonic force threatened the mission of the chosen nation to redeem the world for freedom. These feelings came to the fore in the wake of Russia's toppling of Czechoslovakia and the Berlin blockade in 1948. A Chicago reporter described the "cold fear" that was "gripping people hereabouts." He put his finger on the "reluctant conviction that . . . relentless forces are prowling the earth and that somehow they are bound to mean trouble for us. . . . All winter, confidence in peace has been oozing away. With the Czech coup, it practically vanished."[14] A faint image of the elusive, demonic adversary in the apocalyptic strands of the Bible is evoked in this description of the popular mood in the winter of 1947-1948. The crusade against totalitarianism had somehow failed, and the forces of darkness were "prowling" about once again. The times evoked the feeling of an impending showdown, a sense of standing on the edge of an apocalyptic battle.

The crisis deepened in 1949 with the fall of Nationalist China, the explosion of the first Soviet atomic bomb, and the sensational Alger Hiss case. As Eric F. Goldman wrote, "1949 was a year of shocks, shocks with enormous catalytic force." They "loosed within American life a vast impatience, a turbulent bitterness, a rancor akin to revolt" that were unparalleled in American history.[15] The desire for an easy crusade against the forces of darkness was countered by the fear of vast nuclear destruction. Yet it seemed inconceivable that the chosen nation should have to endure a stalemate. The Hiss case seemed to provide an explanation. As Congressman Richard M. Nixon said after investigating the Hiss case and spearheading its prosecution, "The nation acquired a better understanding, vital to its security, of the strategy and tactics of the Communist conspiracy at home and abroad." Nixon felt that it revealed the "crisis with which we shall be confronted as long as aggressive international Communism is on the loose in the world."[16]

From the perspective of zealous nationalism, the cause of America's frustration eventually clarified itself. The threat to her mission must have come from a demonic conspiracy, centered in Moscow, with its tentacles reaching out to intellectuals such as Alger Hiss and to fellow travelers and liberals who unknowingly supported the party line. It was imperative to purify the camp of such traitors, and Nixon's zealous prosecution of the Hiss case was matched by a flood of incidents all over the country. Loyalty oaths were demanded; extensive security files were gathered on fellow citizens; political beliefs came under the inquisition of "un-American activities" committees. Libraries, schools, and churches were purged of seemingly dangerous books, thoughts, and leaders. The further this cleansing zeal went, the more it conflicted with the cherished traditions of freedom of thought and expression. Heated disputes broke out between zealous crusaders and libertarians. The dilemma was compounded by the frustrating limits of the international situation. Russia was too large to defeat or to occupy, and its development of nuclear weapons quickly led to a stalemate. To maintain a crusade in the international arena required a new level of frustrating double talk. It had to be a crusade that was less than a crusade, an unlimited campaign against evil, but with limits lest a greater evil result. Truman was the first president caught in this dilemma. He picked up the containment impulse from his advisors and translated it into a new form of a limited American crusade. In his message to Congress during the Greek and Turkish crisis in March 1947, he said:

> We shall not realize our objectives . . . unless we are willing to help free peoples to maintain their free institutions and their national integrity against aggressive movements that seek to impose upon them totalitarian regimes. This is no more than a frank recognition that totalitarian regimes imposed on free peoples, by direct or indirect aggression, undermine the foundations of international peace and hence the security of the United States. . . . I believe that it must be the policy of the United States to support free peoples who are resisting attempted subjugation by armed minorities or by outside pressures. . . . We cannot allow changes in the status quo . . . by such methods as coercion or by such subterfuges as political infiltration.[17]

Two worlds appear in this speech, the "free" and the "totalitarian," but the definition is clearly ideological rather than empirical. Turkey and Greece are "free" because they are not under communist domination, not because their citizens enjoy rights of free speech or assembly. One sees similarities here to Wilson's millennial nationalism, with the source of disorder assigned to the nondemocratic peoples and the mission defined as redeeming the world through the spread of democracies. The commitment is remarkably open-ended: "free peoples" anywhere on the globe qualify for aid whether strategically important or not and whether a change in their ruling class actually threatens world peace or not.

The Truman Doctrine commitment to protracted crusade marked a decisive step away from the realistic premises of containment as understood by George Kennan. By the time of his 1949 inaugural address, President Truman had hardened this into an elaborate two-world theory and a commitment to "strengthen freedom-loving nations against the dangers of aggression" by means of defense pacts and economic development.[18] His "Point Four" plan to assist the "free peoples of the world" was an unconditional commitment for the indefinite future. He articulated its goal as a kind of millennial age of peace: "Steadfast in our faith in the Almighty, we will advance toward a world where man's freedom is secure. To that end we will devote our strength, our resources, and our firmness of resolve. With God's help, the future of mankind will be assured in a world of justice, harmony, and peace."[19] This rhetoric appealed to the religious and national sensibilities of the American people and led them in an effort that would occupy them for most of the next half century.

If "one result of containment was the encouragement of a holy crusade against communism," as Arthur A. Ekirch has suggested,[20] it was President Truman who synthesized the two. Despite the resignation of Kennan — who felt that containment had been reduced to its military component — and the protests of other realists, there was little comprehension of how antithetical this synthesis would be to the humane traditions of freedom it sought to enhance. As the Pentagon Papers later revealed, the crusade led immediately to the unwise involvement in Indochina. By the end of 1949, President Truman had approved the policy goal to "block further Communist expansion in Asia." Even so realistic a diplomat as Dean Acheson had succumbed by February 1950 to the mythical picture of aggressive Communism and supported military aid to the French in an early version of the "domino" argument: "The choice confronting the U.S. is to support the legal governments in Indochina or to face the extension of Communism over the remainder of the continental area of Southeast Asia and possibly westward."[21]

The Korean War exposed the fallacy in this synthesis of containment and crusade. At first there was widespread support for the clear-cut solution of battle. President Truman referred to the "complete, almost unspoken acceptance on the part of everyone that whatever had to be done to meet this aggression had to be done."[22] Criticism emerged only after it became apparent that a total war would not be waged. The Russians and the Chinese, who supported North Korea, could not be bombed; the bulk of American troops would be held in reserve to protect Europe while MacArthur's men fought their desperate battles. A crusade Americans could understand and support, but a "police action"? The idea seemed ridiculous, not only because limited war was so antithetical to zealous ideology but also because Truman himself had been so successful in popularizing the stereotype of demonic communist aggression. Americans had not been reared to deal with such demonic aggressors by limited means. The proper way to handle the Beast was to destroy him in the apocalyptic battle!

So in the autumn of 1950 there was a wave of enthusiastic support when MacArthur's troops were authorized to cross the thirty-eighth parallel to create a "unified, independent and democratic Korea." But when the Chinese intervened and President Truman prudently refused to widen the war into China itself, the cauldron boiled over. Americans were enraged and appalled as the United Nations forces were driven back down the peninsula without retaliation against China itself. General MacArthur agitated for a change in policy and was dismissed — which intensified the crisis. The scope of American outrage was indicated by a Gallup poll showing that 69 percent of Americans favored MacArthur and 29 percent favored President Truman.[23]

The issue that MacArthur raised was logical and penetrating, given the assumptions of zealous nationalism. If one is engaged in a crusade against communism, why not carry it to its logical conclusion? He wrote Representative Joseph Martin, the Republican minority leader, that it "seems strangely difficult for some to realize that here in Asia is where the Communist conspirators have elected to make their play for global conquest, and that we have joined the issue thus raised on the battlefield; that here we fight Europe's wars with arms while the diplomats there still fight it with words; that if we lose the war to Communism in Asia the fall of Europe is inevitable; win it and Europe most probably would avoid war and yet preserve freedom. . . . There is no substitute for victory."[24] The ideology here was the same as Truman's, except that it was more consistent. It had the same picture of monolithic world communism, bent on world conquest by force of arms. It betrayed the same apocalyptic mood, the belief that if communism wins anywhere, it will inherit the entire globe, while if it is stopped anywhere, the Beast's power will be thwarted everywhere. Neither MacArthur's nor Truman's vision provided access to the real situation in Korea or Europe, in Moscow or Peking. But it was a vision shared by the American populace as a whole, and from that vantage point, MacArthur's position seemed unassailable: in a crusade there is no substitute for victory. The Book of Revelation would attest to that.

The one insurmountable problem with MacArthur's crusade was the risk of a full-scale war with a country too vast to occupy and too independent to accept infringement of its vital interests. And as close as Korea was to Siberia, it ran a serious risk of provoking Russian intervention as well, particularly if success against the Chinese could be attained. Truman was sensible enough to give up his crusading hopes in the face of such prospects. When the crunch came, his synthesis of zeal and realism disintegrated, and he opted for a stalemate in Korea.

For many Americans, Truman's abandonment of the crusade betrayed the most crucial aspect of the moral heritage. Enormous crowds turned out to meet MacArthur in San Francisco and Washington. After his powerful address to Congress, he was greeted by seven million people in New York City in a "reception that exceeded Lindbergh Day or Eisenhower Day or the excitement of V.J."[25] The Texas Legislature applauded MacArthur when he made this statement: "Never before have we geared national policy to timidity and fear. The guide, instead, has invariably been one of high moral principle and the courage to decide great issues on the spiritual level of what is right and what is wrong. . . . We now practice a new and yet more dangerous form of appeasement . . . on the battlefield."[26]

People believed MacArthur's intimations that "insidious forces from within" America were leading to the Korean stalemate and to America's eventual enslavement to communism.[27] Here was the familiar faith, untainted by considerations of prudence or power politics, a faith shaped by the victories in the Civil War and the Spanish-American War, and now enunciated by a leader who had been victorious in the great world wars. If the crusades worked then, why not now? If the righteous nation was granted total victory over the agents of wickedness through every engagement of the mythic past, what frustrated it now? Could it really be that a dark conspiracy had undermined the land of the free? The only other possibility in the popular mind was to give up the faith itself, and this would imply that those who died in Korea had died in vain. They would not deserve the zealot's honor if their war were less than a divine crusade. In MacArthur's words, to "die in some halfhearted and indecisive effort" was to die without righteous cause. It would not be a matter of dying to make men free.

The issue between Truman and MacArthur was so sharply drawn that it revealed the dilemma of the Captain America complex with definitive clarity. The strands of zeal and realism, joined in various ways since the Puritan era, parted for a moment to show their mutually exclusive character. In the face of the pressures of the atomic age, their synthesis was no longer feasible. If one chose to retain the zealous heritage alone, the results would be suicidal. Only the tradition of constitutional restraint and the common sense of a former haberdasher from Missouri kept the majority of Americans from embarking on precisely such a course in 1950. But since their optimism and heritage kept them from admitting such prospects, the principal result was a frustration so deep and pervasive, so bitter and revulsive, that its effect may yet be felt in American life.

Brinkmanship and the Ideology of Anti-communism

The Eisenhower administration was swept into office by a landslide vote after a campaign that capitalized on that national frustration. The issues of communism, corruption, and Korea were linked in such a way as to appeal to the widespread feeling that subversion and degeneracy had caused the Korean stalemate. The spirit of that campaign is captured in this excerpt from the Republican platform, written by John Foster Dulles, a Truman state department appointee who saw his future with Eisenhower. It speaks to the liberation of peoples under "communist enslavement":

> We shall again make liberty into a beacon light of hope that will penetrate the dark places. It will mark the end of the negative, futile and immoral

policy of "containment" which abandons countless human beings to a despotism and godless terrorism, which in turn enables the rulers to forge the captives into a weapon of our destruction. . . . The policies we espouse will revive the contagious, liberating influences which are inherent in freedom. They will inevitably set up strains and stresses within the captive world which will make the rulers impotent to continue in their monstrous ways and mark the beginning of the end.[28]

This platform linked the zealous crusade with the light-to-the-nations theme, a motif from the tradition of prophetic realism. The world was to be converted by the example of liberty, bringing the "godless" tyranny of communism to its apocalyptic "end." Eisenhower's first inaugural address trumpeted anew the call to arms. Calling for "a conscious renewal of faith . . . in the watchfulness of a Divine Providence," he announced that "freedom is pitted against slavery; lightness against the dark." The enemy he identified was demonic: "The enemies of this faith know no god but force. . . . They tutor men in treason. They feed upon the hunger of others. Whatever defies them, they torture, especially the truth." Yet Eisenhower proposed to work hand in hand with the United Nations, "respecting . . . [it] as the sign of all people's hope for peace." A potent new ideological synthesis is manifest here, one whose legacy long remained influential in the American civil religion. It provides an answer to how the world could be converted when conditions rendered the traditional forms of martial crusading unfeasible.

To arrive at an answer, we must start with the conviction that Wilson's great crusade, which Dulles had served as legal counsel during the Versailles negotiations, failed simply because it had not really been tried.[29] Dulles himself said later: "What was wrong was the spirit which dominated the principal victors. They abandoned initiative and sense of mission. That role was left to be taken over by evil spirits who brought the peace to a quick and ignominious end."[30] He proposed to reactivate that program by the infusion of evangelical, millennial Christianity, the variety prevalent in the liberal Presbyterian circles in which he was reared. The conviction matured in the two international conferences that Dulles attended in 1937. The contrast between the League of Nations consultation in Paris and the World Council of Churches conference at Oxford made an impact on Dulles that his son, Avery Dulles, described in this way: "He found that people of different nationalities were able to reach agreements transcending their short-term national self-interest and prejudices and see things in a much larger perspective. I think the contrast of these two conferences . . . convinced him that Christianity was of tremendous importance for the solution of world problems of peace and international justice."[31]

How would "Christianity" provide the solution? By producing saints who were devoid of "short-term national self-interest"! This has been the theme of countless Protestant sermons in the past hundred years: if people would only be converted to idealism, then war and poverty and labor strife and injustice and every other social problem would be eliminated. Dulles put it this way in November 1944: "If we all concerned ourselves with idealism, of which there is no limit, there would be no competition for possessions. We would wish to share our spiritual values with all."[32] This seems to imply that when everyone becomes Christian, the selfishness that causes world conflict will be eliminated. The illusions of the Book of Revelation are clearly presupposed here: that when the saints alone survive the apocalyptic strife, the millennial era of peace will automatically begin. The saints are intrinsically peaceful, and atheists are inherently destructive; so to convert the latter by American example would achieve Wilson's goal of world peace.

In a speech on January 16, 1945, Dulles spelled out how this millennial ideology could guide the "collaboration" with the Soviets, who obviously did not share the evangelical faith: "We do not want tolerance which reflects a conscious abandonment or lowering of ideals. . . . We cannot agree to solutions which fall short of our ideals if thereby we become morally bound to sustain and perpetuate them. . . . It is the possibility 'of change which is the bridge between idealism and the practical incidents of collaboration."[33] Here is a definition of tolerance that eliminates any permanent coexistence with an adversary. A cold war of indefinite duration is the logical consequence. In this speech the future secretary of state suggested "four principles of conduct" to guide the nation through this protracted crusade. First, "our government should adopt and publicly proclaim its long-range goals. These should stem from our Christian tradition and be such as to inspire and unify us." Here is the theme of proclaiming the high ideals that would convert the heathen and usher in the millennium. When he became secretary of state, Dulles declared that "a first phase of our quest for peace must be to restore our moral influence. . . . The United States must make it clear, clear beyond any doubt, that it has no thought of using economic or military might to impose on others its particular way of life. Unless we do make that clear we shall not be able to assume moral leadership in the world."[34] In short, the chosen nation must lack that fatal self-interest, the bane of power politics, so that its good example would be a light to the world.

There is a complex irony here. The claim of such perfect disinterestedness is so blatantly self-righteous that it could never convert anyone. Moreover, the idea shields one from the realization that the conversion sought is, in fact, precisely an imposition of the saints' "particular way of life." Finally, the pious renunciation of any selfish use of "economic or military might" left the country open to an uncritical use of such force under the impulse of the crusade.

The second principle Dulles mentioned in 1945 was to "fearlessly and skillfully battle" for our ideals. As he later explained, "What we need to do is to recapture to some extent the kind of crusading spirit of the early days when we were darn sure that what we had was a lot better than what anybody else had. We knew that the rest of the world wanted it, and needed it, and that we were going to carry it around the world."[35] But what if there were nations that refused this beneficent gospel? The crusading premise dictates that evil must be either converted or destroyed. Even if such destruction were not a present possibility, in the case of an adversary as large as Russia, the will to battle must remain. For as the third principle implies, the frustration of the saints can never be accepted as anything more than temporary: "No particular set-back need be accepted as definitive." If one is confronted with a situation like that of Eastern Europe after World War II, one may be forced to put up with it for a while, but one should never acquiesce in the matter. To "compromise" would be to give up the faith, to give in to the Antichrist. And the fourth principle in the statement of Christian politics is to judge the worth of an administration by its long-term faithfulness to the mission of world redemption. In other words, a zealous nation should not be measured by the destructiveness of its current policies but rather by the purity of its motives and goals.

The major shifts in Dulles's foreign policy were all implicit in this ideological statement. "Liberation" was the millennial goal, sanctified by the "Battle Hymn of the Republic" and put into modern idiom by Woodrow Wilson. It was to be achieved by international evangelism, in which the righteous nation would win the world for Christ and for peace by its high example. When the world was liberated, it would necessarily accept the tenets of Christianity as Dulles understood them and would thereby presumably cease to be an arena of conflict. The corollary was a rigid stereotyping of the "free world" as invincible, courageous, and just, and of the unconverted "communist world" as doomed to extinction, yet ruthless, cunning, and unjust. Within this ideology, coexistence with the unconverted was excluded: compromise was defined as doing violence to high ideals; neutrality was fence-sitting between Christ and Satan; and accommodations were never accepted on more than a temporary basis. In practice, "liberation" implied a constant crusade by every feasible means to eliminate the adversary — either by conversion or, if he brought it upon himself, by violence. So deterrence, which took the form of massive nuclear retaliation after Dulles's threatening speech in 1954,[36] was the temporary expedient to be used against those who refused such conversion or who insisted on Satanic conversions in return. Any readjustment of frontiers or stabilization of spheres of influence had to be adamantly opposed on the grounds that force was being used to deprive people of their right to hear the gospel. Such acts were defined as "aggressive" and had to be deterred with overwhelming force regardless of the merits of the case.

The thing that baffled Dulles and his followers was how such an idealism could be viewed as self-righteous, provocative, and threatening to world peace. He was particularly piqued when church leaders criticized his version of the crusade. "The Church people," he wrote in 1958 to his brother-in-law, Rev. Deane Edwards, "have been clamoring for a long time for the application of moral principles to public affairs and to foreign relations. Now when we try to do that, and explain what we are doing . . . we are accused of hypocrisy."[37] This was baffling to Dulles because, when one accepted the ideology itself, the hypocrisy was invisible. The theological double talk of the Book of Revelation was so pervasive that the crusade to bring in the millennium through the conversion of the world seemed entirely benign. It kept Dulles from seeing that his ideals of freedom and equality under law were antithetical to his zealous crusade, which stereotyped the enemy and sought either to convert or to destroy him. It would take a staggering series of reverses and crises, the alienation of allies, the hostility of the entire neutral world, and the shattering of every attempt to negotiate, before the nation could begin to recognize the internal contradictions that Dulles was never able to see.

The story of this frustration may be divided roughly into three phases. Until President Eisenhower's heart attack in September 1955, the crusading and realistic impulses within his administration seemed to hold each other in check. Despite the threat to "unleash" Chiang Kai-shek, Eisenhower decided to settle for a stalemate in Korea. His survey of the deep Chinese fortifications convinced him that a rollback was not feasible. It was an embarrassing blow to the liberation policy. Another came when Eisenhower prudently decided not to intervene in the Indochina war. He had supported recommendations for military aid for France, and he echoed the domino theory in his press conferences. But when the clinch came, he was too realistic to commit American troops to an endless land war in Asia.

Dulles, however, made frantic, abortive visits to the Western allies to get support for a coalition to replace France in the war. He was left with the humiliating task of participating in the Geneva Conference, where he was "absolutely immovable," as the Alsops put it, in opposing "a settlement which would or could lead to Communist victory in Indo-China."[38] The purity of his hatred for the negotiations is conveyed in Townsend Hoopes's observations that he attended for a mere week and "conducted himself with the pinched distaste of a Puritan in a house of ill-repute, quite brusquely refusing to shake hands with

Chou En-Lai and instructing the American delegation to ignore at all times the presence and existence of the Chinese delegation."[39] As Louis L. Gerson's study notes, Dulles had felt that any "promise to sustain communist domination of Vietnam, Laos, and Cambodia would be out of the question."[40] Still, under the pressure of the debacle at Dien Bien Phu, Dulles's seven-point memorandum to Mendes-France approximated the final terms of the Geneva Accord.[41] But he refused to negotiate with the communists or to sign the accord because that would have been to condone communist tyranny.

President Eisenhower said that we would respect the terms of the accord without being a signatory, a stance that Thomas J. Hamilton aptly termed "innocence by disassociation."[42] Nothing was allowed to sully the purity of the chosen people. If Harold Stassen is correct, it was Dulles's disapproval that "prevented the United States from granting diplomatic recognition to North Vietnam after the Geneva Conference."[43] It is clear that, immediately thereafter, Dulles began to take over the responsibilities of the French in South Vietnam and to build an anti-communist bulwark there. Studies of the Vietnam and Laotian wars, plus the publication of the *Pentagon Papers,* reveal the pattern of American efforts to encourage those countries to avoid participation in the forthcoming elections. In 1956, the United States introduced additional military personnel into Vietnam in violation of the Geneva limitations.[44]

Early in 1955 this ideology nearly ignited a world war when communist China began to clear its harbors of the Nationalist blockade centered on the islands of Quemoy and Matsu. They had been temporarily fortified during the Korean War to hinder coastal shipping, and they were not included within the defense perimeter in the Mutual Defense Treaty with Chiang in 1954. They had no direct relationship to the defense of Formosa or to the security of the "free world." Yet Dulles threatened publicly to use atomic weapons on Chinese airfields in case of an invasion, and President Eisenhower agreed. Congress passed the vague and sweeping Formosa Resolution; so powerful was the anti-communist ideology that there were only three dissenting votes. The great disappointment was that no U.S. ally except Thailand and the Philippines agreed to fight World War III for the offshore islands. The great crusade to convert the world was failing even to attract the "free nations." But the world was spared the conflagration because China decided to postpone the invasion.

The climax of this first phase of Cold War crises came with the Geneva summit conference of 1955. It had been promoted by none other than Winston Churchill, who had turned away from the crusading ideal after Stalin's death and a taste of Dulles's atomic brinkmanship. The conference represented a real opportunity to settle the issues left over from World War II and thus to bring the Cold War to an end. The diplomatic historian Frederick Schuman describes the prospects after the truce in Korea, the Indochina settlement, and the Austrian Treaty in 1955: "There was every prospect for a negotiated settlement of the Cold War by the end of that year [1955]. Then something went wrong, and the Cold War resumed."

One of the causes was President Eisenhower's heart attack, which "left the direction of American policy in the hands of a secretary of state, who, amid his many virtues, was addicted to the vice of opposing any negotiated settlement of the Cold War."[45] Given Dulles's ideology, it is obvious why he would oppose any real settlement in the consultations after Geneva. It would have meant relinquishing his dream of a Christian NATO and a rearmed Germany under the Christian leader Konrad Adenauer. And, as Gerson explains, "under no circumstances would he accept the Soviet power position in Europe, tolerating covert aggression and sanctifying wrongs in Eastern Europe and elsewhere." The demands of realism proved incompatible with the tenets of zealous ideology. It was not long before the Cold War resumed with more dangerous prospects than before.

The second critical phase in the Eisenhower administration lasted until the resignation and sudden death of John Foster Dulles in 1959. Excepting the refusal to intervene in Hungary, there was probably never a time when the impulse of realism was more conspicuously absent nor the frustration of zealous hopes more complete. To answer the thrust of Soviet influence in the Middle East, Dulles established the Baghdad Pact and sought to coerce Egypt into abandoning its profitable neutrality. He withdrew the promise to support the Aswan Dam project rather than allow communist participation, whereupon Nasser nationalized the Suez Canal. Refusing to acknowledge or support British and French interests in the canal, the administration was shocked by their attack on Egypt in 1956 and piously condemned them in the United Nations. Having alienated the Allies, Dulles allowed matters to drift until 1958, when the United States sent marines to Lebanon to protect a Christian ruler from his Muslim countrymen. That such an intervention was righteous, while the earlier Suez intervention was sinful, was a judgment that could be reached only when one considered ideological factors rather than realistic interests. The possibility of communist influences in Lebanon made the difference. In the Dulles theology, defense of national interests was wrong, but the defense of "principle" was right.

Immediately thereafter, pressure on Quemoy mounted, and again Dulles led the nation to the brink of a world war. The world might be blown up based on zealous principles, but at least it would have the edifying spectacle of seeing the chosen nation in action! That same year the Soviets made a determined effort to settle the anomaly of West Berlin by a new form of coercion. The issue that could have been settled by negotiation in 1955 once again threatened to ignite a general European war.[46]

By keeping crusading zeal as the guideline of American foreign policy, the Eisenhower administration made chronic crises out of issues that could have been settled by compromise. It is questionable whether any administration has evoked more hostility internationally or experienced a more thorough frustration of its stated mission. Zeal and reality were locked in irreducible conflict, yet the chosen nation and its leaders were so righteous and so far from "self-serving" that they were unconscious of the flaw. It was visible to others but never to them.

With the death of Dulles, the third phase of the Eisenhower administration could open. The president asserted himself vigorously to redirect the course of American foreign policy toward negotiation. Openly avowing the goal of coexistence and speaking warmly of neutral nations for the first time, he was cheered by tremendous crowds in India and elsewhere in December 1959. But negotiations required more than good will, and Eisenhower's zealously oriented administration made no adequate preparations for a compromise position at the second summit conference scheduled for May 1960. It used up fruitless months in an effort to appease the French and German allies, who preferred national grandeur to a general European settlement. The mishandling of the U-2 spy plane incident in the Soviet Union provided the final blow. Eisenhower's frank acceptance of responsibility, when in fact he had not authorized this particular overflight and knew little of the precise details, was an admirable act of democratic honesty that helped restore his integrity at home. But it forced Khrushchev into a position of negotiation under duress while his nation's sovereignty was brazenly threatened. Eisenhower's statement that such overflights were necessary and would be continued was a flat rejection of international law, and it placed Khrushchev in an untenable position with respect to the militaristic forces in Russia. The U-2 incident offers a clear example of the tactics of zealous nationalism directly countering the development of coexistence and the enforcement of international law. In any event, the failure of the Paris summit conference was tragic for both East and West. It would be years before a similar opportunity for a major settlement by negotiation would appear.

By 1960 the anti-communist ideology in America had jelled into the form it would take for the next decade and more. Both political parties had contributed to its elaboration; both had supported its tenets in critical situations. And though sophisticated American leaders would increasingly dissociate themselves from its express terminology, they continued to be guided by its premises. The public was so thoroughly indoctrinated by zealous rhetoric that, even when leaders began to dissent in private, they continued to play to popular feelings in their policies and pronouncements.

The Arrogant Missteps of Global Idealism

The presidential inaugural address by John F. Kennedy on January 20, 1961, eloquently expressed some of the perennial features of the civil religion, for example, "the belief that the rights of man come not from the generosity of the state but from the hand of God." The address sees the perennial call to battle as derived from this same God, who encourages believers to be "rejoicing in hope, patient in tribulation," cited from Romans 12:12. The "long twilight struggle" is now to be directed not against a specific external enemy but "against the common enemies of man: tyranny, poverty, disease and war itself." Although these enumerated "enemies" sound abstract, Kennedy's words addressed to other nations had a more bellicose, personal undertone.

> Let every nation know, whether it wishes us well or ill, that we shall pay any price, bear any burden, meet any hardship, support any friend, oppose any foe to assure the survival and success of liberty.

The global idealism of these battle-ready saints who are granted precedence and power over the entire world resounds in such lines, and reaches its climax with the peroration:

> With a good conscience our only sure reward, with history the final judge of our deeds, let us go forth to lead the land we love, asking His blessing and His help, but knowing that here on earth God's work must truly be our own.

Will Herberg's critique of American religion, published a year before this inaugural address, touches on the flaw in these sentiments that would lead Kennedy and his successor into tragic circumstances. From the "point of view of Jewish-Christian faith," Herberg wrote, contemporary American religiosity was naively "man-centered. Not God, but man — man in his individual and corporate being — is the beginning and end of the spiritual system. . . . God is conceived as man's 'omnipotent servant,' faith as a sure-fire device to get what we want."[47] God as a presence imposing an independent standard of justice that every nation and faction should fear is unavailable as human corrective in this scheme. A personal anecdote from Kennedy's secretary, Evelyn Lincoln, suggested that he had scaled down his God to a general with whom he was ready to fight. Following his strained summit in Vienna with Nikita Khrushchev, a thought he had written on a piece of paper fell to the floor: "I know there is a God — and I see a storm coming; if He has a place for me, I believe I am ready."[48]

For combatants in the struggle that would be blessed by God, Kennedy attracted the services of "the best and the brightest," in journalist David Halberstam's ironic phrase, from the great American universities. Combining their super-intelligence with the nation's super-power, Kennedy and his successor, Lyndon Johnson, believed themselves able to solve the otherwise insurmountable problems of poverty and war. There was no place in this supreme confidence for Abraham Lincoln's sober sense that God's righteousness remains transcendent, that the sins of the "almost chosen people" will inevitably be paid for with blood, and that the arrogance of power in any guise is a certain prelude to disaster.

The initial test of Kennedy's zeal for the cause of freedom came with the Bay of Pigs invasion in Cuba — just a few months after his inauguration. The wretched nature of the military operation earned immediate scorn from both liberals and conservatives and may have sown the political disaffection in Lee Harvey Oswald that led him to assassinate Kennedy. A group of 1,400 Cuban exiles, trained and equipped by the United States, were sent to the Bay of Pigs on the premise that their presence on Cuba would lead to a general uprising that would overthrow the government of Castro. Not only was this militarily implausible, given the much larger numbers of heavily armed Cuban and Soviet forces on the island;[49] the United States appears to have deliberately excluded segments of the exile population who could appeal to the same revolutionary sentiments that had brought Castro to power. The Cuban exile forces were quickly slaughtered or captured.

The CIA had apparently designed a failure in hopes that Kennedy would be compelled to unleash the U.S. military. CIA operative Frank Bender had mollified the anxious Dr. José Miro Cardona of the Cuban Revolutionary Council with these words: "Do not worry, once the operation starts, the President will have no choice but to order American forces in." Ernesto Betancourt, who reported this conversation, was an early ally of Castro and had represented him in Washington during the insurrection against the dictator Fulgencio Batista, but had turned against Castro on the issue of communism. Thus he wanted to collaborate with the United States in opposing Castro. In his opinion, the CIA opposed anyone who had a revolutionary background or even a leftist political orientation.

At that time, such an approach was doomed to fail. The only people who had any chance of challenging Castro successfully were those who had fought Batista and, being anti-communist, were rebelling against Castro's betrayal of the revolution. Even for them the odds were remote. Castro had captured the imagination of the Cuban people with his charisma and the economic distribution measures he had instituted, not to mention his appeal to Cuban nationalism.[50]

In effect, the proclaimed commitments of Kennedy to fight "tyranny," "disease," and "poverty" came down in Cuba's case to an issue of control over the forces opposing Castro. Instead of ideals and realistic assessments, Kennedy's CIA persisted in bizarre assassination schemes directed against Castro and fanciful notions about what might trigger an uprising. Betancourt reported that one of General Edward Landsdale's whimsical ideas for destabilizing the Cuban government was the proposal "to send propaganda to Cuba announcing that if the Cubans rebelled against Castro, there was going to be a second coming of Christ. Assuming that the Cubans were completely religious — a completely unwarranted assumption — they were expected to start rebelling in response to that call."[51] Far more ominous were the risks the United States encountered when it discovered the intermediate-range nuclear missiles being installed by the Soviet Union in Cuba.

The principals in this episode — Khrushchev, Castro, and Kennedy — each brought elements of recklessness that threatened to spin the confrontation out of control toward unrestrained nuclear war. One of Kennedy's volatile contributions was the self-righteous stereotype of the American nation that he brought to almost every conflict with the Soviet Union. For example, in the mid-1961 situation in which the East German government built the Berlin Wall to stanch the westward flow of its citizens, Kennedy flaunted the cowboy myth as a relevant guide to the stances of the players.

> The world is not deceived by the Communist attempt to label Berlin as a hot-bed of war. There is peace in Berlin today. The source of world trouble and tension is Moscow, not Berlin. And if war begins, it will have begun in Moscow and not Berlin.
>
> For the choice of peace or war is largely theirs, not ours. It is the Soviets who have stirred up this crisis. It is they who are trying to force a change. It is they who have opposed free elections. It is they who have rejected an all-German peace treaty, and the rulings of international law. And as Americans know from our history on our own old frontier, gun battles are caused by outlaws, and not by officers of the peace.[52]

There were several factors of Soviet intransigence in this situation, but a primary concern was to prevent East Germany from losing its most capable citizens — not a desire to make war. The issue was freedom, of course, but Kennedy's apocalyptic impulse led him to announce in this same speech a large defense build-up in both equipment and personnel — increasing both the military draft and the reserve forces. He also formally announced civilian preparation for nuclear war, complete with "fallout shelters, first aid kits, and other minimum essentials for survival." The object was to save, "in the event of an attack, the lives of those families which are not hit in a nuclear blast or fire." The message to the Soviet Union seemed to be that the American nation was ready for conventional and nuclear war over the issues surrounding the transit of citizens in Berlin.

Given this apocalyptic rhetoric and the U.S.-sponsored attack on Cuba at the Bay of Pigs a few months earlier, coupled with continuing harassments labeled "Operation Mongoose," it is not surprising that Castro and Khrushchev found a common interest in defending themselves with nuclear missiles. Even after the crisis with the missiles, the United States continued to sabotage facilities such as oil refineries, power plants, docks, and ships.[53] When aerial surveillance of Cuba revealed rapidly developing missile sites in October 1962, Kennedy felt that he had to somehow eliminate them. The grave question was how: by bombing the missile sites, by a land invasion of Cuba or a naval blockade, by negotiation, or by making threats? Historian Arthur M. Schlesinger, Jr., who served in the Kennedy White House, gave the gloss to the incident that reminds us of Cold War nuclear brinkmanship: "It was this combination of toughness and restraint, of will, nerve and wisdom, so brilliantly controlled, so matchlessly calibrated, that dazzled the world."[54] The most flattering of the contemporaneous assessments came from Secretary of State Dean Rusk: "We're eyeball to eyeball, and I think the other guy just blinked."

The reality that has unfolded with the declassification of documents and the more open retrospective appraisal of other participants is far less reassuring. In February 1989 a group of senior officials from the U.S., Cuban, and Soviet governments gathered in Moscow to discuss what they thought had happened in 1962. The meeting revealed that each group had acted out of misperceptions, including the failure to know that nuclear warheads had already arrived in Cuba and could be quickly targeted against major U.S. cities. Furthermore, some Soviet commands were equipped with tactical nuclear weapons, and they had the authority to make decisions on the battlefield about their use. U.S. intelligence had estimated the presence of 10,000 Soviet and 40,000 Cuban troops, when the numbers were actually 40,000 and 270,000, respectively. Robert McNamara estimated that U.S. casualties in a land invasion would have been twice as high as military estimates. He concluded: "The horrifying extent to which we misunderstood what was going on is the absolutely fundamental lesson for the future."[55] But this somber spirit of retrospection did not come quickly enough to brake the tragic drift of the Kennedy and Johnson administrations toward other disasters.

Thomas Blanton gave a more realistic assessment of the Cuban missile crisis: "Thus was born the myth of calibrated brinkmanship — the belief that if you stand tough you win, and that nuclear superiority makes the difference in moments of crisis. This myth, midwifed by the Kennedy family and its hagiographers, had untold consequences for the planning of the Vietnam War and the nuclear arms race."[56] This version of the crisis emphasized the invincibility of the superpower, which could always win by facing down and humiliating its adversaries. Kennedy's military advisers, Air Force Chief of Staff Curtis LeMay and Marine Commandant David Shoup, argued that he should follow the mythic logic of bombing and invasion that would presumably prevent a wider conflagration. LeMay made his case: "This blockade and political action I see leading into war. This is almost as bad as appeasement at Munich. . . . I just don't see any other solution except direct military intervention right now."[57]

Fortunately, the Kennedy administration avoided a full-scale military campaign when the crisis was actually resolved by a secret agreement that Robert Kennedy concluded with Soviet Ambassador Anatoly Dobrynin. According to the younger Kennedy's memoir, *Thirteen Days* (1969), the United States had pledged not to invade Cuba and to withdraw its missiles in Turkey. Within the mythic framework for the crisis established by President Kennedy, the need for secrecy was obvious. The United States could not concede that it was making "a deal," negotiating with a reasonable partner, making a concession that admitted any aggressive intent on its own part — as represented by the presence of the Jupiter missiles so close to the Soviet border. The Kennedy administration wanted to maintain the image of the United States as a fierce but selfless antagonist that would "pay any price, bear any burden" anywhere in the world to carry out the fight against world Communism. Having failed to acknowledge the shortcomings of the zealous myth, its logic led toward the tragic denouement in Southeast Asia.

Defeated Superheroism in Vietnam

When Vice President Lyndon B. Johnson unexpectedly assumed office in November 1963, after Kennedy's assassination, he was philosophically prepared for the task of maintaining the superpower mythos in the Vietnam context.

Kennedy had sent him to Vietnam in 1961 to become familiar with the situation. As diplomatic historian Michael H. Hunt observes, "Johnson returned militant on the need to stand firm in the defense of the 'young and unsophisticated nations' of Southeast Asia, emphatic on the need to attack 'hunger, ignorance, poverty and disease,' and nearly apocalyptic on the dire consequences of defeat."[58] He had sat in the councils of power where the United States contemplated arranging the coup that resulted in the assassination of South Vietnam's President Ngo Dinh Diem — just a few weeks before President Kennedy's assassination — first arguing against it and then acquiescing in it. Johnson offered his pledge of support to General Minh, who temporarily emerged as the reigning power after the murder of Diem and his brother Ngo Dinh Nu. Regardless of who was in power (ten governments appeared in rapid succession during an eighteen-month period), Johnson justified support for those governments in terms of the "war against the forces of enslavement, brutality, and material misery," while designating any schemes of neutrality as "just another name for a communist take-over."[59]

It was later revealed that Johnson's public words were contradicted by his private thoughts and conversations with those he trusted. In a telephone call before his re-election in 1964, he expressed to Senator Richard Russell of Georgia, chair of the Armed Services Committee, his fears of the zealotry shown by the circle of policy advisers he had inherited from Kennedy. He compared their recklessness to General Douglas MacArthur's in Korea.

> JOHNSON: Well, I spend all my days with Rusk and McNamara and Bundy and Harriman and Vance, and all those folks that are dealing with it and I would say that it pretty well adds up to them now that we have got to show some power and some force and that they do not — they are kind of like MacArthur in Korea — they don't believe that the Chinese Communists will come into this thing. But they don't know, and nobody can really be sure, but their feeling is that they won't, and in any event, we haven't got much choice. . . . I don't think the American people are for it. I don't agree with [Senator Wayne] Morse and all that he says, but . . .
>
> RUSSELL: Neither do I, but he is voicing the sentiment of a hell of a lot of people.[60]

Senator Morse from Oregon was one of the few members of Congress who stood firmly against the Vietnam War from its initial phases. He and Senator Ernest Gruening of Alaska were to record the only two congressional dissents against the open-ended Gulf of Tonkin resolution in 1965.

Lyndon B. Johnson's inaugural address on January 20, 1965, reaffirmed the narcissistic civil religion that Kennedy had popularized. He conceded that "we have no promise from God that our greatness will endure," since "we have been allowed by Him to seek greatness with the sweat of our hands and the strength of our spirit." However, "we are a nation of believers. Underneath the clamor of building and the rush of our day's pursuits, we are believers in justice and liberty and union, and in our own Union. We believe that every man must some day be free. And we believe in ourselves." The emphatic final line here reveals the central conviction: American civil religion was now centered in the belief in its own superpower. Johnson asserted that because of such self-affirming beliefs, America's enemies will always be thwarted, because they cannot see that "from the secret places of the American heart came forth the faith they could not see or that they could not even imagine. It brought us victory. And it will again." As events disclosed, however, the attempt to maintain this conviction in the face of the frustrations in Southeast Asia required lies and self-deceptions that Johnson could not sustain for himself or for others.

In *Reaching for Glory: The Johnson White House Tapes, 1964-1965*,[61] historian Michael Beschloss describes how Johnson rammed through the Gulf of Tonkin Resolution in August 1964. On the pretext of a minor naval confrontation between American and North Vietnamese forces, this resolution provided legal justification and congressional support for widening the war into aerial campaigns against North Vietnam. That the president knew this to be false was revealed in his statement the following year, as reported by Beschloss: "For all I know, our Navy was shooting at whales out there." In contrast, Johnson reiterated the standard confidence of triumphalist civil religion to a Washington audience in August 1965 — that "America wins the wars that she undertakes. Make no mistake about it!"

The White House tapes Beschloss studied indicate that Johnson didn't really believe this, that indeed he predicted to intimates, "America could never win the war in Vietnam." He repeatedly confided to his wife, Lady Bird, and to Senator Richard Russell (D-GA) that there was no way of winning the war but that a withdrawal of American forces would result in the collapse of other countries in Asia and Europe. In view of America's superpower, Johnson did not want to become "the first president to lose a war," so escalation followed escalation as lie followed lie. Johnson's will to soldier on in the cause he could not match to his triumphalist rhetoric was thwarted by voices within his own Democratic party: Senator George McGovern (SD), Senator J. William Fulbright (AR), and especially Senators Eugene McCarthy (MN) and Robert F. Kennedy (NY), both of whom launched rival presidential campaigns against Johnson with the premise that the Vietnam War was morally wrong. Kennedy was especially eloquent in expressing the insights of prophetic realism. In his campaign speech of March 18, 1968, he opposed the war as "deeply wrong" and expressed his willingness "to bear my share of the responsibility, before history and before my fellow citizens." He rejected the seductive appeal of stubborn persistence as a way of delaying the recognition of failure: "Past error is no excuse for its own perpetuation. Tragedy is a tool for the living to gain wisdom, not a guide by which to live." The chorus from Sophocles' *Antigone,* rebuking the harshness of King Creon, embodied the wisdom that Kennedy wanted to impart to American policy in Vietnam. He quoted: "All men make mistakes, but a good man yields when he knows his course is wrong. The only sin is pride." Kennedy seemed haunted by Lincoln's fears that a just God might make a severe judgment against a nation that pursued such destructive warfare.

> Can we ordain to ourselves the awful majesty of God — to decide what cities and villages are to be destroyed, who will live and who will die, and who will join the refugees wandering in a desert of our own creation?[62]

Senator Kennedy lost his chance to act further on these principles, either as senator or as president. He was assassinated less than four months later during a Los Angeles campaign event. However, his opposition to the Vietnam War policy heightened the frustration and sense of futility for Lyndon Johnson. As an expression of his diminished faith in the cause, Johnson refused to authorize the additional 200,000 troops that General Westmoreland had requested to further bolster the war effort. He also diminished the U.S. role in the fighting.[63] His frustration led to his announcement on March 30, 1968, that he would not seek a second term in office, an extraordinary step for a politician so driven by the desire for power.

Although Johnson's will was broken by the surprising successes of McCarthy and Kennedy — and by mounting criticism of the war's morality — the American people remained preponderantly in thrall to the myth of America's undefeatable military power. They would reject Vice President Hubert Humphrey in favor of Richard Nixon, a man who had made a significant career out of zealous conflict with communists.

Zealous Nationalism and the Loss of Honor

Richard Nixon came to office understanding that the American people were impatient for a resolution of the Vietnam War. However, his evasive campaign spoke of bringing "an honorable peace" that would avoid reneging on any pledges or betraying any trusts. James Chace writes that with the appointment of Henry Kissinger as secretary of state, "an entirely new construct of U.S. foreign policy emerged. . . . The Nixon administration, adopting Bismarck's belief that ideology was foolish and policy was 'the art of the possible,' mitigated the adversary relationships that had prevailed between America and Russia and between America and China. . . . In dealings with friend and foe alike, however, Nixon's carefully managed retreat was often accompanied by jingoist rhetoric."[64] In chapter 10 below, we lay out the evidence that Mr. Nixon was an artful zealot whose jingoism was for public consumption. He employed zealous rhetoric to oppose any changes in the status quo that appeared to favor communist interests, and therefore was more than willing to cooperate with anti-communist dictators in Greece, Chile, Portugal, and parts of Africa. Above all, Nixon was emphatic that whatever the United States did should not impair its reputation as the world's great superpower. In his 1970 speech announcing the invasion of Cambodia, he stated the imperative this way:

> If, when the chips are down, the world's most powerful nation, the United States of America, acts like a pitiful, helpless giant, the forces of totalitarianism and anarchy will threaten free nations and free institutions throughout the world. It is not our power but our will and character that is [sic] being tested tonight. The question all Americans must ask and answer tonight is this: Does the richest and strongest nation in the history of the world have the character to meet a direct challenge by a group which rejects every effort to win a just peace, ignores our warning, tramples on solemn agreements, violates the neutrality of an unarmed people, and uses our prisoners as hostages?[65]

In this vision, everything turned on whether the nation would expand the war one more time, overthrow one more government that had sought a position of neutrality in the Southeast Asian conflict. With America's reputation at stake and the evil of the adversary unrestrained by the years of harm we had inflicted, Nixon could only envision more conflict as the path to peace. His bombing and invasion of Cambodia destabilized the country and prepared the way for the murderous triumph of the Khmer Rouge.

In formulating a variant of the civil theology of America's place in the world, Nixon did not differ significantly from the self-centered nationalism of Kennedy and Johnson. He acknowledged that "the times were on the side of peace" because "the people of the world want peace." To all those who had been troubled by the millions of lives affected by the American conduct of the war in Asia, he had these soothing words: "I know America. The heart of America is good." Because of our inner righteousness, the response to "a crisis of the spirit" is "an answer of the spirit." And, "to find that answer, we need only look within ourselves." There we will find "the simple things, the basic things — such as goodness, decency, love, and kindness." It is hard to know whether these pallid affirmations meant anything to Nixon. They had no cutting ethical or theological edge.

Yet Nixon knew that American support for the war was rapidly declining and that it was important to withdraw U.S. troops quickly. When he was inaugurated for a second time in 1973, the American ground troops were effectively absent, and the United States was fighting on behalf of South Vietnam via bombing campaigns. By the time of his inauguration, after Nixon had decisively defeated George McGovern for president, a peace treaty with North Vietnam stood on the point of implementation. Yet McGovern's strongly affirmative positions on a negotiated peace looked too conciliatory and unworthy of a superpower.

In his second inaugural address on January 21, 1973, Nixon once again sounded the self-centered, nationalistic themes that had marked the turbulent Cold War years under Kennedy, Johnson, and his first administration:

> Above all else, the time has come for us to renew our faith in ourselves and in America. In recent years, that faith has been challenged. . . . Let us be proud. . . . Let us be proud that in each of the four wars . . . in this century, including the one we are now bringing to an end, we have fought not for selfish advantage, but to help others resist aggression. . . . Let us be proud that by our bold, new initiatives, and by our steadfastness for peace with honor, we have made a breakthrough toward creating in the world what the world has not known before — a structure of peace that can last, not merely for our time, but for generations to come. We are embarking here today on an era that presents challenges as great as those any nation, or any generation, has ever faced. We shall answer to God, to history, and to our conscience for the way in which we use these years.

The traditional millenarian hope of an endless era of peace presided over by the chosen nation that echoes in these final lines is rendered dependent on American faith in itself. These lines affirm the grandiosity of a selfless superpower that measures itself with the greatest nations in history. Although there is a routine fragment of realism in the reference to being answerable to God, the main thrust here is on overcoming the shame of defeat and re-establishing national honor no matter what it might cost in human life. In this destructive impasse, any hope of restoring honor was bound to be frustrated. When Mr. Nixon's lies and abuse of power came to light, they resulted in the first presidential resignation in American history. But the country never came to terms with the deaths of two to three million Asians that the Captain America complex had inspired. The failure of the wars in Southeast Asia was the appropriate season for national soul searching, but instead the country turned to even more unrealistic forms of mythic politics.

7 The Ascendancy of Mythic Politics

"Let's look ferocious."

Henry Kissinger, about how to respond to
the *Mayaguez* incident in 1975[1]

Reagan was annoyed when his defense initiative was dubbed "Star Wars."
Richard Perle, however, his brilliant young assistant secretary of defense,
told colleagues that he thought the name wasn't so bad. "Why not," he said.
"It's a good movie. Besides, the good guys won."

Frances FitzGerald, *Way Out There in the Blue: Reagan,*
Star Wars, and the End of the Cold War[2]

In the wake of zealous nationalism's frustration in Southeast Asia, the American civil religion moved into a new mythic phase. Sober reassessments of the national aims and policies were distracted by symbolic forms of politics and foreign policy infused by mythic fantasies. While determined "never again" to become involved in a military conflict that could not easily be won, the Captain America complex continued in new forms whose links to reality were nonetheless more tenuous. As FitzGerald's citation above suggests, American political consciousness was increasingly attuned to the archetypes from popular entertainments.

Artificial Euphoria and the *Mayaguez* Episode

When the humiliating end of the Vietnam War came in the spring of 1975, the character of "Vietnamizing" the conflict became clear. The fate of Southeast Asia would be determined by Vietnamese and Cambodian forces — this in exchange for 587 U.S. prisoners of war, who began coming home in 1973.[3] Because the U.S. government had persisted in believing that additional military appropriations for Cambodia and South Vietnam would stave off disaster, it was stunned by the speed and completeness of the final victory against its allies. Tens of thousands of Vietnamese agents, officials, secretaries, maids, and others who had been promised a timely exit to America were abandoned in the airlift's final desperate hours. On April 17, 1975, the Lon Nol government of Cambodia fell, as the U.S. military and diplomatic contingent fled from Phnom Penh to avoid capture by the successful Khmer Rouge forces. Twelve days later, in neighboring South Vietnam, the city of Saigon fell to the advancing North Vietnamese and Viet Cong forces. The remaining U.S. diplomatic and military advisers escaped in a massive emergency airlift, the last stages of which were carried out in a scramble from the courtyard and roof of the U.S. embassy in Saigon. Film reports carried these events throughout the world. In this context, President Gerald Ford left his notch on the weapon of zealous nationalism — in a largely symbolic, mythical manner.

During the last two weeks of May 1975, much of the nation's feature news was focused on the story of a commercial, American-owned ship named the *Mayaguez*. This ship, carrying cargo to a port in Thailand, was seized at a distance of eight miles from the Cambodian island of Poulo Wai. Within a few days, the U.S. government launched a large-scale military operation to rescue the captive crew — which had been released unharmed shortly before the operation began. The actual sequence of events was not publicly clarified for several weeks; but in the immediate wake of the events, the government and popular press alike celebrated the story as one of heroic rescue.

When the ship and its crew were seized on May 12, the incident was immediately interpreted by most government leaders as a deliberately humiliating provocation. The U.S. Senate and House spent hours discussing the urgent need to redeem U.S. honor through a show of power. Congressman C. W. Young (R-FL) asked, "How long is the United States going to be kicked around . . . ? This is but the latest in a series of insults to the most powerful nation in the world."[4] Congressman Robert Baumann (R-MD) charged that "our desire for detente and disengagement has led some people to wonder whether we are on our way to becoming patsies for the world."[5] Another congressman blustered: "It is hard for me to stomach the treatment our government is taking from pipsqueak governments. . . . It is about time we as Americans put back our shoulders and throw out our chests and act like we are proud of what we are."6 Senator Robert Dole (R-KS) echoed that line: "We cannot allow ourselves to be at the mercy of the whims and vagaries of small nations that may entertain illusions about our will or about their ability to confront us."7

The truculence of the Congress was matched in the executive branch. Secretary of State Henry Kissinger and President Gerald Ford agreed that the seizure of the freighter represented a challenge to American world power that merited a severe reprimand. According to Ford's autobiography, Kissinger and Vice President Nelson Rockefeller advocated B-52 strikes on the Cambodian mainland if tactical aircraft support from carriers could not be employed.8

Kissinger wanted to look "ferocious." Ford also saw the *Mayaguez* incident as an opportunity to repair the nation's ailing military image: "In the wake of our humiliating retreat from Cambodia and South Vietnam in the spring of 1975, our allies around the world began to question our resolve. . . . Rhetoric alone, I knew, would not persuade anyone that America would stand firm. They would have to see the proof of our resolve. The opportunity to show that proof came without warning."9 The perceived affront to American power thus demanded more than mere retrieval of the seamen. A symbolic message had to be sent to the world about America's "will," directed especially at the small nations who were tempted to assert their sovereignty. The United States, having initiated a search for diplomatic resolution through Peking and the United Nations, abandoned the effort after less than forty-eight hours and launched its military operation.

The Cambodians had taken the crew to the mainland to interrogate them about their mission and to determine whether their ship contained weapons for use against them. Although crew members, like the government in Washington, feared that they might be held for months and tortured into making embarrassing confessions before a world audience — as had happened with the *Pueblo* incident in Korea during 1968 — the crew was actually treated politely. Then, apparently having convinced themselves that the *Mayaguez* had no hostile military purpose, the captors decided to release the crew. They were no doubt fearful of American surveillance and reprisal. Crew members were asked to sign "manifests" that included statements such as: "Forty crew members very friendly to people of Cambodia. Good friends . . ." and "The people of Cambodia no like war and want peace and . . . have forty friend in this crew."10 Some crew members resisted a voice vote on these "manifests," but prudence eventually prevailed and they were allowed to leave for the return trip to the *Mayaguez* on a Thai fishing boat.

An hour after their release, the military operation ordered by Washington had begun. The White House and the state department had received a message from the Cambodians fourteen hours before the beginning of the rescue attack: the message did not explicitly mention the crew but simply indicated that the ship was being released. Not knowing about the crew's disposition and concerned that any hesitation would be taken as a sign of weakness, President Ford and his advisors ordered the assault despite the promising diplomatic indications. As the crew of the *Mayaguez* sailed back toward their ship, they were almost strafed by attacking Phantoms, Corsairs, and Intruders. They saved their lives from the attacking rescue force by waving white shirts on the deck.

Meanwhile, the ground assault group landed in helicopters on the island of Koh Tang, where faulty intelligence of the military command had placed the crew. Reports given to the 175-man Marine assault force estimated a small defending force on Koh Tang of twenty to thirty soldiers.[11] Instead, the Marines encountered withering ground fire from well-placed, heavily-armed Cambodian regulars, who immediately destroyed four of the attack helicopters and damaged six others during the engagement. Eighteen marines were lost at Koh Tang, and fifty others were wounded. The assault force fought for fourteen hours, finding it almost impossible to escape from the beach. An additional twenty-three Marines died in a helicopter crash en route from Thailand to reinforce the attack group. After heavy naval artillery and aerial bombardments by the U.S., the Marines on Koh Tang eventually withdrew in the damaged helicopters to their ships.

In related actions on the mainland of Cambodia, tactical bombers attacked an air base at Ream, a naval yard, and an oil refinery at Kampong Som. President Ford and Secretary of State Kissinger argued that the threat posed by military craft and the presence of troops in the region required the bombing. The U.S. government was initially thrilled by its decisive show of force and the return of the crew. President Ford called a press conference after midnight on May 15 and made the following statement:

> At my direction the United States forces tonight boarded the . . . *Mayaguez* and landed at the island of Koh Tang for the purpose of rescuing the crew and the ship, which had been illegally seized by Cambodian forces. They also conducted supporting strikes against nearby military installations. I have now received information that the vessel has been recovered intact and the entire crew has been rescued. The forces that have successfully accomplished this mission are still under hostile fire, but are preparing to disengage. I wish to express my deep appreciation and that of the entire nation to the units and the men for their valor and their sacrifice.[12]

Ford clearly meant to leave the impression that the attacking forces at Koh Tang had effected the rescue. He gave no indication that the Cambodians had released the crew through their own diplomatic initiative. Nor was there any hint of the scale of casualties, which would be disclosed only after several days of inquiries and reluctant disclosures.

In the afterglow of the victory claims, the government minimized casualties and errors because of the apparent psychological gains for the nation. Ford felt that the *Mayaguez* had worked "to ignite confidence in the White House . . . it had an electrifying reaction as far as the American people were concerned. It was a spark that set off a whole new sense of confidence for them too."[13] This exuberant mood of renewal was widely shared in Congress. Representative Jack Kemp (R-NY) asserted on the floor of the House that this kind of leadership was "vital to the restoration of American confidence. In a world in which some had reason to doubt the will of the United States to protect its own interests, the President has demonstrated that we will not tolerate the taking of our ships or the kidnapping of our citizens."[14] There were a few members of government who pointed out that the War Powers Act of 1973 limited the president's military initiative to "a national emergency created by attack upon the United States, its territories or possessions, or its armed forces."[15] The commercial freighter *Mayaguez* and its civilian crew hardly fit this statutory definition of a "national emergency." Critics also emphasized that the Cooper-Church Amendment of 1973 categorically prohibited additional bombing in Cambodia. However, these voices of reason and restraint were largely ignored in the mood of immediate euphoria. Later, military historians analyzed this euphoric moment, lamenting the losses and expressing amazement that the United States escaped a larger disaster. In *A Very Short War*, John F. Guilmartin, Jr., summarized his misgivings in this way:

> [O]n Koh Tang . . . U.S. forces approached the brink of tactical and operational disaster, with policy implications that can only be described as grim. . . . For Communist Cambodia, a fourth-rate power by the most charitable estimate, to inflict an unequivocal military defeat on the United States would have entailed immense damage to American credibility and prestige.[16]

Although temporarily gratifying, mythic politics entailed risks that would later result in such humiliating failures.

Carter's Failure at Domestic Superheroism

By the fall election of 1976, when President Ford faced the Democratic nominee Jimmy Carter, the mood of celebration about American power had worn off. Vietnam followed by Watergate had made Americans suspicious of Washington leaders and of government itself. James Earl Carter, who preferred the more down-home "Jimmy," sensed this mood and exploited it in his electioneering. Because he had served only a single term as Georgia's governor, his lack of experience thus became a virtue: he attacked his future associates as the "confused, bloated, bureaucratic mess in Washington. . . . I'm not a member of Congress, so I'm not responsible for letting that horrible mess develop."[17]

Carter played the role of the innocent outsider, the Everyman figure with wisdom enough to set the nation right after the frustration of the macho paradigm in Watergate and Vietnam. He invited people to trust that his vague pastiche of policies would produce a miraculous change in America. The launching of his campaign in the small town of Le Mars, Iowa, made an indelible impression. A small, informally clad figure with a quiet voice and a friendly, intelligent face, Carter played the quintessential role of the selfless Everyman heading to Washington to clean things up. He won the Democratic nomination in a campaign stressing that he was not part of the national establishment and was uncorrupted by the taint of special interests. The physical appearance of this outsider from Plains, Georgia, seemed precisely what the country yearned for after the disappointments of martial heroism. Carter's television advertisements "concentrated on the candidate as a farmer and working man, talking about his life and family and asking voters to trust him. . . . They also included the lines: 'I'll never tell a lie, I'll never avoid a controversial issue. . . .'"[18]

The care with which Carter conformed to the outsider, Everyman role was typified in a crucial press conference in Plains, Georgia, on June 9, 1976, when primary victories and political commitments officially placed him in control of the nomination. As Martin Schram observed, Carter wanted to tell the political reporters the good news, "but first he had to attend to one detail: the selection of his press conference attire. Carter chose denim — freshly pressed blue jeans and a matching jacket. A careful choice aimed at showing that he was no standard establishment candidate."[19] He extended the humble demeanor to his inauguration by refusing to ride in the presidential limousine through Washington's streets. He chose instead to walk holding hands with his wife, Rosalynn.

Carter's presidency — like his very successful post-presidency — was

While the U.S. Embassy staff in Iran was held hostage during 1979-1981, this image of a humiliated Jerry Miele became an icon for America's sense of innocence.

Credit: © 1981, Newsweek, Inc.

marked by his open and deep religious faith. He had been a Southern Baptist Sunday school teacher in Plains, and he unashamedly brought his faith to the White House. He took seriously the president's role as a peacemaker and thus brought the Panama Canal Treaty to fruition in 1977, which began the process of diffusing a long-standing conflict about the ownership and control of the canal. In the most inspired international achievement of his presidency, Carter managed to bring together President Anwar Sadat of Egypt and Israeli Prime Minister Menachem Begin in 1978 at Camp David, Maryland. After twelve days of negotiations, they established a framework for a treaty that ended the formal state of war between the two nations, established diplomatic relations, and provided for Israel's withdrawal from the Sinai Peninsula. The Camp David Accords also called for the gradual establishment of Palestinian autonomy in the Gaza Strip and West Bank. Had other American presidents been as creative and persistent as Carter was in his attempt to bring peace to the Middle East, the principal actors might have moved beyond the deadly stalemate in which they find themselves locked at the beginning of the twenty-first century. In his successful role as a humanitarian and peacemaker since his presidency, Carter has continued this role as trusted mediator among implacable adversaries. He has, in a remarkable manner, fused the mythic role of the nonviolent superhero and outsider with his sense of responsibility to work for peace.

However, the limitations of a mythic approach to foreign affairs was revealed by the hostage situation in Iran, which dominated the second half of Carter's presidency. Although Carter's basic instincts as a president lay in the direction of peacemaking, the so-called "hostage crisis" called forth the sense of collective innocence so central to zealous nationalism. But rather than striking in angry retribution, Carter quickly took on a public pastoral role as comforter of the afflicted innocent. Just five days after the incident was touched off in November 1979, Carter was already meeting with family members of the Iran embassy personnel — commiserating with them and assuring them of his efforts. Further, he made his relationship known to the nation with an announcement by his press secretary.[20] Throughout the period of captivity, Carter publicly confessed his emotional turmoil over the situation. On the campaign stump at Lyndhurst, New Jersey, in 1980, he said, "No day has gone by, no hour has gone by when I was awake that I wasn't thinking about and often praying for those hostages."[21] In his presidential memoirs, *Keeping Faith*, Carter described even more painfully the visceral impact on his conduct: "Although I was acting in official capacity as President, I also had deep feelings that were almost overwhelming. The hostages sometimes seemed like part of my own family. . . . I knew and had grown to love some of the members of their families, and had visited them in Washington and even in their hometowns around the country."[22]

The extent of diversion from other issues in government was so acute for Carter that he convened his National Security Council one hundred times during the first 180 days of the captivity to discuss the Iran hostages.[23] Yet he seemed reluctant in the policy negotiations to deal very directly with the underlying grievances of the Iranians. He was so irritated by their violation of international standards of conduct that he couldn't take seriously their accusations about prior breaches of international citizenship by the United States. Despite his information that Iranians continued to resent the intrusive U.S. role in the overthrow of Mossadegh in 1953, the role of the CIA in training the repressive SAVAK, the support of the dictatoral shah, and the failure to acknowledge the grievances of the Muslim community led by the Ayatollah Khomeini, Carter repeatedly insisted that *these* Americans were "innocent" because they were only embassy personnel: "All of those people are innocent. All diplomats are innocent," he said in frustration to the secret intermediary Christian Bourguet.[24] American innocence became a leading theme in most of his public comments concerning the Iran hostage crisis. When he took to the campaign trail for his re-election in 1980, "the capturing of the innocent hostages" was his refrain when discussing Iran.[25]

In April 1980, in consultation with his National Security Council, President Carter authorized "Operation Blue Light," a commando-style rescue mission that was frustrated by desert sand storms and the accidental crash of a helicopter at the landing site. Eight servicemen died. Photos of the burned wreckage were shown by Iranian authorities eager to present it as a symbol of American impotence.[26] The failure of this rescue mission, however unlikely its prospects for returning with live hostages, probably sealed Carter's fate with the electorate. With neither diplomacy nor military power working to bring the captives home before election day, the country went through an election in which the archetypes from the American monomyth ascended to a crucial role.

Reagan and the Ephemeral Triumph of Macho Superheroism

The election campaign of 1980 pitted a macho hero who was also untried in national politics, but attuned to the ideology of the *Star Wars* films, against a failed hero with a touch of the innocent Heidi-redeemer in his public persona. Despite differences in specific policy proposals, Ronald Reagan and Jimmy Carter tried to create a similar impression as outsider figures, matching the monomythic scheme of heroes who lack roots in the community they are called to save. Both claimed to be far removed from the mess in Washington: Carter continued in his pose as a farmer from Georgia, and Reagan as an actor-rancher from California. Both claimed to be above traditional party politics, selflessly dedicated to the public good. Each offered incredible resolutions to complex political and economic problems — public miracles whose believability rested entirely on the image and good intentions of the candidate himself. Reagan promised to raise defense spending by a large amount, increasing the size of the armed forces while decreasing the total number of federal employees. He promised to reduce domestic spending while resolving social problems such as crime and unemployment, and to stimulate the economy with a massive tax cut. George H. W. Bush, a candidate during the Republican primaries, harshly identified this scheme as "voo-doo economics." But neither the common sense details nor economic self-interest in the traditional sense seemed to carry a great deal of weight with the American electorate. They voted overwhelmingly for the image of the macho superhero. As Martin Schram observed, Reagan succeeded in getting elected "because he was able to employ an appeal more fundamental than government policies. He skillfully mastered the ability to step through the television tubes and join Americans in their living rooms. . . ."[27]

James Conaway wrote a penetrating analysis of the mythical dimension of this political choice a month before the 1980 election. Conaway talked with Reagan's campaign coordinator, Roger Stone, who observed that "Ronald Reagan is a very nonpolitical person." As a description of a man who had campaigned for several decades with his eye on the presidency, this remark is utterly incomprehensible — except in the light of monomythic politics. Reagan persistently managed to play the role of the unattached superhero, what Conaway calls "a professional political neophyte . . . his manner suggests that he would rather be mending fences or riding one of his horses high above the Pacific Ocean." In a striking allusion to what we have identified as the axial decade for the creation of the American superhero in the 1930s, Conaway predicted that Ronald Reagan would become "the public receptacle of fifty years of mythmaking. . . . I think many people will vote for him because, when that curtain slides shut behind them, they can pull a lever for James Stewart, Robert Redford, and John Travolta."[28]

The same appeal held good in the election of 1984, which witnessed the rise of the so-called "gender gap." Although most American males continued to disagree with Reagan's policies, a majority of them, strikingly higher than the proportion of females, continued their support of him. A Republican media consultant suggested that, in the 1984 election, "it's the perfect gentleman versus the cowboy. . . . Reagan is a healthy dose of macho, and Mondale is part of the Brie-and-chablis crowd." The election had become a test of personal masculinity, in which Mondale inherited Carter's role as an innocent Heidi. A Democratic consultant conceded that Reagan "took a bullet in the chest and survived, and all of America saw it." A young engineer attending a Democratic rally in Detroit described Reagan's unique appeal: "It's a John Wayne type of thing — you know, the Cavalry." The aide to an important Democratic leader concluded: "Men like his swagger. They'd like to have swagger themselves."[29]

In an era when politics took on this monomythic cast, most contemporary Americans preferred the stride of Luke Skywalker or John Wayne no matter what their policies might be. The choice between mythic images thus upstages the wisdom of common people who lack miraculous abilities, the traditional hope of democratic politics. Political scientist James David Barber pointed with concern to this pattern: "America is drifting into a mode of political thinking that is not only illusory but consciously, even proudly so. Both Republicans and Democrats alike are afflicted with this malady. . . . As David A. Stockman . . . summed up the White House system, 'Every time one fantasy doesn't work they try another one.'"[30] What Barber found most alarming and puzzling about this abandonment of pragmatism is the public acquiescence, even when preposterous policies fail to produce the promised miracles.

A crucial policy component in Reagan's heroic approach was his creation of super military power to hold perceived enemies at bay. From the beginning of his political career, he linked strident anti-communism with a commitment to build American military strength to an unassailable level as the essential step toward world peace. The consistent rationale, as Garry Wills has suggested, was "that terrorists will stay away from jet planes if America acts like a cowboy."[31] Reagan repeatedly argued that the incomplete application of military power was the reason for the loss of the Vietnam War. In his view, we should have bombed Indochina back to the stone age.

When the Iran hostage crisis came during an election year, however, the American public began to resonate fully with Reagan's appeal. Charles William Maynes, the editor of *Foreign Policy* magazine, described the national mood in 1980: "As America's uneasiness over changes on the international scene rises, there are more and more blatant demands that we should impose our views through the threat of or use of military power."[32] But, in fact, the threats of international terrorism and of worldwide economic disruption were not resolvable by inflating American strategic forces and training rapid deployment groups. Having propelled ourselves into our greatest peacetime expansion of military power because of the Reagan presidency, we discovered at the end of its second term that the threats remained, as became evident in the situation producing the Persian Gulf War — a situation never really resolved by military power to this day.

The Mirage of Invulnerable Defense

Nowhere was the monomythic appeal of super military power more apparent than in the Strategic Defense Initiative, promoted by President Reagan as a means to abolish the threat of nuclear weapons by providing an invulnerable shield against missiles. True to the selfless and strictly defensive image of superheroism, he promised that this system would be shared with the Soviets once it was developed, thus producing the peace everyone dreamed about. This proposal has been aptly named "the Star Wars system," reflecting, in the words of Bruce Bawer, "a real and significant parallel between Reagan's approach to the world and that of the forthright fantasymongers."[33] Despite the fact that a vast majority of specialists with knowledge of defense affairs declared it impractical, destabilizing, and ruinously expensive, its development went forward. An official in a defense firm described the appeal of this selfless scheme: "The idea took on a life of its own, with almost spiritual overtones. It became an act of faith to believe in Star Wars. . . ." The fact noted by defense analyst Fred Reed that "Star Wars, if it works, will be an *offensive weapon* of absolute power" has been little noticed by the American public, though "the Russians have noticed, as have the Star Warriors."[34]

After the failure of the Iceland summit, in which Reagan's "Star Wars" scheme made him unwilling to accept the most dramatic offer in Cold War history to reduce nuclear weapons, foreign affairs specialists began to ask why his commitment was so firm despite all evidence to the contrary. After sketching the concern about the danger of the scheme, James Cracraft writes: "The mystery, I suggest, is why President Reagan and his closest advisers cannot grasp the nature and depth of this concern, which most of the watching world shared; why they can't grasp it, and then deal with it."[35] The answer to this puzzle is what Anthony Lewis identified as "Reagan's Dream": the president is a "believer in dreams. He attaches himself to some visions so strongly that no facts can shake him off."[36] As David Broder observed, "On the issue of SDI's feasibility, Reagan is as optimistic as he is about the economy and the deficit. The deficit will disappear, the economy will grow forever and, by the same alchemy of spirit, laser beams and particles and technologies yet undreamed of will stop nuclear ballistic missiles in their flight. . . . I believe; therefore it is." The dream was utopian, with a distinctively monomythic slant.[37]

The passage of time since Reagan first dreamed of the protective shield has brought additional evidence of its origins in fantasy. Frances FitzGerald's major study of Reagan's vision has drawn together several strands of evidence. She calls our attention to the findings of film scholar Michael Rogin, who reviewed Reagan's movies and discovered that, in *Murder in the Air* (1940), he played an agent maintaining the secrecy and security of "the Inertial Projector," which "stops and destroys anything that moves." It had just the qualities sought for in Captain America's religion of defense. An admiral in the film reports that the inertial projector "not only makes the United States invincible in war, but in doing so, promises to become the greatest force world peace ever discovered." Rogin also noticed the language of *Torn Curtain* (1966), an Alfred Hitchcock movie in which an American (played by Paul Newman) says, "We will produce a defensive weapon that will make all nuclear weapons obsolete, and thereby abolish the terror of nuclear warfare."[38] FitzGerald also recounts the overly optimistic misunderstandings of the Patriot missile's performance in the Persian Gulf War, as well as the technological chicaneries offered by weapons scientists as they have contrived to demonstrate the feasibility of defensive missile-seeking technology.[39]

Many observers have been struck by the irony of the circumstance that the box-cutter-based attacks of September 11 have emboldened President George W. Bush to abrogate the 1972 Anti-Ballistic Missile Treaty with Moscow so that America can go its own way to develop the next generation of nuclear weapons. This renunciation is probably a tactical move toward the renunciation of the 1967 Outer Space Treaty, which was designed to keep the skies free from orbiting weapons platforms. Secretary of Defense Donald Rumsfeld had already announced his intention to dismantle that treaty.[40] Reagan's legacy clearly continues to have vitality in leading America down an exceptional path that rejects the guidance and cooperation of others.

Illusions of National Innocence

Reflecting on this tendency during the Reagan years, Arthur Schlesinger, Jr., described "a mighty comeback of the messianic approach to foreign policy" in the decade of the 1980s: "The convictions that presently guide American foreign policy are twofold — that the United States is infinitely virtuous and that the Soviet Union is infinitely wicked."[41] Although Reagan's campaign attacked Carter's pacific tendencies as a sign of national weakness, he was more than comfortable with Carter's faith in the mythic blamelessness of Americans. He also accepted Carter's pastoral role with families of captives. Reviewing the White House records, one discovers a significant stream of personal meetings and phone calls for families and released hostages. For example, he met with the Marilyn Klinghofer family (from the *Achille Lauro* cruise ship hijacking), with Nicholas Daniloff (held in Moscow in 1985 against the release of Gennady Zhakarov from U.S. detention) and his family, and made a personal call on Rev. Benjamin Weir after his release in Lebanon.

A Reagan innovation of the captive presidency — which we might also have seen if Carter had been re-elected — was the White House ceremony for returning captives. These rituals openly affirm the innocence of American power and the Puritan sense of ourselves as the chosen people, living in the "city set upon a hill." As Reagan signed a "Day of Thanksgiving" proclamation for their freedom, he said, "God watched over his servants during this difficult time of testing."[42] On the following day, at a massive White House celebration to which 6,000 dignitaries were invited, he quoted the 126th Psalm: "Now our mouth is filled with laughter and our tongue with shouts of joy. The Lord has done great things for us; we are glad."[43]

To the passengers of TWA Flight 847, who were received at the White House in 1985, Reagan emphatically restated the theme of moral purity: "None of you were held prisoner because of any personal wrong you had done to anyone; you were held simply because you are Americans. In the minds of your captors, you represented us."[44]

One of the most explicit expressions of the Captain America complex in recent history was the invasion and brief occupation of Grenada. President Reagan's address on Lebanon and Grenada on October 27, 1983, evoked an immediate increase in support for the invasion — from 64 percent to 86 percent of those polled by ABC News. A *USA Today* survey showed the increase jumping from 48 percent to 68 percent, which was closer to the results of other polls.[45] By whatever measure, the response was remarkable. An examination of the rationale in Mr. Reagan's address reveals the abiding power of the conspiratorial strand within this complex to shape perceptions of the world. The address linked three widely separated and distinct events in the Far East, the Middle East, and the Caribbean as part of a terrorist conspiracy centered in Moscow. The president began as follows:

> My fellow Americans, some two months ago we were shocked by the brutal massacre of 269 men, women and children, in the shooting down of a Korean airliner. Now, in these past several days, violence has erupted again, in Lebanon and Grenada. . . . The events in Lebanon and Grenada, though oceans apart, are closely related. Not only has Moscow assisted and encouraged the violence in both countries, but it provides direct support through

a network of surrogates and terrorists. It is no coincidence that when the thugs tried to wrest control of Grenada, there were thirty Soviet advisors and hundreds of Cuban military and paramilitary forces on the island.[46]

In characterizing the airliner incident earlier, he had laid the groundwork for implicating Soviet power in the worst kind of conspiracy. Refusing to concede the possibility of mistakes for which the American military is notorious, he sought to create the ugliest possible picture of Soviet perversity in the incident.

> Despite the savagery of their crime, the universal reaction against it, and the evidence of their complicity, the Soviets refuse to tell the truth. . . . And make no mistake about it, this attack was not just against ourselves or the Republic of Korea. This was the Soviet Union against the world and moral precepts which guide human relations among people everywhere. It was an act of barbarism, born of a society which wantonly disregards individual rights and the value of human life and constantly seeks to expand and dominate other nations.

Reagan also demanded "an apology and an offer to join the rest of the world in working out a system to protect against this ever happening again."

A more objective appraisal of these events would indicate that their causes and motivations are quite distinct. The downing of the Korean airliner was a tragic instance of bureaucratic and military bumbling, an expression of a long-standing territorial paranoia in which the Soviet pilots literally had no idea of the actual identity of their target. The suicide bombing of the Marine headquarters in Beirut was a typical act of Islamic terrorism whose antecedents can be traced to centuries of religious warfare grounded in principles that are as hostile to Soviet ideology as to Western imperialism. And the execution of Prime Minister Bishop of Grenada, which precipitated the American invasion, was the result of a power struggle between factions in the Grenadian revolutionary movement, the Cuban authorities reacting with conspicuous coolness to the violence that threatened the credibility of their position.

The link between these distantly related events is an expression of American national ideology that tends to simplify world problems as if they all stemmed from a single conspiracy, at that time centered in Moscow; it sees innocent victims threatened by a demonic force whose cunning stratagems encircle the world. America sees itself as the selfless redeemer nation whose task is to protect the defenseless by means of its military interventions. As Reagan said of the marines killed in the headquarters building in Lebanon, "They've given willingly of themselves so that a nearly defenseless people in a region of great strategic importance to the free world will have a chance someday to live lives free of murder and mayhem and terrorism."[47]

Under the spell of these mythic conceptions, the American public perceived the rescue of the medical students on Grenada and the successful capture of the island as a resolution of the rage and frustration it felt over the two earlier disasters. The happy ending had been achieved by violent action against the wicked just in the nick of time. One of the most striking expressions of this coherent national ideology was the videotape of the rescued students cheering the American rangers and waving their index fingers with the sign of number one. America's status as the "greatest nation on earth" was confirmed by the successful completion of the rescue operation.

In the ceremony President Reagan held for the returned American medical students from Grenada, he made the theme of the president as rescuer explicit for the entire world as he read from the letters of appreciation written to him. He spoke of the "heroic rescue mission of our young Americans [the soldiers]" and implied that without his decisiveness in ordering the invasion, the medical students would have become hostages.[48] The president thought that he had, in effect, prevented another Iran from happening. It was a compelling instance of the new form of mythic politics.

The invasions of Grenada and Panama, as well as the mining of harbors in Nicaragua, were flatly in violation of American commitments under international law.[49] Despite a formal commitment by the United States to the International Court in 1946, the Reagan administration withdrew from compulsory jurisdiction in 1985 while the harbor mining incident was under review. In the following year, the court declared the United States to have violated international law in a variety of ways in connection with Nicaragua. In the words of Senator Daniel Patrick Moynihan, this was the "first time in the history of the Court that the United States was found in violation of international law in a matter involving the use of force against another nation."[50] Moynihan expressed justified indignation at America's abandonment of long-standing commitments: "In two centuries of national existence no more pusillanimous act was ever contemplated, much less carried forward, by American officials responsible for our relations with international tribunals."[51] The zealous components in our American ideals had triumphed over the tradition of "prophetic realism," over our commitment to coexistence under law.

Reagan's denunciation of the Soviet Union in the Korean airline incident would come back to haunt him late in his administration. On July 3, 1988, the U.S. warship *Vincennes* was on patrol in the Persian Gulf to protect the transit of oil tankers. Acting on its radar data in the belief that an Iranian F-14 fighter jet was approaching, the *Vincennes* shot down an Iranian A-300 airbus with a missile. All 290 passengers died. Reagan apologized for "the terrible human tragedy" but called the downing "a proper defensive action." He also insisted that there was no legitimate comparison between the Korean airliner incident and the destruction of the Iranian Airbus: "Remember [that with] the KAL, a group of Soviet fighter planes went up, identified the plane for what it was and proceeded to shoot it down. There's no comparison."[52] The U.S. press joined into this spirit by focusing on the "Captain's Anguish" *(Newsday)* and the "Captain's Agony" *(New York Post)*. R. W. Apple of the *New York Times* was a lonely voice in America's press when he published an article on mistakes entitled "Military Errors: The Snafu as History."[53]

The Gulf War and the Lost Chance for Prophetic Realism

As George Herbert Walker Bush took the oath of office as president in 1989, he expressed a sense of developing triumph over the evil empire that Reagan had so consistently denounced: "The totalitarian era is passing, its old ideas blown away like leaves from an ancient, lifeless tree. A new breeze is flowing, and a nation freshened by freedom stands ready to push on." So confident was the elder Bush about America's role that he showed disdain for the notion of historical contingency: "There are times when the future seems as thick as fog; you sit and wait, hoping the mists will lift and reveal the right path. But this is a time when the future seems a door you can walk right through into a room called tomorrow." The happy tomorrow that Bush saw was one in which history had seemed to end in the triumph of America, allowing it to turn inward to find its ideals.

> For the first time in this century, for the first time perhaps in all history, man does not have to invent a system by which to live. We don't have to talk late into the night about which form of government is better. We don't have to wrest justice from the kings. We only have to summon it from within ourselves. We must act on what we know.[54]

This sunny, cheerful, Reaganesque form of the Captain America complex was difficult for President Bush to sustain when he had to deal with the greatest challenge of his presidency, a moment in world affairs that had a significant impact on America's civil religion. It can be best understood in light of the historical background of Iraq's invasion of Kuwait. Iraq claimed the right to annex Kuwait on the grounds that it was originally part of the territory associated with Baghdad and Basra during the period of Turkish occupation and before. This was a fabrication. The area of Kuwait was never a part of the Ottoman Empire, and the Arab clan controlling it had been there since around 1750. Kuwait's independence was confirmed by Turkey and Great Britain in 1913, and Kuwait sided with the Allies in World War I, when the people of Iraq's current territory were still under Turkish rule and thus on the side of the Central Powers. There was also no legitimate basis for a border dispute, as the Iraqis claimed: Kuwait's borders had been established years before Iraq's, which were themselves a highly artificial construct of postcolonial decision-making in the 1920s (Iraq achieved its independence in 1932). The boundary dispute that arose after Kuwait gained its freedom from Great Britain was resolved in 1963 by a formal acceptance of the current borders by the Iraqi parliament. As for the Iraqi claims about alleged slant drilling from the Kuwaiti side of the Rumaila oil fields, this was repeatedly proposed by Kuwait for adjudication at the International Court, which was refused by Iraq. In their summation of this issue, Lawrence Freedman and Efraim Karsh say:

> During the Iraqi campaign preceding the invasion of Kuwait, there was hardly any reference to Iraq's claim to Kuwait. . . . Even in the immediate wake of the invasion, the Iraqi media failed to mention Iraq's "historic rights" over Kuwait, instead presenting the invasion as a temporary emergency taken at the request of the "liberal regime" established in Kuwait instead of the "reactionary" al-Sabah dynasty.[55]

The invasion of Kuwait was the case of a larger neighbor's aggression against a smaller country for old-fashioned motives such as financial gain and the acquisition of additional power. From the perspective of international law, it is a far clearer case than the invasion of South Korea by North Korea in 1950. In Iraq's case, the worsening economic situation after the conclusion of the war with Iran jeopardized its formidable arms build-up for the domination of the Mideast and the settlement through arms of the Palestinian issue. The desire to resolve domestic problems by expansionist schemes is reminiscent of events in the 1930s and '40s. The invasion of Kuwait had genocidal implications in that Iraq undertook efforts after the invasion to erase Kuwaiti national identity, to incorporate its territory into Iraq, and to resettle the area with pro-Iraqi families.[56] The analogies to Nazi designs on Czechoslovakia, Poland, the Ukraine, and Russia — as well as Japanese policies in Manchuria and Korea in the 1930s — are anything but trivial.

As the crisis developed and President Bush consulted with Allied leaders such as Margaret Thatcher of Great Britain, his response to the unexpected invasion was to abandon the unilateral strategy of a mythic superpower that had been popularized by Reagan. He turned to the Security Council of the United Nations, whose Resolution #674, passed on October 29, 1990, held Iraq and its leadership liable for war crimes and violations of the U.N. Charter, U.N. Resolutions, and the Geneva Accord. This resolution offered an opportunity to fulfill the vision of prophetic realism, if the United States had chosen the measures within the U.N. Charter itself. However, rather than granting authority for military action to the Security Council's Military Staff Committee as envisioned in Articles 45-47 of the U.N. Charter, and placing all allied troops under U.N. command, the Bush administration pushed through Security Council Resolution #678 on November 29: it authorized individual states to use military forces "cooperating with the Government of Kuwait" while keeping the Security Council informed about the outcome.

The consequence of this decision, motivated by the fear of losing freedom of action through the Military Staff Committee's leadership, was that when the ultimatum ran its course on January 15, 1991, the Allied forces, organized and led by the Americans, quickly expelled the Iraqis. But they had to cease military operations at Kuwait's border. If they had followed the U.N. Charter, there would have been legal authority for forces under the Military Staff Committee to invade Baghdad and apprehend Saddam Hussein for trial before an international tribunal. Thousands of lives lost in subsequent revolts against Hussein and in the suffering of the civilian population under the largely ineffective oil embargo and the decade of aerial bombardments might have been spared.

The rationale President Bush used for his national constituency employed remnants of the Captain America complex rather than articulating the realistic vision of responding to aggression through the United Nations. His State of the Union speech expressed the stock claims of American virtue: "Our cause is just. Our cause is moral. Our cause is right." Bush's speech to the National Religious Broadcasters on January 28, 1991, provided a significant departure from this mythic ideology. It was the first time, as far as we know, that an American president explicitly articulated a just-war theory during a conflict, albeit in a somewhat garbled manner. It was particularly significant that Bush linked the just-war theory to the United Nations — invoking the United Nations and its resolutions as the "just authority."[57] A weakness of the just-war theory was its lack of categories to distinguish between a police action supported by the United Nations (an act of collective self-defense on the basis of article 51) and traditional wars waged by nation-states in pursuing their own goals.

Another problematic side of President Bush's speech was his confusion between holy-war and just-war theory. To claim God's unambiguous favor for one side of a conflict and to abandon the premise that war is inevitably sinful departs from Christian theories of realism and just war. Bush's appeal to the memory of the Civil War Lincoln shows the movement from a skepticism that characterizes prophetic realism to the certainties of zealous nationalism. He quoted Lincoln as saying, "My concern is not whether God is on our side, but whether we are on God's side." But Bush's spin on Lincoln's humility about identifying his own cause with God's was to assert the following: "My fellow Americans, I firmly believe in my heart of hearts that time will soon be on the side of peace because the world is overwhelmingly on the side of God."[58] The younger George Bush would inherit and repeat this nationalist turn in identifying God as the American partner in waging war on terrorism.

Clinton's Frivolous Use of Mythic Politics

When Bill Clinton took office in 1993, he showed few signs of affecting either the zealous or the prophetic course of America's civil religion. Rather than articulating a vision for the world, Clinton's campaign had focused on the need to rebuild domestic economic prosperity; and he included some national policy goals, such as universal health care. Reaching out to conservative voters, he initially framed his programs in biblical language, bestowing the title "A New Covenant with the American People" on the Democratic national platform.[59] The heart of this covenantal call to renewal was, in the words of his speech accepting the nomination, to be "a solemn agreement between the people and their government, based not simply on what each of us can take, but what all of us must give to our nation." In that same speech he used biblical language to chastise George H. W. Bush for his lack of vision: "But remember what the scripture says: 'Where there is no vision, the people perish.'"[60] Presenting himself as the problem solver with the right vision seemed to be a modest form of Jimmy Carter's approach to politics.

The battering Clinton's initiatives took from angry opposition forces during his first term revealed the inner Clinton. Rather than being a large spirit tightly wrapped around a bundle of core principles, Clinton seemed to be a rather small person who wanted to endure adversities that threatened his reputation or privilege. The innocuous platitudes scattered through both of his inaugural addresses prefigured his tenacious instincts for survival in the face of personal threat. In his first inaugural he said:

When our founders boldly declared America's independence to the world and our purposes to the Almighty, they knew that America, to endure, would have to change. Not change for change's sake, but change to preserve America's ideals — life, liberty, the pursuit of happiness.

Looking outward to the world, Clinton declared:

Today, a generation raised in the shadows of the Cold War assumes new responsibilities in a world warmed by the sunshine of freedom but threatened still by ancient hatreds and new plagues. . . . When our vital interests are challenged, or the will and conscience of the international community is defied, we will act — with peaceful diplomacy whenever possible, with force when necessary.[61]

The leaning toward rhetorical antitheses suggested a willingness to compromise, the mark of prophetic realism; but the great question that hovered over the inaugural platitudes was whether any core of principles could survive overly generous accommodations. In an essay entitled "The Protean President," Thomas B. Edsall focused on Clinton's "political malleability" and argued that, "if Clinton has a central strength . . . it is the capacity to adapt politically to adversity and the threat of defeat."[62] As Clinton accumulated more enemies who hobbled his gait in pursuing gay rights, health care, abortion rights, gun control, and welfare reform, his platitudes took on an even blander cast. By the time of his second inaugural address, he was uttering statements such as, "We must keep our democracy forever young," and "America demands and deserves big things from us — nothing big ever came from being small." He also called on Americans to "build our bridge — a bridge wide enough and strong enough for every American to cross over to a blessed land of new promise."[63] But he called for no particular initiatives that would help us "keep our democracy young" or "build our bridge."

Despite differences in political orientation, Bill Clinton seems most similar to the paradigmatic artful zealot, Richard Nixon. Whereas President Nixon posed as a macho redeemer figure, President Clinton brought the flavor — lacking in comparable religious substance — of President Jimmy Carter's Southern evangelism. In this pose, he resembled a Heidi redeemer who "felt" everyone's "pain" and was remarkably adroit in effecting psychological conversions — to his own point of view. The artful simulation of repentance in the prayer breakfast on September 11, 1998, which traded on his knowledge of the Southern "conversion" experience, was actually consistent with his artful simulation of liberalism; yet when he was about to be exposed by women, he always smeared them, despite his stated principles. His commitment to constitutional process was so thin that he allowed the country to teeter for months on the edge of a constitutional crisis, finally compelling his party colleagues to vote against impeachment under threat of withdrawing their funding in the next election. Clinton's bottom line was his continuation in power.

Lies mark the artful zealot. Andrew Sullivan concluded that Clinton had "taken the principle of cynical duplicity to a new and chilling level."[64] Senator Bob Kerrey, a Clinton ally who observed his behavior at close range, noted wryly that "Clinton's an unusually good liar. Unusually good."[65] Richard Roeper observed that Clinton's speeches concerning Monica Lewinsky confirmed that "he is a liar. A cheat. A conniver. A manipulator. And we love him."[66] Artful lies actually marked his entire political career, as biographer David Maraniss observed on the basis of precise details.[67] Political scientist Stanley Renshon discussed the significance of Clinton's violation of the bond of trust with voters, suggesting that "the fabric of democracy is in danger as the psychological adhesive that holds it together loosens."[68] Bill Clinton clearly felt he was super, that he was above the law, and that anything he wanted to do could be done. Sullivan writes that Clinton believed

> . . . he could get away with almost anything. Which is why he shamelessly corralled shifty businessmen through the White House in return for illegal campaign dollars, chatted on the phone with Dick Morris while Morris played footsie with a prostitute, and cavalierly carried on an affair in his very office with an employee half his age. These are the actions of a man who has come to believe he is beyond the moral measure of anyone else and that nobody has the capacity to catch him. So now that he is caught, it is little surprise that his response is not contrition but outrage.[69]

The impact of a liberal president who was really a Nixon in sheep's clothing was to deepen the already troubling cynicism about the political system and the fourth estate on one hand and to discredit liberal causes on the other. In chapter 10 we discuss the Nixon case, which by some measures was the more serious example of artful zeal, in part because of the huge loss of life in Southeast Asia that it entailed. Clinton's artfulness appears frivolous in comparison: its policy goals were ultimately subordinated to merely preserving his own reputation. But it had enormous implications for his ability to respond to national threats posed by Osama bin Laden late in his second term.

Clinton's presidency of self-preservation became, by default, reactive to world events. To his credit, he did play a constructive role in helping to defuse some of the burning conflicts that came on his watch in government. He played a role in brokering a peace agreement in Northern Ireland. In 1993 he tried to defuse a conflict in Somalia and bring humanitarian relief. However, when eighteen soldiers died in a firefight, he quickly withdrew U.S. forces. He made a vigorous, last-minute effort in 2000 to bring Arafat and Barak to agreement in sessions at Camp David. He pushed for the Dayton Peace Accords, which brought some measure of peace to Bosnia. In 1998 he struck back at Osama bin Laden's training camps in Afghanistan with cruise missiles after the bombings of U.S. embassies in Kenya and Tanzania — a gesture that looks prescient in hindsight. But the ongoing Monica Lewinsky scandal made it difficult to separate strategic wisdom from the manipulative diversion of public attention so cynically laid out in the 1997 movie *Wag the Dog*. Clinton's call to arms against terrorism was so little heeded that it could not even survive as a campaign issue in the presidential election of 2000.

One of Clinton's most troubling legacies in terms of civil religion came with the war in Kosovo and the air campaign against Serbia. Under the leadership of indicted war criminal Slobodan Milosevic, Serbia was engaging in the ethnic-cleansing practices that had marked its behavior in Bosnia — the killing of entire villages and the forced movement of populations.[70] As a relatively small territory, Kosovo appeared to be a situation in which U.N. peacekeepers could separate the combatants and provide time for negotiated settlements. But instead of seeking an internationalist route through the United Nations — where he anticipated obstruction from Russia and China — Clinton chose to use the NATO alliance as an umbrella for American bombing, which raised constitutional issues at home and engendered enormous ill will abroad. Though the United States itself was not under attack by Serbia, President Clinton and Secretary of State Madeleine Albright wanted to intervene on humanitarian grounds.

While the air campaign did weaken Milosevic's hold in Kosovo, the United States paid a substantial price in world opinion for the errors that are typical of an aerial bombardment, particularly those that target urban areas for "precision bombing." Human Rights Watch, an international organization, issued a report in which it identified four areas of NATO indifference to civilians: "The use of cluster bombs in populated areas; attacks in populated areas during the day, when civilians were most likely to be present; attacks on mobile targets without ensuring that they were . . . military; and striking targets with little or no military value despite a substantial risk of civilian death." For example, NATO had bombed radio and television stations.[71] One of the great ironies was that NATO offered the prevention of ethnic cleansing as a rationale for the bombings; yet the practice continued as the bombs fell.

NATO had anticipated that an air campaign would take a mere two days, but it found that it needed seventy-eight days to achieve its objectives.

The most egregious failure of the bombing campaign came when U.S. planes destroyed the Chinese embassy in Belgrade. According to an account in the *New York Times*, the CIA had employed its Counter-Proliferation Division for the job of picking targets, an unaccustomed role for which it had no background knowledge. This division provided a document for President Clinton's personal approval that identified the building as a warehouse structure — the "Yugoslav Army procurement headquarters."[72] The embassy was not entirely destroyed, because some of the bombs that penetrated the building did not explode. Nonetheless, three Chinese citizens died in the bombing, resulting in numerous protests against American embassies. The American contention that it was a mistake could not be readily accepted, since maps of Belgrade indicate the embassy's location. The incident aroused wide suspicions that President Clinton's administration, in alliance with NATO, wanted to punish one of the major powers that disagreed with its policies in the Balkans.

Clinton's government, which had tried to frame itself initially within the appealing language of biblical covenant, had hardly fulfilled the promise of that myth. Vander Slik and Schwark conclude that the concept of a "new covenant" had been "a modestly successful rhetorical device in the vocabulary of Bill Clinton."[73] However, they suggest that the emptiness of the covenantal pledge was conveyed in his 1992 speech accepting the Democratic nomination. There he invoked the language of the Pledge of Allegiance as his theological context for the nation's work: "There is no them; there is only us. One nation, under God, with liberty and justice for all. That is our Pledge of Allegiance, and that's what the New Covenant is about." Rather than achieving a genuine renewal of prophetic realism that this biblical concept might have evoked, Clinton covered himself with conventional patriotism whose purpose was, finally, nothing more than to save his own skin from opponents who found him unworthy of the office. In his instance, the path of mythic politics led into a pitiful frivolity that discredited the idealistic side of American civil religion.

8 The Rapturous Rebirth
of Millennial Zealotry

*You know, I turn back to your ancient prophets in the Old Testament and
the signs foretelling Armageddon and I find myself wondering if we're the
generation that is going to see that come about. I don't know if you've noted
any of those prophecies lately, but, believe me, they certainly describe the
times we're going through.*

President Ronald Reagan's comments to the executive director of the
American-Israeli Public Affairs Committee in October, 1983[1]

One of the most distressing aspects of the contemporary world is the proliferation of mutually antagonistic apocalyptic movements — Christian, Jewish,
Islamic, and Hindu — offering roads to heaven that are paved with the
corpses of those they detest. Given the power of a few determined individuals
to take lives or to derail processes of pragmatic negotiation, our future may
depend on finding models of faith and reason that will lead such movements
beyond their current apocalyptic pessimism.

The Recent Popularity of the Doom Boom

The most visible form of American millennialism of the past two decades can
be seen in the message of prominent television evangelists, who have advocated an end-time scheme in which the final battle of world history will occur

131

April 30, 2002

Sun

SUNSATIONAL DOUBLE ISSUE

SECRETS OF BIBLE'S WOMEN PROPHETS,
FAR-OUT FUTURE FASHIONS & MORE IN...

PROPHECY

BONUS 30-PAGE MAGAZINE IN

BIBLE OMENS WARN...

ARMAGEDDON HAS BEGUN!

Middle East inferno heralds Final Battle against forces of evil

U.S. $2.79 / $3.95 Canada

THE SAVAGE Mideast conflict is the beginning of the last chapter of mankind's turbulent history. And and hide in caves, trembling as civilization The Bible warned that this day would come changed our ways and followed the teaching: carpenter of Bethlehem. That didn't happen. "We have sowed the seeds of our own destru

The tabloid *Sun* reflected the firm faith, held by numerous millennial-apocalyptic groups, that Israel offers the path to Armageddon and world purification.

Credit: © Sun, American Media Entertainment, Inc.

very soon, before which true believers will be "raptured" from their homes and automobiles and enjoy paradisiacal bliss while the rest of the world burns. The Reverend Jerry Falwell set forth his vision of divine catastrophe this way:

> You'll be riding along in an automobile. You'll be the driver perhaps. You're a Christian. There'll be several people in the automobile with you, maybe someone who is not a Christian. When the trumpet sounds you and the other born-again believers in that automobile will be instantly caught away — you will disappear, leaving behind only your clothes and physical things that cannot inherit eternal life. That unsaved person or persons in the automobile will suddenly be startled to find that the car suddenly . . . crashes. . . . Other cars on the highway driven by believers will suddenly be out of control and stark pandemonium will occur on . . . every highway in the world where Christians are caught away from the driver's wheel.[2]

After this highly selective holocaust — which will be followed by nuclear war, in the opinion of some advocates of apocalypse — a new world will be created in which the saints will rule a peaceful kingdom for a thousand years. Those chosen to be saved will be spared any suffering during the terror that comes after the Rapture. According to Falwell, "If you are saved, you will never go through one hour, not one moment of the Tribulation." An earlier broadcast evangelist, Carl McIntire, seemed to feel a sense of glee at the prospect of seeing so many others die: "Thank God, I will get a view of the Battle of Armageddon from the grandstand seats of the heavens." Readers of Hal Lindsey's *Late Great Planet Earth* were offered the spectacle of a "quadrillion megaton explosion" that would kill billions of people.[3]

This apocalyptic theology has advanced from the fundamentalist fringes of American culture into the mainstream during the past quarter century, and it is reflected not just in the messages of televangelists but also in best-selling books, instructional videos, and feature movies, and promoted by thousands of Websites and religious bookstores.[4] The apocalyptic fantasies of these materials now shape a radicalized form of civil religion that delights in the prospect of American participation in battles that will bring world history as we know it to an end on the plain near the ancient Jewish city of Megiddo — the so-called Battle of Armageddon.

In a parallel movement, thousands of Islamic jihadists have yearned for a conflagration that would exterminate Israel, restore global dominance to the religion of Mohammed, and usher in an eternal era of peace. At the same time, Jewish fundamentalists share visions of setting off the conflict that would rid them of Arab pressure for all time. They have been supported in this hope by American end-time enthusiasts, who see in Israel the flash point for their own apocalyptic scenario. For millennial hopes in these mutually antagonistic forms, this world conflagration would be the ultimate, allegedly redemptive, conflict between zeal and jihad.

There would be some comfort in imagining that these eager anticipations of global doomsday lie merely on the crazy fringes of political life; but they have on occasion reached into the highest levels of American government. For example, in the fall of 1983, President Ronald Reagan said that recent events were leading him to think of Armageddon. In the quotation at the head of this chapter, the reference to the Battle of Armageddon reflects how closely President Reagan was attuned to a popular form of the public pulse. He had risen to public prominence when he gave "The Speech" as a spokesman for General Electric, where he clarified his vision of the Soviet antichrist as the nation's enemy: "We are faced with the most evil enemy mankind has known in his long climb from the swamp to the stars. . . ."[5] Reagan was also aware that his own election in 1980 was aided by thousands of churches that had entered the political process for the first time under the leadership of Rev. Jerry Falwell, who was committed to these ideas. But when even a secular president begins to use this language to describe foreign-policy developments, the contagious power of a certain strand of popular apocalyptic imagination is evident.

The president reinforced the sense of the influence of end-timers by offering briefings and seminars for evangelists, who spread messages of doom through radio and television. Donald Wagner reports that on March 19, 1984, Reagan invited 150 conservative Christians to the White House, including Jim and Tammy Bakker, Jerry Falwell, Tim and Beverly LaHaye, Hal Lindsey, Pat Robertson, and Jimmy Swaggart. Briefings were provided by figures such as Bud McFarlane, who was later a principal in the Iran-Contra affair, indicating that this was more than a social tea for friends.[6]

In the rest of this chapter we provide an introduction and critique of this popular strain of American millennialism, and then show some striking parallels in other cultures currently involved in religiously toned violent struggles. A common set of ideas underlies widely popular books such as Jerry Falwell's *Listen, America!*[7] and Hal Lindsey's *The Late Great Planet Earth*, the all-time religious best-seller in American religious history, which claims sales of some 40 million copies worldwide.[8] And those sales have been dwarfed in turn by the remarkable success of the *Left Behind* series by Tim LaHaye and Jerry B. Jenkins, which even markets materials aimed at children.[9]

For the sake of those to whom such books represent a strange and uncanny universe, we discuss the origin and persistent role of these millennial ideas in America, because a grasp of this history, which seems so alien to the modern mind, is crucial to understanding the unique threat their enactment poses in a time of jihad. Our conviction is that some of the militant and imprudent aspects of current American behavior are directly related to the increasing predominance of this millenarian outlook, which correlates closely with the secular apocalyptic, superheroic fantasy. In both systems a violent redeemer figure from the superhuman realm is expected to rescue the innocent from demonic adversaries just in the nick of time.

The Background of Millennial Theology

Although the dating scheme employed by Hal Lindsey and Jerry Falwell is oriented to such twentieth-century events as the establishment of Israel, the threat of nuclear destruction, and the challenge of militant Islam, there is nothing new about millennialism. The idea of a thousand-year kingdom that would follow a great battle between the forces of God and the forces of the demonic realm originated in Jewish pseudepigraphic writings;[10] it is mentioned only once in the Bible (Rev. 20:1-7), one of the most influential passages in Holy Writ:

> Then I saw an angel coming down from heaven, holding in his hand the key to the bottomless pit and a great chain. And he seized the dragon, that ancient serpent, who is the Devil and Satan, and bound him for a thousand years, and threw him into the pit, and shut it and sealed it over him, that he should deceive the nations no more, till the thousand years were ended. After that he must be loosed for a little while.
>
> Then I saw thrones, and seated on them were those to whom judgment was committed. Also I saw the souls of those who had been beheaded for their testimony to Jesus and for the word of God, and who had not worshiped the beast or its image and had not received its mark on their foreheads or on their hands. They came to life again, and reigned with Christ a thousand years. The rest of the dead did not come to life again until the thousand years were ended. This is the first resurrection. Blessed and holy is he who shares in the first resurrection! Over such the second death has no power, but they shall be priests of God and of Christ, and they shall reign with him a thousand years.
>
> And when the thousand years are ended, Satan will be loosed from his prison. . . .

In this grandiose vision of the future, Satan, after the great battle that destroys his forces, will be disabled for a thousand years while the saints rule the earth. Only at the end of this period, according to some interpretations, will the New Jerusalem come to earth.[11] This scheme has been hotly debated throughout the course of church history,[12] occasionally inspiring apocalyptic movements such as the Montanists between the second and fourth centuries, the Franciscans in the thirteenth century, the Hussites in the fifteenth century, the Anabaptists and Münsterites in the sixteenth century, and the Mormons, Seventh-Day Adventists, and Jehovah's Witnesses in the nineteenth and twentieth centuries. Most other Christian groups followed Augustine, who spiritualized the millennial kingdom and identified its fulfillment with various forms of Christendom; others rejected millennialism altogether.

As we have seen in chapter 5, the American civil religion was millennial from its very beginnings in the seventeenth century. The Great Awakening of the 1750s and '60s produced what Nathan Hatch has called "civil millennialism," in which the colonies were to play the role of the saints in the millennial kingdom of God.[13] Catherine Albanese observes that "in important measure, it is millennialism" that stands at the center of the distinctive religiosity and civil religion of the United States. "Sometimes it has been the dominating millennialism which takes its cue from visions of the final battle when good will triumph over evil. Other times it has been the innocent millennialism which seeks to make utopia in the uncorrupted landscape of the United States."[14]

The belief that the millennial age has already arrived is one of the distinctive features of the American mentality, producing a peculiar sense of national innocence, optimism, and superiority. Jonathan Edwards was one of the formative figures in shaping the conviction that the millennium had commenced in the Great Awakening of the 1740s.[15] Others saw the coming of the millennium in the successful conclusion of the American Revolution and the beginning of the nineteenth century. It is now clear that a fairly large group of American Protestants had become postmillennialist by the 1830s and 1840s: they believed, in effect, that the millennial kingdom had begun in North America.[16] This belief was sustained in the North by their victory in the Civil War. Americans with a more secular outlook expressed the postmillennial outlook with convictions concerning progress, expansion, and Manifest Destiny.

The impulse toward social reform in the nineteenth century reflected this postmillennial outlook. The prohibition and suffrage movements were sustained by the idea that Protestant citizens were the saints called to reform the world. The "social gospel" movement at the dawn of the twentieth century was a "secularized form of this postmillennialism."[17] These causes were advocated in the optimistic hope that conflict and poverty could be eliminated. Insofar as liberals from Methodist, Presbyterian, Congregationalist, and other mainline churches shared this optimistic orientation toward social reform, they were acting out of a postmillennial ethos, even though they were not always conscious of it. The willingness of the country to participate in great crusades "to make the world safe for democracy" by defeating Spain in 1898 and Germany in 1918 derived in part from this same postmillennial spirit.

To understand the revival of premillennial perspective in the last several decades, we need to describe the experiences of those who rejected optimistic postmillennialism in the nineteenth century. A number of sectarian groups arose after the 1830s to repudiate the notion that life was improving because the millennium had come to America.[18] Reflecting the experience of farmers and industrial workers, who had often suffered during the frequent depressions in American history, this viewpoint had some elements of realism. It also rested on broad biblical foundations that resisted identifying already existing worldly kingdoms with the kingdom of God. In the 1830s, Joseph Smith founded the Mormons as the "Latter-Day Saints," who would become the first fruits of a millennial kingdom shortly to be established in America. William Miller taught that the millennium was still to come, and he set several dates for its arrival in the 1840s, founding the Seventh-Day Adventists and other denominations.[19] In the 1880s, Charles T. Russell began the Jehovah's Witness movement, which proclaimed the invisible spiritual presence of Christ in a forty-year period that would culminate in 1914 with the dawning of a millennial kingdom. These groups were saying in effect: "We do not believe that America is already a millennial nation. A great catastrophe is yet to come. Our task is to awaken the nation to its premillennial situation."

In *Living in the Shadow of the Second Coming,*[20] Timothy P. Weber has shown that American fundamentalism was dominated by this pessimistic, premillennial outlook in the latter decades of the nineteenth century. The Niagara Bible conferences and the revival meetings that produced institutions such as the Moody Bible Institute, hundreds of Bible colleges, and the Billy Sunday tabernacles shared this perspective. They were pessimistic about the moral and spiritual state of the world. With the exception of the Mormons, these groups did not participate actively in the American political process. Up until the past two decades, these groups for the most part remained skeptical, pessimistic outsiders to the American dream and civil religion. And while this was a minority viewpoint, it was the source of the contemporary explosion of Christian millennialism. The ingredient that allowed this millenarian theology to come to a position of later dominance surfaced only toward the end of the nineteenth century: it is the modern doctrine of "the Rapture."

Calendars for the Rapture

The term *rapture* derives from the Latin translation of a biblical passage in 1 Thessalonians 4:17, where Paul explains that when Christ returns, dead believers will be rejoined with those still alive when they are all caught up together in the air *(simul rapiemur cum illis in nubibus obviam Domino in aera)*.[21] This obscure verse played a minor theological role until the 1830s in Great Britain,[22] when it became crucial for the first time within the Plymouth Brethren, established by John Nelson Darby.[23] Margaret Macdonald, a prophetess within the Darby circle, reportedly had a vision that the meeting with the Lord in the air would occur before the tribulation that was expected in the seven-year period before the warfare ushering in the millennial kingdom.[24] This new idea of a "pretribulation rapture" subsequently crystallized as a widely shared conviction among British, Canadian, and American fundamentalists in the 1880-1890s. It was fused into a dispensational view of biblical history in Oxford University Press's *Scofield Reference Bible* (largely unchanged since its original publication in 1909), one of the most widely used reference books in current Protestantism that remains untouched by the ethos of the Society for Biblical Literature and other scholarly groups.[25] Its premises that we are in the final "dispensation" of world history, and that the contradictions within Scripture reflect the divine law in earlier dispensations, have made the *Scofield Bible* a highly appealing resource during the time of nuclear anxieties instigated by the Cold War, anxieties now brought back to life with the emergence of international terrorism. Hundreds of Bible colleges, led by the influential faculty of Dallas Theological Seminary, have promoted these ideas.

Hal Lindsey's books popularize the doomsday system he learned at Dallas Theological Seminary, and the lack of originality has done nothing to impair the book sales that have made this doomsayer, who expected the end of history several decades ago, into a millennial millionaire.[26] According to Donald Wagner, he also used his special prophetic insights to build "a consulting business with a clientele including several members of Congress, the Pentagon, the CIA, Israeli Generals, and . . . Ronald Reagan." Given the dominance of such thinking among broadcast evangelists[27] and the unsurpassed success of the more recent *Left Behind* empire,[28] some form of rapture theology has arguably become the "mainstream" of American religion.[29] The conflicts within fundamentalism about the exact date of the Rapture have been the most widely discussed theological issue in the culture.[30] Its impact on American politics goes hand in hand with modern dating schemes for the Rapture. Since the tendency of currently popular millennialism is to suppress the memory of the Rapture's frequent and awkward rescheduling, we would like to offer a historical review.

A new scheme for dating the events of what Hal Lindsey called *The Terminal Generation*[31] crystallized in the first decade after World War II. Its premise was that the re-establishment of Israel in 1948 marked the beginning of the final era of world history. Assuming that a generation in the biblical sense is no more than forty years, this meant that the final battle would occur no later than 1988. In Lindsey's version of this scheme, the Rapture was expected to occur before the tribulation, which would begin seven years before 1988, at the latest.[32] This dating scheme was presented by Lindsey and others in a cagey manner, leaving the arithmetic to the reader and never claiming exactly when during this forty-year period the end would actually occur. They repeatedly intoned Jesus' saying about no one knowing the day or the hour. Yet Lindsey and others persistently and forcefully made the claim that the generation that began in 1948 was indeed the final generation.[33] Critics of this view could only offer a far less exciting skepticism, but they never had as much impact as Hal Lindsey, Jerry Falwell, Pat Robertson, and other prominent end-timers.[34] Some of the criticism related not to the date of the Rapture but to its sequence in the end-time scenario.[35]

The flurry of reports in local papers concerning end-time preparations and predictions in the early 1980s indicated that some people took this dating scheme seriously. For instance, the *Chicago Sun-Times* carried an article (April 29, 1981) with the title "Believers Standing By for Ascent into Heaven." It provided the account of a group in Arizona that accepted the Lindsey prophecy very seriously indeed. The *Winston-Salem Journal* (October 2, 1981) reported that "a religious community, with branches in Kansas, Texas and Scotland, has set the date for the Battle of Armageddon. . . ." There was an ironic report in the *Sioux City Journal* (May 7, 1980): "Due to analytical difficulties, the end of the world has been rescheduled for today, according to a religious sect. The world was supposed to have ended last week, according to Charles Gaines. . . ." In a 1990 millennial failure, Elizabeth Clare Prophet, leader of the Church Universal and Triumphant, gathered together her faithful — many of whom had abandoned work, personal property, and family relationships — at a site in rural Montana. April 23 was her predicted date for a nuclear apocalypse initiated by the Soviet Union. When it did not occur, she claimed that the prayers of her followers had prevented it from taking place. What had actually happened, she said, recalibrating her schedule of doom, was "the start of a 12-year 'dark cycle' during which the Four Horsemen of the Apocalypse would stalk the planet."[36] Harold Camping, who commanded a 53-station Family Radio Network, began predicting that the world would end between September 15 and 27, 1994. His books on the subject — *1994?* and *Are You Ready?* — were reported to have printings of 80,000. On September 28, 1994, he conceded to *Christianity Today* magazine that "apparently it was incorrect."[37] What was not widely recognized in any of these disappointments was the impact of such millenarian speculation on the American civil religion.

That the Rapture should have occurred no later than 1980-81 is connected with some important political developments. In 1978, just before the latest date on which the Rapture was supposed to have happened, one of the most remarkable political movements in American history suddenly emerged. Under the leadership of Jerry Falwell and other Rapture advocates, the Moral Majority movement attracted the political involvement of tens of thousands of fundamentalist pastors and churches that had never been involved in the political process before.[38] Transcending almost a century of suspicion regarding the evil arena of politics, they entered into alliance with conservative Catholics, Lutherans, Mormons, and nonapocalyptic fundamentalists whom they had traditionally damned.

In the conviction that the final crisis of world history was at hand,[39] the Moral Majority movement promoted candidates and policies suited for Armageddon, including a stronger nuclear force and enlarged military budget, a resistance to any compromise with the Soviet Union, an unquestioning support of Israel, a rejection of Palestinian claims for autonomy, and an uncompromising position on moral issues such as abortion. They saw these moral stances as preparation for righteous victory in the forthcoming apocalyptic conflagration. Despite the alliance with nonapocalyptic groups, the impetus and all of the state and national leaders of the Moral Majority movement reflected the conviction that the Rapture was virtually within sight. It was, in fact, expected within two years, a detail that correlates with the curious and substantially unexplained loss of momentum in 1981 and its fatal shift into the "Liberty Federation" in 1986.[40] In the early 1980s it also spawned a large number of sectarian groups that separated themselves from society in the expectation of the millennium.

The impact of this movement on American political life has been enormous, far larger than the rather short-lived movement itself would indicate. It contributed decisively to the election of Ronald Reagan in 1980 and brought into office the entire generation of recent leadership within the Republican party, including Newt Gingrich, Dick Armey, Tom Delay, and others. Within a short time it had largely transformed the conservative Republican party, which had hitherto been committed to federalism, capitalism, and the international rule of law, into a millenarian party resistant to federal authority, hostile to the traditional American politics of compromise, and profoundly suspicious of international law and peacekeeping. The Christian right also reached out to the conservative Likud bloc in Israeli politics, encouraging it to resist any efforts at compromise with Palestinians. They had already begun their war-like incantations as a reaction to President Jimmy Carter's peace initiatives for Israel, taking out newspaper ads that read: "The time has come for evangelical Christians to affirm their belief in biblical prophecy and Israel's divine right to the land."[41] Rapture theology also brought an extraordinarily combative tone to American politics, matching the vocabulary of an apocalyptic holy war.[42]

Although the dating scheme based on 1948 failed, rapture theology in North America has hardly lost a beat. It negotiated one of the smoothest transitions through the minefield of apocalyptic failure that history has to report. What may very well have been the first phase of this rescheduling occurred in a Hal Lindsey lecture in Toronto in 1980. Lindsey was beginning to discuss whether the anchor for the terminal generation might be the recapturing of Jerusalem rather than the establishment of the Jewish state. Since Jerusalem's recapture took place in 1967, it would bring the end of the terminal generation to 2007 at the latest, and the beginning of the tribulation period thus came to the satisfying round number of 2000.[43]

The media evangelist who first adopted this new schedule was apparently Pat Robertson, whose ascendancy in the last two decades appears to correlate with his timely adoption of the new dating scheme.[44] Many recent books on the Rapture promote this scheme[45] or a variant that brings the 1988-2000 period into focus as the time of the end.[46] While this latest date for the Rapture has now passed, Paul Boyer reports that "prophecy popularizers, like their predecessors over the centuries, are proving extremely resourceful in restructuring their scenario."[47] While the flurry of books on the Rapture continues unabated, there is considerably more modesty on the matter of specifying the date of the end. Some writers claim that this is the final generation without setting a specific date,[48] while others remain in the tradition of vague forecasting, without specifying that the present age is the end time.[49] Lindsey's own Web site, HalLindseyOracle.com, now adopts a cautious stance that favors the continued sale of millennial products, one of which is *The Last Days Chronicles*, advertised with these words:

> *The Last Days Chronicles* is an exciting newspaper dedicated to examining that evidence — taken directly from the daily news, and showing how what looks like chaos to the world is proof positive that God's Plan for the human race is moving forward according to a clearly defined, pre-determined

schedule. Nobody knows exactly when the Lord will return, but He gave us specific signs of the time, and He promised us that "when you see these things begin to come to pass, then look up and lift up your heads, for your redemption draws nigh."

Lindsey's prediction here has become almost too vague to matter. Others even go so far as to abandon the current expectation, claiming that Christ returned in some other sense at the end of the Jewish-Roman War around 70 CE, and that his final coming is unpredictable.[50] Seventh-Day Adventist materials continue to emphasize that in some sense the last generation has arrived, but they refrain from setting precise dates.[51] By any measure, the interest in the Rapture remains intense while honest recognition of the failed expectations waits on some distant horizon.[52] The situation partially resembles the New Testament coping with the *parousia*'s postponement: evidence is fragmentary, elusive, and lacking the kind of detail that would allow insight into the process of rescheduling the Rapture. But the impact on American political life continues.

Recent Forms of Millennial Civil Religion

Some forms of millenarian ideology advance a theocratic version of the civil religion. For example, in *America's Dates with Destiny*, Pat Robertson argues that in colonial times America was founded as a "Christian nation," and he reviews its history to "call America once again to its spiritual heritage."[53] He shows that America is God's nation in a unique sense, and that evangelicals who accept Robertson's new apocalyptic theology are its best citizens. In *The Secret Kingdom*, Robertson calls on millenarians to become political leaders so that when the battle of Armageddon comes, in the very near future, the country will play its ordained role on the side of the angels. Christians need to "be ready for the new world order that appears to be rushing toward us."[54] After the battle that will destroy communism and other hostile powers, "God's people will rule with Him, in that peaceful reign under the laws of the Kingdom."[55] In maintaining this theocratic vision throughout, Robertson muddles the idea of church-state separation.

In a fund-raising newsletter following his success in the presidential primary election in Michigan, Robertson declared exuberantly: "The Christians have won . . . ! What a breakthrough for the Kingdom!"[56] "The only precedent" for America's constitutional government "was established thousands of years before by the tribes of Israel in their covenant with God and each other," the classical period of Israel's attempt at theocracy.[57] Robertson associates outstanding political leaders with theocracy rather than with the Enlightenment and the vision of limited government. For example, he sees James Madison, who provided the theoretical basis for accepting the Constitution, as actually a "fundamentalist" whose ideas are consistent with "the new right."[58] It follows that "studying the Constitution is like studying the Bible."[59] Robertson praised Ronald Reagan for reflecting "a return to the spirit of the Pilgrims, the spirit of 1776, the spirit of Washington, Jefferson, and Lincoln."[60] He criticizes the ACLU's efforts to defend constitutional rights as destroying "this nation's spiritual heritage."[61]

When people are taught that correct beliefs and membership in the proper sect will guarantee their escape from the tribulation and hence from the threats of nuclear annihilation or terrorism, the proponents of those views have inserted an element of escapism into the civil religion. This comfortable vision of the end is actually unprecedented in Christian eschatology. Prior to the 1830s, Christian apocalyptics taught that believers would have to suffer for their faith. The realism of these earlier apocalyptic theologies is consistent with the sayings of Jesus, Paul, Hebrews, and the prophets — and greatly at variance with the modern teaching. While the appeal of such an escapist doctrine in a time of threatening circumstances is obvious, its effect on a voting public is ominous. It tends to reinforce the escapism of mass entertainment, in which innocent communities are rescued by superheroes who arrive in the nick of time to destroy the wicked.

Such fantasies in religion and entertainment have their political embodiment in the belief that a super-president and the availability of superior military power will provide final security in a threatening world. According to this doctrine, even in a nuclear holocaust, whether imposed by an enemy nation or nameless terrorists, the innocent will escape, survive, and prevail. Even if life as we know it is destroyed, following the plot of Hal Lindsey's books, it will be restored by divine power, and a new millennium will be reborn out of the ashes. In the Christian Broadcasting Network's propaganda, Regent University will be restored after the holocaust to usher in a new era of global peace and prosperity, with Pat Robertson or his successor at the helm.

The current form of millenarian civil religion tends to view current events as they affect the future consummation. Prudential considerations and the preservation of life become irrelevant. The apocalyptic scheme "conditions all our expectations," in Stephen O'Leary's words, allowing even a nuclear war to become "a perverse fulfillment of divine destiny."[62] The Battle of Armageddon is to be welcomed, and any effort to adjudicate conflicts through international cooperation is to be viewed as the temptation of the

Antichrist. This was represented in Pat Robertson's book *The New Millennium,* which warned against the potential of collective action under the United Nations because it might work in the long run against Israel's interests: "Saddam Hussein has set the machinery in motion which one day will bring the military force of world government against Israel."[63] In Robertson's scheme, the greatest threat to peace was not Saddam Hussein but the United Nations. This tendency has also surfaced in the reactions of some fundamentalist publications to the events of September 11, 2001.[64]

The modern form of Rapture theology divides the world into true believers, those who will be rescued from the tribulation, and the rest of the inhabitants of planet earth, who will suffer because of their sins. This sustains the popular feeling that Americans are innocent while their adversaries are full of malice; or, in the context of internal politics, that political opponents are evil and should be opposed on principle.[65] This theology rejects compromise, which is the essence of the American constitutional system's checks and balances, on principle. Gridlock in government, which naturally results from such intransigence, is to be welcomed on principle.

The same principles govern foreign relations, which render a Rapture-expectant public more vulnerable to conflict, more resistant to international institutions that require America to place itself alongside other nations in having only one vote or submitting to the same standards of international law. This theology sees every compromise with America's adversaries as a betrayal of divine trust; every effort to achieve arms control and to reduce the danger of accidental nuclear wars is a sellout to the demonic powers. Similarly, it views efforts to deal with pollution or global warming as futile and counterproductive. While Rapture advocates do not currently wish to promote a global ecological crisis, they are convinced that God wills it and thus that there is absolutely nothing humans can do to stop it. Thus, along with a preoccupation with military preparedness, this theology shows an unrelenting hostility to international agencies that work toward peace or the resolution of ecological issues.

Jerusalem and the End of Days

A striking feature of the current world is that other cultures have developed forms of millennial thinking that parallel those dominant in the United States since 1970.[66] A distilled essence of such fantasies and their inherent dangers has been conveyed by Gershom Gorenberg's remarkable study *The End of Days: Fundamentalism and the Struggle for the Temple Mount,* which documents how Christian, Jewish, and Muslim millennial apocalyptics have brought their combative instincts to focus on Temple Mount (Al-Haram al-Sharif) in Jerusalem. Based principally on interviews with those who wish to make Temple Mount the launching pad for their version of cosmic redemption, Gorenberg's book shows us these forces in a mutually destructive array, with each party absolutely certain that God wants the other party destroyed as the price of world redemption. America's Christian Right pushes for a foreign policy that will trigger favored scenarios from Revelation. Some want to destroy the Muslim Dome of the Rock and build a new temple to trigger the Second Coming of Jesus and the Tribulation.[67] Benjamin Netanyahu, as prime minister of Israel, worked directly with Jerry Falwell and the Christian Right to undermine the Oslo Accords. Netanyahu's policy adviser, David Bar-Illan, found America's Christian Right as supportive as his own Likud party, since they were "opposed to giving up any land. It belongs to the Jews. . . . They oppose aid to the Palestinians. Yes, they see the conflict in black and white."[68]

Jewish groups have directed violent deeds at the Arab presence on the Temple Mount. One advocate, Gershon Solomon, puts it this way: "Instead of the Dome of the Rock and mosques, the flag of Israel and the Temple." Several advocates and violent activists are American Jews who espouse the Daniel scenario in which a time of trouble comes, followed by a waking of the dead for final judgment.[69] Rabbi Zvi Yehudah Kook, a seminal figure in the history of the Gush Emunim movement, declared in the wake of the 1967 war, which was seen as a new miracle and promise from God to make Israel's dominance over its biblical territories permanent and unqualified: "There are people who speak of the beginning of redemption in our day. Open your eyes and see that we are now in the middle of redemption."[70] Impatient Israelis, who accepted this redemptionist premise, thought that the timetable could be accelerated by violent action, by destroying the Muslim Dome of the Rock. The plan, in the words of Haim Ben-David, a Golan Heights settler and conspirator, "was a stage in the spiritual redemption of the Jewish people. What was new for me was that this spiritual action would lead to a physical action."[71] The conspirators were foiled in their attempt to blow up the Muslim Temple, so they turned to other acts of violence, such as entering the Hebron Islamic College in 1983 with bullets and grenades, killing three and wounding thirty others.[72]

In a similar vein, Muslim apocalyptics see Jews in the vicinity of the Temple Mount and the Wailing Wall and their American allies as demonic infidels whose unholy presence must be purged by the sort of violence that end-time Jews and Christians have in mind for them. Indeed, this vision has drawn some of its scriptural support from Muhammad himself. The scholar David Cook has followed Islam's popular apocalyptic writer Said Ayyub, who uses the Christian apocalyptic texts — Daniel, Ezekiel, Isaiah, and Revelation — to identify the United States, in partnership with the "anti-Christ Jew," as the "chief enemy of Islam."[73] Cook reports that Ayyub's book *Al-Masah al-Dajjal (The Anti-Christ)*, which resembles Hal Lindsey's *Late Great Planet Earth,* has been a best-seller in Egypt and has inspired hundreds of others in the same mold.[74]

Gorenberg sees common textual and historical threads in these mutually nullifying visions of the end: "Christianity's scriptwriters reworked Judaism, and Islam rewrote both."[75] They all agree that Jerusalem is the setting and that the past, present, and future temples hold the keys — sacral and physical — to the end of days that will consume their enemies and exalt the members of their own faith as never before. In searching for the correct religious spirit in which to approach the future, Gorenberg quotes from Darrell Fasching's ironically titled *The Coming of the Millennium: Good News for the Whole Human Race.* Fasching feels revulsion for Hal Lindsey's Hitler-like vision of "apocalyptic purification of the earth through violence and death." Fasching's vision is a Christianity in which "welcoming the stranger, the person unlike yourself" is an ethical imperative.[76] Gorenberg's own conclusions are written in the spirit of prophetic realism:

> A de jure division of holy space is not only a political concession. It should be seen as a religious achievement. There's a profit in getting less than everything. The symbolism of publicly affirming the partition of the holy places is that Islam and Judaism will live side by side, neither victorious over the other.[77]

Yet he does not envision that everyone will surrender something in the interest of a common future, commenting that "the most extreme, those who have invested themselves most in the dream of here and now, are likely to refuse to retreat. For some the appeal of catastrophe would beckon."[78] Perhaps their appeal will diminish as the "religious achievement" of accommodation permits calmer, more prosperous lives.

We find such a conclusion more latent with promise than that of Mark Juergensmeyer in his *Terror in the Mind of God: The Global Rise of Religious Violence.* He believes that common to those movements promoting divinized cosmic warfare for political goals is a rejection of a secular state that promotes materialism and individualism. His prescription for a safer, less violent world thus requires a compromise between secular and religious values:

Religion gives spirit to public life and provides a beacon for moral order. At the same time it needs the temper of rationality and fair play that Enlightenment values give to civil society. Thus religious violence cannot end until some accommodation can be forged between the two — some assertion of moderation in religion's passion, and some acknowledgment of religion in elevating the spiritual and moral values of public life. In a curious way, then, the cure for religious violence may ultimately lie in a renewed appreciation for religion itself.[79]

While we agree that the role of religion needs to be recognized, we fear excessive emphasis on taming religion to permit civil peace. While we agree that secular values can moderate the zealous impulse, we favor Gorenberg's more positive view that some strands of religion explicitly counter the visions of righteous violence that have become so common in the world. We also believe that the Enlightenment, although it has historically worn secular dress, owes much of its wisdom to the strand of prophetic realism in the Bible that has always run side by side with the impulses of zealous nationalism. Ideals of respecting conscience, encouraging compromise, relying on nonviolent means of conflict resolution, and removing religion from the jurisdiction of state power had religious roots before they were adopted by reason.

Responsible Uses of the Apocalyptic

We believe that it is incumbent on all believers to struggle against the lethal impulses that lie within their own religious traditions. Although claiming to be consistent with the religious traditions emanating from the Bible, these Jewish, Christian, and Islamic forms of millennial zealotry that have emerged in recent decades reject the entire strand of biblical realism, from the Old Testament prophets down to Jesus and Paul. An important insight of biblical research is that there are forms of apocalyptic thinking that encourage a sense of historical responsibility and a humane attitude toward neighbors. For example, the apostle Paul combined apocalyptic urgency with a peaceful ethic, as J. Christiaan Beker has shown.[80] Paul's ethical admonitions were in support of love and reconciliation, not apocalyptic violence. And while he clearly expected the end of the world to come shortly, he resisted any form of date-setting: "As for prophecies, they shall fail . . . but love endures" (1 Cor. 13). We have here an example of responsible apocalyptic thought, taking the possibility of a holocaust seriously, but not giving up on the preservation of the world and its inhabitants.

One could make a similar case about the books of Mark, or Hebrews, or 1 Peter, all of which are apocalyptic writings that offer responsible ethical resources for the difficult final transition into the time of jihad. They offer a corrective to contemporary millennialist theologies, taking demonic threats to humanity seriously and refusing to fall prey to current ideologies, but not despairing about the potential of love and coexistence between competing persons, races, classes, or empires. Without these realistic resources, the millennialist theologies regnant at the present time pose as ominous a threat as the apocalyptic literature of the first century did on Jewish culture. That literature contributed to the destruction of Jerusalem as a result of the zealous war against Rome, a conflict that both Jesus and Paul sought to avert. They took up the ancient prophetic vision of coexistence and nonviolent conflict resolution whose biblical expression is honored by Judaism and Islam as well as Christianity. But to follow that vision requires a renunciation of millennial zealotry that threatens to turn the time of jihad into another self-imposed holocaust.

We must also recognize the corrective that the sense of the apocalyptic has aroused in the peace movements — both secular and religious — with the specter of nuclear warfare. Paul Boyer's history of American responses to nuclear weapons reminds us that scientists joined hands with religious activists in questioning America's innocence in using the atomic bombs at Hiroshima and Nagasaki.[81] The confluence of many movements in the 1980s — Clergy and Laity Concerned, Computer Professionals for Social Responsibility, SANE, Freeze, Catholic bishops, and others — exerted an important influence on President Ronald Reagan, who responded by distancing himself from Hal Lindsey, Jerry Falwell, Pat Robertson, and other Christians who relished the prospect of Armageddon. The very alarmed peace activists helped create an atmosphere in U.S. politics that welcomed the Intermediate-Range Nuclear Forces Treaty of 1987. The United States and the Soviet Union agreed to do away with their intermediate- and medium-range land-based missiles, which were scattered across the European and Soviet terrain, facing one another at frighteningly close distances.

President Reagan, who had so often declared Soviets the embodiment of the most intolerable evil in history, traveled to Moscow in pursuit of an arms agreement. The public rewarded him with approval ratings in the 70 percent range, with 72 percent endorsing his conduct of Soviet relations.[82] That episode demonstrates the important role for an informed and politically active sense of danger to humanity. Today's world is hardly beyond peril from nuclear arms and threatens to slide back toward nuclear unilateralism on the part of the United States, where millennialism continues to fuel the Captain American complex.

9

The Global Popularization of Zeal and Jihad

Everything I did, I did for God, the Torah of Israel, the people of Israel, and the land of Israel.

Yigal Amir, a law student who assassinated Israeli Prime Minister Yitzak Rabin in hopes of derailing the Oslo peace process[1]

"Truly there is only one death," he said, repeating the words of a famous Muslim martyr, "so let it be the path of God."

a smiling boy who has prepared himself for death, speaking on a Hamas videotape[2]

We have demonstrated a peculiar involvement of mass culture in violent movements of the past several decades. Although explicitly religious motivations are often present, they are modified and expressed through the media and symbols of popular culture. These contemporary movements also arose at a time when the American monomyth had gained global ascendancy as an entertainment product. The most sophisticated, cheapest, and thus most widely dispersed films and television programs came from Hollywood and New York, spreading the message of regeneration through violence across the entire world. Captain America's ideology thus became a dominant theme not just in the United States, but it began to appear in other parts of the globe

149

with access to modern media. Religious and secular zealotry and jihadism, not new phenomena in history, had always promised to rid the world of evil-doers who appeared to threaten the survival or preeminence of their particular group, culture, or nation. The American monomyth's colorful, convincing enactments of redemption through violence lent a new emotional power to these indigenous forms of zealotry and jihadism. The mythic brew that arises out of the encounter of conflicting zealous myths has given the world a new urgency to considering a kind of "spiritual disarmament" — a retreat from the captivating narratives of divinely sanctified destruction and a turn toward the traditions of peaceful restraint from the violent tendencies that exist in every religion.

Because of their relative importance in ongoing struggles over terrorism, we begin here with some Islamic conceptions of jihad and then move on to describe Israeli zealotry. Then we characterize similar trends elsewhere in the world. It is surprising to discover the similar rationales for violence in these movements, despite their differing historical circumstances and diverse cultural backgrounds. The Captain America complex, with its peculiar tension between zeal and realism, surfaces even in groups that claim to despise everything American. We shall see that the moments of jihad actually began before September 11, 2001, and that its explosions have destroyed buildings and slaughtered bystanders far beyond Manhattan Island.

The Recent Militarization of Jihad

We have observed in chapter 2 that the concept of *jihad* in Islam is not necessarily related to terrorism. Most Muslims interpret jihad as "the effort to live in the way that God intended for human beings," as Karen Armstrong and others observe.[3] John Esposito's authoritative study points in the same direction:

> Jihad, "to strive or struggle" in the way of God, is sometimes referred to as the sixth pillar of Islam, although it has no such official status. In its most general meaning, it refers to the obligation incumbent on all Muslims, as individuals and as a community, to exert themselves to realize God's will, to lead virtuous lives, and to extend the Islamic community through preaching, education, and so on. . . . A related meaning is the struggle for or defense of Islam, holy war.[4]

This latter sense — of *jihad* as holy war — is derived from biblical roots, according to Esposito, in the belief shared by Muhammad and some Jews and

Christians that "God had sanctioned battle with the enemies of the Lord."[5] This side of the Muslim tradition follows the same biblical patterns of Elijah and Jehu that influenced American zealotry, as we traced in chapters 5-7.

In the eighteenth and nineteenth centuries the traditional Islamic concepts of "renewal *(tajdid)* and reform *(islah)*," closely related to jihad, were used to demand "a return to the fundamentals of Islam."[6] A wave of revivalism swept over the Islamic world, of which the Wahhabi movement in Saudi Arabia has proven to be the most influential. Muhammad bin Abd al-Wahhab (1703-1792) taught that the political weakness of Islam resulted from its deviation from "the straight path," and that a holy war should be fought against resisters.[7] He advocated a puritanical form of Islam, rejecting music and decorative arts in any form and favoring simple prayers and unostentatious piety — opposing both the excessive veneration of Muhammad and the worship of holy places and shrines. He also became known for extreme punishments against offenders, providing the inspiration for the religious police in Saudi Arabia and Afghanistan. In the words of Tariq Ali, "He also insisted on . . . beatings and more: adulterers should be stoned to death, thieves should have limbs amputated; criminals should be executed in public."[8] Stephen Schwarz offers the impression that Wahhabism is "stripped-down Islam" — simple, violent, intolerant, and "fanatical beyond measure."[9]

In cooperation with a local tribal leader, Muhammad bin Saud, the founder of Saudi Arabia's current dynasty, the Wahhabi warriors subdued and united most of Arabia. Their propensity for violence was infamous: "For example, the Wahhabis fell upon the city of Qarbala in 1801 and killed 2,000 ordinary citizens in the streets and markets."[10] Their iconoclastic zeal "destroyed Sufi shrines and tombs . . . [and] led to the destruction of sacred tombs in Mecca and Medina, including those of the Prophet and his companions."[11] Wahhabism retains its importance up to the present because of its standing as the official interpretation of Islam in Saudi Arabia and is dominant in many other parts of the world.[12] Because Saudi Arabia has used its wealth to spread Wahhabist beliefs around the globe, many of the mosques in the United States have been founded with their gifts. Estimates of Wahhabist influence in these temples varies widely, with the highest estimate expressed by Stephen Schwartz: "In the U.S. 80 percent of the mosques are estimated . . . to be under the control of Wahhabi imams, who preach extremism. . . ."[13]

This is the form of Islam that Saudi Arabia exported to Pakistan and Afghanistan; it dominates the widely popular schools sponsored by local mosques in Pakistan, from which the now discredited Taliban movement in Afghanistan sprang. According to Pakistani journalist Ahmed Rashid's account entitled *Taliban*, Osama bin Laden "used his wealth and Saudi donations to build Mujaheddin projects and spread Wahhabism amongst the Afghans."[14]

Although there were occasions in Islamic history when the martial dimension became dominant, it was not until the 1970s that a strand arose to claim violent jihad as the sole legitimate form of religious intensity.[15] The initial success of Arab armies against Israel and the Oil Embargo in 1973, the Iranian Revolution of 1978-79, and the invasion of Afghanistan in 1979 "served as catalysts for Islamic revivalism" that brought jihad into ascendancy.[16] Radicals insisted that "jihad against unbelief and unbelievers is a religious duty," that the establishment of Islamic law and government is a religious obligation, and that Christians and Jews should no longer be tolerated as "people of the book" because of their involvement in Zionism and colonialism.[17] Another factor has been the humiliation of having fallen so far behind the West in economic and political development.[18]

During the 1970s, Omar Abder Rahman, the blind theologian who was later imprisoned because of his role in the 1993 attack on the World Trade Center, wrote a 2,000-page dissertation at the famous Azhar University at Cairo in which he argued that the only legitimate form of jihad was to use the sword to force unbelievers either to accept the Islamic faith or to submit to Islamic rule. He argued further that Islam had always been imposed by force and that it must be so in the future.[19] Abdes Salam Farag, one of Rahman's disciples involved in the assassination of Egyptian premier Anwar Sadat, wrote an influential pamphlet claiming that martial jihad was the sixth pillar of Islam.[20] Even in a religion lacking a centralized theological authority, this was an astounding alteration of the long tradition of Islam's five pillars, or five basic religious obligations. Ali Ben-Haj, a leader in Algeria's "Jihad-Party," took this one step further when he described jihad as the third pillar of Islam, ranking it just below the obligations to observe monotheism and prayer.[21] The teacher of Osama bin Laden, Dr. Abdullah Azzam, crisscrossed the world to recruit converts to this radical view after the Soviet invasion of Afghanistan in 1979. This charismatic teacher wrote "The Lovers of the Virgins of Paradise," which promised immediate access to a harem of beautiful virgins for each soldier who dies in the service of jihad.[22] His approach to conflict was starkly simple: "Jihad and the rifle alone: no negotiations, no conferences, and no dialogues."[23] It appears that this radicalized form of Islamic jihadism is particularly popular in circles influenced by Wahhabi, which brings us to the case of Osama bin Laden.

The seventeenth of fifty-two children of a Saudi millionaire, Osama bin Laden was a bright and ambitious young businessman who began to read radical Islamic literature toward the end of the 1970s. Soon after the Soviet occupation of Afghanistan in 1979, he joined the jihadic resistance movement under the influence of Prof. Abdullah Azzam, who taught at the International Islamic University in Islamabad. Azzam was one of the founders of the Palestinian Hamas movement, and he promoted a radical form of jihad not only against the Russians but against the entire non-Islamic world.[24] Secretly sponsored by Pakistan, financed by the Saudis, and supplied with weapons by the CIA, bin Laden assumed leadership as a coordinator of the resistance movement. His immense personal wealth, organizational abilities, Saudi background, and personal charisma over a twenty-year period led to his preeminence in the global movement of Islamic jihad.[25] He formed the al Qaeda terrorist organization, which has cells all over the world and has trained tens of thousands of recruits for suicidal terrorism at camps located in Afghanistan and elsewhere. Although bin Laden has no formal religious education, he became an eloquent spokesman for jihadic terrorism and "established himself as one of the most momentous figures in contemporary Islamic history," in the assessment of Ruel Marc Gerecht.[26] As a wealthy businessman who chose hardship in Afghanistan and was "persecuted" in country after country, "bin Laden evokes the prophetic tradition" of Muhammad.[27] The components of his ideology, derived primarily from Abdullah Azzam, comprise a virtual mirror image of the Captain America complex.[28]

Bin Laden's disciples are taught that they are Allah's select warriors in the war against America, the West, and all non-jihadic Muslims. They envision a vast conspiracy in which dishonorable Muslims give tacit support to the Christian "crusaders" of the West. The massacres of innocent Muslims from Bosnia to Chechnya are, in bin Laden's view, the result of "a clear conspiracy between the USA and its allies . . . under the iniquitous United Nations."[29] In a militant Islamic magazine published in Australia, bin Laden described this allegedly aggressive conspiracy against innocent Muslims as follows:

> What bears no doubt in this fierce Judeo-Christian campaign against the Muslim world, the likes of which has never been seen before, is that Muslims must prepare all possible might to repel the enemy, militarily, economically, through missionary activity, and all other areas. It is crucial for us to be patient and to cooperate in righteousness and piety and raise awareness of the fact that the highest priority, after faith, is to repel the aggressive enemy that corrupts the religion and the world. Nothing deserves a higher priority, after faith, as the religious scholars have declared.[30]

Here we see martial jihad advanced to a preeminent place among the pillars of Islam, following the rationale developed by Omar Abder Rahman and

Abdullah Azzam. There was thus a substantial theological rationale in bin Laden's "Declaration of War Against the Americans Occupying the Land of the Two Holy Places," issued in 1996. This war will result in "the establishment of a castle of the Muslims, a [new] Caliphate" of the golden age to come, as formulated in *The Encyclopedia of the Afghan Jihad* compiled by al Qaeda.[31] By overcoming the dominance of the non-Muslim Western world, the holy law of the Koran will reign supreme in the entire world, redeeming it from degeneracy. World redemption is the assured goal of this violent campaign, because Allah wills it.

As for the jihadic warriors willing to lay down their lives for the holy cause, paradise is promised on a more immediate timetable. Osama bin Laden's warriors are taught a doctrine developed by Abdullah Azzam: their bodies would never deteriorate after death, and each would be granted a harem with seventy-two beautiful virgins who would never menstruate, never suffer from migraine headaches, and never be in a bad mood. In return for a momentary pain of death, they receive a "payment that lasts for eternity."[32] The suicide bombers are like the superheroes of American fantasy, who can never really be defeated: their willingness to take the law into their own hands in the struggle against evil will not only redeem the world but will result in eternal honor for the heroes themselves. But in contrast to American superheroes, they will achieve a marvelous sexual fulfillment in return for their deeds.

It is clear that this jihadic interpretation is countered by a more realistic and humane tradition within Islam itself.[33] Terrorism that causes civilian casualties is actually a violation of Islamic law. The *Sahih Moslem,* the official collection of Muhammad's sayings, explicitly forbids the killing of women in times of war. Sura 4 of the Koran also forbids the killing of fellow Muslims. Yet in many terrorist attacks, including the one on September 11, 2001, both women and Muslims were killed.[34] Marianne Williamson reports a conversation with the Mufti, the supreme cleric in Egypt, while they were both visiting India. He told Williamson's group of clergy and laypeople: "I am aware that for most Americans, when you hear the word *Islamic,* you usually hear the word *terrorist* in the same sentence. I wanted to speak with you to make sure you understand that Islam is a religion of peace. Every people has a dark element — a group which does not represent the larger group well. Obviously, we have ours. But please do not think that Islamic terrorists represent true Islam, any more than Christians who commit violence in the name of God represent true Christianity, or Jews who commit violence in the name of God represent true Judaism."[35]

Yet it must be recognized that Islamic radicalism can appeal to a body of texts in which Muhammad himself speaks words such as the following: "Behold! God sent me with a sword, just before the Hour, and placed my daily sustenance beneath the shadow of my spear, and humiliation and contempt upon those who oppose me."[36] Moreover, Islamic radicalism is a flight from the modern world, according to sociologist Karin Priester. It seeks to return to a time before the Enlightenment when people were subordinate to religious authority. Since it views divine authority as incontrovertible, there can be no "freedom of speech, freedom of the press, religious freedom, or freedom of conscience, so that the exercise of fundamental rights becomes a matter of blasphemy."[37] To struggle against this legacy is as great a challenge to Islam as the struggle against the Captain America complex poses to American Christians and Jews.

Zealous Fervor in Israel

Just as the American monomyth developed in an interplay between artistic imagination and historical events, some of the mythic guideposts for Israel reflect its calamities and triumphs. Cardinal moments that continue to live in the memory of Jewish people include the experience of diaspora after clashes with the Roman Empire in the second century, the steady experience of pogroms and expulsions in Europe — culminating in the Holocaust — and the contentious founding of the modern state of Israel in 1948. Always facing hostility from Arabic populations within and along its borders since then, Israelis fought a series of wars that gave them the opportunity to expand the boundaries of the territories they claimed as their own. An especially victorious moment in these conflicts was the 1967 "Six Day War" against Egypt, Jordan, and Syria, which resulted in Israeli control over the Sinai Peninsula, the Golan Heights, and the West Bank of the Jordan River (formerly belonging to Jordan), including East Jerusalem.[38] Although all Israelis and their sympathizers understandably share the "never again" mentality that demands a secure state, this mentality contains associated elements of zeal that work against possibilities for a peaceful state. Some of these reflect a strand of Israel's own history of violent zealotry, while others reveal the influence of the American tradition of mythic zealotism, for example Rabbi Meir Kahane of Brooklyn, a man who settled in Israel, formed a fundamentalist political party (Kach), and called for the violent expulsion of Arabs.

Reflecting a much older history of zealotry that Israel has ritually cultivated is the story of Masada, associated with the unsuccessful war of independence from Rome in the first century CE. In retaliation for this rebellion,

Rome obliterated Jerusalem and the Second Temple. Among those who had instigated the revolt and refused to be pacified were the most extreme Zealots, known as *Sicarii* ("dagger men"), who practiced terrorism and assassination, often attacking fellow Jews whom they considered too friendly to Rome. They were known to poison food eaten by Romans and to contaminate the water supply of Jerusalem. The historian Flavius Josephus recounts a story from the revolt against Rome (66-73 CE) of the Sicarii at the fortress-like rock of Masada. From their elevated and protected position at Masada they managed to resist capture for three years. When the Roman ramparts finally threatened to breach their fortress, the group reached a decision that every one of them, including women and children, should die rather than surrender. In the words of Josephus, "Every one of them dispatched his dearest relations. . . . So these people died with this intention, that they would leave not so much as one soul among them all alive to be subject to the Romans."[39]

Out of this episode came the term "Masada complex," defined by Susan Hattis Rolef as "the conviction that it is preferable to fight to the end rather than to surrender and acquiesce to the loss of independent statehood."[40] And from such unpromising historical materials, many in Israel have constructed an uncompromising answer to the Holocaust. For several decades, the Israeli military sought to make the Masada complex a part of the national ethos. In fact, until 1991, Israeli soldiers swore an oath: "Masada shall not fall again."[41]

The pessimistic, suicidal behavior of the Zealots at Masada bears little resemblance to Israel's more recent history. Its emergence as a Mideast superpower has brought its national mythos into synchronism with America's triumphalist tales of victorious vengeance over despised foes. Israel's founding in 1948, achieved in the shadow of the Holocaust after terrorist actions against Britain's Palestinian Mandate, fulfilled the Zionist hope of re-creating a homeland secure from centuries of anti-Semitic depredations. During the 1967 War with Egypt and Syria, in which the great powers refused to intervene, Israel won decisive victories and tripled the land it controlled with the loss of only 777 of its own soldiers. "Our basic objective will be to destroy Israel," had been the announcement by President Nasser of Egypt.[42] But David seemed to grow in strength under the attack of its neighboring Goliaths.

However, the Yom Kippur War of 1973 had a less thrilling outcome. Attacked by Egypt in the Sinai and by Syria in the Golan Heights, Israel was shaken by the forces who were so well armed by the Soviet Union and who fought with much greater effect than they had in 1967. This time 2,522 Israeli soldiers lost their lives in the effort to stave off a disastrous defeat.[43] Secretary of State Henry Kissinger played an important "shuttle diplomacy" role in bringing this conflict to an end, but this circumstance emphasized for many Israelis a loss of power to determine their own destiny. In the view of several interpreters of the Israeli national mentality, a kind of depression set in. Sociologist Amia Leiblich, in *Tin Soldiers on the Jerusalem Beach,* saw the war's impact as inducing a feeling of vulnerability, the belief that anything could happen. "Something very basic in society broke down, our view that our strength can prevent all bad."

Political scientist Charles Liebman spoke about "the myth of defeat": "society insisted on calling it a defeat . . . because it shattered a lot of the dreams and fantasies that Israelis had . . . following the Six Day War, as well as the notion that somehow Jews were safe here." Ya'acov Hisdai, a reserve colonel who served with the Agranat Commission, saw great psychic losses: "The Israeli self-confidence, the optimism, the feeling of the justice of the cause, all that fell apart on Yom Kippur." Hisdai also saw it as a crisis in Israel's interpretation of the justice of its power: "Up until 1973, there was a synthesis between rightness and strength. There was a feeling that we must be right since we win the wars, and winning the wars shows that we are just and right."[44]

Given the endangered myth of superpower, the moment was ripe for the resurgence of the ancient passions of zealotry. To a marked degree, those passions came to expression in fundamentalist movements such as Rabbi Kahane's Kach party, its offshoot "Terror Against Terror" (TNT in Hebrew), and in the orthodox religious party Gush Emunim ("Bloc of the Faithful") — each having an affinity for violent, suicidal acts of resistance against peace. Kahane's state-entwined theology is simple: "God wanted us to come to this country and create a Jewish state." And Kahane gave this imperative from God an exclusivist twist: "God wants us to live in a country of our own, so that we have the least possible contact with what is foreign." In Karen Armstrong's summary, "Kahane's theology sees enemies everywhere, enemies that are ultimately one and the same, whether they are Christians, Nazis, blacks, Russians or Arabs. Everything is seen from the perspective of Jewish suffering, and vengeance for that suffering."[45] The Gush Emunim theology is similarly absolute in its perspective. Responding to the Camp David Accords of 1978, the Gush Emunim Rabbi Eleazar Waldman decried it as a surrender to evil that would destroy the entire world:

The Redemption is not only the Redemption of Israel, but the Redemption of the entire world. But the Redemption of the world *depends* upon the Redemption of Israel. From this derives our moral, spiritual, and cultural influence over the entire world. The blessing will come to all of humanity from the people of Israel living in the whole of its land.[46]

According to Ehud Sprinzak, a scholar who has studied fundamentalist movements in Israel for several decades, the Gush Emunim did not officially sanction violence by its followers, though in fact an "underground" developed in which members of the sect secretly carried out acts of terror against Arabs.[47] The "Jewish Underground," led by two Gush members, Yeshua Ben Shoshan and Yehuda Etzion, planned attacks on Arab officials, schools, and the Muslim shrine at the Temple Mount, killing or wounding Arabs in several incidents. An operation to destroy the mosque at the Temple Mount was foiled. From his jail cell, Etzion published a tract that set forth his redemptionist vision of violence:

> The expurgation of the Temple Mount will prepare the hearts for the understanding and further advancing of our full redemption. The purified mount shall be — if God wishes — the ground and anvil for the future process of promoting the next holy elevation.[48]

Etzion felt no "constraints of political reality" because they governed only "those who live by the laws of existence," rather than the law of God. In his mind, the purgative violence would bring about "the transformation from the State of Israel to the Kingdom of Israel."[49] In a theocratic vision parallel to that of the late Ayatollah Khomeini in Iran and the Wahhabist Taliban in Afghanistan, Etzion envisioned a regenerated state controlled by priests.

Another advocate of violent actions against Muslims was Dr. Baruch Goldstein, an American physician who followed Rabbi Meir Kahane's Kach party, which had been disqualified from representation in the Israeli Knesset because of its racist provocations. Gershom Gorenberg, in *End of Days: Fundamentalism and the Struggle for the Temple Mount*, observes that Goldstein was married by Kahane and served as a party representative on the town council in Kiryat Arba, an Israeli West Bank settlement.[50] After treating two fatal victims of Hamas violence, he espoused Kahane's doctrine of holy violence. (Kahane had himself been murdered in New York during 1990 by a Muslim extremist.) Goldstein's eulogy for the two victims of Hamas, in the description of an observer at the funeral, "called for vengeance" and argued that those present were pathetically "guilty of their deaths before heaven" because of self-imposed restraints.

In addition to feeling vengeful guilt, Goldstein feared the momentum of the Oslo peace process being carried forward by Prime Minister Rabin. Like Kach and Gush Emunim, he believed that trading land for peace was an unholy compromise. To derail the process, he undertook a mission of conflagration in 1994 at the Muslim Tomb of the Patriarchs. Putting on his soldier's uniform and taking a submachine gun, he fired more than 100 shots at Muslims engaged in their Ramadan prayers, killing twenty-nine of them and wounding more than a hundred.[51] Goldstein himself was killed in the melee that ensued with surviving worshipers. While many Israelis were horrified by Goldstein's murderous attack, others offered praise and quickly elevated him to the status of a martyr. In his own Kahanist perspective, Goldstein was carrying out "'a religious act and a sacred mission' in which the very name of God was being sanctified."[52]

At a yeshiva in Kiryat Arba, where Goldstein's body was brought, Rabbi Dov Lior praised the killings as acts "for the sake of Jewish honor and to sanctify the name of heaven."[53] Goldstein's admirers have created a shrine and a book honoring him, *Baruch Hagever,* its title meaning "This Man, Baruch" and "Blessed is the Man."[54] He had conformed to the zealous model of Phinehas, whose murders had matched the zeal of Yahweh (Numbers 25). The biblical paradigm was confirmed by a conversation Allan Brownfeld had with a young Jewish activist at Dr. Goldstein's grave near Hebron. The young activist said that "the war with the Arabs did not begin with the intifada in the 1980s, or even with the establishment of the state of Israel. It goes back 'to biblical times' . . . indicating that the present-day Arabs are simply the modern descendants of the enemies of Israel described in the Bible for whom God has unleashed wars of revenge. Ultimately, he thought that the warfare could end, but only when Arabs leave the land and Israel is, in his view, complete."[55]

Goldstein's zealous murders had an understandable effect on the peace process for Israel. It gave the Palestinian organizations Hamas and Islamic Jihad a new argument for violence against Israelis, particularly in light of the fact that Israeli Defense Force security for the Tomb of the Patriarchs was exceptionally light on the day that Goldstein struck. After Ramadan ended, Islamic militants — who also share opposition to the peace process — began their new tactic of suicide bombings against randomly selected groups of citizens inside Israel.[56] And those grisly episodes of violence gave other opponents of the peace process a new justification for dramatic retaliations, thus inducing additional fears about the loss of biblical lands to the Arabs.[57]

Stepping forward in another burst of anger at pragmatic efforts toward the reconciliation of Arabs and Israelis was Yigal Amir, a 27-year-old law student who could not accept the idea of Palestinian self-rule in a territory that he saw as divinely destined for Israel's control. On November 4, 1995, at a rally in support of the Oslo Peace Accords in Tel Aviv, Prime Minister Yitzak Rabin spoke in the spirit of ancient Israel's prophetic realists. He addressed the crowd somberly and without redemptive promises of prospects for withdrawing from the often bloody West Bank territory that Israel had controlled for twenty-eight years: "This is a course fraught with difficulties and pain. For Israel, there is no path without pain. But the path of peace is preferable to the path of war."[58] After the singing of "The Song of Peace," as Rabin was leaving the rally, he was fatally shot in the back by Yigal Amir. During his arrest, Amir proclaimed, "I acted alone on God's orders and I have no regrets"; and on the day of his sentencing in court, Amir was righteously defiant about his murder of the prime minister. After his conviction, he uttered the words at the head of this chapter, that he had acted in behalf of "God, the Torah of Israel, the people of Israel, and the land of Israel."[59]

Spiraling Sanctified Violence

The ideals and deeds of the fundamentalist zealots in Israel are matched almost symmetrically by the Hezbollah movement in Lebanon and the Hamas "human bombs" movement mentioned in chapter 2. The Shi'a theologians of divine violence have insisted on a wholesale remaking of the world. The Ayatollah Bager el Sadr said: "The world today is how others shaped it. We have two choices: either to accept it with submission, which means letting Islam die, or to destroy it, so that we can construct it as Islam requires."[60] The Hamas movement has claimed more than 200 lives since the first human bomb exploded in 1994. The Hamas variation of Islam is yet another inventive way to sanctify violence through divine associations. The name *Hamas* itself means "zeal" or "enthusiasm." In his quest to understand the linkages between religion and violence in the contemporary world, Mark Juergensmeyer interviewed Dr. Abdul Aziz Rantisi, a physician and one of the articulate spokesmen for the suicidal violence. Dr. Rantisi objected to the term "suicide bombing" that has been used frequently in the press. He preferred the word *istishadi*, which means "self-chosen martyrdom," within a framework of belief where "all Muslims seek to be martyrs."[61] In his view, the targeting of noncombatants is permissible because this is a time of war. Rantisi believes that Israel seeks to destroy Islamic nationalism, pointing to the failure of Israeli soldiers to prevent Baruch Goldstein's attack on Muslims at Hebron as evidence. In the context of Israeli violence against Palestinians, he claims that the bombings are legitimate self-defensive acts of war, regardless of who dies. The spiritual leader of the Hamas movement, Sheik Yassin, has rejected the standing of the Palestinian authority to act peacefully on behalf of Muslims because there "is no such thing as a secular state in Islam."[62] Another physician associated with Hamas, Mahmoud al-Zahar, has spoken about Hamas's "final goal" in terms that echo the totalism of bin Laden:

It is to establish an Islamic state in Palestine, in Egypt, in Lebanon, in Saudi Arabia — everywhere under a single caliphate. There is no room for a Jewish state in this. . . . We will not tolerate a non-Islamic state on Islamic lands.[63]

Apart from its warlike struggle against Israel, Hamas engages in charitable programs that give the organization a peaceful face through its distribution of medicine, food, and educational opportunities. Unfortunately, its commitment to carry forward its struggle under the mantle of sacred violence probably guarantees that new Yigal Amirs and Baruch Goldsteins will appear to act out their rage against a peace process that would protect the rights of those they are determined to expel entirely from Israel.

The deadly spiral of sanctified violence in Israel has the power to make a militarized society increasingly acceptable to ordinary Israeli citizens. The scholar Ehud Sprinzak, writing more than a decade ago about the murder of Rabbi Meir Kahane, made these observations about his effects — despite the marginal status of his Kach party in Israeli politics:

The Israel that Kahane has left as a legacy is far different. It is still democratic, open and free. It is also brutal and violent. Its schools, universities, military camps, markets and synagogues are increasingly filled with populist chauvinism and crude anti-alien sentiment. Most noticeable are neo-religious ideas about redemption, the expurgation of the Temple Mount, the indivisibility of the Land of Israel and the necessity to transfer the Arabs out.[64]

In the ensuing decade of violence and counterviolence, we see policies for detention, segregation, the assassination of leaders, urban killings of Palestinian youth who throw rocks, the retaliatory destruction of homes, and military assaults on the instruments of Palestinian governance. Journalist Thorsten Schmitz observes that during the fall and winter of 2001 militant nationalism reigned supreme in Israel, lending passionate support for violent governmental policies.[65] However acceptable these practices become in mainstream politics because of atrocities from the Palestinian side, they merely bring about more of the same. By the spring of 2002, the spiral of violence reached levels that shocked the world; and another human bomb group, the Al Aqsa Martyr's Brigade, began to claim victims in the streets and business places of Israel. The dilemmas of security that both Israelis and Palestinians face offer a strong argument for the kind of coexistence that the prophet Isaiah envisioned. To continue in the path of zealous violence is disastrous for both sides. The looming heritage of Masada should contain a message relevant to all: that zealous violence can never achieve its redemptive goals, because in contrast to the myths, heaven refuses to intervene. This was clear even to David Ben-Gurion, a Zionist who fought a war to found the modern state of Israel. Alexander Zvielli describes Ben-Gurion's desire to find a middle path, even in the midst of violence:

> On August 23, 1946, David Ben-Gurion sent a message from Paris to a Mapai [labor party] conference in Palestine. His advice was: "Not Masada and not Vichy!"

Engaged in a bitter struggle with the British, Ben-Gurion perceived Masada as a symbol of hopeless resistance; and Vichy, the Nazi collaborationist government of France in the early 1940s, of course, meant a corrupt state of complacency. Ben-Gurion was thus warning the Yishuv that both Masada and Vichy were unacceptable to Judaism and Zionism. His view was shared by Yitzhak Ben-Zvi, Menachem Begin, and many other national leaders and historians who questioned the wisdom of educating people with a narrative that ends in suicide. Resisting the call of Masada — of all those symbolic Masadas that beckon us with their visions of relentless violence — is an important call to heed in our time.[66]

Aum Shinrikyo in Japan

Looking at the world beyond Islamic and Jewish militancy is hardly encouraging. As the bipolar structures of the Cold War lapsed, the world has once again become the scene of holy warfares of the sort that inspired thinkers of the Enlightenment to finally conceive a formal separation of church and state. For centuries of European history, visions of holiness, enforced by the power of government, had proven to be recipes for cyclical acts of violence and counterviolence. The warriors who conducted the Crusades and the internecine Christian wars on the European continent were little deterred by the Sermon on the Mount or the other resources of prophetic realism within the Judaeo-Christian tradition. And the terroristic visions of holiness in the twentieth century seem unaffected by these earlier historical experiences of disillusionment because they focus on purity and spiritual proofs of zeal rather than on pragmatic survival. The list of destructive moments can be extended far beyond the scope of this book, but a few more examples should suffice for the points we want to make.

In Japan, Shoko Asahara, a charismatic leader, persuaded highly educated, technically sophisticated followers to work with him in a scheme of bringing world redemption. He had attained enough respectability to receive invitations from universities for speaking engagements about his ideas on spiritual development. Generous financial gifts from followers allowed his organization to purchase significant quantities of weapons. By 1995 the wealth of his Aum Shinrikyo organization had reached perhaps as much as $500 million.[67] Indiscriminately eclectic in his taste for sources, he had visions of Freemasons and the CIA in demonic conspiracy. He also accepted the term "Armageddon" from the Book of Revelation, imagining that by killing enough people in Japan he could bring about the moral transformation of the world. Refashioning a concept from Buddhism, he projected that the coming Armageddon would spare those who had accumulated a protective quantity of good *karma:* "They will survive and create a new and transcendent human world."[68]

The scientists working for Aum Shinrikyo explored assorted weapons of mass destruction, especially botulism, cyanide, and the gases VX and sarin. Robert Jay Lifton relates that one of Aum's weapons specialists recorded a question from the master that had a chilling effect once it became known in Japan: "How much is a nuclear warhead?"[69] The weapons were important to Asahara because of his belief that he would personally begin the war of Armageddon depicted in the Book of Revelation. In a sermon that mentioned criticisms directed against his organization, he suggested that "we must kill as soon as possible all those opposed to the supreme truth."[70] Lifton cites estimates that Asahara's organization had murdered as many as eighty people, some of them dissident members of his sect who had become suspicious about its ultimate goals. The most audaciously destructive theological innovation of the Aum scheme was a notion that the righteous killing of everyone in the world could confer immortality on sinful people who might perish for eternity if allowed to live out the normal course of their lives. In one manuscript designed for members of the sect only, Asahara articulated a doctrine of mercy killing that proclaimed "the right of the guru and of the spiritually advanced to kill those who would otherwise fall into the plains of hell."[71] Asahara had designated this sort of redemptive murder *(poa)* and had composed a kind of chant for his followers:

> I will *poa* all wrongdoers.
> I will do whatever is required for the salvation of the world. . . .
> I will not stop this practice before I die from it. . . .
> Now as the Bible explains, Armageddon is finally approaching.

> I will join the holy army to *poa* all wrongdoers. . . .
> *Poa* is world salvation.[72]

Acting to serve this vision, Aum's members released vials of deadly sarin gas in a Tokyo subway station on March 20, 1995. Twelve people died and some 5,500 required medical treatment for their symptoms. The police pursued Shoko Asahara for more than two months, eventually finding him hidden in a coffin-like structure at his compound called Satian No ("Supreme Truth").[73]

Shoko Asahara and his Aum Shinrikyo organization offered a prefiguration for the appearance of Osama bin Laden. At the center of their convictions lies the furious certainty that the world's purification requires the potentially limitless death of others. Their contempt for pragmatic compromise, combined with a willingness to use weapons of mass destruction, signifies that the apocalyptic religious imagination has been captured by the armaments of secular government — chemical, biological, and nuclear. However diabolical those weapons are intrinsically, their use has been restrained previously by the pragmatic sense that government has the responsibility to ensure that life goes on. The concept of absolute purity accepts no such obligation.

Seeking Responsible Forms of Zeal and Jihad

The germs of zealotry appear to be generic to humans as they form groups. Given the fierceness of their rivalries over land and power, it is tempting to harden and sharpen the weapons with a layer of divine sanctity. The battles between Protestants and Catholics in Northern Ireland, the blessings of the Serbian Orthodox Church for the making of "Greater Serbia" in the 1990s, the violence of actions coming out of the Christian Identity and Operation Rescue movements in the United States — all demonstrate that the pacific teachings of Jesus have not immunized Christians. The attacks and counterattacks by Sikhs and Hindus, and by Hindus and Muslims, in India demonstrate the failure of another major religion, Hinduism, to quell the absolutist impulses of its adherents in confronting adversaries.

Reinhold Niebuhr analyzed a link between patriotic crusading and the universal tendency toward individual selfishness in *Moral Man and Immoral Society:*

> The man in the street, with his lust for power and prestige thwarted by his own limitations and the necessities of social life, projects his *ego* upon his nation and indulges his anarchic lusts vicariously. So the nation is at one

and the same time a check upon, and a final vent for, the expression of individual egoism.[74]

Niebuhr also saw clearly that religion could add an inflammatory element to the destructive altruistic patriotisms. In a world of profoundly diverse faiths, a transcendent religious commitment to the democratic spirit was imperative:

> It demands that each religion, or each version of a single faith, seek to proclaim its highest insights while yet preserving an humble and contrite recognition of the fact that all actual expressions of religious faith are subject to historical contingency and relativity. Such a recognition creates a spirit of tolerance and makes any religious or cultural movement hesitant to claim official validity for its form of religion or to demand an official monopoly for its cult.[75]

Every culture has episodes of zealous violence, either in the past or the present. If we could carefully examine the episodes of genocide, the mass destruction of civilizations and cultures, they may all relate to this human tendency that now surfaces in so prominent a form since September 11, 2001. That is why it is inappropriate at the present to concentrate a crusade against Islamic terrorism, as if this were part of an "axis of evil," the center of a single vast conspiracy against the "free world." It is far more appropriate for us, while seeking forms of international law enforcement, to probe our own religious traditions, employing the tools of historical-critical research, to find resources that might transform zeal and jihad into more responsible and humane dimensions that match our professed political values. It has become more timely than ever to recall John Saltmarsh's injunction from *Smoke in the Temple* (1646) concerning religiously inspired warfare:

> Let us not assume any power of infallibility toward each other . . . for another's evidence is as dark to me as mine to him . . . till the Lord enlighten us both for discerning alike.[76]

An important starting point must be reasserting a philosophical distinction between logical certainty and mere psychological conviction. This distinction lay at the heart of the separation of church and state that brought a measure of religious peace to Europe and the United States. Common to every contemporary movement that promises salvation through the destruction of others is the doubtful warrant of intense certainty. The incompatibility of mutually destructive claims to certainty argues for a measure of self-critical humility. We are not recommending here a rationalist model that counterposes reason against faith. The staggering losses of population under communism demonstrate that official atheism — priding itself on its reasonable view of the world — can wield the guns and garrotes of certainty as destructively as can the most fervent Christian, Hindu, Jew, Muslim, or Sikh. Nor do we recommend a life without myth. Rather, we recommend the cultivation of myths associated with prophetic realism — tolerant myths that make it possible to live with others who do not share the same beliefs. Indeed, without better myths and a self-critical fidelity to the realistic religious resources that each tradition has inherited, the entire world could come to resemble the ruins at the foot of Manhattan Island.

10 Consumed by Zeal and Jihad

And the Lord said to Moses, "Phinehas the son of Eleazar, son of Aaron the priest, has turned back my wrath from the people of Israel, in that he was zealous with my zeal among them, so that I did not consume the people of Israel in my zeal. Therefore say, 'Behold, I give to him my covenant of peace . . . because he was zealous for his God, and made atonement for the people of Israel.'"

Numbers 25:10-13

What Germany was to Nazism in the 1940s, Iran is to terrorism today. Whatever other countries it strikes, therefore, the U.S. can put an end to the Jihad-mongers only by taking out Iran. We must not only wipe out Iran's terrorist sanctuaries, its training camps and its military capability. We must also do the equivalent of de-Nazifying the country, by expelling every official and bringing down every branch of its government. . . . It requires invasion by ground troops, who will be at serious risk, and perhaps a period of occupation. But nothing less will "end the state" that most cries out to be ended.

from "It Is Time to Declare War," a full-page ad placed by
Leonard Peikoff, founder of the Ayn Rand Institute, in
The New York Times, The Washington Post, and numerous
university newspapers on September 20, 2001[1]

Gazing with horror at the jihadic impulses directed toward it, America needs to re-examine the kind of zeal that has marked its own history. What kind of violence toward others — and self-destructiveness — has come out of our zeal? Has it become a permanent part of the nation's psychic identity? What is the nature of the zeal that marks American nationalists? How does it lead to violence and self-destruction? Can the American psyche survive without it? These questions, derived from the history of zealous nationalism, can best be approached through an analysis of the linguistic and mythic roots of zeal. After defining the basic phenomenon, we examine the varieties of hot zeal, cool zeal, and artful zeal. We explore the sense in which these forms tend to consume both the zealot and his victim. Finally, while accepting the need for zeal, we propose a prophetic model for its healthy transformation.

Zeal in the Bible

The origins of the word "zeal" clearly reveal its psychological and moral dimensions. According to Norman Snaith, the Hebrew term *qānā'* comes from an ancient Semitic root meaning "to be dyed dark-red, black," signifying the deep emotion of rage that arouses such color in the face.[2] This fundamental connotation of red-faced rage is implied in the references to the "consuming" of zeal (Ps. 119:139; 69:9) and to the "burning heat" of zeal (Ps. 79:5; Ezek. 36:5f.; 38:19; Zeph. 1:18). Johannes Pedersen points out that zeal could be described as a fire "because it burns in the soul and makes the cheek glow. Yahweh speaks with the fire of his [zeal], it devours the whole earth."[3] Pedersen goes on to note the relationship of zeal to righteousness: "All righteousness is rooted in him [Yahweh], therefore he defends every breach in it. . . . Yahweh's hatred of sin is in its essence based on the fact that sin is inimical to life. It creates disaster in the soul, but at the same time it is a breach in Yahweh's will, a disobedience which offends against his honour."[4] Yahweh's zeal was therefore a constant state, a function of his righteousness. From this point of departure one can grasp the moral and psychological reality underlying the seemingly disparate aspects of the Hebrew term, which connotes jealousy, envy, rage, and striving.[5]

During the first century CE, zeal is primarily understood as an "eschatological intensification of the Torah," with emphasis on Israel's purity and freedom, the refusal to acknowledge Rome's legitimacy, and an expectation of the millennial consequences of armed rebellion.[6] The range of this biblical term is approximately the same as for the Islamic word *jihad*, which involves striving to realize Allah's will, to reform the world — by violence if necessary — to match the ideals of Islam.[7] What links these ideas is the reaction of the self to violations of its sense of right. Whenever the norms one accepts are thwarted by an adversary, zeal arises. Thus a standard definition of biblical zeal as it surfaced in the first two centuries of the Christian era is: "behavior motivated by the jealous desire to protect one's self, group, space, or time against violations."[8] Jealousy and zeal are thus similar inasmuch as the reaction of the lover at the displacement of the beloved's affections resembles the reaction of the moralist at the violation of his principles. In fact, it is an accident of the English language that the two terms "jealousy" and "zeal" are derived from a single Greek root, *zēlos*.[9] This has caused considerable confusion, because "jealousy" came to receive a negative connotation, while "zeal" remained basically positive. That the Old Testament God (in the older translations) was referred to as "jealous" became inexplicable, and that "zeal" itself is morally ambivalent was only rarely grasped.

The prototype of zeal for the biblical tradition was Phinehas (Num. 25).[10] He broke into the marriage tent of an Israelite man and his Midianite wife to spear them both with one thrust, spurred by his conviction that such intermarriage had violated the purity of Israel and brought about a plague as punishment. The striking thing is that this prototype closes the gap between divine will and human rage. A short circuit occurs by which Phinehas' zeal is flatly identified with Yahweh's. This so absolutizes human zeal that it justifies the elimination of due process of law and breaks across any restraint of social custom. Phinehas does not wait for a proper Hebrew trial but breaks into the taboo area of the trysting tent to act as judge and executioner. The later priestly tradition affirmed Yahweh's delight at this atrocity "in that he was jealous with my jealousy among them" (Num. 25:11). Phinehas came to be viewed as a prototype of faith, the hero of a long and violent succession of zealots.

The proof of Phinehas' rightness lay in the claim that he "turned back" Yahweh's wrath against Israel, redeeming her from the plague. By claiming this, the priestly writers of Numbers 25:11 formulated a theory that has had a long and deadly impact: it assumed that reverses suffered by the chosen people, whether sickness, famine, or defeat, were due to divine wrath against internal enemies. The traitor within the camp became the source of evil. Therefore, to rid the chosen people of such internal sources of corruption was to save the nation. The zealot became the redeemer, cleansing the nation by violence so that its triumphant destiny could be restored.

The model of Phinehas remains attractive today within the United States, where a so-called "Phineas Priesthood" has developed among members of the Christian Identity movement; its themes are its opposition to government authority, racial intermarriage, and abortion. One of the criminally convicted members of Christian Identity, Walter Eliyah Thody, confessed to some twenty bank robberies whose object was to finance assassinations of those favoring "one-world government." Declaring his right to murder those who disagree with him, he said: "We're having to fight to keep our country. Killing is normally murder. . . . Theft is theft. But if you're in warfare, then those same acts are acts of war. I'm at warfare against the enemies of my country." *Christian Century* magazine summarized Thody's endorsements of crimes "committed to avenge a transgression against God's law or the U.S. Constitution."[11] This emphasis on vengeance that is unconstrained by ordinary law helps explain the significance of William Pierce's book *The Turner Diaries* for the Christian Identity movement. It also points to the kind of zeal that Timothy McVeigh, who was deeply influenced by *The Turner Diaries*, lived out when he chose to destroy the Murrah Federal Building in Oklahoma City.[12]

Hot Zeal in Its Modern Embodiments

Three distinctive forms of zeal have been transmitted from the biblical tradition to the modern world. The first of these, *hot zeal*, is active, direct, and violent in its outcome. Driven by the conviction that God desires the annihilation of the wicked, it carries out the bloody task without a twinge of conscience. Its heroes stand in the succession of Phinehas: Samuel, who hacked the pleading Amalekite king to pieces before the altar of Yahweh at Gilgal; Elijah, who slew the prophets of Baal with his own sword on Mount Carmel; and Elisha, who called for the annihilation of the Moabites.

Hot zeal assumed decisive importance in Anglo-Saxon mentality during the Puritan Revolution — with its campaign to cleanse England of the presumed corruption of Catholicism. Under its impetus, altars were desecrated, works of art were destroyed, theaters were closed, and opposing clergymen were lynched. Fiery Puritan preachers, including the extremist "Fifth Monarchy Men," interpreted political resistance and desires for moderation as demonic forms of corruption. Their sermons and pamphlets urged the crowds to turn on one enemy after the other in furious succession. The rationale for annihilation that hot zeal provided was perfectly exemplified by Oliver Cromwell's command to massacre the Catholic survivors in the siege of the Irish town of Drogheda. He insisted that "this was a righteous judgment of God upon these barbarous wretches, who have imbrued their hands in so much innocent blood."[13] Michael Walzer notes a decisive difference between this revolutionary zeal and the spirit of the French Calvinist nobility, held

In the week of November 26, 2001, both *Time* and *Newsweek* delivered their news with the spirit of hot zeal by placing bin Laden in their imaginary gun sights.

Credit: © 2001, Time, Inc.; © 2001, Newsweek, Inc.

back by a certain nostalgia for the traditions of feudal chivalry: "There was too much regret, an emotion on which Calvinism does not thrive."[14] Hot zeal of the Anglo-Saxon variety was conspicuously lacking in regret, untouched by the plight of the victim and unconcerned about the social aftermath of the massacre.

William Styron has imagined the manifestation of hot zeal in his novel *The Confessions of Nat Turner*. He suggests that moral rage, nourished by reading the Bible, developed within Nat Turner a sense of divine mission to massacre slave owners in Virginia. It was a rage banishing all regret. The narrative depicts Nat reflecting for years on the necessity of "pure hatred." After a brutal slave owner forces two of his slaves to fight each other to exhaustion for the entertainment of a crowd, Nat Turner's rage finally overcomes its last vestiges of regret and prepares to break forth as hot zeal: "My heart seemed to shrivel and die within me . . . and rage like a newborn child exploded there to fill the void: it was at this instant that I knew beyond doubt or danger that . . . the whole world of white flesh would someday founder and split apart upon my retribution, would perish by my design and at my hands."[15] When the butchery of the rebellion was over, Nat was asked in his jail cell whether he regretted killing the children along with their parents. "'No, sir,' I replied calmly, 'no, I feel no remorse.'"[16] Here is a zeal so nurtured by the tradition of Phinehas that the rage of the self becomes the rage of God, eliminating any hindrance from mercy or due process. A bloody massacre, which finally consumes the zealots themselves, is the logical consequence.

The definitive expressions of hot zeal in the American experience were John Brown's raids at Pottawatomie Creek in Kansas and Harpers Ferry in West Virginia. This antislavery crusader's favorite line was: "Without the shedding of blood there is no remission of sins."[17] He believed that the sin of slavery could be atoned — and the nation redeemed — only by annihilating slave owners in the style of Phinehas. With his four sons and three other followers, he dragged five proslavery settlers out of their cabins at Pottawatomie Creek and hacked them to death. He was convinced that the raid was "decreed by almighty God, ordained from eternity."[18] Consequently, Brown had not the slightest regret about the murders he committed. Mrs. Doyle, the wife and mother of three of the men Brown killed, commented, "If a man stood between him and what he thought right, he would take that man's life as coolly as he would eat breakfast."[19]

When national atonement failed to come about as a result of these murders, Brown denied his participation in the event and planned the raid at Harpers Ferry. In one sense it was a farcical affair, so poorly planned and executed that the anticipated slave uprising could not possibly have succeeded. Brown's disdain for rational planning was perfectly consistent with the impulse of hot zeal: if the raid was God's will, God would see to its success. The logic of this position should have led him to infer from the debacle that it had not been God's will after all; but after his dissimulating testimony aimed at avoiding such an inference, he gained the conviction, as Allan Nevins put it, that he had "fulfilled a mighty destiny," and that God "would yet overmaster all opposition to his divine decrees."[20] The note he left with the jailer as he went out to the scaffold restated the zealous creed that would inspire the North in the subsequent Civil War: "I, John Brown, am now quite certain that the crimes of this *guilty land: will* never be purged *away;* but with blood. I had as I *now think: vainly* flattered myself that without *very much* bloodshed it might be done."[21]

One indication of the powerful appeal of this ideal was the response it aroused in the North, which culminated in the passionate marching song of the Union armies, "John Brown's body lies a-mouldering in the grave." Preachers such as Wendell Phillips eulogized Brown as "the impersonation of God's order and God's law, molding a better future, and setting for it an example."[22] Ralph Waldo Emerson extolled him as the "man to make friends wherever on earth courage and integrity are esteemed, the rarest of heroes, a pure idealist, with no by-ends of his own."[23] Henry David Thoreau picked up the theme of pure idealism and connected it directly with the Puritan heritage: John Brown was "one of a class of whom we hear a great deal, but, for the most part, see nothing at all — the Puritans. . . . They are neither Democrats nor Republicans, but men of simple habits, straightforward . . . not making many compromises, nor seeking after available candidates."[24] As far as Thoreau was concerned, the gaunt old man on the scaffold embodied an ideal that derived not merely from the Puritans but from Christ himself: "Some eighteen hundred years ago Christ was crucified; this morning perchance Captain Brown was hung. These are the two ends of the chain which is not without its links. He is not Old Brown any longer; he is an angel of light."[25]

Thoreau viewed the connection between Brown and Christ, in effect, through the Book of Revelation's lens. An uncompromising grip on the truth in the face of opposition by a corrupt government — one that begs to be purified or destroyed — this was the link Thoreau had in mind. In formulating his case, Thoreau secularized the zealous war tradition for America. Standing in the forefront was an emphasis on holding the transcendental truth without political compromise. If one held faithful, he was justified in short-circuiting the due process of law and even the democratic process itself. Thus an image of the violent idealist arose from John Brown's grave to capture the imagination of an increasingly secularized America. The secular idealism is clearly visible in Thoreau's peroration concerning the hot zeal of John Brown:

> He was a superior man. He did not value his bodily life in comparison with ideal things. He did not recognize unjust human laws, but resisted them as he was bid. For once we are lifted out of the trivialness and dust of politics into the region of truth and manhood. No man in America has ever stood up so persistently and effectively for the dignity of human nature, knowing himself for a man, and the equal of any and all governments. In that sense he was the most American of us all. . . . He could not have been tried by a jury of his peers, because his peers did not exist. When a man stands up serenely against the condemnation and vengeance of mankind, rising above them literally by *a whole* body — even though he were of late the vilest murderer, who has settled that matter with himself — the spectacle is a sublime one.[26]

A number of crucial motifs, whose religious origins were soon to be forgotten, are inserted here into the mainstream of American popular consciousness. They provide the raw materials for countless detective stories, comic books, cowboy Westerns, and commencement addresses: the distaste for the compromises required by the "dust" of democratic politics, the disdain for the institutions of due process of law, the desire for total solutions by holding to pure ideals, the inclination toward violence and its justification on grounds of idealism, and the "sublime" superiority of such an image of manhood. The myth of an idealistic superhero who redeems his community by selfless violence is here set on its path through the American imagination.

John Brown, of course, remains a polarizing figure for readers of American history. Russell Banks, who wrote a novel about Brown entitled *Cloudsplitter* (1995), made this remark that echoed the sympathies of Frederick Douglass and W. E. B. DuBois: "The reason white people think he was mad, is because he was a white man and he was willing to sacrifice his life in order to liberate black Americans."[27] While racism doubtless does account for much of the historical revulsion against the deeds of John Brown, there were contemporaries of Brown who immediately recognized the tragically self-destructive quality of crusading such as his. Ken Chowder, in his overview of Brown as an early American terrorist, records these judgments:

> Leaders of the Republican party organized anti-Brown protests; "John Brown was no Republican," Abraham Lincoln said. Even the *Liberator*, published by the staunch abolitionist William Lloyd Garrison, called the raid "misguided, wild, and apparently insane."[28]

Both Lincoln and Garrison were pragmatic enough to see the tragic potential in Brown's tactics, regardless of the cause to which he was wedded.

Hot zeal has been remarkable in its power to inspire establishment and anti-establishment figures alike, shaping actions on both the right and the left in American politics. It provides a common denominator between persons and movements that appear at first glance diametrically opposed. For instance, Theodore Roosevelt evoked the image of heroic battle when he declared at the Bull Moose convention, "We stand at Armageddon and battle for the Lord." As Winthrop Hudson has shown, the image was used by other national leaders, including William McKinley, William Jennings Bryan, and Woodrow Wilson, as well as their predecessors in the political arena.[29] Yet it also inspired the anti-establishment Ku Klux Klan, which emerged after the Civil War and again after World War I to battle against government's "corruption" of the zealous ideal by including African-Americans and foreigners. The heroic dimensions of this battle were eloquently set forth in Thomas Dixon's novel *The Clansman* (1905) and its film version, *The Birth of a Nation* (1915). In the case of the KKK, the zealous ideal was explicitly grounded in the biblical tradition, as Imperial Klokard ("Lecturer") William James Mahoney insisted in the 1920s:

We magnify the Bible as the basis for our constitution, the foundation of our government, the source of our laws, the sheet-anchor of our liberties, the most practical guide of right living, and the source of all true wisdom. Furthermore . . . we honor the Christ as the Klansman's only criterion of character. And we seek at His hand that cleansing from sin and impurity, which only He can give.[30]

Since these ideals were thought consistent with the religious heritage, they provided cleansing, so that a lynching did not arouse a sense of guilt: if the zealot was selfless, his violence could redeem. So far as the mythic premises were concerned, Roosevelt and Mahoney were in agreement.

While many commentators believed that the tradition of hot zeal came to an end in the frustrating jungles of Southeast Asia some thirty years ago, it is striking to observe how the same sentiments emerged in the wake of September 11, 2001. Senator John McCain, one of the few heroes to emerge from the Vietnam War, called early and impatiently for relentless war against terrorists:

Fighting this war in half measures will only give our enemies time and opportunity to strike us again. We must change permanently the mindset of terrorists and those parts of Islamic populations who believe the terrorist conceit that they will prevail because America has not the stomach to wage a relentless, long-term, and, at times, ruthless war to destroy them. We cannot fight this war from the air alone. We cannot fight it without casualties. And we cannot fight it without risking unintended damage to humanitarian and political interests.[31]

Among those who do not walk the corridors of power in Washington, the exhortations were even more zealous than McCain's call to "let the killing begin." Leonard Peikoff's prominently printed statement as newspaper ad, a portion of which appears at the head of this chapter, calls for an attack that would destroy every agency of government in Iran. Peikoff rejects any requirement to link our military behavior with any particular harm inflicted on the United States: "We do not need to prove the identity of these creatures, because terrorism is not an issue of personalities." Iran seems especially suitable to him as a target because it was the first country, in 1951, "to nationalize a Western oil company." In his view, the oil of the Middle East "rightly belonged to those in the West whose science, technology and capital made its discovery and use possible." He also approves of Secretary of Defense Donald Rumsfeld's reported refusal to rule out the use of nuclear weapons in fighting against terrorists. Peikoff also advocates fighting the war "in the manner most beneficial to the American cause, regardless of the suffering and death this will bring to countless innocents caught in the line of fire." And he relishes "the excellent words of Paul Wolfowitz, [that] we must end states who sponsor terrorism." This is hot zeal beyond anything that John Brown, who had to kill his victims one at a time, could imagine. In Peikoff's vision, entire nations may be exterminated through the use of nuclear weapons: "The choice today is mass death in the United States or mass death in the terrorist nations." The position taken by Peikoff in the post–September 11 world, though founded on the atheistic individualism of Ayn Rand, has remarkable affinities to the millennial apocalyptics who relish massive conflagration in the expectation that a redeemed and purified world will emerge.[32]

The Dominance of Cool Zeal

Standing in contrast to hot zeal is *cool zeal*, which is passive: it prefers to let others dispatch the victim and is concerned that the saint not be defiled in the regrettable course of battle. While Phinehas and Elisha were prototypes of hot zeal, the biblical books of Daniel and Revelation provide inspiration for the cool variety. In Daniel the saints never actually put the villains to death. This is a crucial motif in the familiar tale of Daniel in the lions' den, which provided a model for American heroism. The conspirators had sought to find something wrong with Daniel, but "they could find no ground for complaint or any fault, because he was faithful, and no error or fault was found in him" (Dan. 6:4). So they devise a scheme to get the king to sign a decree forbidding prayer, which Daniel's faithfulness forces him to disobey. They immediately cast him into the lions' den; when the king finds him alive the next morning, Daniel speaks with all the modesty of the cool saint:

> "My God sent his angel and shut the lions' mouths, and they have not hurt me, because I was found blameless before him. . . ." And the king . . . commanded that Daniel be taken out of the den . . . and those men who had accused Daniel were brought and cast into the den of lions . . . they, their children, and their wives; and before they reached the bottom of the den the lions overpowered them and broke all their bones in pieces. (Dan. 6:22-24)

The moral attractiveness in this ancient form of massacre was that Daniel himself played no direct part. His God saw to it that the lions did the job.

The author of Daniel suggests that the saint must keep himself aloof from the battle, pure and blameless while other agencies wipe out the evildoers. The premises and the outcome are precisely the same here as in the tradition of hot zeal. Evil derives from the behavior of certain persons who must be destroyed before God's kingdom can be restored. The same pattern appears in Revelation. There, too, the saints keep their robes white by allowing divine agencies to massacre the wicked. They repose in contemplation of the wicked burning in angelic sulfur pits. Their Roman persecutors and religious rivals will be destroyed, they are assured — but not by their own saintly hands.

We encounter this concept in such materials as the "The Battle Hymn of the Republic." Here the Lord himself is seen executing judgment through the agency of his Northern marching legions. But in order to fit into Revelation's fastidious tradition, the hymn sidesteps the fact that Union soldiers actually kill their enemies. If death comes to the Union soldier, he is "transfigured" by his Christ-like unselfishness; if death comes to the Confederate soldier, he has been cut down by the "terrible, swift sword" of God. Thus a traditional battle-song theme — the joy of killing the enemy — is completely sublimated in cool zeal. It is as if the Lord alone pulls the triggers while the soldiers serve as faithful and guiltless channels of remote-controlled wrath.

Several curious aspects of the American character become comprehensible when we recognize these conventions of cool zeal. One is the compatibility of the widespread pacifist sentiment with warlike behavior. Americans consider themselves a peace-loving people, having heard Christian messages about loving the enemy, and being nurtured as skeptics of the militarism seen in other nations. Many Americans feel that war is intrinsically wrong and harbor dreams of its abolition. Yet when war breaks out, they tend to conduct it with obsessive relentlessness. John Hay wrote from Paris in 1898 about his attitude toward the Spanish-American War: "I detest war, and I had hoped I might never see another, but this was as necessary as it was righteous. I have not for two years seen any other issue."[33] A pacifist public with a penchant for total war is an anomaly that continues to puzzle foreign observers. But it fits perfectly with the premises of cool zeal; for the nation so inured remains fastidiously pure and free from base motives such as hatred or avarice, while allowing the violent process of presumably divine retribution to take its course. That such a public could rapidly shift from a predominantly pacifist sentiment to a martial crusade, as it did in World Wars I and II, is thus not a sign of fickleness but a logical consequence. That such a public could regret and condemn the Vietnam War and yet tolerate the most intensive bombing in history for the sake of peace is equally logical.

The concept of cool zeal also explains the striking recurrence of appeals to pure motivation in American war pronouncements. The Spanish-

American War was "not a war of conquest . . . of envy or enmity . . . of pillage or gain," wrote the editorialist Henry Watterson in 1898.[34] President Wilson insisted in his declaration of war message of 1917 that "we have no selfish ends to serve. We desire no conquest, no dominion."[35] President Nixon constantly reiterated the selfless character of the Vietnam War. His long-term goal, as he told Allen Drury, was "first to get this war ended in a way that Americans can look back upon not ashamed, not frustrated, not angry, but with a pride that in spite of our difficulties we have been totally unselfish."[36] Such sentiments are not merely gratuitous exercises in self-righteousness; they are drawn from the ethos of cool zeal with the aim of preserving the purity of the saints in the midst of the apocalyptic carnage.

Finally, the model of cool zeal may help to explain something of the interplay between Manifest Destiny and the eradication of the American Indians so eloquently detailed in Dee Brown's story about 1890 South Dakota, *Bury My Heart at Wounded Knee.* The doctrine secularizes the apocalyptic wrath and battle themes of Revelation and Daniel, offering a nineteenth-century way to justify genocide as the regrettable price of divinely ordained progress. It was used, for example, by General Carleton after the decimation and subsequent deportation of the Navahos from their ancestral homes in New Mexico in 1864:

> The exodus of this whole people from the land of their fathers is not only an interesting but a touching sight. They have fought us gallantly for years; they have defended their mountains and their stupendous canyons with a heroism which any people might be proud to emulate; but when at length, they found it was their destiny, too, as it had been that of their brethren, tribe after tribe, away back toward the rising of the sun, to give way to the insatiable progress of our race, they threw down their arms.[37]

Shielded by the idea of remote-controlled wrath, Americans found it virtually impossible to assess blame for genocide. When one surveys the long series of massacres, reaching from King Philip's War in 1675-1676 to the Battle of Wounded Knee in 1890, Americans virtually never alleged or confessed individual responsibility for them. Well-publicized excesses such as the Sand Creek Massacre were occasionally condemned, but the responsible policy-makers were never brought to trial. By and large, the saints felt as guiltless in those engagements as Daniel felt about the fate of his enemies in the lions' den.

The consequences of this mythic rechanneling of responsibility were clearly visible in the wars in Southeast Asia. When the peace of the "free world" was threatened in the mid-1960s by "communist subversion," America turned first to mercenary troops and to superheroes such as the Green Berets. It was widely believed at the time that if they had only been given a free hand to shoot the outlaws down on Main Street, Hanoi, the outcome would have fit the mythic expectation.[38] But when conditions hindered a quick and clean victory, and the situation worsened, the American government pursued the immensely unpopular measure of sending in a half million ground troops. The result of so direct and massive an involvement of the saints in a dubious war was national division. The tradition of cool zeal had led us to expect more hygienic solutions. As General Lewis Puller said, "What the American people want to do is fight a war without getting hurt."[39] The mythic structure did not provide for hundreds of American deaths per week in so remote and sticky a cause. A large percentage of Americans began to disapprove of the war, not because it was inhumane or unjust but because its intractability threatened the substance of the national myths.

However, when the Nixon administration withdrew American ground troops and intensified aerial bombing, widespread resistance to the war faded again. As long as retribution was enacted by remote-controlled means, at little cost to the peaceful community of the saints, it was tolerated. The majority of Americans viewed it as a regrettable necessity, imposed by the recalcitrance of our enemies, but fully justified at whatever cost in civilian enemy casualties because of the purity of our motives. The public reaction to the murder trial and conviction of Lt. William L. Calley, Jr., for his part in the My Lai massacre in March 1968 was a case in point. Calley had taken his platoon into a village and killed some 500 unarmed men, women, and children before being interrupted by officers from other units who were sickened by what they witnessed.[40] But millions of Americans were outraged at the guilty verdict, and at least three-quarters of those polled approved President Nixon's intervention in Calley's behalf. "The Ballad of Lt. Calley" sold 300,000 copies in three days, according to one report.[41] In the June 1972 issue of *Psychology Today,* Kelman and Lawrence described the puzzles this presented to the scholarly community:

> Social scientists were at a loss to explain the widespread disapproval of Calley's trial. Rarely do 70 percent of a national sample agree on anything, especially current political issues; yet here were all sorts of strange bedfellows: hawks and doves, liberals and conservatives, whites and blacks, young and old, rich and poor, veterans and nonveterans. The standard dichotomies did little to predict which groups supported Calley and which did not. Nor could one predict a person's attitude by knowing whether he supported the war and the military.[42]

Kelman and Lawrence found that 67 percent of those polled felt that most Americans in Calley's position would shoot villagers if ordered to do so. The study concluded that submission to governmental authority was the key to the striking separation of individual responsibility from the killings one performed. But this conclusion was belied by the fact that passionate Calley supporters on local draft boards protested by refusing to carry out their lawful duties.

Calley was a typical impassive killer of the cowboy type defined in the western genre. He acknowledged that he did not feel he was killing human beings at all. Without personal malice or any other objectionable emotion, he was coolly enacting the remote-controlled retribution called for by his national ethos. And most Americans thought it grossly unfair to condemn him when he was being responsible to his calling. It shattered the mythic ideal that excused any killing for the sake of freedom as long as it was done with decent motives. As one respondent said to Kelman and Lawrence, "If they are going to train people to be good professional cool killers and send them out to war and tell them they're back of them and put them in an area where they *have* to fight and then let the men down — it's wrong to draft them."[43] It was like hauling the cowboy back from the golden sunset and convicting him for manslaughter after he had been forced into the duel that redeemed the town.

Artful Zeal's Destructive Legacy

While both cool and hot zeal are the moral reactions of a self that is deeply grounded in traditional ideals, there is a third form: the reaction of a self that is grounded in the will to power. *Artful zeal* is motivated by the desire for mastery, usually in the form of political advantage. In a calculating manner, it seeks the appearance of zealous behavior to win the support of the public. It is unscrupulous in its exercise of power because it is unhindered by respect for life. It emerges in a society that has begun to doubt and to modify the zealous ideals. And although those who practice artful zeal may not be sincere followers of an ideal prototype, there is a biblical character who perfectly embodies its structure and consequences. His name is Jehu.

The setting for Jehu's purge in 842 BCE was the struggle between the zealous Yahwist prophets and the Dynasty of Omri, which was incorporating Canaanite elements into the culture of Israel in the north. The prophet Elisha arranged to have the officer Jehu anointed as Yahweh's new king while the legitimate monarch, Jehoram, was recovering from battle wounds in the summer palace in Jezreel. The scene was cleverly arranged to make it appear that an ambassador from Yahweh had selected Jehu (2 Kings 9), but it was in fact simply a "military coup."[44] Jehu mounted his chariot and drove furiously toward the palace at Jezreel before King Jehoram could be forewarned. He shot the king with his bow and dispatched his cousin, Ahaziah, the visiting king of Judah, at the same time. Then he went after the old queen mother, Jezebel. He threw her down from the upper window, and she was trampled to death by Jehu's warhorse. In a laconic description of Jehu's remarkably nonchalant behavior in the midst of the bloody slaughter, 2 Kings 9:34 reports: "Then he went in and ate and drank."

From this point on, the story of Jehu becomes one of atrocity equal to some in today's world.[45] He arranged to have the seventy sons of Ahab executed, putting their heads in two grisly piles at the gate of the city. Then he went to work on the rest: "So Jehu slew all that remained of the house of Ahab in Jezreel, all his great men, and his familiar friends, and his priests, until he left him none remaining" (2 Kings 10:11). Several days later, he was traveling north and came upon a caravan in royal attire. Discovering that they were relatives of Ahaziah, the king of Judah whom he had already slain, he "slew them at the pit of Beth-eked, forty-two persons, and he spared none of them" (2 Kings 10:14). It was immediately after this massacre that Jehu had a revealing encounter with Jehonadab, a reactionary religious leader. Jehu invited the latter into his chariot with these words: "'Come with me, and see my zeal for Yahweh.' So he had him ride in his chariot. And when he came to Samaria, he slew all that remained to Ahab in Samaria, till he had wiped them out" (2 Kings 10:16). Clearly it was the artful appearance of zeal that Jehu sought. If he had truly been caught up in passion for Yahweh's cause, he would not have been concerned that it be seen by the molders of public opinion. His real goal was to establish a political dynasty, not to achieve some religious purpose, as he revealed in his slaughter of the Yahwist-inclined family of Ahaziah. He achieved his purpose when a properly impressed prophet produced an oracle legitimating his new dynasty:

> And the Lord said to Jehu, "Because you have done well in carrying out what is right in my eyes, and have done to the house of Ahab according to all that was in my heart, your sons of the fourth generation shall sit on the throne of Israel." (2 Kings 10:30)

The remainder of Jehu's actions reveal the same artful capacity. To wipe out the remaining believers in Baal Melqart, the Phoenician deity crucial to the former dynasty's alliance system, Jehu posed as a fanatical Baal worshiper for a time. He invited like-minded persons to enter the Baal temple with him and convincingly took part in the ceremonies before calling in his troops for the blood bath. At this massacre, as usual, he had a Yahwist fanatic on hand for public relations purposes (2 Kings 10:23).

But there is a limit to the most artful manipulations, and inevitably the discrepancies between appearance and reality show themselves. The massacres isolated Israel from its former allies in Judah and the Phoenician states.[46] After destroying the administrative and economic leadership of the Northern Kingdom, Israel, he was unable to defend the state against the neighboring Arameans. He was defeated in battle after battle, losing substantial portions of his monarchy's territory in the process, finally placing himself in vassaldom to Assyria to protect his dynasty. Since this involved allegiance to the gods of Assyria, no true zealot could have taken such a step. When one recognizes that Jehu thereafter tolerated local forms of Baalism (2 Kings 10:29), there are grounds to agree with those who doubt his sincerity. Owen Whitehouse put it bluntly: "He posed as a religious zealot."[47] But the long-term consequences of such artful rule were extremely grave. It was Jehu who ushered in the long dark age of Assyrian assimilation, and thus he popularized violence to such a degree that the subsequent self-destruction of the Northern Kingdom became inevitable.

The experience of Jehu's fallen kingdom helps us examine the beginnings of artful zeal among American leaders at the time of the Vietnam War. *The Pentagon Papers* reveal quite clearly the gap between official ideology and actual political goals. While the official rhetoric of "why Vietnam?" emphasized the reactive nature of the U.S. action, the government steadily and secretly pursued what military historian Richard H. Schulze, Jr., has described as sabotage and terror in North Vietnam. His book *The Secret War Against Hanoi: Kennedy's and Johnson's Use of Spies, Saboteurs, and Covert Warriors in North Vietnam* describes naval bombardments, sabotage teams, psychological warfare, and other disruptive acts, all begun before this country admitted that we were at war in South Vietnam.[48]

While public pronouncements stressed defending against Communist aggression, preventing a domino effect and honoring our commitments, it was the fear of political consequences that guided policy-makers. Stanley Karnow explains: "Having suffered through the Joe McCarthy era, the Democrats felt especially vulnerable on the Far East issue. After all, they had 'lost China' and pursued a 'no-win' Korean policy. Thus they came to believe that for domestic political reasons they could not afford another setback in Asia. Or as James C. Thomson formulates the decisive consideration: 'They thought that they had to hold Saigon in order to hold Washington.'"[49] This political motivation revealed itself over and over again through the highly contrived dissemblings of the Johnson Vietnam policy. The president himself admitted in justifying the 1965 escalation to his close advisers, "This is a bad year to lose Vietnam to the Communists."[50] It was always a "bad year" to face reality in Indochina because the administration feared the reaction of a zealous public. This helps to explain what Daniel Ellsberg called the "process of immaculate deception" on the part of three administrations. They consistently disregarded skeptical intelligence reports and knowledgeable opinion about the prospects in Vietnam in the hope that they could postpone the inevitable until after the next election.

There were differences during the 1960s and '70s in the artful rhetoric used to shield the political goal from public view. President Johnson sought to combine the dove-pleasing style of political realism with hawk-pleasing zealotry. He veiled his decision to escalate the war in realistic-sounding speeches warning against "committing a good many American boys to fighting a war that I think ought to be fought by the boys of Asia to help protect their land."[51] *The Pentagon Papers* reveal that there was a consensus in the administration to enlarge the war as early as the September prior to the November 1964 elections; but operations were delayed because "the President was in the midst of an election campaign in which he was presenting himself as the candidate of reason and restraint as opposed to the quixotic Barry Goldwater."[52] The abortive but highly publicized peace overtures were likewise "contrived more to placate American doves than to achieve a genuine settlement."[53] When the nation found itself in a large-scale war within months after the election, the rhetoric shifted to the vintage motifs of zeal. But the art was far too apparent to be convincing. A credibility gap emerged, and President Johnson was so severely hampered that he was forced to announce his decision not to seek reelection. The public could not accept so wide a war under the aegis of a mixed rationale of realism and zeal. Johnson regained his credibility only after he assumed the cool role of savior without political ambitions, relying on zealous rhetoric alone during the last months of his presidency. We now know, via the White House tapes secretly recorded by Johnson, that he felt a dreadful certainty that the war could never be won. Yet he was compelled to soldier on because America never loses wars.[54]

The art of Richard Nixon was much more successful. He relied from the start on the premise of cool zeal that a millennial peace can be assured only by a remote-control victory in which the saints incur no blame. Within the secure protection of this mythic structure, his maneuvering room was substantial, and the gaps between ideology and reality evoked low levels of public concern. He combined bellicose statements about refusing to accept defeat with suitably unselfish protestations about his own lack of political motivation. As he put it in the Cambodian invasion speech, "I would rather be a one-term President than be a two-term President at the cost of seeing America become a second rate power and see this nation accept the first defeat in its proud 190-year history." Combined with the promises to "end the war . . . to win a just peace" and to "avoid a wider war," this selfless motivation formed a mythic structure so tight that the public found it irresistible. That the invasion was in effect a widening of the war by taking responsibility for yet another regime, thus avoiding the onus of acceding to a communist victory in Cambodia, was clear for anyone to see. That the president's goal was precisely to become a two-term executive by avoiding such an onus was also apparent. But the public overlooked such discrepancies. To admit their force would be not simply to oppose Richard Nixon but to break with the national myth. The facade was unassailable because its enunciator fit himself so perfectly into the pattern of the unselfish savior. Vice President Spiro Agnew claimed this in connection with the Cambodia speech: "In times of crisis, presidents have always seemed to rise above self-interest and politics."[55]

The Vietnamization policy as a whole was a distinctive product of artful zeal. As a military strategy it was absurd from the outset. What rational person could believe that we would force the other side to relent by withdrawing our troops? That we could get our prisoners home by refusing to compromise? That we could improve the faltering morale of a client regime by infusing it with more weapons? That we could prevail in an essentially guerrilla war by reliance on bombing? The policy made sense only as an attempt to manipulate political opinion at home. This explains the frequent announcements of a future withdrawal of American troops — all scheduled for completion in 1972, an election year. It explains the constant reports of progress in the face of all evidence to the contrary. These devices ingeniously disarmed critics at home. But shrewd observers repeatedly pointed out the re-election strategy on which Vietnamization was based. Walter Lippmann described the dominant role of Nixon's desire not to "let anybody charge him with having lost the war" and his conviction that "he had to end the war in his first term if he wanted to be re-elected."[56]

There was one action, however, that convinced even the true believers that President Nixon's zeal was more artful than real: this was his visit to the People's Republic of China, which led many right-wingers to denounce him. For years he had preached the dangers of "aggressive international communism." He had accused John F. Kennedy of being soft on communism because of his desire to modify the U.S. stance toward the Chinese islands of Quemoy and Matsu. In the third television debate, on October 13, 1960, Nixon had noted with pride: "I continued to hammer hard on the general theme that in the struggle against World Communism we could make no greater mistake than to submit to blackmail — that surrendering a relatively small and unimportant area under threat of war would never satisfy an aggressor but would only stimulate and encourage him to step up his demands."[57] The Chinese communists, in short, were incorrigibly wicked agents with whom one ought to battle but never compromise. Yet in his 1971 announcement of the impending visit to China, Nixon referred to it as "a major development in our efforts to build a lasting peace in the world." It would be, as the final lines of the address claimed, "a journey for peace — peace not just for our generation but for future generations on this earth we share together."[58]

Except for the inflated image of millennial peace, this was the language of realistic coexistence, not zeal. And when the president actually shook hands and ate with Chou En-lai, true believers in the United States were apoplectic.[59] Was this not the same demonic communist leader whom John Foster Dulles, Nixon's erstwhile idol, had refused to greet at Geneva in 1954? Given that agreement to the One China principle, a negotiated settlement of the Taiwan dispute, and withdrawal of our forces from Taiwan and the Taiwan Straits were prerequisites for the visit, one wonders what led the president to move so far from his earlier stand. James Reston noted that in return for these concessions Nixon gained no practical result other than "a relaxation of tension as an argument for reelection."[60] But what could be more to the point? After persuading the zealots of his faithfulness to the cause, why would anyone object to his performing a dramatic gesture to win the support of the realists? Had not Eisenhower achieved his highest peaks in popularity after being cheered in foreign capitals as an emissary of peace? It made perfect political sense. But no convinced zealot would have done it.

This is not to reduce the issue of artful zeal to the simple matter of insincerity. The artful zealot may be fully convinced in his own mind that the cause for which he fights is God's cause; he may feel that his own political mastery embodies the divine will. Only the discrepancies between ideology and behavior offer a glimpse of the real grounding of the system — not in the divine will but in the will to personal power. The true zealot, whether hot or cold, is absorbed in his cause. He derives his significance not from the exhilarating battle itself, nor from his own triumph in the battle, nor from the political results for himself, but rather from the justice of God. There is a motif in "The Battle Hymn of the Republic" that states this quite powerfully: "Glory, glory, hallelujah, His truth is marching on." A person's transition into artful zeal is marked when he begins to derive his significance not from God's triumph but rather from the prestige or meaning that thereby accrues to his group or himself. Jehu sought the prestige of a dynasty and used the rhetoric of zeal to establish it.

President Nixon sought the meaning of his life in mastering crises, an opportunity that the presidency supremely offers. His book *Six Crises* reveals that it is not the triumph of some cause that to him was ultimate but rather the personal sense of mastery in the midst of the battle. The "six crises" were not occasioned by wandering into beleaguered towns and helping them out by engaging in regrettable duels on Main Street. They were all battles for Nixon's own prestige. Here was a man who sought such battles as the "easiest" times in life, the moments of his most creative challenges. These were, in the language adopted from American pietism, his "mountaintop experiences."

The price for these experiences of mastery was exorbitant, but since it was paid mostly in Asian blood, the American public remained largely unconcerned. It was only when Nixon violated the law and the Constitution in the Watergate affair that the country became seriously concerned. The revelations of Nixon's prevarications in the White House tapes and his consequent loss of public support led to the resignation of this artful zealot. But in the scales of divine justice, which measure the value of every human life — whether Asian or American — as equally precious, something far more important than the fate of a particular presidency was at stake. Even decades after these events, the country still has not acknowledged, nor grieved, nor sought to atone for, the atrocities it committed in the futile effort to gain "peace with honor." They make the destruction of the World Trade Center appear tiny in scale. As the history of Jehu indicated, artful zeal yields an awful legacy.

The All-consuming Nature of Zeal and Jihad

The destructiveness of zeal manifests itself first within the person of the zealot. From Shakespeare's Othello to Melville's Captain Ahab, and down to characters such as Adam Stanton in the novels of Robert Penn Warren, this process has been traced by sensitive writers. It is expressed in a single pithy sentence of the psalmist: "My zeal consumes me, because my foes forget thy words" (Ps. 119:139; cf. 69:9). The writer of these lines burns with indignation at the behavior of sinners. What makes their actions so infuriating is the conviction that what they do is against God's law. This short circuit of zeal diminishes the self by the fire of its own rage. The zealot admits no thoughts to his mind except those brooding on the boundless affront to divine justice and picturing the anticipated vengeance. The world becomes divided into the bitter camps of those few who stand with the zealot and those against him. Neutrality becomes a reproach, prudence a betrayal. This isolates the self, and a sign of its lost equilibrium is the obsessive repetition of first-person-singular pronouns: "My zeal consumes me, because my foes forget thy words." The self in effect becomes the sole axis of the universe. In absolutizing its own rage, it assumes a burden far too heavy for finitude to bear. Under its weight the self loses its sense of freedom as well as the openness that is required for creativity. It feels driven by necessity to a violent outcome for which it can no longer envision alternatives. In short, as the biblical tradition has always affirmed, idolatry first enslaves and then consumes the idolater; it then destroys everything he or she touches.

The inner constriction of idolatrous zeal places its stamp on every phase of action. The human values consumed within the zealot himself are destroyed also in the community he seeks to redeem. Despite the myth of a Captain America who always disappears from the scene at the end so that his behavior does not further influence the peaceful community, zealotry leaves ineradicable scars on the society it seeks to redeem, Robert Penn Warren's theme in *The Legacy of the Civil War*. He notes the change in mentality that resulted from the triumph of zealous exponents of "higher law," such as the Northern abolitionists who "claimed a corner on truth by reason of divine revelation. The man who is privy to God's will cannot long brook argument, and when one declines the arbitrament of reason, even because one seems to have all the reason and virtue on one's side, one is making ready for the arbitrament of blood."[61] Warren cites Stanley M. Elkins' thesis that the sense of responsibility in post–Civil War society came to be "transformed into implacable moral aggression: hatred of both the sinner and the sin." Added to this was the increasingly popular longing for the apocalyptic moment, the "total solution . . . to purge in violence the unacknowledged, the even unrecognized tension."[62] Warren refers to this as "higher-law-ism," the principle that one man plus God is the majority and thus can shed blood in his name and for his presumed cause.

Contrary to popular belief, the greatest danger in the United States does not lie in the excesses of hot zeal. Our dominant myths condition us to be wary of overt anger and extremism. Much more serious in its potential for destruction on the American scene is cool zeal. The widespread adulation of the cool superhero opens the door to impassive killings with good conscience for the sake of redeeming the community. The killer is misled by the myth to believe that he is responsible solely for pure motives but never for the consequences. According to Robert Penn Warren, "The man of righteousness tends to be so sure of his own motives that he does not need to inspect consequences."[63] The public seems to assume that fate will take care of the happy ending for the most dubious battles so long as the motives are pure. Given the risks of total war in the atomic age and the automated character of limited warfare, in which the directors and even the agents are so shielded from their victims that regret cannot emerge, a structure of cool zeal has ominous possibilities indeed.

Of the three forms of zeal, however, it is the artful variety that is finally the most insidious. Since it is tied to the drive for power rather than to any transcendent norm of justice, it is impervious to regret. One searches in vain through the state papers of Nixon and Kissinger for any semblance of regret or grief for the hundreds of thousands of deaths their policies produced. Protected by playing the role of cool saviors, such leaders are not restrained by public disapproval.[64] Their protestations about innocent motives are sufficient to defend the most blatant misuse of power. Such individuals will despise constitutional precedents and make political use of the very religious leaders and traditions that could stand in judgment of them, as the equally artful Bill Clinton showed. The only things they fear are the cracks in the zealous facade. That they will consider journalists and congressional investigators as mortal enemies is logical. They need to make every effort to restrict access to the truth, to protect the vital image from public scrutiny. Lacking the restraint of conscience, and having access to enormous powers, such leaders pose a far greater threat to a democratic society than do any foreign terrorists.

The Need for Modest Zeal and Jihad

Since consuming zeal derives from our dominant religious tradition, its antidote should be sought in that same tradition. We should begin with the central insight of the prophetic message of the Bible, embodied in the First and Second Commandments.[65] Although they do not explicitly mention zeal, they have directed our analysis of the idolatrous character of short-circuited zeal. The First Commandment — that one should have no other gods before Yahweh — calls on the faithful community to refrain from giving its ultimate loyalty to finite principles, institutions, or myths. In its initial form, the commandment did not require that one deny the existence of such factors, but merely that one cease to hold them as ultimate. The Second Commandment is simply the reverse side of this admonition: that one refrain from worshiping any "graven image" of ultimate reality, whether it be in the form of a visual image or an abstract definition. Both commandments deal with the avoidance of idolatry. They serve to protect rationality and humanity itself by freeing it from bondage to manmade principles, institutions, or ideologies.

The relevance of these commandments to the problem of zeal should be obvious. Taking the First and Second Commandments seriously would prevent one from falling prey to the fatal short circuit between human rage and divine rage. Zeal would then lack the power to consume, because it would never be able to claim ultimate approval for its definitions of the right or its strategy to deal with what it deems wrong. It would take itself less seriously and would respect the restraints of custom and law. Taking these commandments seriously would also serve to protect the community from the arbitrary actions of the self that constantly tend to absolutize its own goals and to infringe on the lives of others in attaining them.

We would be falling prey, however, to some of the worst habits of the Puritan mentality if, having noted the grave dangers of zeal, we were now to eradicate it completely from American ideology. It is not zeal itself, but the absolutizing of zeal, that is destructive. Only when the fatal short circuit occurs between human and divine rage does idolatry commence. Short of this barrier, however, zeal is an absolutely essential component of the moral life. If we are committed to love and justice, for example, we must strive for them even though we are incapable of devising their perfect definition or even of making a precise discrimination in their application. It is also clear that pursuing perfection, while driven by the lure of positives, cannot be done without the vigorous rejection of the alternatives.[66] This point was grasped in an interesting but problematic article by the Unitarian clergyman Horace Bridges, published in the *Atlantic Monthly* when the United States was entering World War I. He wrote of "a duty of hatred, an imperative of conscience prescribing resentment, as unconditional as the very law of love itself; nay, the law of resentment is the necessary complement of the law of love and pardon."[67] Though Bridges went on to define the German war effort in the categories of absolute and bestial evil, which overstated the case, his point is nonetheless valid: there is a duty of hatred, but it remains healthy only so long as a person continues to act on the premise that his or her hatred is not identical with God's hatred.

To deny the necessity of zeal and to eliminate it from American morals would open the door to indifference or nihilism; without zeal for some righteous purpose the American moral sense could disintegrate. It could fall into the apathy that precedes aimless and utterly destructive violence, as Rollo May suggests.[68] Or it could seek only selfish ends, using weaker nations for its own profit and destroying those who resist or interfere. The prospects of vast American power, unrestrained by the internal flywheel of its own sense of moral obligation to mankind, are terrifying. The search for terrorists under every tree — and the strategy of coping with them by bombing them — could transform the rest of the globe into a replica of the denuded and pockmarked landscape now visible in parts of Indochina.

We must grapple with the paradox of zeal, namely, that when it takes itself with ultimate seriousness or betrays its impulse with apathy, it sickens and becomes destructive. To confront this would require giving up our propensity for total solutions and discovering some procedures for muddling through. To face this paradox would be to acknowledge our finite situation and take up the complex tasks that all other nations must face. But there are resources in the more realistic portions of the biblical message that may guide the development of procedures to keep zeal responsible.

One resource is the approach taken by Jesus concerning the zealous rage that was so popular a feature of religious and political life in his time. It was widely assumed that righteous zeal was one of the clearest signs of devotion to God and his law. The law forbade the sinful expression of rage and lust, but it did not attempt to suppress these emotions. The "evil urge" and the "good urge" were viewed as the spontaneous and uncontrollable heritage of the sons of Adam, and it was pointless to hold a man responsible for anything but his actual deeds.[69] In an environment dominated by myths of zealous nationalism, these assumptions provided the perfect justification for idolizing rage. It was very easy to identify one's spontaneous anger as a God-given call to enact judgment on some malefactor. Zealous murders were very much the vogue, and the religious parties in Jesus' time fought and killed each other with ferocious zeal.[70] Over and over, this zeal generated atrocities against the Samaritans or revolts against the Romans.

Jesus was dealing with one of the foremost social and political problems of his time when he challenged the traditional attitude toward anger:[71]

> You have heard that it was said to the men of old, "You shall not kill; and whoever kills shall be liable to judgment." But I say to you that every one who is angry with his brother shall be liable to judgment; whoever insults his brother shall be liable to the council, and whoever says "You fool" shall be liable to the hell of fire. (Matt. 5:21f.)

If anger was subject to divine judgment, two important consequences followed: it was not automatically identifiable with divine zeal, as the dominant religious tradition in the first century encouraged people to believe; and it was a matter for which persons were to be held responsible. This countered both the short circuit of zeal and the resignation to Adamic urges. To accept Jesus' view is to abandon the claim that one's anger is identical with that of the divine judge, so that any action derived from such anger would automatically be approved. Killing in God's name thus turns out to be murder. Furthermore, the wording of Jesus' statement carries a clear reminder of one of his basic theses, that the enemy is a "brother." To "insult" him or to call him "Thou fool!" is to lose sight of shared humanity and to prepare the way to annihilation.[72] The remarkable advice Jesus gave elsewhere to "turn the other cheek" and "walk the second mile" was aimed at recognizing precisely this essential brotherhood. To love your enemy and pray for those who despitefully use you (Matt. 5:44) was the logical climax of this new doctrine of responsibility.[73] It redirected zeal to a healthy concern for justice in relation to the life of one's enemy.

It is important to note that this approach is a far cry from what is suggested by Bible interpreters schooled in the tradition of cool zeal. Jesus does not say, "Be not angry! Repress zeal! Be a nice person!" Generations of well-meaning Christians have misunderstood Jesus' statement in this way. He explicitly does not say it is wrong to be angry, but rather that "everyone who is angry . . . shall be liable to judgment." These are not in any sense the same thing. The one is a call to repression, which ends up in hideous forms of remotely enacted wrath, disguised by hypocrisy; the other is a call to mature responsibility not only for the moral rage itself but also for its actions and aftermath. Jesus was not the slightest bit concerned, as the tradition of cool zeal has been, with preserving the image of the self from unfortunate emotions; rather, he was concerned with preserving the health of the self and protecting the neighbor from zealous behavior.

For zeal to be responsible, it must acknowledge the limitation of its moral vision and still dare to act in prudent faith. Only when zeal is fixed steadfastly on transcendent justice, which stands forever beyond the limitations of human achievements, can it remain both effective and humble. The critical need is for a pilgrim zeal,[74] striving for the lasting city but never arriving; moving forward with courage and prudence, but never overrating the results; and respecting persons because of their intrinsic value in the eyes of divine righteousness. Such pilgrim zeal may be glimpsed in the life and thought of Abraham Lincoln and in some of the best of American literature. Other nations and religious traditions have comparable resources that are as cogent for jihad as for zeal. There is now a global necessity to make use of these resources before it is too late.

11 Evil as a Grand Conspiracy

How can we account for our present situation unless we believe that men high in this Government are concerting to deliver us to disaster? This must be the product of a great conspiracy, a conspiracy on a scale so immense as to dwarf any previous such venture in the history of man. A conspiracy of infamy so black that, when it is finally exposed, its principals shall be forever deserving of the maledictions of all honest men. . . . What is the objective of the great conspiracy? . . . to diminish the United States in world affairs, to weaken us militarily, to confuse our spirit with talk of surrender in the Far East and to impair our will to resist evil. To what end? To the end that we shall be contained, frustrated and finally: fall victim to Soviet intrigue from within and Russian military might from without. Is that farfetched? There have been many examples in history of rich and powerful states which have been corrupted from within, enfeebled and deceived until they were unable to resist aggression.

Senator Joseph McCarthy in a speech delivered
before the U.S. Senate on June 14, 1951[1]

It should not be hidden from you that the people of Islam had suffered from aggression, iniquity and injustice imposed on them by the Zionist-Crusaders alliance and their collaborators, to the extent that the Muslims' blood became the cheapest and their wealth as loot in the hands of the enemies. Their blood was spilled in Palestine and Iraq. The horrifying pictures of the massacre of Qana, in Lebanon, are still fresh in our memory. Massa-

192

cres in Tajakestan, Burma, Cashmere, Assam, Philippine, Fatani, Ogadin, Somalia, Erithria, Chechnia and in Bosnia-Herzegovina took place, massacres that send shivers in the body and shake the conscience. All of this and the world watch and hear, and not only didn't respond to these atrocities, but also with a clear conspiracy between the USA and its allies and under the cover of the iniquitous United Nations, the dispossessed people were even prevented from obtaining arms to defend themselves.

from "Declaration of War against the Americans Occupying the Land
of the Two Holy Places (Expel the Infidels from the Arab Peninsula),"
a message from Osama bin Muhammad bin Laden to his Muslim
Brethren all over the World Generally and in the
Arab Peninsula Specifically, August 1996[2]

In his statesmanlike account of the origins of the Vietnam War, Louis J. Halle describes the impact of conspiratorial thinking on American policy. Believing that every frustrating diplomatic feature of their world had been devised by evil adversaries, American planners came to misunderstand completely the nationalistic thrust of Ho Chi Minh and his movement, to link them prematurely with the Chinese Communists, against whom they were seeking to maintain their independence, and to take over the abortive French efforts to sustain a pro-Western regime there. "From the beginning the West was governed by the myth of a single conspiracy for world conquest under the direction of a satanic band in the Kremlin to whom all who called themselves Communists, the world over, gave blind obedience."[3] Since the mid-1950s, it should have been evident how little the Russians actually were able to control events in allied countries. The split between Russia and China, preceded by the independence movements in Communist countries of Eastern Europe, gave the lie to the conspiracy premise. Nevertheless, the United States committed itself to the civil war in Indochina on false premises and was unable to disentangle itself even after signing peace agreements.

What are the sources of this variant of conspiracy theory, which has had such pervasive effects on the American mind and America's policies? What answers can it give concerning the origins of evil in the social realm? How does the theory find and interpret evidence and how do those processes energize zealous nationalism? How did it mesh with such Cold War motifs as the "domino theory," the defense posture based on enemy capabilities rather than political probabilities, and the unwillingness to compromise on international issues? Now that the Cold War has ended, why has a theory focused on a conspiracy of evil remained so compelling an explanation of the shocking events of September 11, 2001?[4] In providing tentative answers to these questions, we can set the stage to show the relevance of Jesus' campaign against the conspiracy theology so popular in his time.

Conspiracy Theory in the Bible

The negative connotation of "conspiracy" and its use in explaining the origin of misfortune are closely related to the development of zealous nationalism. One can discern in the Phinehas tradition the beginnings of a conspiracy theory in which the actions of a few evil members of the chosen people evoke the wrath of God (Num. 25). It could be "turned back" only by the elimination of the source of corruption. But in a cultural situation where the ultimate source of evil was thought to be Yahweh himself and where no demonic counterforce to Yahweh was thought to exist, a fully developed conspiracy theory of evil could not arise. Israel's traitors occasionally associated themselves with her enemies, as in the case of Phinehas' antagonist, who married a Midianite woman. Yet it was disobedience to Yahweh's law on the part of Israelites themselves that brought down wrath upon them. In this sense, the early period of Israel's thought affirmed human responsibility for evil.

Only after the exile, during the period of Persian domination (538-323 BCE), did the basis for a full-blown conspiracy theory begin to appear. This was the period when dualistic thought patterns, probably influenced by the Zoroastrian religion of Persia, began to infiltrate the theology of Judaism. God was seen opposed by a demonic counterforce, surrounded by legions of evil angels who stirred up opposition on earth against the agents of righteousness. In the Persian empire, where the majority of Jews lived for this 200-year period, Ahura Mazda, the god of light, was thought to have called the emperor to wage war against the god of darkness and his conspiratorial throng. External and internal enemies of the empire were assumed to be the pawns of this demonic force. Thus history became a battleground between the armies of good and evil. It was precisely during this period that the idea of a devil and his demonic army of spirits began to appear in Judaism. And in this milieu a conspiracy theory of evil emerged for the first time, virtually taking its modern form, in the Book of Daniel.

The stories of Daniel and his friends Shadrach, Meshach, and Abednego present evil as deriving neither from the great empire that held Israel captive nor from the sin of the chosen people themselves. They portray foreign emperors in a benign light, even at times as Yahweh's servants, and faithful Jews had no compunctions about serving their administrations. As for the heroes, the author of Daniel took great pains to portray their innocence. They faithfully served both the empire and the laws of God, refusing the corrupting food and drink of the palace, yet doing their duty honestly without hope of personal gain. They prayed three times a day, kneeling in the direction of Jerusalem. There was no evil in them. They did not even sin inadvertently, since they came from families that taught them the details of the Jewish law. For as the author insisted, they were of the Jewish "nobility, youths without blemish, handsome and skillful in all wisdom; endowed with knowledge [of the Torah], understanding learning, and competent to serve in the king's palace" (Dan. 1:3-4). Untouched by the foibles ascribed to earlier heroes of the Israelite faith, such as David, these perfect men were not thought susceptible to the tragedy that befell others. The author of Daniel portrays evil as a result of the conspiracy of evil people. For example, after Daniel has been made prime minister under King Darius, the "presidents and satraps" began to oppose him. Finding it impossible to discover "any ground for complaint," they worked out a plot and came "by agreement to the king" (Dan. 6:4-6). They set forth the suggestion that no one in the empire should make a petition to anyone but to the king himself. The king signed it with the naivete of someone as untouched by evil as Daniel himself. When Daniel was caught praying to God at his usual time, he was apprehended by the plotters and thrown to the lions. Thus evil came to the perfect man as punishment for his spiritual fidelity.

Of course, the conspiracy could not really harm Daniel, because he was so righteous that the lions would not touch him. He survived the night in the lions' den, and the next day the conspirators were themselves thrown into it to be devoured. A decisive element in the conspiracy theory was that the good guys always come out unscathed, a theme that worked about as well at the time Daniel was written — when the faithful Jews were being slaughtered by Antiochus Epiphanes — as it has ever since. But when precisely the same plot replayed in the case of Daniel's three friends, and they survived in the fiery furnace "without a hair singed . . . nor any smell of burning" (Dan. 3:27), a myth was born. It was the myth of the saints in battle against the grand conspiracy.

The myth received extensive elaboration in the apocalyptic books written between the second century BCE and the New Testament period. The idea of fallen angels, who disobey God out of jealousy, emerged to explain the origin of Satan. The creation stories were reinterpreted to emphasize that Satan's voice beguiled Eve and led to the fall of humankind. The older Hebrew conception of evil as originating with willful human disobedience was dismantled, and humans emerged as pawns of demonic or angelic forces. Determinism altered the traditional ideas of human freedom and responsibility.

History increasingly became the battleground between cosmic forces of good and evil, and people were called upon to take sides in the ineluctable war. By the Roman period some people believed that demonic forces had taken over the world empire itself. In apocalyptic materials found at Qumran, the "sons of light" were called to prepare themselves for battle against the "sons of darkness," who conducted earthly policies of "Belial," prince of demons (1QM 1:1-5). Against whatever odds, victory would be inevitable, for God would not allow the conspiracy against his justice to prevail.

The classic form of the myth of the grand conspiracy is set forth in the Book of Revelation.[5] It explains evil as emanating from Satan, who inspired the heretics within the church; the opposition from the side of the Jewish synagogues, called "Satan's synagogue" by the author (Rev. 2:9; 3:9); and the persecution by the Roman Empire, the "beast" from Satan's deep (Rev. 13). These institutions tempt the faithful into false worship and kill them when they retain their integrity. Posed against Satan's horde is the heavenly army of God, repeatedly entering battle until evil is annihilated. History moves inexorably from the primeval battle between Michael's angelic army and the Satanic horde (Rev. 8:2–11:18) to the current struggles between the church and the bestial empire (Rev. 11:19–15:4). The stages of these battles are seen as predestined by God, so that the seer can reveal to his audience ahead of time the sequence of the catastrophes. Seals are opened and bowls of wrath are poured out in orderly succession. There is no doubt about the ultimate goal of world history: it will be the final destruction of the demonic grand conspiracy and all who serve it.

The solution to the problem of evil will be the victory of the lamb. Paul Minear's commentary on Revelation points out that the terms "victor" and "victory" dominate each major section of the Apocalypse.[6] The saints alone will enjoy the fruits of the victory. As Revelation 2:26-27 indicates, they will have the pleasure of keeping the subsequent world forcibly under their control: "To the victor who keeps my works until the end, I will give him power over the nations, and he shall rule them with a rod of iron, as when earthen pots are broken in pieces." This is spelled out in Revelation 20, where the saints reign with Christ for the millennial period while Satan is chained in the pit — "so that he might seduce the nations no more till the thousand years were over" (Rev. 20:3, Minear). One final battle remains, in which Satan and his cohorts will be destroyed and thrown into the lake of fire. Then in the heavenly Jerusalem, with evil completely banished, the saints will rule triumphantly forever. This passage thus affirms the total solution to the problem of evil in the end as accessible to the people of God: "The victor will inherit all these things" (Rev. 21:7, Minear).

Other key assumptions of the grand conspiracy are related in Revelation to this grandiose scheme of victory over evil. If the saints are to rule, they must be perfectly righteous. Revelation 14 describes the 144,000 saints: "No lie was found in their lips; they are faultless" (Rev. 14:5, Minear). The stereotype of the enemy is equally radical. Agents of Satan are utterly lacking in human qualities. Even after fearsome punishment, they remain incorrigible idolaters, murderers, sorcerers, and fornicators (Rev. 9:20f.). Since they are irredeemable, their destruction is the single aim of God and his saints. Although the saints are not directed to take up the sword, lest they besmirch their white robes, they cry out for annihilation: "How long until you [God] judge and avenge our slaughter by the earthdwellers?" (Rev. 6:10, Minear). That the entire world may be destroyed in this slaughter is a delightful prospect for the saints (Rev. 16:19-21).

Those who accepted this vision of the grand conspiracy and its ultimate destruction through the apocalyptic battle would be willing to accept the prospects of such a battle at any appropriate moment; it was perfectly logical that the world needed to be destroyed to cure the source of evil.

A Realistic Theory of Evil

The books of Daniel and Revelation offer a fully developed conspiracy theory of evil. To understand the impact of this theory, we must distinguish between its main characteristics and prophetic realism. We begin with its interlocking premises, and then move to its consequences, demonstrating its appeal to those schooled in the tradition of zealous nationalism.

The traditional doctrine of universal, willful sin crucial to prophetic realism maintains human responsibility for evil. In the creation story in Genesis, the desire of humans to be "like God, knowing good and evil" (Gen. 3:5) in some absolute sense, led to the eating of the forbidden fruit and brought in its wake the poisonous residue of alienation and violence. In contrast, the conspiracy theory assumes that evil originates in the demonic realm and is not the fault of humankind at all. A fully developed conspiracy theory thus requires the existence of a devil, a cosmic counterforce to the divine will. This malevolent agent must be equipped with vast and cunning powers; it must be capable of infiltrating the web of historical experience, luring its willing and unwilling agents into its wicked design. One must imagine a vast network of historical and angelic agents of this malevolent design. Individual agents may indeed believe that they are acting righteously, but the person with insight into the grand conspiracy knows better: they are nothing but the unwitting tools or fellow travelers of Satan.

The conspiracy theory also demands a break with the traditional biblical doctrine of human freedom, an essential component of personal responsibility. The prophetic premise is that those addressed by the divine word are capable of changing, of repenting so as to avoid the disaster that might otherwise overtake their sinful behavior. This must be replaced by a deterministic doctrine if the conspiracy theory is to reach its full development. Since humans are merely the pawns of cosmic forces, their particular backgrounds and personal aims in life need not be considered. Evil people must be destroyed because they are the extension of the demonic force; it is never assumed that they act out their own desires for mastery or justice. Likewise, the saints are not fully accountable for their deeds because they are being used by God. The good or evil they do, such as acquiescing in the destruction of the world, is God's doing, not their own. Human responsibility is limited to the matter of faithfulness to the force whose pawn one has become.

The prophetic tradition views humans as involved in the tangled web of their own sin, social alienation, and international pressures, in which the best they can hope to achieve is a modicum of justice by the grace of God. In contrast, the conspiracy theory believes in a total cure for the problem of evil, a cure that will be accomplished by the violent elimination of the satanic agents. This may be accomplished by God or one of God's mysterious agents, or it may require the work of an army of the saints. But there will be no muddling through. Evil, like a problem of plane geometry, is susceptible to a perfect solution.

History is thus the arena of cosmic warfare. Its plot is never visible in the struggle of the actors on the darkling plain, but only in the forces of good and evil that loom over the battlefield. The complex knot of historical causation, so baffling a puzzle to the historian, can be cut with one stroke of the sword. It is the grand conspiracy of Satan that gives shape to history. Only when the apocalyptic battle itself is fought can history reach its climax and be dissolved in the golden light of the eternal Jerusalem. There the saints will live forever in perfect peace, no longer harassed by the agents of wickedness. In the meantime, the responsibility of the saints is not to guide history creatively or to take steps for human betterment, but simply to be faithful to God's side in the cosmic struggle. It matters little whether their zeal is hot or cool; the important thing is that right triumph, though the world itself be destroyed in the process.[7]

The conspiracy theory eliminates the need or possibility for any pragmatic assessment of historical or political factors. A person privy to the grand conspiracy knows ahead of time. The only interest in details relates to ascertaining the stages in the predestined course of history. The peculiar motives of individual actors and the variations in national or individual temperament are irrelevant in assessing probabilities for the future. Power factors play no role. Though a handful of the saints be surrounded by foes, their ultimate triumph is assured. They will gladly participate in the apocalyptic battle because they already know the outcome: after the incineration of the world, they will inherit the heavenly Jerusalem.

The conspiracy theory also eliminates the need to improve the institutions of government. The saints in Daniel are perfectly content to work for the Persian empire so long as it exists, since after the demise of the last earthly empire, they will directly rule the earth. They do not anticipate how they will carry out this rule — either in Daniel or in Revelation — because the complex institutions of due process of law and division of responsibility will be unnecessary once the world is rid of the source of evil. In the meantime, why concern oneself with striving toward justice in the empire by means of institutional reform? Even the most radical reforms cannot thwart the power of the grand conspiracy! And once it is destroyed in the apocalyptic battle, only the saints will be left — and surely they will need no institutions of law and order. Once the world is made safe for democracy, the saints will take care of themselves in perfect harmony.

Finally, the conspiracy theory eliminates the possibility of compromise. With the world divided between the forces of God and Satan, no neutral space remains. To agree to live in harmony with those who are against God is to break faith and join the demonic ranks of the grand conspiracy. There is nothing worse than coexistence with evil. As the angel said to the church of Laodicea in Revelation 3:16, "Because you are . . . neither cold nor hot, I will spew you out of my mouth." The danger of neutrality, of course, is that it beguiles the saints to weaken their preparedness for battle and thus is one of the most treacherous devices of Satan. As for the compromises required in the democratic political system, they are unspeakably filthy. Preferable is a system where the saints exercise absolute power and do not have to give up their faith by compromising.

These premises and consequences interlock to produce a complete worldview, with a precise definition of good and evil, an explanation of their origins, and a knowledge of the historical process by which they battle one another for supremacy. It offers the true believer a completely satisfactory explanation for the presence of adversity in the experience of the chosen people. Once its premises are admitted, it is a logical and appealing ideology. It assures a chosen people of its perfect virtue and its right to an unproblematic existence in a world without evil. It gives meaning to the present dark moment in history and sustains the resignation of the saints to whatever destruction unfolds in the course of the battle. Above all, it provides the assurance of a perfectly happy ending. That it is idolatrous to assume to themselves God-like vision and responsibility for punishment does not seem to occur to the saints. After all, did they not learn of the grand conspiracy from the Bible it-self?

Grand Conspiracies in American Politics

The impact of this conspiratorial theory on American thinking was visible from the outset. As Bernard Bailyn has suggested, American leaders in the late eighteenth century widely shared the conviction that they were facing a de-monic conspiracy in the court of George III. Evoking Daniel's saintly aura, their Declaration of Independence spoke of "their own patient sufferance" and "humble petitions," which were meant to answer "the design to reduce them under absolute Despotism" or "absolute Tyranny." The curious fact was that the English court itself held a virtually identical premise — with the an-gelic and demonic roles reversed. With both sides struggling against the pre-sumed influences of the devil's grand conspiracy, neither would pull back from the brink. War became inevitable.[8]

When the perfect society anticipated by the saints failed to appear after the Revolution, the conspiracy theory offered ready explanations. One thinks of the remarkable series of hysterical campaigns and political battles that mark American history. In the 1820s it was the anti-Mason movements: as a secret organization, the Masons were perfect targets for the accusation of in-volvement in the grand conspiracy. The controversy started when William Morgan, who had written an anti-Masonic tract, was abducted and presum-ably murdered in upstate New York. Four persons were found guilty of kid-napping him and got off with light sentences, but no evidence for murder was actually found. Nevertheless, there was a popular feeling that the Masons had gained revenge and controlled both the courts and the federal government. Anti-Masonic newspapers and clubs sprang up all over the North; Anti-Masonic Party candidates were elected to local and state offices. Several states even passed laws to require secret societies to make annual public reports so that any conspiracy could be kept within bounds. The party played a decisive role in the national election of 1832, and it was several decades before the con-viction that the Masons were conspiring to subvert and control the republic died down.

With the Irish immigration of the 1830s, the accusation of conspiracy shifted to the Roman Catholics. Nativist American parties sprang up to counter that presumed threat to the republic. They imagined that "Romish" plots were aimed at subverting the public school system and ultimately taking over the nation in the service of the pope. Those middle decades of the nineteenth century saw the emergence to prominence of the Know-Nothing Party, which demanded the exclusion of all recent immigrant Americans from political life. The idea was that, since evil was brought in from the outside by foreign agitators, one could purify the republic by having nothing but Americans in control. In fact, former President Fillmore ran as the Know-Nothing candidate for president in 1856. Samuel Morse, the inventor of telegraphy, wrote a book entitled *Foreign Conspiracy Against the Liberties of the United States*. It is a curious and ironic attestation to the omnipresence of the conspiracy motif that, following the demise of the Know-Nothing Party after 1856, its enemies crowed about their triumph over a dreadful conspiracy. Indiana Congressman George W. Julian concluded that the Know-Nothing movement had been "a horrid conspiracy against decency, the rights of man, and the principle of human brotherhood."[9]

The history of the struggles between the North and the South in the decades before the Civil War indicates the importance of the conspiracy theory on both sides. David Brion Davis's book *The Slave Power Conspiracy and the Paranoid Style* notes that the Northerners interpreted Southern power in the Senate, the passage of runaway slave laws, and the blockage of northwestward expansion as a vast conspiracy to impose slavery on the entire nation.[10] The Southerners in turn were obsessed with the thought of abolitionist conspiracies, both inside and outside the South, that they perceived were aimed at gaining control of government so as to impose rule by blacks. Both sides thought Satan was maliciously guiding the behavior of their antagonists. This contributed to the South's secession in 1860, when the Republican party, sympathetic to the abolitionist cause, gained power. As Eric Foner's study of Republican ideology has shown, Southern fears were not entirely groundless.[11] For the Republicans were determined to stop what they considered to be a conspiracy of the Supreme Court, the administration, and slave interests. Historian William W. Freehling has observed that the paranoia on both sides was fed by the actual political possibilities: "What historians, no less than psychiatrists, must remember is that monstrous fears feed on monstrous realities."[12] However, to view these realities purely as the result of some demonic conspiracy, which could only be cleansed by violence, was to thrust the struggle from the purview of the democratic political system and onto the bloody battlefields of the Civil War.

Another example of the conspiracy theory of evil was the "Red Scare" of 1919-1920. Having made the entire world safe for democracy, the nation sought to return to "normalcy" after the armistice. It was shocked by labor unrest and a series of bombing incidents that now appear to have been staged by various groups and persons who were unconnected to any general conspiracy. But Attorney General A. Mitchell Palmer and his chief of investigation, J. William Flynn, were certain that these events were part of a gigantic plot to overthrow capitalism and establish a communist-style government similar to the one emerging in Russia. Unprecedented raids by government agents netted several hundred radicals and labor organizers, some of whom were summarily deported without trial. Hundreds of others were detained and savagely beaten by mobs and policemen before it was determined that they were completely unconnected to any subversive activity. The Sacco and Vanzetti case, a widely publicized miscarriage of justice, was a direct product of this atmosphere. Long after the Red Scare and its excesses were over, the legacy of an "underlying fear of radicalism and the proclivity for intolerance" remained to influence American politics.[13] It resulted in the emergence of dozens of patriotic societies that took up the task of rooting out Bolshevik conspirators from churches, schools, colleges, and labor unions. It encouraged the passage of restrictive immigration laws, for as General Leonard Wood summed it up, "We do not want to be a dumping ground for radicals, agitators, Reds, who do not understand our ideals."[14] The excesses of the Red Scare could serve as a significant warning about the current erosion of constitutional standards in the "War against Terrorism."

The consequences were even more serious when a similar hysteria broke out in the 1950s. After the defeat of the Nationalists in China and the emergence of the Iron Curtain in Europe, the frustration of American hopes was explained by what Eric F. Goldman called the "Great Conspiracy." The premise of this theory was that the "hated developments could all have been prevented. . . . The rise of Communism around the world did not result from long-running historical forces; the red advances came from the Alger Hisses, who had contrived to bring them about."[15] Senator Joseph McCarthy's speech before the Senate on June 14, 1951 (cited at the head of this chapter) claimed that the secretary of state himself had participated in the communist conspiracy. Despite the groundlessness of McCarthy's charges, there was an enormous readiness on the part of the American public to receive them. President Eisenhower reacted passively to the charges and simply let McCarthy play out his preposterous crusade by attacking the U.S. Army itself in nationally televised hearings. But there was an evangelical fervor to the pro-McCarthy rallies in those years, endorsed by many clergymen, and they ascribed enormous cunning to the demonic enemy within and without. Communist triumphs were all assumed to have been precisely planned and directed from headquarters in Moscow. A pro-McCarthy magazine, *Counterattack,* blacklisted a popular television singer because a communist paper had listed her as a supporter of their candidate for councilman in New York. *Counterattack* said their proof was unequivocal because "the *Daily Worker* is very accurate; they never make a mistake."[16]

That such statements were patently ridiculous detracted nothing from their power to convince Americans — or from their destructive consequences. Un-American activities committees, in brazen disregard of civil rights, began their search into the private lives and beliefs of citizens. Antisubversive laws were passed and loyalty oath campaigns were inaugurated, severely crippling key governmental agencies such as the state department, not to mention state universities and other institutions. Outstanding specialists in Far Eastern affairs, both in the government and outside it, were harassed or fired from their positions, producing a gap in experience and wisdom that contributed to the subsequent disastrous American policies in Asia. Police and intelligence agencies were fundamentally altered by the conspiratorial fever, producing for the first time in American history a pattern of surveillance of American citizens that often runs substantially outside public control.

FBI director J. Edgar Hoover gave voice to this counterconspiracy zeal for years, linking organizations of dissent or mere political opposition with the demonic communist plot. As late as 1968, he testified before the Commission on the Causes and Prevention of Violence that "communists are in the forefront of civil rights, anti-war, and student demonstrations, many of which ultimately become disorderly and erupt into violence."[17] Hoover even placed wiretaps on the phones of Dr. Martin Luther King, Jr., in the conviction that the campaign for racial equality must have been communist-inspired.[18] Such government harassment is a much more dangerous departure from democratic principles than anything a communist conspiracy could have accomplished. It reveals the incompatibility of the conspiracy theory with American ideals and procedures.

In the literature of the John Birch Society and Billy James Hargis's "Christian Crusade," the complete panoply of these assumptions came to expression. Those campaigns explicitly linked the communist conspiracy with Satan. Hargis insisted: "It is apparent upon examination that Communism cannot be of human origin, for human beings are of themselves incapable of total corruption. Only Satan could inspire in human beings complete dedication to utter folly, unspeakable horrors, and total untruth. Only Satan can be the inspiration for Communism. . . ."[19] Hargis's magazine viewed America, in a contrasting stereotype, as the "Christian country, led by the Spirit of the Living God."[20] Attempts at coexistence are "simply the first stage in the building of a world government of the Anti-Christ."[21] Hargis rendered his entire system invulnerable to criticism by flatly identifying his viewpoint with that of God himself. "Those of us who have been in this fight against Communism know beyond a shadow of a doubt that what we do is of God, and those who oppose this conservative effort are not fighting us — they are fighting God."[22]

The idolatrous swagger of the grand conspiracy theorists makes the most preposterous accusations and offers the most unlikely explanations. Without batting an eye, the John Birch Society could claim that Dwight D. Eisenhower was an undercover agent of the communist movement. Society founder Robert Welch stated the mythic premise:

> Communism is never anything but a drive for power or position or glory or wealth on the part of the Insiders at the top. . . . These insiders impose the components of Communist tyranny on a people and on the world, subtly, skillfully, deceptively, and with patient gradualism. . . . This is why nothing else that you do to oppose collectivism or immorality or revolutionary vandalism really matters, unless you expose the Conspiratorial drive behind them.[23]

What makes the nonsense plausible is simply the conspiracy premise itself. No evidence is required; indeed, none can be provided because everything is really controlled by the mysterious beings "at the top."[24] The power of the message derives from the fact that it offers a consistent and internally logical treatment of the conspiracy myth at a time when the established authorities have been forced to swerve from it under the impact of reality.

At the same time, we must observe, a similar pattern of conspiracy theory manifested itself in the language of the Left. Rather than communism as the agency of the grand conspiracy, it perceived the great evil to be the military-industrial complex, whose mysterious tentacles were thought to reach into every area of government and daily life. In place of the pseudo-Christian terminology of the far Right, it used the well-worn maxims of Marxist ideology. The Left viewed history as the battlefield between "dialectical historical forces" correlated with historically "progressive and reactionary social classes," and it called on the public to take up the role of violent saviors who would destroy wickedness through "revolution," which was sure to be victorious. Jerry Rubin, who helped give 1960s Leftism a street-theater quality, advertised the purity of the cause in this way:

We were dirty, smelly, grimy, foul, loud, dope-crazed, hell-bent and leather jacketed. We were a public display of filth and shabbiness, living-in-the-flesh rejects of middle-class standards. . . . We were outlaw forces of America displaying ourselves flagrantly on the world stage.[25]

The new revolutionaries considered secular saints of the Left as pure and undefiled as those in Revelation, albeit because of their lack of material self-interest rather than their adherence to some religious code. They still perceived the wicked as irredeemable and thus doomed to annihilation. On the crazy fringes of the revolutionary Left no sentiment or act seemed too extreme if it reflected the purity of their destructive intent. Speaking of the Weather Underground group, Todd Gitlin remarked, "The Weathermen were a rage, not an argument. They were the foam on a sea of rage."[26] Bernadine Dohrn, a member of the Weathermen celebrated the ritual murders carried out by the Charles Manson "family": "Dig it! First they killed those pigs, then they ate dinner in the same room with them, then they even shoved a fork into the victim's stomach." Jerry Rubin joined in the festive spirit by visiting Charles Manson in prison. He wrote: "I fell in love with Charlie Manson the first time I saw his cherub face and sparkling eyes on national TV. . . . His words and courage inspired [me] . . . and I felt great the rest of the day, overwhelmed by the depth of the experience of touching Manson's soul. . . ."[27] The ghoulish glee of such a "revolutionary" spirit matches the relish of the saints in Revelation over the sinners burning in the eternal fires.

The impact of such thinking on campus discourse was almost fatal in the 1960s and '70s. The outer edge made any intermediate position, no matter how extreme, seem more reasonable. With zealots on both sides seeking not the discovery of new truth but the destruction of grand conspiracies, the possibility of an open forum is virtually nil. This was the case particularly regarding the Vietnam War. The President's Commission on Campus Unrest in 1970 noted the "chilling effect on rational academic discourse" that such conspiracy thinking had caused:

As opposition to the war grew and the war continued to escalate, explanations of America's involvement in it became more radical. From having been a "mistake," the war was soon interpreted by radical students as a logical outcome of the American political system. They argued that what was most objectionable was not the war itself, but rather "the system" that had entered, justified, and pursued it. . . . The university, too, came to be seen as a part of "the system," and therefore it became a target — as distinct from an accidental arena — of antiwar protest.[28]

Educators were unprepared for this massive outpouring of counterconspiracy zeal, because they were convinced that the era of ideology was long since past and that the secular mindset would naturally be free of the evangelical heritage of America's past. What had actually occurred was a translation of the conspiratorial model into secular terminology. Americans differed violently in the terms and details, but for the most part they had not broken free from the conspiratorial premises themselves.

Their susceptibility to conspiracy theories was, of course, nourished by the existence of real conspiracies. Robert A. Goldberg's study *Enemies Within: The Culture of Conspiracy in Modern America* demonstrates how facts feed the disposition to find hidden plans. The Soviet Union did, after all, seek to harm America through secret plots. Accepting the Warren Commission's official account of the Kennedy assassination required a suspension of reasonable doubt.[29] And the events of September 11 demonstrate conspiracies of unsurpassed hostility toward America. Yet all such schemes lack the administrative centralization of control that marks the grand conspiracy and justifies the relentless animosity of those obsessed by conspiracy.

Michael Barkun's study of conspiracy theories about a demonic "New World Order," which arose in connection with the year 2000, shows the effect of three similarly irrational beliefs: "that nothing happens by accident, that everything is interconnected, and that nothing is as it seems."[30] This produces "a bizarre kind of pseudo-scholarship" that endlessly searches for a conspiratorial link between unconnected events. There is a constant effort "to unmask the invisible interlocking directorate that allegedly rules the world. And, since nothing is as it seems, those who appear powerful may actually be impotent puppets, while the truly powerful lie concealed and must be exposed."[31] This conspiratorial orientation cannot be overturned by contrary evidence, because the very fact that prestigious authorities and institutions reject such preposterous theories "is taken as evidence that those claims are really true" because they are themselves part of the grand conspiracy.[32] In the light of the past several decades, it seems clear that such thinking has behavioral consequences.[33]

Conspiracy Theory and the Vietnam War

If blame is to be assessed in the tragic U.S. involvement in Indochina in the 1960s and '70s, neither a conspiracy of the Right nor one of the Left should be singled out. It is the seductiveness of the conspiracy theory itself that should be blamed. A case can be made that, if it were not for the widely accepted premises of the conspiracy theory, the United States would never have drifted into so ill-advised a war in an area so strategically insignificant. As Kahin and Lewis have pointed out, the United States initially encouraged the Vietminh independence movement and sought to dissuade the French from re-establishing a permanent colonial rule there after 1945.[34] The publication of Ho Chi Minh's correspondence with President Franklin Roosevelt indicates the extent to which the Vietnamese themselves hoped for the application of American principles of self-determination. It was only after the fall of Nationalist China and the rise of the conspiratorial Cold War mentality that the United States began to support the French. Kahin and Lewis observe:

> Major support for the French was not given until mid-1949, when communist rule was established in China. . . . In accordance with these new American priorities, France's position in Vietnam was now described in terms of the Free World's stand against communist expansionism, and Washington ceased to perceive the war in Vietnam as primarily a local colonial conflict. Now linked to the Cold War, Vietnam was regarded as an area of strategic importance to the United States.[35]

Ho Chi Minh's long-term goals were lost sight of in the sudden belief that he was the cunning agent of a demonic campaign. Hans Morgenthau has described the crucial significance of this "demonological conception of the world in which the United States is pitted in ineluctable conflict against other nations of incalculable power and infinite cunning. . . . Our involvement in the Vietnam war is similarly justified by this demonological conception of the world which assigns to the United States the mission to defend the Free World against aggression and subversion from the Communist conspiracy."[36] Having made this fatally conspiratorial assessment of the Vietnamese independence movement, it was logical that America would take up the task of the French after their collapse in 1954. The basic rationale for American involvement was first formulated by the National Security Council in February 1950: "The neighboring countries of Thailand and Burma could be expected to fall under Communist domination if Indochina is controlled by a Communist government. The balance of Southeast Asia would then be in grave hazard."[37] The council's paper of January 1954 repeated this dire prediction: that if "any single country" is "lost" to communism, the rest of the dominos would likely fall, starting with the rest of Southeast Asia, then India and Japan, ultimately endangering the security of Europe itself.[38] That the vastly different countries and movements in Asia could be decisively influenced by a single event, or that the various religious and nationalistic impulses were somehow reducible to a single factor — this could be believed only by those who had no detailed knowledge of the multifarious peoples and cultures of Asia. But it required no evidence. The conspiracy theory itself supplied the proof. The *Pentagon Papers* state this unequivocally: "The domino theory and the assumptions behind it were never questioned" — from 1949 until the disastrous American military involvement fifteen years later.[39] Only the powerful influence of the myth of the grand conspiracy can explain the adherence to this improbable dogma by Dulles, Eisenhower, Rusk, McNamara, Bundy, Johnson, and Nixon. Millions of otherwise intelligent citizens followed their lead.

Given the mythic certainty of the domino theory, it was no surprise that American intelligence organizations provided so little in the way of realistic guidance for policy-makers. For the most part, intelligence reports simply reflected the myth itself, overlooking evidence to the contrary. Louis J. Halle points out this chronic shortcoming, which affected not only the conduct of the Vietnam War but American foreign policy as a whole during the Cold War period: "The tacit assumption that the intelligence experts in Washington made, when they set themselves to interpret the vast arrays of data before them, was that of a conspiratorial movement."[40] With such an assumption, alarming but ultimately misleading reports continued to bombard American leaders, spurring them further and further into the quicksand of an unwise war. The myth of the grand conspiracy produced a vicious cycle of self-delusion in which the best resources of a sophisticated intelligence system simply confirmed what had been a false position from the beginning. The myth played a particularly decisive role in the official thinking of the armed forces themselves. Lewis H. Lapham describes the resulting "military theology" as a closed system of moralistic tenets quickened by a conspiracy theory of evil in the Vietnam War period: "The Army also resembles the medieval church, preserving what every good officer believes to be 'the true American virtues' in the midst of a decadent temporal society riven by disillusion and despair."[41] The definition of good and evil includes a traditional, puritanical code of personal ethics, but its living core is the conviction that there is a grand conspiracy, which the Armed Forces feel they are fighting, and which manifests itself in every adverse criticism. After a visit to Fort Knox, Lapham noted that the officers ". . . liked to refer to the *Louisville Courier-Journal* as *Izvestia;* at the Pentagon it is fashionably humorous to refer to the *Washington Post* as *Pravda*."[42]

The certainty that this mythic perspective provides in assessing the probable behavior of one's antagonists was revealed in a statement by General Thomas S. Power in the late 1960s:

Soviet rulers are not like the leaders of other nations with whom one can reason and conclude agreements to be approved and honored by the people whom they represent. . . . The military aspects of the Communist threat represent just one phase of the most insidious and gigantic plot in history.[43]

With particular reference to the Chinese communists, Power said, "Once they have succeeded in building up a sufficient stockpile of nuclear weapons and delivery vehicles . . . [they] will doubtless embark on a major and sustained campaign of aggression against their neighbors." These predictions appear preposterous in the cool light of history, yet the Bush administration rhetoric in 2002 directed at an alleged "axis of evil" reflects a similar conspiratorial premise. There is, in fact, no evidence that the bitter enmity between Iran and Iraq has given way to cooperation in international terrorism, or that either is associated with an almost completely isolated North Korea. It is difficult to avoid the conclusion that mythic certainty continues to prevail over all contrary evidence. When political and military leaders so blindly follow such counsel into one debacle after another, one is tempted to pose Jesus' sarcastic question: "Can a blind person lead a blind person? Will they both not fall into the pit?" (Luke 6:39). In this case it is the peculiar blindness of claiming to see everything. Under the influence of the myth of the grand conspiracy, reality disappears from view and the nation is advised repeatedly to enter unwise crusades that undermine the very democracy they are intended to save.

Paths away from the Grand Conspiracy

The tradition of prophetic realism contains some resources to counter this peculiar blindness. Since Jesus' contemporaries were on the verge of a crusade against what they perceived as the ultimate source of evil, his efforts to counter the premises and consequences of conspiratorial theology seem to be particularly relevant. As we noted in chapter 4, several of the nationalistic movements in Judaism were convinced that the source of evil lay in the influence of foreigners — particularly in the rule of Rome. From the beginning of Jesus' ministry, his departure from the widespread premises of the grand conspiracy was noticeable. His opening sermon in Nazareth reversed the expected sequence of the kingdom of God in relation to the destruction of evil. He announced "good news to the poor . . . release to the captives . . . recovering of sight to the blind," and liberty for the oppressed (Luke 4:18) as coming "today," before the apocalyptic battle against the source of poverty, slavery, blindness, and oppression was fought. The audience was surprised and irritated, only to have Jesus reiterate the point that foreigners such as those in the Gentile areas of Sidon and Syria would enter the kingdom of God before the Jews themselves (Luke 4:24-28).[44] He barely escaped being lynched by his own townsmen at this suggestion that the hated Gentiles would be accepted by the messianic kingdom rather than be destroyed in its coming (Luke 4:29f.). Were these not the same peoples whom Deuteronomy and Daniel had targeted for annihilation, and whom the zealots aimed to massacre as members of the grand conspiracy?

Jesus worked out his radical break with the popular myths of his time in a fundamental way in the temptation experience early in his ministry, which he later apparently told to his disciples in parabolic form. The parable portrayed the devil as a tempter who set the seductive motifs of the grand conspiracy before Jesus as strategies for ushering in the kingdom. Jesus' first temptation was to use divine power to eliminate the evil of poverty. To "turn stones into bread" would be to fulfill the paradisiacal conditions that the zealots were envisioning after the destruction of Satan's hordes, who they thought were taking food from the mouths of Jewish children. Jesus rejected this temptation as a demonic urge to transcend the human situation: we do not overcome the problems of life by eliminating evil but by living in the midst of it through faith in God's word: "Man does not live by bread alone, but by every word that God utters" (Matt. 4:4).

Jesus' second temptation was to be given assurance in advance about the outcome of his ministry: to throw himself down from the pinnacle of the Temple to test whether the angels will "bear you up" is to gain precisely the kind of certainty that the grand conspiracy seemed to offer. Jesus judged this, too, to be a demonic distortion of the finite situation of humans in relation to God's future: "Scripture says again, 'You are not to put the Lord your God to the test'" (Matt. 4:7). The ideals of the great crusade against the sources of evil, in which victory is assured in advance no matter what the odds, are crumbling here under the impact of divine reality. And Jesus struck the final blow when, in the third temptation, he rejected the theocratic dream itself: the rule of the entire world by the saints after the demise of Satan. He equated falling prey to such a dream with worshiping the demonic. "Once again, the devil took him to a very high mountain, and showed him all the kingdoms of the world in their glory. 'All these,' he said, 'I will give to you, if you will only fall down and do me homage. But Jesus said, 'Begone, Satan! for it is written, "You shall do homage to the Lord your God and worship him alone"'" (Matt. 4:8-10).

This is a penetrating and comprehensive rebuttal of the theology of the grand conspiracy. Jesus has exposed its subtle distortions of God's will into a graven image of human dreams, its flagrant violation of respect for God's open future, and its pretensions of being virtuous enough to carry out God's rule on earth. But most shocking of all, he has denoted as demonic not the presumed source of evil in the form of foreign conspiracies but rather the very belief in the theology of the grand conspiracy itself! The mystique of evil, which has fascinated true believers from Daniel to the John Birch Society, from the Book of Revelation to the *Left Behind* novels and videos, Jesus has deftly set aside and replaced with a realistic appraisal of the moral depravity of a particular political program. What is demonic is not some alien conspiracy against the good but rather the religious and political perversions by those who presume to act on God's behalf.

The main lines of Jesus' subsequent ministry all radiate from this decisive starting point. Each of them stands in stark opposition to modern — as well as ancient — forms of conspiracy theology. Rather than wait for some violent process to cleanse the world of evil so that the saints could inherit the kingdom, he openly celebrated its presence in a world where evil still remained. To these festivities he invited sinners and outcasts, even Roman collaborators and their arch-enemies, the zealots and zealot sympathizers, whose alienation he overcame through the indirect process of celebratory love. He attacked the common stereotypes in brilliantly designed parables, which evoked new visions of humanity and common sense from his listeners. His attack was so thoroughgoing that he refused to be addressed with the honorific title "Good Rabbi": "Why do you call me good? No one is good except God alone" (Luke 18:19). To fall prey to the conspiracy theory's myth of perfectly good saints is to claim for humankind what is rightfully due only to God. And if this realistic insight were to be accepted by the pious defenders of the "free world" and "Christian America," the self-righteousness that is essential for the conduct of the conspiratorial foreign policy would dissolve.

As for the idea of the "demonic" itself, Jesus clearly refused to take it with the obsessive seriousness of his fellow religionists — then or now. He used the dualistic language of his time, but he refused to ground his thinking in anything but the reality of God. He taught his disciples to live in relation to the Father alone and thus to leave the solution to the problem of the demonic in God's hands. A line from the Lord's Prayer is a case in point: "Lead us not into temptation but deliver us from the evil one" (Matt. 6:13). While humans are pictured as capable of avoiding demonic temptation, they are incapable of saving themselves from the power of the demonic itself by futile crusades; God alone is capable of such deliverance. Thus humans are set free to live in the midst of evil possibilities without becoming so obsessed in the effort to transcend their finite situation that they destroy themselves and the world. Jesus interpreted his healing ministry, which he conducted in the style of first-century exorcisms, as a means of setting people free from demonic compulsions and opening to them the possibility of a restored life in relationship to God: "If I by the power of God cast out demons, then is the kingdom of God come to you" (Luke 11:20). It adds up practically to the annulment of the demonic as a ruling factor in human life. Jesus expressed this thought in his ecstatic pronouncement concerning the impact of the healing ministry: "I saw Satan fall like lightning from heaven!" (Luke 10:18).[45]

Accepting this interpretation of Jesus' ministry would cut the nerve of conspiracy thought, which ascribes the dominant role in history to the demonic and then takes up demonic methods in the crusade. It would allow people to incorporate Jesus' realistic assessment of the demonic potential of the religious impulse itself. It was Peter's preference for the zealous approach to the problem of evil in Israel that elicited Jesus' harsh command, "Get behind me, you Satan!" (Matt. 16:23). He warned against religious leaders who wear the peaceful clothing of sheep, "while underneath they are ravenous wolves" (Matt. 7:15). He reserved his fiercest denunciations for the religious establishment itself for so encouraging self-righteousness that its converts become "twice as fit for hell as you are yourselves" (Matt. 23:15). To accept this would also enable people to adopt Jesus' political pragmatism: "Or what king will march to battle against another king without first sitting down to consider whether with ten thousand men he can face an enemy coming to meet him with twenty thousand; if he cannot, then, long before the enemy approaches, he sends envoys and asks for terms" (Luke 14:31f.).[46] One would also acknowledge the wisdom of Jesus' refusal to chart the future kingdom by some conspiratorial design: "But of that day and hour [of the kingdom's final coming] no one knows, not even the angels in heaven, not even the Son; only the Father" (Matt. 24:36).[47] Politics would then evolve into the prudent business of responding to reality rather than attempting to mold it to suit our cravings for certainty about the future. Rather than making cataclysmic efforts to reshape the world, we could settle down to the task of gradually humanizing it.

The change in perspective would be particularly fruitful with regard to the coexistence of various racial, religious, and economic groups in one democratic society. So long as they are imbued with the impulse of the grand conspiracy, such groups will be locked in lethal combat with each other, precisely as they have been for decades in the Middle East and Northern Ireland, with each side seeing the devil behind the other's barricades. The only hope is to take the realistic point of view that evil and good are so inextricably mixed in mortals that precise solutions are impossible and consequently that coexistence under law is essential. This kind of realism is characteristic of the prudent landowner in Jesus' parable of the wheat and the weeds (Matt. 13:24-30). The weeds in this parable are probably the poisonous darnel, which looks identical to wheat in its early stages of growth.[48] The weeds are admittedly bad, but the parable casts doubt on humans' ability to make a precise separation. The conspiratorially oriented audience would have been drawn into the parable by the cleverly repeated motif that "an enemy" was responsible for the bad seed. Their natural response, both in first-century Israel and in modern America, would be to tromp out to the field with the servants and rip the offending weeds out by the roots.[49] The landowner convincingly observes the counter-productivity of this approach: since the weeds and the wheat look so much alike, the crusade will destroy them both (Matt. 13:29).[50] God alone can separate precisely between good and evil; humans must devise the means to live together in the meantime.

After the sad experiences of the last half century, it is time for Americans rigorously to separate themselves from the pretension of the grand conspiracy: it is as incompatible with the democratic process as it is with the message of prophetic realism. Where there is concrete evidence of conspiracies — and particular conspiracies surely exist without being "grand" — to violate the law, they must be exposed and prosecuted by legal means. Terrorism in its various forms poses a particularly difficult challenge to the legal systems of nations and the international community. Attention to root causes of conflicts must go hand in hand with law enforcement in what is likely to be a long and costly struggle. But it is quite another matter to believe, as many today give evidence of believing, that all evil in the world is caused by a demonic conspiracy. To act on the premise of the grand conspiracy in the name of Americanism or Christianity or Islam remains a classic instance of wolves in sheep's clothing: no matter how convincingly they bleat, the results of their crusades are bloody annihilation. All one needs to do is look closely at the results of such mythic thinking — in the leveled city of ancient Jerusalem, in the bloody alleys of Belfast, in the shredded jungles of Vietnam, and in the wreckage of Afghanistan.

12 Stereotypes of Good and Evil

It's true we Americans don't know very much about you Japanese, and never did — and now I realize you know even less about us. You can kill us, all of us, or part of us. But, if you think that's going to put the fear of God into the United States of America and stop them from sending other fliers to bomb you, you're wrong, dead wrong. They'll blacken your skies and burn your cities to the ground and make you get down on your knees and beg for mercy. This is your war — you wanted it — you asked for it. And now you're going to get it — and it won't be finished until your dirty little empire is wiped off the face of the earth.

a captured "Doolittle flyer" over Japan in the
Hollywood movie Purple Heart (1944)[1]

The American enemy, driven by its ambition to conquer the world, is coming to attack us, and as the breath and odor of the beast approach, it may be of some use if we draw the demon's features here. Our ancestors called them Eibusu or savages long ago, and labeled the very first Westerners who came to our country the Southern Barbarians. To the hostile eyes of the Japanese of former times they were "red hairs" and "hairy foreigners," and perceived of being of about as much worth as a foreign ear of corn. We in our times should manifest a comparable spirit. Since the barbaric tribe of Americans are devils who come from the West, we should call them Saibanki, or Western Barbarian Demons.

from a Japanese magazine article, "Naming the
Western Barbarians," October 1944[2]

Radical stereotypes are the logical corollaries of the conspiracy theory. They form images of perfectly good saints locked in battle with perfectly evil villains. This division of the world into good and bad people is a crucial component of the Captain America complex, visible in World War II, the Cold War of 1945-90, the Vietnam War, the Gulf War, and the current "war on terrorism." None of these struggles would have occurred as they did without such stereotypes. John W. Dower's *War Without Mercy,* from which this chapter's epigraphs are taken, argues that American and Japanese stereotypes became especially vicious in 1944, contributing to the exceptionally heavy losses of life suffered by both sides before the final searing conflagrations in Tokyo, Hiroshima, and Nagasaki. The Japanese were stubbornly reluctant to surrender to "demons," and the United States proved willing to incinerate Japan's civilian populations by the hundreds of thousands to bring the war to a conclusion. As General Curtis LeMay, planner of the Tokyo raids that killed between 80,000 and 100,000 civilians described it, they were "scorched and boiled and baked to death."[3]

Is it a mystery that some American soldiers collected the ears and teeth of slain Japanese, but those in Italy and Germany did not do so?[4] Would Americans have been willing to resort to the destructive tactics that were used in Indochina if we had visualized our antagonists as white Christians? A similar question needs to be posed for other cultural traditions. When another nation is defined as "the great Satan," or a whole people as immoral terrorists, the stage is set for their violent destruction. To explore the process of stereotyping is to grapple with one of the most volatile components of the current global situation.

Stereotyping occurs in all cultural traditions but takes different forms because of different psychological and historical complexities in each case. Therefore, our analysis should begin not with stereotyping in general but with the most important ideological source of the American civil religion, namely, in the biblical tradition as appropriated by our colonial predecessors. After briefly tracing the historical development, we propose to describe the images of the "good guys" and the "bad guys" popularized by the present form of the Captain America complex. We will deal with the impact of these images on our behavior in some detail: the encouragement of reflex action in foreign policy; the justification of military annihilation; the encouragement of official dishonesty for the sake of a public image; the erosion of the ideals of democratic equality and due process of law; and finally, the use of stereotypes in justifying violence. At that point we may be in a position to grasp the contribution of the Bible's realistic tradition toward the task of humanizing the stereotypes that encourage holy war. We begin by measuring the dark side of the biblical tradition that shaped the peculiar stereotypes of the Captain America complex.

The Rise of Stereotypes in Biblical History

Contrary to reasonable expectation, biblical history's early phases did not manifest a particularly striking tendency toward stereotyping. There was sufficient provocation in the early tribal warfare, the experience of slavery in Egypt, and the long struggle with the Canaanite city-states. But, for some reason, highly consistent stereotypes did not arise. In the Song of Deborah (Judges 5), one of the earliest fragments of Hebrew poetry, both the chosen people and their enemies retained an essential humanity, despite the passionate excesses of warfare. This helps to explain how the Israelite tribes could have lived in relative harmony so intermixed with the Canaanite city-states for hundreds of years. It sheds light on the relative ease with which David later incorporated these foreign population groups into his empire, some of them becoming well-known exponents of Israel's faith. The early history of Israel contained many examples of foreigners whose noble behavior belied the traditional image of Israel's enemies. Uriah the Hittite, the husband of Bathsheba, clung vigorously to the standards of Israel's zealous warfare even while at home (2 Sam. 11); Ruth the Moabite put aside the enmity of long warfare to migrate to Israel with her bereaved mother-in-law; and Job was admired for his wisdom, although he came from Edom, that usually despised area of resistance against Israel. The tribal enmities, however primitive and ferocious, did not eliminate the possibility of exceptions.

This was really quite an amazing state of affairs, given the long tradition in the early Yahwist faith of resistance against foreign elements. It was not until the seventh century BCE that the situation changed to make more rigid stereotypes possible. The Book of Deuteronomy developed the earlier prophetic critique against Canaanite religion into a comprehensive rationale for the national decline. National reverses were supposedly due to God's wrath at the widespread acceptance of foreign religion and culture by Israel. The solution that Deuteronomy proposed was to wipe out the corruption by centralizing cultic activity in Jerusalem while eliminating foreigners. The command was to destroy the "Hittites, Girgashites, Amorites, Canaanites, Perizzites, Hivites and the Jebusites. . . . The Lord your God will give you victory over them. Your part is to exterminate them, never parleying with them, never pitying them" (Deut. 7:1f.).

This program was a decisive step toward a rigid stereotyping of the enemy. To be sure, Deuteronomy did not encourage a parallel stereotype for the

Jews themselves. Since "of all nations you are the smallest" (Deut. 7:7), there was no reason to boast, except in the power of Yahweh. Deuteronomy, with its exhortation to sincere worship and social justice, seemed to assume the very real possibility that Israel might fall short of her calling. But it nonetheless called for the annihilation of many of the groups accepted into Israelite life during the earlier period — stereotyping them as the source of corruption.

Although this could not be carried out completely in the short decades between the Deuteronomic reform and the fall of Jerusalem in the sixth century BCE, it decisively shaped subsequent religious trends. Under the pressure of the Babylonian exile, the impulses toward racial purity and avoidance of foreign contamination became more and more central. By the time of Ezra and Nehemiah's restoration in the next century, the maintaining of racial purity, even at the price of breaking up marriages with foreigners, became a religious obligation. With the written law defining the obligations of religion in an exclusive sense, the world came to be divided into Jews and the Gentiles — foreigners whose very touch would corrupt the faithful. The realistic vision of Israel as a finite and partially sinful people began to give way to a stereotype that simply reversed the image of the enemy.

The stereotyped images of good and evil peoples is particularly prominent in the Psalms. Martin Buber discussed the terminology of the enemy nations in Psalm 14:

> The nations are "shameless" and godless, their habits are "corrupt" and "abominable"; among them, as is repeatedly said, there is none that does good. . . . In contrast, the people of Israel, which is "oppressed" and "eaten up" by this society of evil-doers, is apparently described as a "proven generation," whose refuge is God and whom God will free from the others and restore to their former glory.[5]

Buber weighs the possibility that these enemies might be within Israel itself, but even so, this would imply a virtually impassable "rift" within Israel itself; so he confesses that he "cannot be satisfied . . . with a simple division of Israel, just as I would not be satisfied with such a division of the human world."[6] Peter Riede has provided an extensive analysis of these images of the enemy as wild animals or hunters of innocent victims in other Psalms.[7] A particularly noteworthy example of mixing these heartless metaphors describing the pagan enemies comes in Psalm 57:

> I lie in the midst of lions
>   that greedily devour the sons of men;

> their teeth are spears and arrows,
>> their tongues sharp swords. . . .
> They set a net for my steps;
>> my soul was bowed down.
> They dug a pit in my way,
>> but they have fallen into it themselves.
> My heart is steadfast, O God,
>> my heart is steadfast!
> I will sing and make melody. (Psalm 57:4-7)

As Riede observes, these enemies "not only constantly chase and hunt the man praying, but they also shame him and attack his sense of human dignity."[8] They not only have the superhuman power of the wildest animals but are as stealthy and traitorous as hunters who camouflage traps for their victims. Only God can preserve the faithful from such insidious foes, a theme that receives full development in contemporary entertainments that depict the power of supervillains on so immense a scale that a superhero is required to rescue the innocent.[9]

The stereotyping process culminated in the books of Daniel and Revelation. Here the saints are entirely pure and their antagonists entirely corrupt and beastly. Here the tendency visible in some of the Psalms extends into grotesque stereotypes of enemy empires:

> Daniel said, "I saw in my vision at night, and behold . . . four great beasts came up out of the sea, different from one another. The first was like a lion and had eagles' wings. . . . And behold, another beast . . . like a bear. It was raised up on one side; it had three ribs in its mouth between its teeth; and it was told, 'Arise, devour much flesh.' After this I looked, and lo, another like a leopard, with four wings of a bird on its back; and the beast had four heads; and dominion was given to it. After this I saw in the night visions, and behold, a fourth beast, terrible and dreadful and exceeding strong; and it had great iron teeth; it devoured and broke in pieces, and stamped the residue with its feet." (Dan. 7:2-7)

Such enemies evoke no sympathy; they destroy for the sheer pleasure of destruction. In view of their bestial nature and evil deeds, there is no hope of their conversion. Each empire destroys its predecessor, and now the saints face the most terrible threat of all, the fourth beast with its great iron teeth in the form of the Hellenistic mercenaries. Daniel is spared by God, not because he possesses equivalent military force, but because he "was found blameless" in God's eyes (Dan. 6:22). The term used here measures perfection by the standard of cultic purity: the one who has not violated the commandments is "blameless" or "untainted" from any source of corruption. The question of proper or improper motivation does not arise to cast doubt on this neat framework of perfection.

The word "saint" also occurs frequently in Revelation as a technical term to depict radical separateness from corruption. A typical statement of this conception appears in the description of the heavenly Jerusalem after all sources of corruption have been banished: "Into it will come nothing unclean, nothing corrupt, nothing false, only those included in the Lamb's book of life" (Rev. 21:27). Such passages assume a legalistic and predominantly cultic definition of perfection. The saints are those who refuse to worship the corrupt "beast" of Rome (Rev. 20:4), who "have not defiled themselves with women" (Rev. 14:4), and who "keep the commandments of God and the faith of Jesus" (Rev. 14:12). They are those in whose mouths "no lie was found, for they are blameless" (Rev. 14:5).[10] Matching the purity of their behavior is the white robe of the saints in Revelation, and the author explicitly links this to legal obedience: "Now the fine linen signifies the righteous deeds of God's people" (Rev. 19:8). The author connects this purity to a passive endurance of persecution rather than with active resistance, again highlighting the concern not to smear the saints with the blood of their corrupt victims. But this hardly rules out the saints' explicit hatred of their enemies. Before God's throne they cry out for vengeance against their persecutors (Rev. 6:10),[11] rejoicing in the thought that the aftermath of apocalyptic victory will take the agents of Rome into the torture of eternally flaming sulfur pits, where "the smoke of their torment will rise for ever and ever" (Rev. 14:11).[12] Obviously, this definition of saintly purity has nothing to do with replacing the motivations of hatred with those of love. If the saints keep proper distance from "corruption," they have neither flaw nor sin.

Matching this stereotype of the saints is that of the wicked. They are inevitably foreigners in the Book of Daniel, persons who do not conform to the strict laws of righteousness in the Torah. But there is as little interest in their actual motivational structure as there is in the case of the saints themselves. They are introduced simply as enemies and rivals, who inexplicably oppose the saints. Daniel 3:8 is typical: "It was then that certain Chaldeans came forward with malicious accusations against the Jews." The visions of Daniel 7 extend this evil stereotype to the great empires of the author's past and present, each depicted as a grotesque beast. The worst of all is the "fourth beast," which represents the reign of Antiochus IV, who was persecuting the Jews at the time Daniel was written.

> And a fourth beast I saw last, fiercer, and stranger, and more powerful yet. It had great teeth of iron, ready to crush and to devour, and those it spared it would trample down with its feet . . . and out of its head grew ten horns. Even as I watched them, a new horn grew up in the midst of the others, and three of them must be plucked away to make room for it; eyes it had, this new horn, like a man's eyes, and a mouth that talked very boastfully. (Dan. 7:7-8)

This last-born beast is interpreted in Daniel 7:21f. as Antiochus Epiphanes, who in the second century BCE made "war against the saints, and prevailed over them, until the judge appeared, crowned with age, to give them redress, and their turn came to have dominion." By characterizing the enemy as bestial, the writer accomplishes several things. He has explained the destructive impact of the empires, because they are inhuman from the start; and there can be no sympathy when such bestial entities are destroyed in the end. This may relate to the seemingly inexplicable behavior of Daniel's rivals, allowing the reader to see that their conspiratorial behavior is a natural consequence of their bestiality. At any rate, an enormously significant development has taken place here that allows ferocious stereotypes to develop. For if one's political enemies are actually beasts for whom wanton destruction is natural, there is no hope except for their annihilation.

In the New Testament, Revelation is the book that develops this inhuman theme further by characterizing the government of Rome as follows: "And the beast that I saw was like a leopard, its feet were like a bear's, and its mouth was like a lion's mouth" (Rev. 13:2).[13] It utters blasphemies and makes "war on the saints," deriving its capacity to perform "great signs" from the fact that it exercises the authority of the satanic "dragon." The source of bestiality is therefore precisely defined as demonic, which makes the stereotype even more rigid than in the Book of Daniel. The author groups all of his enemies under this rubric, even though many of them have no function in the Roman government: "But as for the cowardly, the faithless, the polluted, as for murderers, fornicators, sorcerers, idolaters, and all liars, their lot shall be in the lake that burns with fire and brimstone" (Rev. 21:8). The author regards these persons, including those Christians whom he considers heretics, as incapable of repentance, even after the punishments described in Revelation 8, 9, and 16.[14] If such people will not see the light even after having been "bombed back into the stone age" — to use the idiom of the modern American civil religion — then one can only conclude that they are incorrigible and deserve the final sweep into the lake of fire. What other solution is there for the bestial servants of the dragon?

American Adaptations of Ancient Stereotypes

The connection between these stereotypes and their modern counterparts should already be apparent. One need sketch only briefly the style of their transmission. The Puritans were so deeply imbued with Daniel and Revelation that the use of such terminology became habitual, and the moderating tradition of biblical coexistence was overlooked. Alexander Leighton of 17th-century England wrote that, though his Puritan colleagues desired peace, they had to recognize the bestial quality of their rivals. "But we must understand with whom we live in this world, with men of strife, men of blood, having dragon's hearts, serpent's heads."[15] The only solution for this kind of stereotype was one of violence. So, Leighton continued, it behooved the saints to "work with one hand and with the other hold the sword." As this spirit manifested itself on American soil, it was quickly matched by an equally rigid stereotype of the purity of the saints. They alone carried forward the faith betrayed in England; they alone ruled as the saints were destined to rule. After the American Revolution, this feeling of superiority over European forebears assumed remarkable proportions. John Adams' letter to Thomas Jefferson on Nov. 13, 1813, claimed nothing less than millennial sainthood for Americans: "Many hundred years must roll away before we shall be corrupted. Our pure, virtuous, public spirited, federative republic will last forever, govern the globe and introduce the perfection of man."[16]

How were such paragons to live in a world of sinners? The answer was they could not. Those who clung most ferociously to their own stereotype of virtue were willing to declare eternal war on those who fit their stereotype of wickedness. One thinks of William Lloyd Garrison's blanket condemnation of Southern leaders: "They ought not to be allowed seats in Congress. No political, no religious co-partnership should be had with them, for they are the meanest of thieves, and the worst of robbers. . . . We do not acknowledge them to be within the pale of Christianity, of republicanism, of humanity."[17]

That the enemy is not human and therefore deserves annihilation has been one of the most frequently repeated legacies of Daniel and Revelation. During World War I, the Germans were portrayed as bloodthirsty "Huns," completely devoid of human attributes. An advertisement in *The American Magazine* pictured some American troops during World War II praying with their chaplain "that the people back home will understand that here in this green hell the enemy is not a man but a devil . . . [that] we fight for the right . . . of all men to live and grow in a world where every man may keep forever free from hatred, greed, and tyranny — his home — his country . . . and his God. Amen."[18] Here are both sides of the stereotype in their essential form, set in the context of apocalyptic warfare to make the world "forever" safe for the saints: the enemy is demonic, and the saints are perfectly pure, no matter what they may do in the battle. These images have been presented in so many movies, stories, comic books, and newspapers that they have etched themselves firmly in the national consciousness. Although the identification of the enemy may change through the centuries from Cavalier to Royalist, to Englishman, to Rebel, to Yankee, to Indian, to Don (Spaniard), to Hun, to Nazi, to Jap, to Gook, to Arab — the form of the stereotype and its apocalyptic solution remain constant. In the quotation at the head of this chapter, an American aviator expressed scorn for Japan's "dirty little empire" that was about to be incinerated. A Japanese journalist replied in the same vein. President George W. Bush, in his 2002 State of the Union address, maintained this tradition by using on several occasions the language of vermin for the nation's enemies: "My hope is that all nations will heed our call and eliminate the terrorist parasites who threaten their countries and our own."[19]

The interchangeable identifications of the righteous and their enemies suggest that a well-defined stereotype has been established in the American mind. A. Dale Tussig made a humorous start at discerning the structure of this system in an article entitled "Education, Foreign Policy and the Popeye Syndrome." Popeye is a significant figure because he has been a national comic-strip and comic-book character since 1929, functioning as an early instructional source for children as they learn how to respond to aggression in an American manner. In the *Popeye* comics, Bluto is the brutish, far larger and more muscular bad guy who constantly picks fights with the American sailor Popeye over the beloved Olive Oyl, to whom they both feel attracted. In each fight, Bluto almost destroys our hero by his unfair tactics. Thrust into extremity, Popeye eats a can of spinach, which Tussig suggests may itself be "symbolic of that which is unpleasant but right and moral." He then uses the same unfair tactics — generally the miraculous "twisker sock" that comes from his spinach-pumped arm — to dispose of his foe.[20] Tussig sets forth the pattern of this stereotype that justifies the hero's violent action: "The three-fold combination of the villain's established evil character, the fact that he attacked first, and his use of dirty and immoral tactics, not only justifies the hero's fighting back, but his complete and total subjugation or annihilation of the villain."[21] This helpful start is quite compatible with the more exhaustive sixfold pattern derived from our analysis of Daniel and Revelation.

Six Features of Popular Stereotypes

1. The most decisive aspect of the contemporary stereotype is the *identification* of the person or movement with one side of the cosmic struggle between good and evil.[22] Dualism of the late biblical variety is essential for such mutually exclusive categories as cowboys vs. Indians, cops vs. robbers, Popeye vs. Bluto, the Jedi and the Empire, or Captain America vs. the Enemy of the Moment. The reader or viewer is tipped off immediately by conventional motifs as to whether a given character belongs to the good or the bad side. So attuned are American children to this scheme that "good guy" and "bad guy" are often the first words they use in describing the cartoons they watch. The villains are pictured in bestial or demonic fashion and the hero in supremely human fashion, along moralistic rather than heroic lines. Often it suffices merely to state which side a person or movement is on. Such stereotyping is also persistent in popular, apocalyptic writers such as Hal Lindsey, who linked "the Soviet Union and China with the demonically inspired kings of the north and the east in the prophecies of Ezekiel and Revelation," as Stephen O'Leary explains.[23] In his book *The Magog Factor*, Lindsey predicts that a coalition of Islamic countries with "irrational leaders" will invade Israel and bring on the apocalyptic climax.[24] The designation of good or evil defines both the character of the sides and the inevitable outcome. When cosmic identification is abandoned, the stereotypes lose both their exclusiveness and their power.

2. The next traits relate to the behavior of the good and bad people or groups. The former is marked by a *defensive* stance and the latter by an *offensive* stance. Clearly reflecting the tradition of cool zeal, the good guy stereotype always includes a passive, peace-loving pattern of initial behavior. Popeye never picks a fight but is forced into it against his will by the most extreme provocation. The cowboy redeemer often rides into the beleaguered town without his pistols, having resolved never to use force again. In contrast, the bad person is always pictured as the aggressor. Like the satanic enemies of Daniel and Revelation, he "makes war on the saints" and always "prevails" for a time. This offensive behavior clearly shows that he does not desire peace at all. He loves conflict for the pleasure of destruction, and this bestial-demonic trait makes it impossible for the normally passive saint to tolerate his existence.

3. While the behavior of the good people is *clean,* that of the bad is "dirty." Although the idea of "fairness" influences the definition of such behavior, popular presentations of the myth make it clear that cleanness in the biblical sense of "untainted" is the more basic category. The saints of Revela-

tion, their white robes shimmering, stand comfortably among contemporary American entertainers. The hero of the older cowboy movies and TV programs was pictured wearing a "white hat," neatly shaven, dust-free, and clean living. The villain was correspondingly portrayed as careless in his dress, filthy in personal habits, and unprincipled in his fighting tactics. Fairness and unfairness were subsumed under the category of cleanliness so conceived, and one always knew by external observation how the two sides would conduct themselves in the inevitable battle. The importance of clean appearance continues to play a decisive role in associating racial or cultural types with the bad guys. Indians, blacks, Orientals, swarthy Europeans, Iranians, Pakistanis, and Arabs tend to be stereotyped on sight. If cleanliness is next to godliness, then darkness must be devilish.

4. Finally, the behavior of the good guys and the bad guys is marked by opposite relationships to the law. The one is *law abiding* and the other is incorrigibly *lawless*. The hero is usually pictured as respecting lawful authority, as politely fulfilling the written and unwritten laws and customs of the community, and as deeply revolted by the lawlessness of others. He rejects the requirements of law only when — as in the American monomyth — the impotent and incompetent community is threatened. The villain usually flouts the laws and customs openly, provoking audience displeasure as much by his demonstration of disrespect as by serious violations. But the plot of the western or criminal story inevitably demonstrates the outcome of such an attitude in the form of murder, robbery, extortion, or kidnapping. It often develops the motif that the bad guys even refuse to abide by their own laws, such as the agreed-upon division of the booty. This points up the incorrigibility of the lawless in a manner quite reminiscent of Revelation. The petty moralism of pietistic religion is frequently more prominent than respect for actual due process of civil law. In the heyday of cowboy movies from the 1920s through the 1970s, the hero was typically pictured as drinking alcohol unwillingly if at all, as refraining from gambling, and as resisting the advances of the flirting maidens. The villain, on the other hand, broke all the pious laws by drinking with intoxicated delight, by obsessive gambling, and by lecherous behavior toward willing or unwilling maidens.

5. Several traits relate more to attitude than to behavior. While the good guys are stereotyped as being *faithful* to ideals, the bad guys are pictured as being so incorrigibly unfaithful that they *refuse to repent*. This is a rather complex attitudinal pattern on both sides. The villains tend to be pictured as completely unprincipled. Even when they promise to "go straight," they prove unable or unwilling to resist the temptation of easy stealing or murder. They are given opportunities in each story to change their ways, and their inevita-

ble refusal to do so prepares the audience to welcome their demise. As in the Book of Revelation, there is no exit but death for those who refuse to repent.

For the hero, faithfulness implies the courage to oppose the villain on grounds of principle alone. He never seems to seek or enjoy the accolades of the community, and in the classical tales, he never rides off with the beautiful girl. In the taking-courage episode before the final confrontation with the bad guy, he decides to be faithful to himself and what he believes is right, without regard to the inevitably cowardly attitude of the crowd. Having so resolved, he becomes curiously immune to criticism if he happens to break one of the ideals or laws in the battle. This is where Popeye's can of spinach fits. He initially desires to stand passively in the face of provocation; but when he receives the clear call to battle, he must faithfully but regretfully obey. He then becomes a channel of divine justice, and whatever he does to win the battle is tolerated. Spinach symbolizes quite effectively the unpleasant obligation to redeem the community through violence as well as the implicit promise of strength so that victory is inevitable. Just as in the Book of Revelation, to be faithful causes one to suffer, but it also qualifies for victory in an apocalyptic battle where no holds are barred.

So conceived, the stereotype combines such seemingly contradictory elements as a perfectly clean and basically passive hero, committed to lawful obedience, carrying out his highest form of faithfulness by not violating the norms of cleanliness, law, and passivity. The dramatic transition from cool to hot zeal is the marrow of the myth — from Clark Kent to "Superman," from Bruce Wayne to "Batman," and from Dick Grayson to "Robin," from the timid Luke Skywalker to the Force-enabled pilot who causes the nuclear incineration of the Death Star.

6. The good guy must maintain his humility even in face of the *arrogance* of his antagonist. As noted above, he must be faithful without exhibiting ulterior motives such as the desire for prestige, for gratitude, for personal gain or even for personal satisfaction. He must derive no pleasure from killing the bad guy — the can of spinach is proof against that, as is Luke Skywalker's remorse over Darth Vader's death in the final battle that ends his life. In the period of waiting for the duel, good guys must exhibit no overconfidence. Like the saint in the apocalyptic tradition, his trust must not be in himself but rather in the cosmic source of justice. For Luke it is the speaking, spiritual presence of the dead Obi Wan Kenobi, through whom the destructive power of The Force flows. Humility, therefore, involves avoiding any objectionable emotion or motive; it manifests itself as coolness, a sense of being utterly detached from the battle even in its midst. In contrast, the bad guy is presented as arrogantly confident of victory, trusting entirely in himself, and overbear-

ing in his demeanor. He consistently sets himself above others, bullying the townsmen and taunting the weak. He appears to act from purely selfish motives. In contrast to the cool good guy, he loses control of his emotions in an objectionable fashion. In a Puritan culture, that in itself is the epitome of arrogance.

These six features of contemporary American stereotypes of good and evil interlock so that when one of them appears, the others are automatically evoked. The negative features evoke a reverse image by which one tends to compare himself favorably with every adversary. The stereotypes provide the set of conventions by which characters in comics, movies, books, and politics are identified as belonging either to God or the devil. They are so deeply rooted in the American mind that the complexity of moral reality comes pre-processed as the product of the stereotype.

Problematic Stereotypes in Recent History

This moral stereotype played a decisive role in the Cold War and in the Indochina conflict. The schematic rendition of strategic reality led us to interpret the Soviet position in Europe after 1945 in overly aggressive terms, although it is now clear that their major goal was to prevent a recurrence of the disastrous invasions of their territory that had so frequently issued from the West. The stereotype led us to view the independence movements in various former colonies as intrinsically dangerous and unwisely to take sides in civil wars. Once a movement or person received the stamp of the bad guy stereotype, our policy would become what Ernest May called "axiomatic." We would deal with foreign countries up to the point that they manifested the traits of evil, and then we would fiercely attack. We viewed them as outlaws for whom no punishment was considered harsh enough.[25] The stereotyped definition of absolute good and evil entailed the theorem of apocalyptic violence. Once the axiomatic chain of inferences began, a process of self-fulfilling expectations was manifested, whereby the nation so treated reacted with hostility. Our belligerent policy toward an "evil nation" provoked responses that served to confirm in our minds the incorrigibility of the enemy.

A similar tendency began to surface shortly after the terrorist attack on September 11, 2001. Classifying Islamic countries whose citizens celebrated the destruction of the World Trade Center as inherently bad and thus worthy of destruction is becoming more and more openly stated. A column written for *The National Review* by Ann Coulter, cited earlier in chapter 1, provides a vivid example of this stereotypical logic. She writes:

This is no time to be precious about locating the exact individuals directly involved in this particular terrorist attack. Those responsible include anyone anywhere in the world who smiled in response to the annihilation of patriots like Barbara Olson. We don't need long investigations of the forensic evidence to determine with scientific accuracy the person or persons who ordered this specific attack. We don't need an "international coalition." We don't need a study on "terrorism." . . . We know who the homicidal maniacs are. They are the ones cheering and dancing right now. We should invade their countries, kill their leaders and convert them to Christianity. We weren't punctilious about locating and punishing only Hitler and his top officers. We carpet-bombed German cities; we killed civilians. That's war. And this is war.[26]

Coulter's accolade of correspondent Barbara Olson, who courageously phoned her husband with a request that he inform the FBI about the hijacking that later crashed into the Pentagon building, is correspondingly simplistic: she was "really nice. A lot of people on TV seem nice, but aren't. . . . But Barbara was always her charming, graceful, ebullient self." This image of perfect innocence in a person killed by the terrorists provides justification for a massive annihilation of populations deemed hostile. It is assumed, of course, that if they became "nice Christians," they would no longer harbor resentment toward the United States because of its policies that they now find repellent.

A sad illustration of the damage caused by such axiomatic judgments can be seen in U.S. policy on China during the early phase of the Cold War. Having stereotypically assessed the virtues of the competing sides during China's civil war, the United States became certain that Satan had triumphed in the communist victory in 1949. We refused to recognize the new regime or to open normal diplomatic relationships. We interpreted every incident from the Korean War to the occupation of Tibet or to the Indian border dispute as originating from Chinese aggressiveness. We then proceeded to encircle China with American military bases and to harass her border provinces with mercenary troops and subversive activities. We encouraged the Nationalist regime on Formosa to sponsor raids, espionage, and blockades of Chinese harbors. Quite naturally, the Chinese responded with hostility; and though this took only verbal form for the most part, Americans interpreted it as confirmation of the demonic stereotype.

Americans recently reconfirmed their hostility to the Chinese in the incident of the U.S. Navy EP-3 reconnaissance plane, which collided with a Chinese fighter plane near Hainan Island on April 1, 2001. The Chinese forced the

U.S. plane to land and detained the crew for twelve days; they tried to force the United States to make an apology for the surveillance and for their own missing airman. Americans saw their crew, which had saved itself by flying with great skill and had surrendered calmly, as heroic. Americans saw the close electronic surveillance of China as a right, though it is not so easy to imagine that they would accept comparable Chinese surveillance near our own military facilities on the West Coast, particularly if one of our airmen had been killed. The episode occurred just two months after an American submarine, accompanied by civilian visitors, had accidentally taken the lives of nine Japanese school children in one of its sudden surfacing maneuvers. And it came just two years after American pilots had "mistakenly" bombed the Chinese embassy in Belgrade, killing some of its personnel.

The power of mutually hostile stereotypes was strong on both sides. The Chinese likely saw the Americans as continuing the Anglo-American colonialist tradition of the Opium Wars and the Open Door Policy, through which China was compelled to cede sovereign rights on their own soil to Europe and to the United States. *The South China Morning Post* commented that the reconnaissance plane event "reeks of Top Gun, Tom Clancy novels and — in real life — of Francis Gary Powers, the U-2 pilot shot down over the Soviet Union in 1960 and jailed for espionage."[27] From the U.S. side, Chinese behavior was seen as contrary to international law — making excessive demands for payment or apologies. Out of such confrontations, driven by negative images of the adversary, can grow much larger conflicts that cannot be contained by diplomacy.[28]

The stereotypes apparent in the EP-3 episode were compounded a few months later, when each party found reasons to disparage each other's truthfulness. The Boeing Company had entered into an agreement to build a presidential aircraft for Jiang Zimen. Because the Chinese did not fully trust the United States in this relationship, it assigned military officers to watch the final outfitting of the plane in San Antonio, Texas. After the delivery of the plane to China, it was discovered that twenty listening devices, capable of being controlled by satellites, had been placed throughout the cabin of the plane. Were the Chinese officers responsible for spying on their own president? Or is the United States implicitly asserting its international right to spy and lie whenever it can get away with it?[29] The obvious financial repercussions for the United States are very clear. As the *Times* (London) pointed out, "The impact of the discovery on US business could be catastrophic for Boeing and other parts of the US aerospace industry because China is one of the fastest-growing parts of the world aviation market."[30]

The power of such stereotyping had terrible consequences in prior historical relationships because it led to the false inference that China was some-how responsible for the situation in Indochina and that the Vietnamese were merely puppets. As Lieutenant General James M. Gavin noted in an interview several years ago, "In '54, '55 and '56, when we first considered going into Southeast Asia . . . we agreed among ourselves in the Pentagon, the planners, that we were really going to war with China."[31] The public now has access to a much more realistic picture of Vietnamese antagonism against China and maintenance of their own nationalistic goals of independence, but this only serves now to underscore the power of the stereotypes to obscure reality for so many years. Allen S. Whiting, of the Center for Chinese Studies at the University of Michigan, testified as follows before the Senate Foreign Relations Committee at the time of the Chinese atomic capability scare:

> I see no basis in fact or theory for attributing a significantly higher likelihood of irrationality to Chinese as compared with Russian decision-makers. . . . The preponderant weight of the evidence shows that the Chinese leadership to date has used force beyond its borders with a consistently deliberate control to minimize the risks.[32]

Whiting went on to warn against the self-fulfilling expectation of evil behavior as manifest in our desire to erect an antiballistic missile defense against the Chinese. It would not be "a guarantee against Chinese irrationality or miscalculation but rather may actually be a further goad to Chinese assumptions of our malevolence and permanent enmity."[33] By assuming that Chinese atomic capability would lead inevitably to atomic aggression, we could act in such a way as to provoke it.

Louis J. Halle noted in this connection a consistent pattern of American miscalculations because capabilities rather than actual intentions were taken into account by military strategists. For example, in the summer of 1950, after the Korean invasion, we decided for the first time to intervene with our own forces in the Chinese civil war by positioning the Seventh Fleet between the mainland and Formosa. President Truman's military advisers convinced him that China might decide to invade Japan: "This argument was plausible only in terms of the principle that military preparations must be based on a possible opponent's capabilities rather than on his intentions. For a variety of reasons it was virtually inconceivable that the new regime in Peking would actually undertake the conquest of Japan, but the fact was that it would have the capability of doing so."[34] The hidden premise of such thinking was the demonic stereotype of the Chinese. It was to be assumed that they would practice aggression if they were given a chance. Their capability was identified with their intentions because they were felt to be depraved. Like the bad guys in the cowboy westerns, the Chinese were expected to break all laws within their capability, so long as the super cowboys did not restrain them.

The stereotypes of the "nice" people in Asia were equally effective in separating American policies from reality. The U.S. government portrayed Chiang Kai-shek and Syngman Rhee as loyal members of the "free world" despite the fact that their regimes were brutally dictatorial. They both had systematically destroyed their political opposition and stamped out free speech. Eventually their abusive policies came to be repudiated by the vast majority of their countrymen. Yet they were sustained by the United States because they were on the right side in the apocalyptic battle. John Foster Dulles responded to some critical remarks by the diplomat George V. Allen, who had studied the behavior of these two leaders: "Well, I'll tell you this. No matter what you say about them, these two gentlemen are modern-day equivalents of the founders of the church. They are Christian gentlemen who have suffered for their faith. They have been steadfast and have upheld the faith."[35] The stereotype of the saints derived from Revelation is visible here. Minor faults might well be present, but keeping the faith in the battle puts people among the elect. If Chiang Kai-shek and Syngman Rhee kept the faith, it followed that they were pure by definition and their actual behavior was beyond scrutiny.

The sixfold typology of the good and evil nations provided the appeal in the speeches defending the U.S. involvement in the Indochina conflict.[36] The public responded to presidential claims that the North Vietnamese were "international outlaws," involved in "aggression across an international border," using dirty tactics such as "indiscriminate shelling" of "civilian population centers," violating "the treaties they had signed in 1954," demonstrating the spirit of "intransigence," and making "arrogant" demands. The picture of the good folks in Asia was equally gratifying. Our side sought only to "win the kind of peace that will last," engaging in bombing for the sake of "protective reaction," offering the fairest and "most generous peace terms," respecting "scrupulously" the neutrality of Cambodia and Laos, and holding firm to faithful "resolve" while engaged in a "selfless cause." Hearing the use of such motifs, a public that was skeptical of the wisdom of the war, suspicious about the virtue of our allies, and utterly weary of hearing Vietnam reports was induced to support its indefinite extension. The amazingly positive public reaction reveals the grave dangers that such primitive conceptions still contain, not only in leading us into an endless succession of unwise crusades against ostensible terrorists around the world but also, as the following section will show, in eroding our own democratic heritage.

Three Negative Effects of Stereotyping

The adverse side effects of stereotyping are often viewed as separate phenomena, unrelated to the process of behaving according to cultural myths. We would like to suggest that several alarming tendencies in current American life are the natural by-products of stereotypical thinking.[37]

First, there is the *growth of official dishonesty*. *The Pentagon Papers* revealed a variety of deceptions, ranging from secret sabotage operations in North Vietnam beginning as early as 1954[38] to the Gulf of Tonkin incident of 1964 and down through the raids on villages and dams in North Vietnam, in which the public was misled, misguided, and misinformed.[39] The military details well known by Vietnamese, Laotians, and Cambodians were classified into secrecy so that the U.S. public could not discover what had occurred. The misleading news reports derived from slanted briefings by military authorities became so habitual that they lost their power to arouse indignation. Yet this was more than merely the power of habit; it was an indication of the power of stereotypes. The goal of official lying is almost always to preserve the image of the good country. Behavior inconsistent with the defensive, clean, law-abiding, faithful, and humble stance demanded by the stereotype must be denied or hidden.

Only belatedly did the public discover heavy bombing of villages along the Ho Chi Minh trail in Laos, which began secretly in 1964 and was steadily and secretly escalated until finally terminated by the Agreement of the Restoration of Peace and Reconciliation in Laos. As Roger Warner wryly notes in *Backfire*, his history of secret U.S. warmaking in Laos, "Neither the Americans nor the North Vietnamese signed the new agreement. To sign it would have meant admitting publicly that they had been fighting there."[40] This secret bombing campaign had been larger than the bombing of South Vietnam and Cambodia. Warner relates that 440,000 tons were dropped in 1971 alone — "nearly twice the amount dropped on South Vietnam and twenty-five times the power of the atomic bomb at Hiroshima."[41] The rationale for such secrecy is obvious, and it has nothing to do with denying vital information to the enemy, who already knew exactly what had occurred. It had a purely mythic rationale: nice countries do not conduct a barbaric war against a small, neutral nation. The democratic spirit in American politics, severely frustrated by such cynical manipulation, finally reacted in great anger as Congress acted to introduce legislative restraints — and forced the duplicitous Nixon from office in the demoralizing Watergate affair.

This leads to a consideration of the second adverse side effect of stereotyping: *its impact on the political process*. The democratic political system is based on the idea of the consent of the governed. Its function depends on widespread acceptance of certain ground rules and a large degree of trust. Rather than relying on coercion, it relies on the willing cooperation of its citizens. What happens to such a system when citizens discover that successive administrations have lied to them, have committed atrocities on their behalf without public approval, and have manipulated the national ethos to their own political advantage? The answer now lies before us. Generations of younger people who have lived through the Vietnam War, the Iran-Contra Affair, and other misrepresentations of American action are losing faith in the democratic process. In smaller and smaller proportions do they even vote in national elections — a mere one-third of them in the national elections of 2000.[42]

Given the usefulness of the stereotypes in winning elections, politicians remain unwilling to confront actual issues. With relatively few exceptions, our presidential campaigns have been waged by image-making. Those seeking to get elected stigmatize their opponents as dangerously evil, which is intended to convince the public that the good candidate should win. The resulting smear campaigns and public-relations lies keep the public from grappling with the policy questions on which their judgment is required. Foreign-policy responses to foreign-based terrorism did not even enter the presidential election campaign of 2000, when George W. Bush emphasized "character in the White House" and Al Gore promised — just as a deep recession was beginning — continuing prosperity for everyone. Unfortunately, this is nothing new. William G. McLoughlin has noted that the "moralistic and pietistic temper has always inspired our political life. There has scarcely been an election in American history since 1796 which was not conducted as a fight between good and evil for the power to steer the ship of state toward the millennial harbor."[43] The long-term effects of such campaigns are anything but democratic. With the candidates presenting mythic stereotypes, the questions on which the electorate's judgment ought to be rendered are submerged. These questions are then decided outside the electoral process. Many bright young people observe such trends and conclude that democracy is incapable of providing justice in the modern world. Since their thinking is often as dominated by stereotypes as is their elders', they sometimes conclude that salvation will come only when their own pure generation comes to power.

A third negative side effect of the stereotypes is their tendency to *erode due process of law and the principle of democratic equality*. The moment someone gets stereotyped as a bad guy, he or she is marked for destruction. As a threat to the order of the saints and as an agent — knowingly or unknowingly — of the demonic realm, he tends to be viewed as lacking the rights of citizenship. His life can be taken without the use of the normal processes of law. Civil rights are designed for the nice people who are intrinsically peaceful, not for the incorrigibly lawless types who threaten the system.

Behavioral scientists have discovered how important such stereotypes are in the minds of torturers. Daniel Goleman reports: "According to experts, the preconditions that can lead someone to become a torturer include a fervently held ideology that attributes great evil to some other group and defines the believer as a guardian of the social good. . . ."[44] Goleman reports on the research of psychologist Ervin Staub, who discovered that "the fundamental psychological underpin of the torturer . . . is in dividing the world into two groups, 'us' and 'them.' . . . This is a view that defines the torturer's victims as an evil group who pose a tangible threat to the social order."[45]

American minority groups have long experienced the effects of this stereotyping. The long and sordid history of lynching, raping, and abusing African-Americans is a case in point. And contrary to the usual opinion in the North, this has not been a tendency peculiar to the former slave states. One should not overlook the anti-Negro laws in Midwestern towns, forbidding blacks to stay overnight within the city limits. One should not lose sight of the fact that the black settlements in the rural areas of the North after the Civil War were for the most part harassed out of existence, their citizens denied equal protection under the law. It was in Omaha, Nebraska, that Malcolm X's father was lynched. The theme was as clear for the blacks as it was for the Indians and many other minority groups.

For the most part, this denial of equal rights to persons stereotyped as bad guys has been exercised by private citizens rather than the law-enforcement agencies themselves. Admittedly, the record is spotty, with many incidents of prison brutality and unfair trials. But the constitutional heritage, with its provision of equal rights in the amendments, has been a bulwark against the popular tendency to treat citizens according to the stereotypes. Supreme Court decisions on the basis of those amendments have progressively developed procedural barriers against prejudicial behavior on the part of law-enforcement officials. What has frequently been lacking in recent decades is forthright leadership on the part of the executive branch of the government in defending such procedures and carrying them out in pursuance of constitutional obligations.

We have witnessed instead the systematic frustration of such equal protection for the sake of winning public approval. In violation of his oath of office, the president has turned away from the task of enforcing the law of the land in order to play politics with the stereotypes. In the context of a "war against terrorism," in which certain groups are deemed guilty because of their religion or culture, the secret military courts authorized by the Bush administration constitute an open invitation to judicial torture. By allowing prejudicial guilt by association to replace the premise of the American legal system — that one is innocent until proven guilty — the door is now open for summary executions and torture such as practiced by Nazi Germany, Soviet Russia, Argentina under the dictatorship, and many other countries.

The call to replace the institutions of equal protection before the law with those of crusading but secretive administrative procedures sometimes finds acquiescence from a zealous public. In the first year of the new millennium, the USA Patriot Act was passed by the U.S. Congress, and executive orders were issued that facilitate precisely this kind of stereotypical treatment of persons who appear friendly to Islamic terrorism. The 124-page act, passed quickly and signed into law by President George W. Bush on October 26, 2001, carves significant chunks out of a constitutional tradition that offers protection against searches or detention without a showing of cause and presses toward large-scale investigations and deportations. Father Robert F. Drinan, who has served in Congress, pointed out that the bill was proposed by the Justice Department, not by the House Judiciary Committee, which had approved its own legislation by a 36-0 margin. He added that the rush to passage, compounded by the scope of the legislation, made it "impossible to comprehend or even read the bill."[46] He also suggested that no evidence was given that the changes in law would have prevented the events of September 11. Enumerating earlier moments of "panic legislation" in American history, he listed the Alien and Sedition Acts of 1798, the cancellation of *habeas corpus* during the Civil War, and the internment of 120,000 Japanese-Americans to whom the nation later apologized and paid reparations. His final assessment of the act's implications was pessimistic:

> In such a climate, almost anything that is proposed as a weapon against terrorism will be approved. Congress rejected all the usual months of reflection and calmness needed for sensible and wise legislation. Its product is one more serious impediment to granting equality and justice to the seven or more million Americans who are of Arab or Muslim heritage.

Tragically echoing Drinan's concern were the hundreds of incidents around the country in which people of Arab, Muslim, Persian, or Sikh appearance were screamed at, assaulted, or even murdered. Stores, homes, and mosques were paint-balled, defaced by hateful graffiti, or burned. People of Arab appearance or distinctive dress felt terrorized in their homes, at their schools or workplaces, and they expressed fears of attending their mosques. While President Bush and government leaders generally sought to stem the tide of irrational hate, they could not prevent the initial destructive surge that will probably instill fear for generations — even among groups who immigrated to this country more than 100 years ago.[47]

These terrorist acts of rage, designed to retaliate against the sources of evil, reflected more than the events of September 11. We have learned from our own popular culture that Arabs share the subhumanity of earlier victims of national rage. Jack Shaheen, an American-Arab who has studied stereotypes for several decades, reported this finding from reviewing eight seasons of television nearly twenty years ago:

> Television tends to perpetuate four basic myths about Arabs: they are all fabulously wealthy; they are barbaric and uncultured; they are sex maniacs with a penchant for white slavery; and they revel in acts of terrorism. . . . The image can best be described as "The Instant TV Arab Kit." The kit, suitable for most TV Arabs, consists of a belly dancer's outfit, headdresses (which look like tablecloths pinched from a restaurant), veils, sunglasses, flowing gowns and robes, oil wells, limousines and/or camels. . . . Yet just a little surface probing reveals that these notions are as false as the assertions that blacks are lazy, Hispanics are dirty, Jews are greedy and Italians are criminals.[48]

Even as other racial and ethnic groups have pressured television and the movies for less derogatory images of their people, Shaheen's "TV Arab" has not really improved. Shaheen's more recent study of the movies, *Reel Bad Arabs: How Hollywood Vilifies a People*,[49] offers a comprehensive review of theatrical films supporting his thesis that Arabs are either "invisible or despicable." The conclusion of his earlier work still seems valid: "The present Arab stereotype parallels the image of Jews in pre-Nazi Germany, where Jews were painted as dark, shifty-eyed, venal and threateningly different people."[50] We know from sad history that such images of Jews, blacks, and other minorities have been accompanied by widespread acquiescence in committing atrocities against them.

Unfortunately, the heart of the USA Patriot Act seems to beat to the stereotype of "the evil ones" that President Bush called on so frequently in leading the nation toward an open-ended war on terrorism. As he signed the legislation against "a threat like no other our nation has ever faced," he defined the character of "the enemy": "They recognize no barrier of morality. They have no conscience. The terrorists cannot be reasoned with."[51] In other words, "they," being subhuman, can only be rooted out and destroyed. Our legislators and executives are hardly alone in thinking of new ways to deal with the new inhumanities with which we are confronted. Along the way, it may be necessary to torture them, in the opinion of Alan Dershowitz, formerly one of the nation's staunchest advocates for strict preservation of the Bill of Rights' letter and spirit. Since September 11 he has repeatedly advocated that the United States join Israel as the world's only democracy that maintains the legal option to authorize the torture of suspects in cases of extreme urgency. Dershowitz believes that his humane contribution to the cause is to require a "judicial warrant" so as "to reduce and limit the amount of torture that would, in fact, be used in an emergency." According to his prescription, torture would be limited to "nonlethal means, such as sterile needles being inserted beneath the nails to cause excruciating pain without endangering life."[52] A further bonus to the tortured person is that "the suspect would be given immunity from prosecution based on information elicited by the torture" — thus checkmating the traditional constitutional arguments against self-incriminating confessions. It does not fill us with a sense of safety to join the company of Israel in this legal innovation, nor can we imagine that the confederates of tortured suspects, learning of such torture, will relent in their conspiracies.

One of the most important movements of the Enlightenment was to develop powerful arguments against judicial torture — the kind of arguments embedded in the Fifth Amendment to the U.S. Constitution. Cesare Beccaria, an Italian mathematician with an interest in crime and punishment, pointed out this "strange consequence . . . from the use of torture" in 1764:

> The innocent person is placed in a worse situation than the criminal, since if both of them are tortured, all circumstances are against the former: for either he confesses to the crime and is condemned, or he is found innocent after having suffered a punishment he did not deserve. The criminal, on the other hand, is in an inherently favorable situation: that is, if he firmly withstands the torture, he is acquitted; he has exchanged a greater punishment for a lesser one. Thus, the innocent cannot but lose, and the guilty can only gain.[53]

Alan Dershowitz does not seem to mind the cost of punishing the innocent in such situations, because he seems confident that errors will never happen. It has always been thus with stereotypes of "the evil ones"; once you have your needles under their fingernails, you can be sure that salvation is near at hand.

Five Strategies to Overcome Destructive Stereotypes

Given the potential of stereotyping to dehumanize both stereotyper and victim, why is it so difficult to overcome? Surely it has long been apparent that it
leads to violence, that it counters the precious heritage of democratic equality, and that it has led us into unwise wars. Educators in particular have long
been aware that stereotyping disguises reality and incapacitates the mind to
make impartial and pragmatic assessments of evidence. Yet experience indicates over and over again the resilience of the stereotypes and their capacity to
resist any argument or evidence to the contrary. No matter how much data
were amassed to disprove popular stereotypes in foreign relations, the power
of the stereotypes seemed to remain. The mistake is to consider stereotyping a
purely intellectual problem, a habit of the mind that can be altered by the infusion of contrary evidence. In actuality it is a religious problem. The American stereotypes of good and evil are beliefs that provide a clear and apparently defensible sense of the identity of and solution to evil and an equally
clear and gratifying sense of national self-righteousness. To give them up is to
acknowledge problematic aspects of one's national or peer-group history. It is
to enter the dangerous and ambiguous realm of relative judgments, with no
hope of absolute certainties and every prospect of incriminating mistakes.
On the intellectual level alone, it is preposterous to think that such advanta-
geous structures would give way under the mere infusion of contrary evidence. Consequently, the liberal tradition in America, hostile toward theology, naive about the tenacity of belief structures, and superficial in its grasp of
human nature, has been ineffective in dealing with one of the crucial components in a long series of irrational policies.

In the realistic tradition of biblical thinkers, however, there are some brilliant strategies designed to grapple with the hold of idolatrous stereotypes.
There are also secular forms of these strategies that have emerged in various
quarters that make plain the potential. In taking the religious tenacity of the
stereotypes fully into account, these strategies avoid the inevitably futile frontal attack. To use Kierkegaard's expression, they "wound from behind." They
usually begin by seeming to take the stereotyping viewpoint with full conviction, drawing the audience into the line of argument or action, and then col-
lapsing the stereotype from within. They lead conversation partners to advance on their own assumptions beyond themselves, to the point where the
stereotypes suddenly appear absurd or immoral, so that their minds can
progress beyond the shadowy land of mythic images into daylight. Their goal
is to humanize individuals and nations by freeing them from the grip of idolatrous stereotypes.

The first strategy is what we call *ironic transposition.* This was used by Amos to powerful effect in his sermon at Bethel, the royal cult center of Israel in the North at the time of the national expansion under Jeroboam II. The Northerners had explained their successes and justified their treatment of enemies by means of stereotypes counterposing God's righteous and elect people and their unrighteous foes. Rather than directly attacking these brutal stereotypes, Amos used them in ironic fashion to condemn Israel's enemies for precisely the same kinds of crimes that Israel herself had committed (Amos 1:3 to 2:3). Only after Amos had the nationalistic audience fully on his side did he transpose the images to give a sudden fresh insight into the impact such stereotyped behavior had already made on Israelite life (Amos 2:6-16).

In the New Testament era, Jesus used this transposition technique, and he combined it with the ironic humor of his parables. In one incident a man burst onto the scene with an abrupt and imperious demand: "Master, tell my brother to divide the family property with me" (Luke 12:13). The Jewish law encouraged the holding of family property in common, with the elder brother directing affairs and dividing the living with the younger. Lacking a legal remedy and apparently finding cooperation with the dominant older brother intolerable, this man was so obsessed with the justness of his cause and the injustice of his brother's hold that he did not even precede his demand with an explanation. Jesus responded at first with a question phrased to adopt the imperious questioner's stereotype of himself as "good." "My good man, who set me over you to judge or arbitrate?" He then told the crowd: "Beware! Be on your guard against greed of every kind, for even when a man has more than enough, his wealth does not give him life." At first glance, this remark would not seem to be directed against the questioner, because from his perspective his brother's greed had caused the problem. But the emphasis on "greed of every kind," and the antithesis between wealth and life, served to juggle the stereotype of absolute right and wrong with its obsessive solution.

Then Jesus launched into the story of the "rich fool" (Luke 12:16-20), which would have moved the crowd to laughter but served at the same time to transpose the stereotype. The questioner and the crowd would see in the "rich man" a stereotype of the wicked materialist, such as the older brother. The rich man's obsessive conversation with himself and his ridiculous behavior of pulling down his barns to build "bigger" ones would strike them as funny. It comes as abruptly as that moment in the old silent movies when a confident, whistling man — proudly outfitted in tall black hat and evening clothes — suddenly disappears down an overlooked manhole. And since the rich man has considered no one but himself in the story, who is to inherit his money? His relatives. But the story achieves more than the relief of a tense situation through laughter. The questioner is made to laugh at precisely the same obsessive behavior in which he himself has just engaged. His laughter helps break the stereotype and enables him to see the illusion concealed in his own desire to be sole manipulator of his portion of the estate. This ironic transposition was designed to make it possible for him to live with this all-too-human and apparently insoluble dilemma.

A second strategy is to *stretch the stereotype* of the righteous person, extending it along the lines of its natural development, so that one can glimpse its grotesque nature. To be effective, it must avoid polemical crudity but precisely use the religious ideals of the audience so that from the outset they can identify themselves in a positive manner with the stereotype that is to be stretched.

Jesus is clearly using this technique in the parable of the Pharisee and the tax collector (Luke 18:10-14). Joachim Jeremias has suggested that in the figure of the Pharisee, Jesus has given us not a caricature but the epitome of the religious ideal common to first-century Jewish piety. The audience would initially identify itself with the Pharisee, who "went up into the temple to pray." Most moderns have entirely missed this point because of their negative stereotype of Pharisees. In the proper fashion of Jewish prayer, the Pharisee does not claim he has earned his superior status: "God, I thank you that I am not like other men, greedy, dishonest, adulterous, or even like this tax collector. I fast twice a week, I give tithes of all that I get." By thanking God for his virtue, the Pharisee affirms God's grace with the conventional humility of that time. Even the comparison of himself with the tax collector would not strike the audience as boastful, because the traditional Eighteen Benediction prayer thanks God that one is not a "Gentile . . . a woman . . ." or some other person unable to assume the burden and blessing of the whole law. Jesus merely stretches the natural lines of contemporary piety in mentioning the morally depraved types. But he has already set the trap: whereas the comparison models in the conventional prayers are those who cannot obey the whole Jewish law, the models for the "greedy, dishonest, adulterous" could just as easily include Jews such as the Pharisee himself.

The subtle stretching of the paradigm of virtue reveals immediately that it is not the blessing of the law that is central for this man, but rather the status of being better than the "rest of men." The comparison with the tax collector likewise stretches the stereotype of the good man. The audience, hostile to the agents of the Roman government, would easily applaud the inclusion. Yet the terrain of popular piety is getting trickier, because presumably the Pharisee was praying to God. Why is he looking around at the tax collector? Although the audience would still identify with the good guy stereotype, they would be aware that something was amiss. But the description of the Pharisee's prayer moved even further in the same direction. To "fast twice a week" and "pay tithes on all that I get" were the extremes in piety. They were points that most people recognized as the height of piety, but at the same time they resented having them imposed on them by the Pharisees. The listeners who had identified themselves with the Pharisees were thus led subtly into issues that had infuriated them as unreasonable burdens that only the rich and leisurely had time to fulfill. Suddenly, the discrepancy with the Pharisee's protestation that he was really not like rich men — "greedy, dishonest" — begins to jar the mind; he makes it even more offensive by his repeated "I . . . I . . . I. . . ." The audience is suddenly in a position to grasp the essential fact: although his prayer is couched in the elaborate disguise of conventional piety, this Pharisee is not praying. He is boasting.

This insight is immediately confirmed by the contrasting picture of the tax collector. He prays in the simple and humble manner prescribed by the prophets and psalms. He acknowledges his human failures and relies entirely on God's mercy. Here is the true form of piety that the Pharisee had elaborately feigned in his prayer. In comparison with this proper humility, the piety of the Pharisee, which the audience initially accepted as normative, now appears truly grotesque. The final line of the parable simply applies the hammer to a structure that is about to crumple from internal tension: "I tell you, this man [the tax collector] went down to his house justified rather than the other." He alone was accepted by God. Given the cultural assumptions of the time, the listeners have to agree. They are led to see the grotesqueness of their own stereotypes of the good guy and to see that the hated tax collector actually is capable of model piety. In being stretched to their logical conclusions, stereotypes that would have resisted any frontal assault have been exploded from within, enabling the listeners to perceive the human realities disguised by the stereotypes.

A third strategy, closely related to the above parable, is *to humanize the Bad Person.*[54] This, too, must be done skillfully, lest the critic fall under suspicion of disloyalty by picturing an enemy as a person of virtue. It must be a fully believable and natural story in which the audience is led on its own assumptions to break with past stereotypes of enemy behavior. Depicting a tax collector as a model of biblical piety achieves such an end, even though it mainly serves in the story to provide the clarifying counterpoint to the Pharisee's hypocrisy.

A more explicit use of this strategy is found in Jesus' classic story of the good Samaritan (Luke 10:29-37). The background of the vicious stereotype of Samaritans as incorrigible heretics and miscegenists is an essential premise of this story, lifting it above the level of a moralistic example, as it is so often understood.[55] When the lawyer asks the question that elicits the story, the issue of cultural stereotypes is really under debate: "And who is my neighbor?" (Luke 10:29). This raised the question whether the command to love the neighbor as oneself relates to enemies, Gentiles, and heretics, a matter that most of Jesus' zealous contemporaries fiercely answered in the negative. Neighbors such as the Samaritans were not to be loved but rather liquidated as hindrances to the coming of God's kingdom. Instead of attacking this vicious stereotype directly, or imposing the demand to love Samaritan neighbors on the unwilling lawyer, Jesus devises a parable that strikes at the root of the problem. It portrays a Samaritan not as the recipient of neighborly love but rather as a humane agent of such love. He sets this up with extraordinary care so as to convince rather than to offend. A Jewish traveler from Jerusalem to Jericho is attacked by bandits and left "half dead" along the barren and dangerous road. When two religious officials "passed by on the other side" without providing assistance, there is a situation of urgent, lifesaving necessity that elicits the sympathy of the hearers. The extremity of the circumstances and the resentment against the callous officials prepare the audience to approve the assistance that come from an otherwise unacceptable source — the Samaritan.[56] To receive such help in an emergency is not morally offensive to one who believes in the stereotype, whereas to render such help to a Samaritan violates the obligation to carry out zealous murder. The story decisively undercuts the stereotype that presumes Samaritans to be bestial, unfeeling, and cruel louts.[57]

Jesus specifically emphasizes the indirect impact of the story in his question to the lawyer at the conclusion of the story: "Which of these three do you think was neighbor to the man who fell into the hands of the robbers?" The lawyer answers, "The one who showed him kindness." And Jesus concludes, "Go and do as he did." The question shifts here from "Who is my neighbor?" to "Who acted in a neighborly fashion?" The shift makes sense because answering the first question directly would require a futile attack on the stereotype. In contrast, Jesus' question evokes the irresistible recognition that the Samaritan indeed fulfilled the commandment of neighborliness. The audience must thus discard the crucial premise of the stereotype: how can all Samaritans be bestial if this one man showed such mercy? Even the sophisticated lawyer has to acknowledge this much, though he still cannot bring himself to use the word "Samaritan" in his reply to Jesus. The parable enables him to shed the blinders of the stereotype and acknowledge the antagonist's humanity.

Similarly, social scientists have discovered that "one of the most important antidotes" to torturing "is to break through the chasm that separates the torturer from the humanity of his victims."[58] Daniel Goleman reports an episode involving a former army officer who had served as a torturer, described in *The Breaking of Bodies and Minds* by Elena O. Nightingale and Eric Stower. He was assigned the task of torturing "a man whom he recognized as his friend since childhood. The officer refused, for which he himself was arrested and court martialed. He has now left Uruguay, given a full account of his participation, and describes himself as 'totally repentant.'"[59] A new and more humane form of social interaction becomes possible when one discovers the humanity of one's opponent.

Jesus developed a fourth strategy by using nonverbal as well as verbal means to *celebrate coexistence* between enemies.[60] The crucial requirement of this method is the effective expression of unconditional acceptance. When two people who are antagonistic because of stereotyped expectations feel completely accepted by a third party, they will act toward him with their guard down. If the trust is deep enough, they will be able to extend such openness to each other. But since the stereotypes have such resistance to direct confrontation, indirect means such as sharing in a festivity or a new common cause are the most effective agencies of reconciliation.

Both in his circle of disciples and in the joyous celebrations of the presence of the kingdom, Jesus used such means to notable advantage. Contrary to the customs of the times, he invited disciples to join him and thus achieved two components of this strategy. He communicated a sense of his acceptance of them in the invitation, but he also was able to make certain that his circle was not merely a gathering of like-minded persons. From various sides of the ideological struggle, Jesus chose people who had acted out the stereotyped roles that made coexistence impossible. He called Matthew the tax collector, a hated Roman collaborator, to be a fellow disciple with Simon the Zealot (Luke 6:15)[61] and Judas Iscariot, whose very name implied membership in the zealot underground.[62] Jesus brought these men into fellowship with hated tax gatherers such as Zacchaeus (Luke 19:1-10), as well as with haughty Pharisees (Luke 14:1-24), despised outcasts, and even prostitutes (Luke 15:1; Matt. 21:31; Luke 7:39). These were groups that opposed each other with the fury that ideological fanaticism provokes. They constantly attempted to destroy each other, and each justified his brutality with the faceless stereotype of the demonic enemy whose destruction is demanded for the coming of the kingdom. The experience of celebrating the presence of the kingdom together served to overcome these barriers with amazing effectiveness.

Jesus instructed his followers to use their creative impulses to restore a spirit of coexistence with people who had acted toward them in hostile fashion. In Matthew 5:38-41, he advises them not to "resist" persons stereotyped as "evil." This implies not giving back in kind, if the Greek expression is taken fully into account — not the passive acceptance of evil so often inferred from the text. The examples make it clear that he envisioned spontaneous gestures to restore relations between equals.[63] When the insulting backhand strikes one "on the right cheek," one should ignore the insult and express willingness to begin again. When the hated Roman legionnaire forces one to carry his pack the compulsory mile, perhaps one might go beyond the legal obligation and treat him as a fellow human being with a heavy burden, rather than as an enemy. The element of spontaneously celebrating coexistence predominates in these examples. Jesus is not in any sense setting up pacifistic rules.[64] The key element is to reach through the mask of the stereotype and treat the "enemy" as a person worthy of concern and personal relationship. Such nonverbal gestures can do more to break down destructive stereotypes than the most closely reasoned argument.

A final strategy is to retain or develop *institutions of coexistence.* Structures of law and custom that allow competing groups to interact peaceably and adjudicate their conflicts through compromise are constantly in danger of being discarded by a zealous public. The fact that such institutions treat ideological opponents as equals may infuriate the parties themselves, but it is absolutely essential in preserving domestic tranquility and affirming the limitations of the stereotypes. Thus the exponents of prophetic realism from the time of Amos to the historical Jesus displayed a marked interest in such institutions. One thinks of Amos's affirmation of the validity of international codes of behavior in the sermon at Bethel, of Isaiah's vision of the international tribunal of justice, and of Jesus' unpopular stand in support of the institutions of Roman justice. In this last instance, the zealots undoubtedly saw his advising his hearers to pay taxes to Caesar as blasphemous; but it fit precisely with his concern to overcome the violent stereotypes that were leading his generation into a disastrous crusade.

Jesus' concern for institutions of coexistence was particularly evident in the cleansing of the Temple, the incident leading directly to his execution. The moneychangers and sellers of sacrificial animals had moved their operations into the Gentile court as a convenience to the Jewish pilgrims, who usually bought their sacrifices in the stalls on the hill opposite the Temple. In addition, the populace of Jerusalem had begun to use the gates on either side of the Gentile court as a shortcut into the city. With the court transformed into a noisy bazaar, dignified worship by Gentile pilgrims was impossible. An institution designed for both Jews and Gentiles was being callously distorted by behavior explicable only on the premise of the vicious stereotype of the

Gentiles as irredeemable. As the account in Mark 11 reveals, Jesus used the hostility of the zealous Passover crowd toward the Sadducee temple authorities to throw their agents out of the Gentile court, but he did so with a rationale that the crowds certainly did not have in mind. "And he taught, and said to them, 'Is it not written, "My house shall be called a house of prayer for all the nations"? But you have made it a den of robbers'" (Mark 11:17). The citation from Isaiah proclaims the ideal of the Temple as an institution of coexistence, a place where all the nations would come to worship. To retain such an institution could contribute to the healthy recognition that stereotyped enemies stand as equals before God.

These strategies may offer current critics of American stereotypes some stimulus for their endeavors. It is a task that should engage the vital energies of an entire generation of artists and teachers, ministers and civic leaders. Avoiding the futile methods of the past and grasping the essentially idolatrous structure of popular stereotypes, they are called to help overcome the stereotypes that have shielded us from reality and led to brutality. This can be accomplished only by those who love people enough to respect the moral passions that grip the stereotypes, and who understand them enough so that their hidden capacities for sympathy and justice can be elicited. We need the resources of the filmmakers, novelists, and artists whose genius is to create new images of humanity. We need the wisdom of community leaders to defend and develop institutions of coexistence such as the Constitution and the principles of the Declaration of Independence. We need the courage of religious leaders to incorporate enemies into their fellowships and to develop the means of tolerant cooperation. We can only hope that they will work with such effectiveness that the world may be spared the senseless tragedies that are always latent in moral imaginations captivated by stereotypes.

13 To Convert Them or Destroy Them

When he saw the blood, it was as though he had drunk a deep draught of savage passion. Instead of turning away, he fixed his eyes on the scene and drank in all its frenzy, unaware of what he was doing. He reveled in the wickedness of the fighting and was drunk with the fascination of bloodshed. He was no longer the man who had come to the arena. . . . Need I say more? He watched and cheered and grew hot with excitement, and when he left the arena, he carried away with him a diseased mind which would leave him no peace until he had come back again. . . .

St. Augustine on his acquaintance Alypius at the Roman games[1]

St. Augustine was repulsed by the brutality of Roman entertainments and doubtless hoped that the coming of Christian faith would significantly change tastes. He could not foresee that the faith itself could ride alongside and often enhance violent currents of succeeding cultures. Like St. Augustine, we are disturbed by the violence in our midst, but part of that distress must fall on why it remains so appealing — especially to Americans — after centuries of exposure to gospel messages of peace and love. There is an aspect of American ideology that seems to condition us to consider our own violence benign. The conviction was nicely put by the line in the Dick Tracy comics at the time of the Robert Kennedy assassination: "Violence is golden when it's used to put evil down." This articulates the pervasive appeal of those moments of righteous violence that we have reviewed in this book. The challenge is to understand the source of its peculiar appeal to us as individuals, as makers of our civic order, and as world citizens who project our power into other lands.

From its beginnings, the idea of righteous violence as means of redemption and conversion has carried the positive aura of moral purity. We begin our analysis by focusing on the origins of this seductive mystique in ancient Israel and its later evolutions in American history. Then we apply the critical resources of prophetic realism that come to us through the voices of Hosea and Jesus so as to clarify the contrast between unconditional love and violence as the means of world transformation.

Redemptive Violence in the Bible

That violence can be redemptive is affirmed in one of the oldest pieces of Hebrew poetry, the Song of Miriam, which celebrates the triumph over the Egyptians at the time of the exodus:[2]

> Sing to Yahweh, for he has triumphed gloriously,
> Horse and rider he has thrown into the sea! (Ex. 15:21)

In sweeping the Egyptians into the sea, Yahweh saved his people from slavery and demonstrated his glorious power both to Israel and to the nations looking on. The community is exhorted to celebrate this act of redemption through song; and there is a note of ecstatic enthusiasm here that concentrates on Yahweh as the agency of magnificent, redemptive violence. In the later elaboration of the song, these motifs — implicit in the archaic fragment — are explicitly stated, revealing the connections between violence and redemption, destruction and conversion (Ex. 15:11-16). Yahweh's violent warfare achieves the "salvation" of his people, which in this context means emancipation from the Egyptians. In having "redeemed" them, he demonstrates his "steadfast love." From the very start of the Israelite tradition, therefore, violence is the means to set men free. Yahweh's glory is visible in his terrible "deeds" and "wonders." He is praised as a "man of war" (Ex. 15:3) who triumphs over the foes of his people, demonstrating his superiority over the other gods (Ex. 15:11). The neighboring peoples tremble because their gods cannot protect them from Yahweh's martial power. They behave quiescently as the Israelites move into their territories. Their acknowledgment of Yahweh's power bespeaks conversion, for, in the primitive context, to worship a god is to affirm his superiority over other forces and to assure oneself of safety under his sphere of protective power.

In the Song of Miriam it is not violence as such but righteous violence that can redeem and convert. The song stigmatizes the violent desires of the Egyptians as boastful, bloodthirsty, and predatory (Ex. 15:9). This immoral form of violence is frustrated by Yahweh's blast of wind, which drives the waters over their heads. This critical attitude toward private or foreign violence frequently appears in biblical material. The Hebrew form of the flood story emphasizes the moral justification of worldwide destruction because of the violence that has spread over the earth in the wake of Adam's fall and the upsurge of violent civilizations: "Now the earth was corrupt in God's sight, and the earth was filled with violence. . . . And God said to Noah, 'I have determined to make an end of all flesh; for the earth is filled with violence through them'" (Gen. 6:11-13). Here the fist of divine violence smashes human violence motivated by mere pride. Noah alone, of all living men, is deemed sufficiently humble and upright to earn his family's preservation. This typical moral structure is stated succinctly in Ps. 11:5: "The Lord tests the righteous and the wicked, and his soul hates him that loves violence." The paradox here is that God hates violence — though supreme in violence himself. Violent humans are to be destroyed by violence because violence is hateful in the hands of humans perceived to be evil. Not until the maturing of prophetic realism was this paradox of divinity rectified, but for American civil religion, the redemptive capacity of righteous violence — in the hands of the right men — still predominates.

Given the prevalence of the conspiracy theory of evil, destructive violence lies in the realm of evil. In Psalm 58 the agents of the foreign gods enact the violent decrees of their vicious idols. In order for Yahweh's righteousness to prevail in the cosmic struggle, the psalmist demands the most bloody forms of annihilation:

> The righteous will rejoice when he sees the vengeance;
>   he will bathe his feet in the blood of the wicked.
> Men will say, "Surely there is a reward for the righteous;
>   surely there is a God who judges on earth." (Ps. 58:10-11)

Here the mystique of righteous violence has taken its mature form. The issue falls not merely between Israel and her political rivals, but between Yahweh and false gods (Ps. 58:1f.). Since the agents of the gods are incorrigible, filled with "the venom of a serpent . . . like the deaf adder that stops its ear" against the truth (Ps. 58:3-5), violence is justified. Harvey H. Guthrie has pointed up this dimension of cosmic incorrigibility: "Vague as to who the 'wicked' are, the psalm ascribes what they are to causes lying beyond their own ability to decide or to set their venomous course. . . . The sovereign of the cosmos himself must intervene if effective remedy is to be realized."[3] The cosmic level of the struggle between God and the demonic constitutes the mystique of violence. The spared believer "rejoices" in the bloodshed, because the righteousness of the cause overcomes any revulsion toward the bathing in the blood of the slain wicked. The righteous survivors, in other words, may indulge in the pleasures of Augustine's perverted friend Alypius.

In Psalm 58 the motif of conversion is again present, even though the enemy itself is too incorrigible to be converted. The last verse of the psalm suggests that "men" in general will be convinced of Yahweh's righteous judgment on the earth when he prevails against the resistance of the other gods. Despite the improbable effectiveness of this kind of missionary rationale, it typifies the tradition of zealous nationalism.

The missional motif appears in the crude expectation of the prophet Zephaniah that all sinful nations will be punished so that they will repent and be converted. Because of their recalcitrance, the prophet envisions that Yahweh will enact his will to "gather nations, to assemble kingdoms, to pour out upon them my indignation, all the heat of my anger; for in the fire of my jealous wrath all the earth shall be consumed. Yea, at that time I will change the speech of the peoples to a pure speech, that all of them may call on the name of Yahweh and serve him with one accord" (Zeph. 3:8f.). Whether anyone would really be converted by this indiscriminate orgy of zealous violence, or whether indeed there would be anybody left to convert — these are questions that apparently do not trouble the prophet. If the heathen are to change their language and learn to pray in Hebrew so as to serve Yahweh "with one accord," conversion is clearly a matter of cultural assimilation. A powerful impulse comes to light here, one that is directly related to the "fire of zealous wrath." When a particular moral or cultural stance absolutizes itself in zeal, as in the vision of Zephaniah, it thrusts itself violently on its adversaries. The desire is either to convert or to destroy the presumed agents of evil; if this version of truth is absolute, everyone else's must conform. From this premise, to convert is actually to destroy.

In the ancient Semitic custom of the "ban," or "devotion" of spoils to Yahweh, one can see the basic similarity between conversion and destruction. At the conclusion of a battle the priests would order the booty and prisoners placed under *ḥerem* ("the ban"), to be destroyed or dedicated to God. This is reported in the biblical account of Jericho's destruction (Josh. 6:17-21). The rationale of *ḥerem* was that the chosen people, in conquest, appropriated the evil realm belonging to the sphere of the rival god. Since it would defile their purity and erode their strength to possess such objects, they had to decontaminate the objects.[4] Depending on the degree of toxic threat to cultural purity, some objects had to be burned, others purified, and others devoted to the holy treasury. The crucial affirmation in this ritual is that the chosen people believed coexistence with the alien realm to be impossible. The choice was to destroy or to convert by radically altering the threatening features. In either case, the duty was to eradicate any distinctive marks of the conquered, alien sphere. In one episode of cultural danger, an individual's appropriation of a part of the Jericho booty so eroded Israel's strength that the next battle resulted in defeat. Only when they had located the source of corruption and extirpated the offender's entire family could Yahweh's wrath be averted and victory be assured (Josh. 7).

Since this entire story is highly idealized — because Jericho was actually destroyed long before Israel's conquest of Canaan, as archaeologists have discovered[5] — it presents a purely ideological impulse. It provided an ideal precedent not only for Jewish behavior in the later period but also for English Puritan and American zealotry. An analysis of the grievances leading to the emergence of the African-American and Native American power movements reveals the consequences of this ideology: conversion on these zealously nationalistic terms has been experienced as cultural annihilation. In other words, converting others in the crucible of purification is simply another way of destroying them. The Taliban's furious efforts at cultural extirpation in Afghanistan follow this same precedent.

We need to examine one final motif: the capacity of righteous violence to bring peace. It surfaces in the story of Achan, the looter of Jericho. With his punishment and the dedication of his booty to Yahweh, Israel was delivered from her enemies: "Then Yahweh turned away his burning anger" (Josh. 7:26). The same motif appears in the story of Phinehas, who in a similar situation averted Yahweh's wrath by killing Zimri and his Midianite wife. According to the tradition, Yahweh declares: "Behold, I give to him my covenant of peace . . . because he was zealous for his God, and made atonement for the people of Israel" (Num. 25:12f.). The future priesthood of Phinehas and his descendants would be granted prosperity and respite from opposition, just as the averting of Yahweh's wrath would signify, for Israel as a whole, the return of success. "Peace" in this ancient tradition had a wider and more material sense than in modern usage; it connoted "the state of wholeness possessed by persons or groups, which may be health, prosperity, security, or the spiritual completeness of covenant."[6] If such wholeness were being ruined by alien corruption, destroying corruption meant restoring peace. A similar logic was implied in the many statements linking a successfully completed war with the idea of peace.[7] To prevail over the enemy is to gain peace because it averts the threat to the well-being of the community. The precedent was established here for the long tradition of seeming double-talk that typifies zealous nationalism: wars for the sake of peace, destruction of enemies to guard the peace, and ultimately — as in the Book of Revelation — the violent destruction of the entire world so that the peace of the saints can be secured.

To summarize, biblical zeal offers a thorough and appealing mystique for violence, making it seem plausible that righteous violence could redeem God's people, demonstrate his superiority over rival forces, and even convert the world to a single faith. This mystique clarifies the proximity of destruction and conversion, and it justifies the most appalling atrocities against alien persons and objects. Violence could even produce peace. With an appeal of this magnitude, it is logical that the grounds for violence often seem self-evident. It also follows that a culture schooled in this tradition will exhibit extremely high levels of violence in both its individual and its collective behavior.

Violence and America's Sense of Mission

The biblical tradition of redemptive violence was popularized in Western culture by the Crusades, and it was then taken up by the Reformation in England. As Michael Walzer has shown, Puritanism developed the crusading impulse of the Old Testament to the logical extreme. Puritan divines visualized God as a God of violent justice, and they called on their people to carry out his purposes in history:

> A warlike God made warlike men. . . . "Above all creatures [God] loves soldiers," proclaimed a Puritan preacher, "and . . . above all actions he honors warlike and martial design." "Whoever is a professed Christian," declared another, "he is a professed soldier. . . ." As there is permanent opposition and conflict in the cosmos, so there is permanent warfare on earth. "The condition of the child of God," wrote Thomas Taylor, "is military in this life." The saint was a soldier — but so was everyone else; Puritans did not recognize noncombatants. "All degrees of men are warriors, some fighting for the enlargement of religion and some against it."[8]

The rationale of such warfare was to destroy the agents of wickedness and thus usher in the era of redemption promised by Daniel and Revelation. Not only would Puritan violence be redemptive, it would convert the world. When God had destroyed evil, root and branch, the last resistance to the truth would disappear. But evil had to be totally annihilated. To say that even women and children were combatants, agents of the force of evil, was to pre-pare the way for the unrestrained application of *herem*.

It is possible to draw from this Puritan outlook direct lines to the peculiar mystique of violence in America. Senator William Fulbright suggested this in his thoughtful speech "Violence in the American Character," which he wrote in the wake of President Kennedy's assassination: "The Puritan way of think-ing, harsh and intolerant, permeated the political and economic life of the country and became a major secular force in America."[9] Fulbright pointed particularly to the impact of the Puritan dogma of absolute good and abso-lute evil, which tends to rationalize violence. When the saints feel called on to take up the task of overcoming such evil, their mission work is marked by in-tolerance, and their warring takes on the harshness of the Old Testament ban.

The implicit connections between zealous mission and zealous warfare come into sharp focus in the accounts of American missionaries. Winthrop Hudson has shown the interlocking character of foreign missions and world redemption, citing Rev. Heman Humphrey's sermon of 1819 at the ordination of the first missionaries to Hawaii.[10] Humphrey compared the mission enter-prise to Israel's conquest of Canaan: "As the nation of Israel was then militant, so is the church now. As the land of Canaan belonged to Israel in virtue of a di-vine grant, so does the world belong to the church. And as God's chosen peo-ple still had much to do before they could come into full and quiet possession of the land, so has the church a great work to accomplish in subduing the world 'to the obedience of Christ.'" Humphrey went on to describe the fortu-itous circumstances that made it appear proper to conquer the heathen for Christ. He challenged "our American Israel" to take up this great task, and his terminology evoked images of a war against wickedness. The missionaries were to look upon themselves "as soldiers in this important expedition. You have set your faces towards Hawaii as part of the 'promised land' which remaineth 'yet to be possessed.'" Mission in this context amounts to cultural annihilation — first purifying the alien sphere of false gods and then assimi-lating them. This is a grandiose conception of world redemption, with the ex-pectation of world peace when the chosen people come "into full and quiet possession of the land." Mission is simply an alternate form of warfare.

The zealous form of mission appears with striking frequency in the writ-ings of missionaries and theologians who were widely influential in shaping the sense of American destiny. John Eliot, the first missionary to the Ameri-can Indians, who helped to found the Society for the Propagation of the Gos-pel in New England, wrote tracts concerning the "wars of the Lord against the Anti-Christ."[11] Timothy Dwight, president of Yale during the Revolution, de-scribed the triumph of America over the "savage nations," with mission and national destiny combined.[12] During the entire colonial period the main motivation for mission was the "glory of God," which would be advanced when he triumphed over Satan's realm.[13] Samuel W. Fischer used similar motifs in his 1860 sermon before the American Board of Missions, entitled "God's Purpose in Planting the American Church." God's purpose was to spread the mission throughout the world: "to form men, to give laws to nations, and to interpenetrate the souls of missions with the truth as it is in Jesus." He interpreted the growth in American power, "the power that subdues and moulds other minds by a law as certain as that which bids the flowers open," as given by God. It would make possible the fulfillment of America's destiny to "lead the van of Immanuel's army for the conquest of the world."[14]

The definitive statement of mission and manifest destiny was made by Josiah Strong, the secretary of the American Home Missionary Society. According to Strong, the English-speaking peoples were being prepared by God to enter the competition with other races for the control of the world. The Christian mission would serve to destroy the cultures of inferior and corrupt peoples and incorporate them into the dominant culture of the chosen race. Now that the westward expansion was completed in America, the new stage could begin — "the final competition of races, for which the Anglo-Saxon is being schooled." America's "peculiarly aggressive traits calculated to impress its institutions upon mankind" will inevitably dominate the world. The result would fit the Darwinian formula:

> Can anyone doubt that the result of this competition of races will be the "survival of the fittest"? Nothing can save the inferior race but a ready and pliant assimilation. . . . The contest is not one of arms, but of vitality and civilization.[15]

Strong's writings gave emotional impetus to the sense of Manifest Destiny that justified campaigns to convert or destroy the adversaries. There was an "Old Testament fierceness" in this doctrine, to use Hans Kohn's words. He cites the Democratic politician and journalist John Louis O'Sullivan, who wrote in 1847: "The Mexican race now see in the fate of the aborigines of the north their own inevitable destiny." As Kohn puts it, "They must be either amalgamated and assimilated or they must utterly perish."[16]

The prevalence of imperialist ideas in more recent times and the basic congruity between zealous mission and zealous annihilation were strikingly illustrated from a conversation Langdon Gilkey reported in *Shantung Compound*.[17] Gilkey was interned in a Japanese prison camp with a mixed group of businessmen and missionaries, several of whom were discussing how Japan should be treated after the war. The less "religious" members of the group agreed that, while the Japanese were cruel and aggressive under the present circumstances, the best thing to do after the war would be "to try to forget this whole business and to bring them back again into the world of civilized and peaceable nations as quickly as possible." But the fundamentalist missionary Baker disagreed with furious urgency:

> Why they're all pagans there, and filled with all kinds of immorality. In fact, they're hardly human at all — look at the way they behave! No, I don't feel any responsibility to them as brothers. If our world is to be ruled by righteousness, we must rid it of these unrighteous groups as best we can. There's no question but what we should crush them completely in order to weaken them permanently as a nation. If necessary, I'd even say we ought seriously to consider depopulating the island.

One might be inclined to dismiss this genocidal sentiment as extreme and atypical, except for the fact that it fits the tradition so precisely. It reveals the basic connections that are disguised by more sophisticated spokesmen. The mystique of violent redemption, either by mission or by war, leads in extremity to just such sentiments.

As the history of the mission to the American Indians reveals, the mystique produced more than mere sentiments. From the beginning, the goal of many missionaries was to destroy the Indian cultures and to replace them with Christian civilization. When the Indians resisted cultural annihilation, they were consigned to *ḥerem,* beginning with the Pequot Massacre of 1637. Captain John Underhill defended this episode by referring specifically to the application of the ban in the Old Testament:

> It may be demanded, Why should you be so furious? But I would refer you to David's War. When a people is grown to such a height of blood, and sin against God and man . . . then he hath no respect to persons, but harrows them, and saws them, and puts them to the sword, and the most terriblest death that may be. Sometimes the Scriptures declareth women and children must perish with their parents. Sometimes the case alters; but we will not dispute it now. We had sufficient light from the word of God for our proceedings.[18]

The rationale of the massacre, in short, was precisely the same as the rationale for mission. The bloodthirsty savages had to be radically decontaminated for inclusion in the kingdom of the saints; and if they refused, annihilation was the logical solution. As one examines the rationale for the Protestant mission to the Indians, as Robert Berkhofer has done in *Salvation and the Savage*, this radical effort at cultural annihilation comes to the fore. Berkhofer writes: "Only a detailed examination of . . . the missionary mentality will persuade the reader how no custom was too picayune for censure and change and no demand too sweeping and drastic in the missionaries' attempt to revamp aboriginal life — in conformity with American ideals."[19] That such efforts were self-defeating from the start should have been obvious. But in the tradition of zealous nationalism, reinforced by biblical precedents, it seemed appropriate that conversion and destruction should go hand in hand. If resistance to the mission necessitated the application of *herem*, it was the fault of the Indians and not of the saints.

The Mystique of Violence in American Wars

The mystique of violence has imparted a distinctive character to American wars; these, in turn, have been decisive bearers of the mystique into a secular era. In the twentieth century at least, Americans have not had to learn it from reading the Old Testament or listening to missionary sermons. They have absorbed it from the traditional presentation of American history, in which the decisive dates are not the births or deaths of political leaders but the beginnings and endings of great crusades. They have endorsed it by experiencing wars to redeem the world for the "four freedoms," or to defend the "free world" against those who would impose dictatorships on their innocent neighbors. Ever since the Mexican War, Americans have taken up the goal of redeeming the world through violence. The historian Ray A. Billington found this motif in attitudes toward the call of Manifest Destiny:

> Every patriot who clamored for Mexico's provinces would indignantly deny any desire to exploit a neighbor's territory. The righteous but ill-informed people of that day sincerely believed their democratic institutions were of such magnificent perfection that no boundaries could contain them. Surely a benevolent Creator did not intend such blessings for the few; expansion was a divinely ordered means of extending enlightenment to despot-ridden masses in near-by countries! This was not imperialism, but enforced salvation. So the average American reasoned in the 1840's when the spirit of manifest destiny was in the air.[20]

It was, of course, absurd to think that violence against Mexico could produce "salvation," or that "enlightenment" could be enforced. But this crusade helped prepare the way for the Civil War in the 1860s. Harriet Beecher Stowe reminded her readers "that prophecy associates, in dread fellowship, the day of vengeance with the year of his redeemed." Hollis Read said in 1861 that the war would break up "Satan's empire," shatter false traditions, and usher in the Golden Age for the entire world.[21] Late in the war, Marvin R. Vincent, a New York preacher, struck a similar note: "God has been striking, and trying to make us strike at elements unfavorable to the growth of a pure democracy; and these and other facts point to the conclusion that he is at work, preparing in this broad land a fit stage for the last act of the human drama, the consummation of human civilization." Vincent went on to raise a rhetorical question: "Who shall say that she shall not only secure lasting peace to herself, but be, under God, the instrument of a millennial reign to all the nations?"[22] Shaped by the mystique of violence, a war that was being fought for political ascendancy between two sections of one country became a redemptive battle to set the whole world free.

As Michael Bellesiles has shown, the Civil War also "altered the national character" and showed "the need for one American to be able to kill another" with a firearm.[23] For the first time in American history, guns had been made widely available by mass production, and they were in popular use. While guns had rarely played a significant role in American life for its first two hundred years, the Colt Company had begun in the 1840s to merchandize its pistols with mythic engravings of men defending their families against Indians with a Colt pistol.[24] It was after the Civil War that the company perfected revolvers that would fire self-contained metal cartridges, which Colt called "the Peacemaker." According to Bellesiles, "The *Wichita Eagle* reported in May 1874 that 'Pistols are as thick as blackberries.' By that time a gun seemed to most men a requisite for their very identity. . . . The Civil War transformed the gun from a tool into a perceived necessity. The war preserved the Union, unifying the nation around a single icon: the gun."[25]

The concept of redemptive violence was translated increasingly into secular terms in the latter part of the nineteenth century. Albert K. Weinberg has traced the rise of the idea of "humanitarian coercion" prior to the Spanish-American War. Leaders began to suggest that "all previous American history had prepared for the realization of the beneficence of force."[26] Underdeveloped countries would have to be brought forcibly into democratic civilization. Theodore Roosevelt wrote in 1895 that force would also be beneficial in reinvigorating the American spirit: "This country needs a war," but the weaklings and "anglo-maniacs" opposed the redemptive process, favoring the cowardly route of peace at any price.[27] Violence would not only restore the morale of the chosen people, but, as many hoped, would shatter the last vestiges of tyranny in the Western Hemisphere. It would usher in the new age of freedom.

During World War I and World War II, the mystique of redemptive violence came to full expression. Antidemocratic forces were seen to be threatening the peace of the saints; but there was a belief that righteous violence could hold them at bay and permit the emergence of democratic governments. President Wilson called for the application of "force, force to the utmost, force without stint or limit, the righteous and triumphant force which shall make right the law of the world and cast every selfish dominion down in the dust."[28] With the victory of this crusade in World War I, the impetus was irresistible to make World War II into a redemptive campaign as well. President Roosevelt's declaration of war message called for a campaign of total victory so that America would never again be threatened by treachery or tyranny. He expressed his belief in the power of violence to transform the world in the prayer he cited in his United Nations message:

> The spirit of man has awakened and the soul of man has gone forth. . . . Grant us honor for our dead who died in the faith, honor for our living who work and strive for the faith, redemption and security for all captive lands and peoples. . . . And grant us the skill and valor that shall cleanse the world of oppression and the old base doctrine. . . . And in that faith let us march toward the clean world our hands can make. Amen.[29]

President Truman appropriated this belief in his message of April 1945, in which he called the nation "to live up to our glorious heritage" by bringing the war to total victory: "America will continue the fight for freedom until no vestige of resistance remains. . . . America will never become a party to any plan for partial victory [for it would] jeopardize the future security of all the world." The country should "lead the world to peace and prosperity . . . to a cleansed world."[30] Here the distinctive shape of the violent mystique is phrased in the secular terms that are now the natural mode of expression for American civil religion. The world is to be redeemed by the total destruction of the enemy; lasting peace is to be secured by the application of violence; and the whole world is to be converted to freedom by the successful crusade.

One feature of the zealous mystique, however, is minimized in these idealistic calls to battle: the application of the ban. With the prevalence of cool zeal, which leads Americans to prefer fastidious detachment from the process of annihilation, they avoided a portrayal of the dreadful means of achieving "unconditional surrender." Newsreels could show dramatic scenes of bombs dropping from the airplanes and the billowing explosions they produced, but no one described in detail to the American public what it was like to be a defenseless civilian during these attacks. Practically no public debate took place on the fateful decision to aim the bombing raids at residential areas as well as military installations. The enemy was to be demoralized by the application of the modern form of *ḥerem* — and thus forced to surrender. A 1943 *Reader's Digest* article entitled "Bomb Germany — and Save a Million American Lives" sets forth the rationale that subsequently became a dogma: destroying Germany's cities would "make it impossible for the enemy to supply his armies in the field and can bring about his collapse from within." The article said that an all-out air campaign could win the war in six to nine months; it offered such inflated hopes without offering any discussion of the moral issue of killing civilians. The article simply noted that "public opinion in America is turning strongly in favor of the Air Plan, just as it has turned in England — for it is the people's own lives that are at stake."[31] Saving the lives of the saints and at the same time bringing a quick peace was a rationale so allied to the traditional mystique that moral objections could scarcely arise. If the new form of violence is universally redemptive, why not use it universally against the enemy, including women and children?

The increasing power of the mystique can be measured against earlier standards of behavior in war. In World War I, Americans had been outraged by German war tactics that were in violation of neutrality and the Geneva Convention. The sinking of civilian vessels on the high seas by German submarines had been a cause of the United States' entrance into the war. American servicemen had avoided killing civilians and had treated prisoners, by and large, according to the laws of war. In World War II, they participated in a strategy of bombing residential areas with hideous new weapons such as incendiary bombs. Once the war was over, Americans disregarded the official Air Force studies that concluded that mass bombing of residential areas had been a mistake. After all, it had raised rather than lowered the enemy's will to resist; and it had been ineffective in slowing down war production. The dogma developed that bombing cities had won the war, or at least decisively shortened it. Therefore, in subsequent conflicts the dogma of redemptive bombing held sway. Down to the present moment, the application of *ḥerem* from the air is the preferred American means of warfare, despite its long-term ineffectiveness and its barbaric level of civilian casualties.[32]

The power of the mystique to silence the moral and practical objections to mass bombing may also be measured against the behavior of allied peoples. The British preceded the Americans in the use of mass bombing but apparently never came to view it as redemptive. For example, revenge for the German bombing of British cities and a desire to demonstrate power to Russian allies appear to have played major roles in the decision to bomb Dresden, one of the most barbaric acts of the war. But in British explanations of the policy one always senses the consciousness that it was a bad business. And in subsequent years they seem to have lacked the curious propensity to see *ḥerem* from thirty thousand feet as the appropriate tactic in every campaign. They refused to use any bombs at all in the nine-year guerrilla campaign in Malaya, a situation analogous to Vietnam. There have been no demands that they use mass bombing to free blockaded districts of Northern Ireland. Despite their own casualties, the British have kept the level of force commensurate with the situation. This is not a function of some higher moral capacity on the part of the British but rather a sign that they no longer fall prey to the mystique of violence. They experienced once what it meant to follow the Puritan dogma that every woman and child is a combatant, and they are not now inclined to believe it again.

There is something distinctly American about the belief in the efficacy of bombing. The fervor with which it is defended indicates that it is a belief structure rooted in the civil religion itself. As the bombs began to fall on cities in World War II, the theologian John Ford was a singular American voice who tried to bring ethical conscience to the practice in his 1944 essay "The Morality of Obliteration Bombing."[33] When one attacks the belief with arguments about morality or practicality, one inevitably encounters the response that bombing shortened World War II, and, in particular, that using atomic weapons against Hiroshima and Nagasaki "saved a million American lives." This is the standard teaching in the history books, and it leads occasionally to the belief that, had we used atomic bombs in Vietnam, we could have won that war easily and cheaply.

The peculiar circumstances of the final phase of the war with Japan need to be considered in evaluating this issue. The terrible losses in the invasions of Iwo Jima and Saipan, the suicides of thousands of Japanese civilians at the ends of those campaigns, and the development of highly destructive kamikaze attacks led American leaders to believe that Japan would commit national suicide before surrendering. From the Japanese viewpoint, "unconditional surrender" was understood to mean disestablishment of the emperor cult, which was central to Japanese culture. Since Japanese efforts to retain their conquests through negotiations had been rebuffed by official Allied circles, the war lingered on. In noting these factors, diplomatic historian Louis J. Halle points out the strange lack of ethical discussion as well as the ironic fact that the August 1945 surrender was conditional after all — because the status of the emperor remained unchanged.[34] The bombing of the two Japanese cities, with its appalling death toll in noncombatants, did bring the war to an end; but the routine nature of the decision to bomb remains haunting. Specialists in Japanese culture were not even consulted about the dropping of the atomic bombs. The ideology appears to have sufficed: if violence is redemptive in a world of demonic adversaries, then total violence must be irresistible.

A self-fulfilling prophecy was thus set in motion to confirm the dogma for a subsequent generation: the enemy that had presumably been recalcitrant was suddenly brought to terms; the war was won by the marvelous new form of *herem;* thus the ultimate violence of atomic weaponry was the best means of achieving peace. President Truman gave the gloss of divine sanction to the atomic bomb when he said to the American people: "We have used it against those who attacked us without warning at Pearl Harbor, against those who have starved and beaten and executed American prisoners of war. . . . We thank God that it [the atomic bomb] has come to us instead of to our enemies; and we pray that He may guide us to use it in His ways and for His purposes."[35]

The articulation of this distinctive American dogma, sanctioned by its piety, readily defined the path into the atomic age. Doctrines of massive retaliation preoccupied the postwar leaders, particularly those most committed to the zealous cause. Americans reacted with amazement against realists in other countries who lacked enthusiasm for redemptive violence. That the world should be destroyed for the sake of American principles seemed self-evident to most Americans, while those in other countries decided that it might be better to be "red than dead." Such an attitude seemed highly immoral to Americans. The mystique had rendered us incapable of comprehending even our allies. With the same ideological blindness, we plunged into the arms race without the slightest hesitation and produced an arsenal of ludicrous proportions. A usually prudent and economy-minded public, still traumatized in other regards by the Depression experience, supported the expenditure of uncounted billions on the machinery of modern *herem.* The gap between prudent necessity and actual investment was and is so overwhelming, and the lack of public debate on the matter so amazing, that only devotion to ideology can explain it. It reveals the religious conviction of a people as vividly as do the long-forgotten pyramids in the jungles of Central America, testimony to the power of primitive obsessions.

Confirmation of the religious, as opposed to the pragmatic, motivations for *herem* can be derived from circumstances noted by the strategic arms analyst Sidney J. Slomich. The United States, rather than taking "advantage of the relatively good political climate of the middle fifties" by reducing the enormous arms expenditures, "plunged, instead, into the awesome orgy of nuclear missile building."[36] In 1972 there was a repetition of the same variety of ideological madness when the U.S. Defense Department announced plans to develop a first-strike missile capacity in the very wake of the agreements reached at the Strategic Arms Limitation Talks (SALT), which should have made such steps unnecessary. Slomich's conclusion in 1968 is even more valid today: "There is something awry when societies reject politics and ethics and look for salvation to weapons of mass destruction."[37] What was really awry, we submit, was the mystique of violent salvation itself.

This mystique has been particularly evident in the American strategy in Afghanistan. The reliance on bombing not only killed an estimated three to five thousand innocent civilians, but it also undermined the goodwill of the Muslim public that was essential in the campaign against terrorism.[38] There is doubtless a military calculus that demonstrates net Afghan lives gained by quickly eradicating a Taliban government that would probably have allowed vast populations to starve. However, given the circumstance that thousands of civilians died before a single U.S. soldier fell of combat wounds on January 3, 2002, it will be difficult to show in the court of world opinion that the United States does not value the lives of its own soldiers far more highly than it does the innocent victims of its preferred style of warfare. Heribert Prantl formulated the underlying moral issues acutely weeks before the first bomb fell on a village in Afghanistan. He described the Bush campaign as "criminal justice . . . the multiplication and intensification of the death penalty" or "avenging one wrong with a similar evil." Reflecting on the imprecision of war as punishment, Prantl pointed out that many innocent people would be drawn into the circle of the victims, characterizing the U.S. action as "a reaction to the murder of thousands of innocent people with a war that will, in turn, cost more innocents their lives." In his final moral judgement, Prantl saw such a war as more primitive morally than the ancient code of *lex talionis,* which was at least governed by a stricter proportionality between offense and punishment while striving to ensure that the victim of the punishment actually be the offender. He found the most compelling analogy in the revenge of clans: "Clans avenge themselves upon other clans. This is an archaic form of mourning. People find the power of death easier to bear when they make use of it themselves."[39]

Jürgen Todenhöfer, a journalist with pro-American sympathies who has frequently visited Afghanistan, developed a substantial case that the bombing campaign was "irresponsible and counterproductive."[40] In view of the unpopularity of the Saudi Osama bin Laden among the majority of the Pashtun tribespeople, financial payments would have been a more effective inducement than bombing. Support of the Northern Alliance and the development of Pashtun resistance in the south could have sufficed to topple an oppressive Taliban regime. To kill innocent civilians who were not involved in the government or in the terrorist movement was immoral and aroused immense hostility not just in Afghanistan but elsewhere in the Muslim world. Every bomb that struck an Afghani civilian increased the desire for terrorist vengeance throughout the Muslim world, thus undermining the very campaign against terrorism that it sought to advance. An egregious example was the mistaken bombing of a convoy that killed sixty-five tribal elders on their way to attend the swearing-in ceremonies of the Karzai government in December.[41] Moreover, Todenhöfer noted that since the CIA had supported Muslim extremists in Pakistan and Afghanistan in the mid 1980s in the struggle against Russian occupation, the United States placed itself in the awkward position of punishing Afghani towns and cities for the consequences of its own previous actions. The appropriate American strategy, in Todenhöfer's view, would have been to rely on forces placed under U.N. command, to employ vigorous means of international law enforcement, to enter constructive dialogue with the Muslim world that seeks to overcome its inferior standing, and thereby to encourage the large majorities who favor tolerance instead of terrorism.

Hosea's Critique of the Mystique of Violence

The consequences of violent ideology, when popularized by publicly sponsored crusades, are extremely grave. And given the appeals of violence that we have noted here, it is difficult to find critical perspectives that promise to have an impact on popular thinking. To unveil the impulses behind the mystique is thus a formidable achievement. It is particularly difficult to achieve during a time of social disintegration and external threats to a nation. During such a period the popular religious leaders tend to preach frantic messages interpreting decay and violence as signs of inadequate devotion to the zealous ideals and calling the faithful to one last crusade against the wicked. Yet this was accomplished in the eighth century BCE by the prophet Hosea for his own culture, at a time when the process of social disintegration was in full swing and the threat of national annihilation at the hands of the Assyrians was acute. Hosea's insights into the cause and shape of violent decay are highly appropriate for the time of jihad. The power of his ideas, and their systematic neglect by a people that claims to take inspiration from the Bible, are evidence of how firmly rooted zealous nationalism is in our culture. We propose, therefore, to use some of his powerful oracles to demonstrate how a courageous thinker faces the challenges posed by the seductiveness of nationalistic violence.

The first Hosean theme to be considered is the relationship between the violent mystique and social disintegration:

You have plowed iniquity,
    you have reaped injustice,
    you have eaten the fruit of lies.
Because you have trusted in your chariots
    and in the multitude of your warriors,
therefore the tumult of war shall arise among your people,
    and all your fortresses shall be destroyed,
as Shalman destroyed Beth-arbel on the day of battle;
    mothers were dashed in pieces with their children. (Hos. 10:13-14)

The agricultural images of plowing and reaping evoke an inexorable process of cause and effect. It exactly reverses what was assumed in the popular religion of Hosea's time. Both the "injustice," involving "a dimension of violence" in the difficult Hebrew original,[42] and the prevalence of "lies" are seen as the direct result of having "plowed iniquity" into the soil. The violent crusades, purges, assassinations, and conquests perpetrated by Northern zealots in the name of the religious mystique were directly responsible for the disintegration. The next verse specifically attacks the militant aspect of public policy.[43] Led on by the mystique of violent redemption, leaders had come to "trust" in their military arrangements. Acting out that trust, they drifted inevitably into wars that were as brutal as the massacre in Beth-arbel, a notorious incident in that time.

The tone of direct accusation in Hosea's oracle should shock us — a "people of the Book" — as much as it did his fellow citizens. Like us, the Israelites were convinced that the world had to be made safe for the chosen people and that the sole threat to the peace came from the enemy. They were as certain as we are that the security risk lay in the enemy's army and not in their idolatrous trust in their own. And they were certain that proper preparedness and righteous interventions would keep war away from their own neighborhoods. "It is better to fight them in Vietnam than in Long Beach," some Americans solemnly assured one another a few decades ago. But that we ourselves may be a source of the disorder — that is unthinkable! We are the chosen people, are we not, the selfless defenders of the free world? How can peacemakers be responsible for wars? Without the penetrating accusation of a Hosea, it is doubtful whether any would come to a more realistic appraisal. In the violent consequences of the mystique is the punishment that such evasion brings upon itself.

Hosea announces the *aspect of divine justice* within the plowing of crusades and the reaping of violence in the most shocking terms possible. He hears Yahweh say:

> I am like pus to Ephraim,
> and like bone rot to the house of Judah. (Hos. 5:12)

James Luther Mays observes that the "comparisons were drawn to the extreme limit, but their boldness is meant to reveal how God in hiddenness is already at work, sapping away the vitality of Ephraim and Judah through the very actions that they initiate and execute. The debilitating effect of their policy is not to be thought of as separate from the effect of his presence in their history."[44] Here is the thesis of Hosea in its most unforgettable form. The moral decay of a society may not always indicate how far it has strayed from the zealous ideals, but rather how much its enactment of those ideals has brought judgment against it. In demoralization and social sickness Hosea saw God acting to carry out an inexorable justice against those who fall prey to the mystique of violence. If these prophetic insights are valid, they would apply to all cultures — atheist, Christian, Hindu, Jewish, or Muslim — that focus their national energies on zealous crusades to destroy their enemies.

Accepting Hosea's analysis, it follows that there must be a *repudiation of the zealous myths*. As long as a society is awed by the violent deeds of its heroes and leaders, it will tend to follow their example. If the popularization of violence is the means by which disintegration occurs, then it must be exposed and stopped. Hosea makes a daring attempt in this direction when he condemns the most thoroughgoing zealot of them all, the founder of the dynasty in power. As we showed in chapters 4 and 10, Jehu had carried out a political purge with the full support of the zealots of his time. He was the heroic warrior whom the dynasty and the public sought to emulate. He mercilessly killed the wicked Jezebel and enacted the ban against other enemies of the state. His vigor in chariotry and skill with the bow were models for the bold men of Israel. It must have seemed both blasphemous and treasonous, therefore, when Hosea condemned the mythic ideal of *ḥerem* on the plain of Jezreel and predicted Yahweh's repudiation of the nation for emulating it:[45]

> And Yahweh said to him, ". . . I will punish the house of Jehu for the blood of Jezreel, and I will put an end to the kingdom of the house of Israel. And on that day, I will break the bow of Israel in the valley of Jezreel." (Hos. 1:4f.)

We can grasp the audacity of Hosea's attack on the mythic ideal of the current regime when we remember that both the prophet Elisha and the zealot Jehonadab enthusiastically supported Jehu's purge. Hosea pits himself against the dominant religious ideals of his time — and ours. His words reveal a concern about the bloodshed in the massacre and the consequences of popularizing militarism, symbolized by the "bow" that would one day be broken.[46] It is important to note that this prediction of the shattering of Israel's military establishment was fulfilled when Tiglath-Pileser swept over Israel in 733 BCE. Having followed the mythic ideal into the imprudent war against Assyria, Israel had to suffer the consequences. By attacking the myth, the prophet aimed at freeing his people from its idolatrous grasp before it was too late.

One logical consequence of the mystique of violence, in Hosea's view, was the *popularization of crime and brutality*. In the following oracle he visualizes Yahweh as charging his people with forsaking the truth of religion in their violent crusades and with violating the commandments concerning respect for persons. Crimes of violence are the logical products of misunderstanding obligations to God, and the very land itself suffers and loses its productivity because of such violence. Hosea sets forth in unforgettable images the interrelationship of ecological decay, destructive personal behavior, and the false mystique:

> Hear the word of Yahweh, O people of Israel;
>> for Yahweh has a controversy with the inhabitants of the land.
> There is no faithfulness or kindness,
>> and no knowledge of God in the land;
> there is swearing, lying, killing, stealing, and committing adultery;
>> they break all bounds and murder follows murder.
> Therefore the land mourns,
>> and all who dwell in it languish,
> and also the beasts of the field,
>> and the birds of the air;
>> and even the fish of the sea are taken away. (Hos. 4:1-3)

This sweeping condemnation must have amazed those engaged in zealous violence. It implied that, contrary to the popular mystique, no crusade or murder then being performed was a matter of covenant loyalty to God. It cut the very nerve of zealous nationalism, which assumed that God called people to exercise faithfulness by killing sinners. Moreover, Hosea's oracle flatly insisted that the religious consensus contained no knowledge whatsoever of God. Deluded by zeal, religionists had a completely distorted perception of Yahweh's justice. The result of this radical perversion was to legitimate antisocial behavior.[47] Each crime Hosea mentioned is a breach in the respect for persons that was implicit in covenant loyalty to Yahweh. "Swearing," for instance, was "an imprecation or malediction invoking a divinely caused misfortune on another"; it was a matter of gaining precisely the vengeance in personal matters that zealous nationalism sought in public matters.[48]

The *connection between public zealotry and private violence* should be obvious. If it is proper to kill without trial in zealous campaigns, why should it be wrong in cases of personal injustice? If one can lie in connection with the crusade against evil, why should it be objectionable when the individual is pitted against personal threats? If leading citizens become rich and gain power through their participation in public crusades, why should commoners not be justified in taking what they need if their motives are pure? Once infected by the short circuit of zeal, in which the aims of the self are identified with the aims of God, one finds it natural to break across all restraints. Life becomes cheap.

The Hosea oracle provocatively portrays the *ecological results of violence.* That the land itself should "mourn" and the beasts "languish" may strike one at first glance as a curious fragment of ancient superstition. How could such "a loss of vitality by land and population . . . a terrible diminution of life-forces which tends to a total absence of life" be related to the violent mystique?[49] A quick glance at what happened to the land of Palestine as a result of zealous crusading may provide a clue. Forests were ravaged for siege timbers and campfires; vineyards and orchards were destroyed by raiding troops and abandoned by depopulated villages; waterways and irrigation systems were damaged and fell into disuse; pastures and grain fields were trampled by battles and ruined by neglect when their owners were killed, subsequently to be eroded beyond usefulness. Streams were polluted and wells poisoned. Between the violent campaigns, survivors directed their vital energies toward military preparedness rather than constructive agriculture and industry. The landscape of Palestine began to assume the appearance it has presented in modern times: barren, denuded of natural forests, lacking in vineyards and orchards, eroded by the winter rains, and parched by summer heat. A land flowing with milk and honey was ruined by the mystique of violence.

Surely a similar "mourning" and "languishing" of the very earth itself is visible today as well. In the United States, how long has it taken for the ravaged South to recover its strength or productivity after the Civil War? Have the desert canyons of the Navajos ever regained their fertility after the marvelous peach orchards and fields and livestock were destroyed by American soldiers more than a hundred years ago? How many generations will it take for the poisoned fields and blighted forests of Indochina to regain their verdure? If the still-ruined terrain of Verdun is any guide, it may never happen. The shattered, shell-torn earth, like the now-barren hills of the Palestinian wilderness, may be permanently ruined by the modern methods of *ḥerem.*

The violent mystique causes a *perversion of justice*. By encouraging brutality and crimes against others, it gradually drives a society into corrupt practices. The institutions of law and order, whose aim is the preservation of life through the equal treatment of all persons, begin to condone violence against certain groups and types. The principle that a person is innocent until proven guilty is set aside in the case of certain enemies of the state. Suspects are tortured on the premise that they are guilty anyway and are incapable of responding to anything but brute force. One by one, the constitutional protections of the rights of citizens drop away until the government changes from an agency of justice to the very opposite. Hosea describes the perversion caused by the spell of the violent mystique in a sharply formulated oracle directed against the legal and religious authorities of his time. Though they were ostensibly Yahweh's ministers of impartial justice, they had been "making a quarry of others instead of being their protectors and benefactors."[50]

> Hear this, O priests!
> Give heed, O house of Israel! Hearken, O house of the king!
>   For judgment pertains to you; for you have been a snare at Mizpah,
>   and a net spread upon Tabor. (Hos. 5:1)

The image of a trap for wild game reveals the callousness in the treatment of fellow human beings. It is a suitable image for modern forms of police brutality and dehumanized court and prison systems that the time of jihad is likely to produce. If violence is truly redemptive, and if the source of evil is identifiable on the basis of popular stereotypes, then the constitutional protections can be dispensed with. The presumably guilty parties are issued an immediate form of violent justice, whether their guilt has been proven before an impartial bar of justice or not.

One of Hosea's oracles portrays in telling fashion the capacity of the violent mystique to *undermine respect for law and order*. It cites the cynical remarks of his fellow countrymen who experienced the perverted forms of violent justice:

> For now they [the disillusioned citizens] will say:
>   "We have no king,
> for we fear not Yahweh,
>   and a king, what could he do for us?"
> They [the authorities] utter mere words;
>   with empty oaths they make covenants;
> so judgment springs up like poisonous weeds
>   in the furrows of the field. (Hos. 10:3-4)

If the king's justice is partial, based on stereotypes and executed in impatient violence, why should those who experience it continue to offer their respect? And if such perverted justice is really Yahweh's justice, as it claimed to be, let God be damned as well! The result is a growth of lawlessness, in which the social cement of respect for authority has dissolved. But the prophet sees the source of such "poisonous weeds" much more clearly than do the typical supporters of the Captain America complex. The source is in the very defenders of the perverted law and order, who call violence justice and who discard the priceless treasure of equality before the law.

A final consequence of the violent mystique is the *militarization of foreign policy*. If the exercise of military power is thought to be redemptive, ridding the nation of threats to its existence, then the tedious and humble business of accommodating the nation to living with reality falls into disrepute. Diplomacy gives way to militarism. George F. Kennan noted such a process in connection with the development of the containment policy in the 1950s. American leaders thought of it in strictly "military terms." Kennan claims that the U.S. government "failed to take advantage of the opportunities for useful political discussion when, in later years, such opportunities began to open up, and exerted itself, in its military preoccupations, to seal and to perpetuate the very division of Europe which it should have been concerned to remove."[51] Donald McDonald explains: "Foreign policy becomes militarized when, at critical moments, it is the military who seem to offer the crisp, definite, tangible options — while those who argue for negotiation, diplomacy, and respect for the decent opinion of mankind seem to be offering the unattractive, endlessly prolonged, and inconclusive options."[52]

Human experience belies the easy promises of military solutions. The promises they seem constantly to offer turn out to be tracks into the swamps of endless violence. The Vietnam debacle was an excellent example. Hosea has a succinct description of this paradox: that the clear-cut solution of militarism drives a nation into far worse dilemmas and dangers than it initially confronted. He likens the military option to the east wind of Palestine, the searing sirocco that destroys everything green in its path:[53]

Ephraim [i.e., Israel] herds the wind, and pursues the east wind all day long; they multiply falsehood and violence; they make a bargain with Assyria, and oil is carried to Egypt. (Hos. 12:1)

Like the militarized foreign policy, the wind from the eastern desert is clearcut, tangible, and undeniably potent. But it seems to defy herding. A nation can devote itself to the task with all the care of the German general staff and all the resources of the Pentagon, but the sirocco too frequently runs amok. Rather than achieving what it promises, it redoubles the "falsehood and violence." All the shrewd arrangements of military diplomacy in Hosea's time, such as the vassal treaty with Assyria and the bribing of Egypt to help break it,[54] could not provide protection from the cycle of destruction.

This oracle renders a telling judgment on the self-defeating policies that America has followed in the past generation. How much have our military alliances and interventions added to our security? Has militarized diplomacy really been effective in Southeast Asia or in Latin America? Have we been any more successful than ancient Israel in taming the east wind? Are crusades against terrorism likely to augment our safety, when the underlying causes remain unresolved? If we are honest, we must admit the cogency of this oracle: the mystique of violence has proved anything but redemptive in our own recent experience. Rather than holding violence at bay, or keeping evil within bounds, it has added to it ten- and twenty-fold. Like the sirocco, the mystique of violence has led us to destroy everything that seems to stand in our way.

The scope of American destructiveness in Southeast Asia has never been officially acknowledged. The nearly sixty thousand American dead are widely mourned, but the millions of Asians dead or displaced from bombing campaigns, infantry operations, and the mass murders that followed our destabilization of Cambodia are viewed benignly as the cost of our good intentions.[55] No reparations have been paid and, with the exception of a few minor actors, no legal accountability has been sought for those responsible for this holocaust, despite the fact that the path of policy was repeatedly paved with cynical lies. In its national intransigence about these errors, the United States has matched the callous indifference of the communists, who also slaughtered the innocent furiously as they ascended to dominance. The contrast with the efforts of German churches and government agencies to overcome the consequences of the Jewish Holocaust since 1945 is stark. Perhaps the technology of aerial bombing is an important factor in that most of the Southeast Asian deaths occurred off-camera — yielding no face-to-face encounter with Americans. For the most part, the *ḥerem* was administered from the safe distance of thirty thousand feet, with carpet bombing that killed every living creature within a target area. The few instances in which Americans witnessed — via photography or television — the bitter harvest of our tactics resulted in pressure against the continuation of the war.

But it must be acknowledged that in activities like the Phoenix Program, the U.S. calmly financed, helped organize, and countenanced the large-scale arrest, torture, and extra-judicial killings of individuals suspected of supporting the Vietcong opposition to the Republic of Vietnam. Praise for the program's "success" continues to be expressed in publications such as ABC-Clio's recent *Encyclopedia of the Vietnam War,* which reports, "[F]rom 1968 to 1972 captured VCI [Viet Cong Infrastructure] numbered around 34,000; of those 22,000 rallied to the RVN [Republic of Vietnam], while those killed numbered 26,000."[56] Apologetics for U.S. military involvement in the Phoenix Program continue, relying in part on the fog of statistics about the circumstances of killing and in part on redirecting attention to the larger situation of the war and its selfless intent. Mark Moyar's *Phoenix and the Birds of Prey: The CIA's Secret Campaign to Destroy the Viet Cong* is representative in suggesting that national leaders rather than military officers deserve blame for "excesses" in the program: "They chose to enter the type of war in which unjustified arrests and killings are unavoidable." But even those leaders can fall back on the higher justification, because "[p]reventing the spread of Communism was a noble goal."[57] When the saints stumble in the path to world redemption — engaging in acts that would ordinarily be regarded as political terrorism — they can be forgiven.

Following the logic of the east wind, there were scarcely any limitations in the level of destruction routinely inflicted. The laws of war appeared helpless to harness the gale. Richard Wasserstrom's thoughtful study of this process sets forth the consensus that prevailed in government circles: "The laws of war permit and treat as legitimate almost any practice, provided only that there is an important military advantage to be secured."[58] The destructive logic of the east wind brooks no arbitrament of law, of reason, or humanity. If violence is redemptive, then one must be willing to follow it to the end.

The classic statement of this logic was offered by an American major during the Tet offensive early in 1968. The town of Ben Tre had been overrun by Viet Cong attackers, so American fighter bombers carrying bombs, rockets, and napalm were ordered in to level it. The number of casualties in the town of thirty-five thousand is unknown, but military observers estimated that at least five hundred civilians were killed. The officer explained that "it became necessary to destroy the town to save it."[59] For many critics of the war, this statement was the epitome of absurdity; but it fit precisely into the structure of the violent mystique: the application of *ḥerem* is sometimes necessary to redeem a town from the grip of evil. If bombing saved the world in World War II, it could surely save a river town in the Mekong Delta. The logic of the east wind was never more clearly stated.

Overcoming the Illusions of Redemptive Destruction

Is there anything that can reverse this awful process of destruction, which has so often replayed in subsequent campaigns where purifying angers have raged against the people of Croatia, Kosovo, Serbia, Gaza, Rwanda, Chechnya, Iraq, and East Timor? What spiritual and ethical resources can set people free from the perverse sirocco of violence? Hosea was the first thinker in world history, so far as we know, to wrestle with this question in something like its modern form. James D. Smart describes his legacy in this way:

> Hosea came to see most clearly the fearful dilemma of man's evil. Sin, by its disruption of the personal relation on which life depends, brings blindness, callousness, and despair, which lead to yet more violent sin. The human being, once started on this disastrous downhill course, is helpless to stop the tragic cumulative process. There must be an intervention from beyond. Someone, with love for the sinner in spite of the sin, must break in upon the deadly process and by sheer grace create for the prisoner of sin and death the possibility of a new beginning. This was Hosea's final word concerning God.[60]

Hosea develops this theme in the following oracle, which pictures Yahweh in daring terms as the lover who will "allure" his people, taking them into the "wilderness," which was the site of their covenant relationship during the time of the exodus and the wandering. Yahweh would draw her away from the site of Canaanite civilization, with its manipulative attitude toward the world and its reliance on coercion. He would also reverse the dread legacy of *herem*, which had so perverted the substance of the faith. The prophet describes Yahweh as calling to his people:

> Therefore, behold, I will allure her,
>   and bring her into the wilderness,
>   and speak tenderly to her.
> And there I will give her her vineyards,
>   and make the Valley of Achor a door of hope. (Hos. 2:14-15)

Achor was the barren, rock-strewn site where Achan and his family were presumably stoned for violating the terms of *herem*. This horrible tradition will be reversed so that the Valley of Achor will no longer symbolize wrath and death. It will become the hopeful path into the verdant vineyards of the future. The chapter proceeds to describe the restoration of harmony between humans and their natural world that would come in the wake of this reversal. "And I will make for you a covenant on that day with the beasts of the field, the birds of the air, and the creeping things of the ground; and I will abolish the bow, the sword, and war from the land; and I will make you lie down in safety" (Hos. 2:18). The power of God's love would evoke a sense of repentance that would mark the end of the rule of the violent mystique over the human heart (Hos. 14:3). It would one day draw Israel away from her self-destroying militarism that set the very balance of nature awry.

This strategy of redemptive love was also cultivated by Jesus of Nazareth. What for Hosea had remained but eloquent words came into concrete human experience in the life of Jesus. The passionate love of God came to earth, full of sensual, yearning, creative power. Jesus expressed love to people obsessed by the mystique of violence, as well as to those suffering under its brutal impact. It proved as redemptive as Hosea had promised. Small groups of restored persons began to emerge, and they reached out to others in their violence-prone society, with a vigor and joy which only love can produce.[61]

With violence relegated to the nonredemptive role of enforcing civil law and order so that people may survive together until they all have been set free from the poisonous residue of a crippling past, love came into its own. It accepted enemies just as they were, in the very midst of alienation, offering them a chance to break free. Its form of conversion was the very opposite of *ḥerem:* it offered antagonists a possibility of remaining true to themselves while accepting others as they themselves felt accepted. Redeemed by the power of such acceptance, the races, the sexes, the generations, and the classes discovered that they could exist together. The joy of reconciliation and the new stimulations to creativity served to confirm the power of love and make its further communication a matter of pleasure. Thus a new form of mission emerged. Rather than thrusting itself upon the neighbor in the zealous demand to lose identity and be absorbed into the superior community of the saints, it offered restored relations with neighbors precisely as they were. Unconditional acceptance replaced aggression, joy took the place of rage, and a zeal for love overcame the zeal to destroy.

Two paths thus lie open to those who would reform American society today, or take up her calling to serve the world. There is the way of redemptive violence, which may take the form of the great revolution or the great crusade: this path promises to shatter injustice with a righteous fury, punishing the evildoers, emancipating those who have been exploited, and making the world safe for virtue. But there is also the way of redemptive love: its promise is less clear-cut, and it leads to much less predictable results. For when love is enacted, people become free. New impulses awaken that no one can master ahead of time. So this is the way for the audacious and the large in spirit, those who can live without idols and face an uncertain future unafraid. It is for those who dare to coexist with all sorts and conditions of fellow human beings. Those who follow it will be thrust out into the no-man's-land between the rigid fronts of zealous conflicts — out among the wounded, the shell-shocked, and the lost. Their impulses of creative love will draw them into the prisons and the ghettos, onto the streets and the way stations, even into the lands that have been ravaged by our crusades. Whatever their occupation or place of service, they will give way to the spontaneous impulse within them to overcome alienation with love, despair with joy. They will seek and save the victims as well as the violent ones, not by pious admonitions or zealous evangelism but by the sort of unconditional acceptance they themselves have received. Many of them will perish in the times ahead, victims of hatred and suspicion. But their work will redeem, even as they forgive their executioners and pray for the lynching mobs. They stand in a great and noble company, not with Elisha and Jehu and John Brown, but with Hosea and Jesus and Saint Francis and Martin Luther King.

The age of jihad is one in which these two paths, which have been hopelessly confused in the American mind, stand as sharply opposed alternatives, awaiting our choice. The same alternatives lie open to Islam, Hinduism, Judaism, and every other set of principles that dares to face honestly the strategies of conflict. If our path is to be redemptive love under the aegis of international law enforcement, then we must repudiate the mystique of violence and its policies once and for all. And if it is to be the path of violent zeal or jihad, we should drop all pretensions of carrying out the goals of love and equal justice for all. Hypocrisy merely adds extra flavors of bitterness to the ashes of holy war. These two paths are mutually exclusive, as Hosea demonstrated some 2,600 years ago. It is time for this prophet, whom Judaism, Islam, and Christianity all acknowledge as authoritative, to finally come into his own.

14 Neither Humiliation nor Defeat

If you obey the voice of Yahweh your God, being careful to do all his commandments which I command you this day, Yahweh your God will set you high above all the nations of the earth.

Deuteronomy 28:1

If, when the chips are down, the world's most powerful nation, the United States of America, acts like a pitiful, helpless giant, the forces of totalitarianism and anarchy will threaten free nations and free institutions throughout the world. It is not our power but our will and character that is [sic] being tested tonight.

President Richard Nixon, announcing the
invasion of Cambodia in May 1970[1]

In his speech defending the invasion of Cambodia, President Nixon gave voice to a theme of twentieth-century history: "We will not be humiliated. We will not be defeated." He went on to declare his willingness to suffer political death, if necessary, in order to prevent such reversals: "I would rather be a one-term President than to be a two-term President at the cost of seeing America become a second-rate power and see this nation accept the first defeat in its proud 190-year history." In view of the fearsome consequences of this invasion, which destabilized Cambodia and prepared the way for the

273

murderous Khmer Rouge, the national psychology of humiliation merits investigation.

What is there about defeat that evokes the feeling of political suicide? Similarly, as we noted in chapter 6, the rationale in the Vietnam War during Lyndon Johnson's administration also voiced fear of the first American defeat. Have not other nations experienced defeat and yet survived and even recovered with more strength and determination than before? Why should a reversal in so obscure and distant a battlefield as Indochina seem to threaten the very foundation of American pride? And why should President George W. Bush's success in Afghanistan have led fundamentalist Christians to conclude that he was God's predestined leader — especially considering that they had earlier supported his election with declining interest? Dana Milbank observes that "only 15 million of the 19 million religious conservatives who should have voted went to the polls in 2000." Nevertheless, after September 11, 2001, "conservative Christians tend to view Bush's recent success as part of a divine plan." "I've heard a lot of 'God knew something we didn't,'" said Ralph Reed, who once led the Christian Coalition: "In the evangelical mind, the notion of an omniscient God is central to their theology. He had a knowledge nobody else had: he knew George Bush had the ability to lead in this compelling way."[2]

The key to answering these questions was suggested by the historian D. W. Brogan. While discussing Vietnam and the mounting impatience about that seemingly unwinnable war in 1967, he noted that "the desire to be right as well as victorious is deeply embedded in the American psyche."[3] David L. Larson similarly suggested that our isolation from the realities of international power "is primarily due to the Puritan ethic. Or, that 'somehow, some way, right will prevail over might.'"[4] We can see a presumptive connection between being right and being victorious. And the obvious corollary of such a position is that to be defeated is to be wrong. Given this premise, accepting defeat is acknowledging national guilt, perhaps even giving up the "favored people" concept. If the implications are really so drastic, a zealous nation might be willing to take the most desperate steps, even flirting with self-destruction, to avoid defeat. Conversely, victory produces a sense of having been led by God and thus being able to defeat any foes anywhere, as seen in the exultant American attitude after driving al Qaeda and the Taliban from the cities of Afghanistan in the winter of 2001.

To account for this phenomenon, we must trace the impact of the biblical models of the triumphant God and his victorious people as understood in the moral framework of right producing victory and wrong producing defeat. We need to explore the zealous interpretations of defeat and examine the psychic impact of unresolved defeat. After noting the disastrous consequences of refusing defeat, we will draw on the resources of prophetic realism to suggest creative alternatives.

Victory as the Reward for Piety in the Old Testament

The Song of Miriam summons the faithful community to break forth in ecstatic song, for Yahweh "has triumphed gloriously" (Ex. 15:21). The song portrays Yahweh especially as the powerful warrior (Ex. 15:3), invincible in battle. Psalm 24 calls forth the liturgical question, "Who is the king of glory?" The answer is prescribed: "Yahweh, strong and mighty, Yahweh, mighty in battle!" This tradition developed into the highly stylized promises of victory that were announced before battle in every instance of zealous warfare. The promises were stated in the past tense, as if the victory were already complete before the battle had opened:[5]

> And Yahweh said to Joshua, "See, I have given Jericho into your hand." (Josh. 6:2)

> "Do not fear or be dismayed. . . . I have given the king of Ai into your hand." (Josh. 8:1)

The Israelites who heard and believed such promises went into battle with "the perfect certainty of victory."[6] It was as certain as any event that had already occurred, and to doubt this meant doubting the power of Yahweh himself. The exhortation not to fear the enemy but to believe in Yahweh, so frequently connected with promises of victory in the early accounts of zealous warfare, may actually have been the earliest form of the Israelite faith.[7] And there is little doubt that it was an effective force in evoking the courage to face enemies who were often better armed and trained than the Israelite peasant volunteers.

From a rather early time in biblical history this faith had to confront the uncomfortable fact that victories did not always come as expected. The Israelites were defeated by desert tribes at the time of the invasion of Canaan, as well as by the Philistines, culminating in the loss of the Ark of the Covenant at the battle of Aphek, a loss that nearly shattered the tribal confederacy (1 Sam. 4). In the later period came defeat — and ultimately the destruction of Israel and Judah — at the hands of the great empires. Any one of these defeats could have led to the dissolution of faith in Yahweh as a triumphant God. What kept this from happening was the development of the "Deuteronomic principle," which linked Israel's virtue with victories and her sin with defeats.

In its classic form the "Deuteronomic philosophy of history, with its rhythm of righteousness-prosperity and wickedness-ruin," offered a simple but harsh explanation of defeats.[8] They were due to the wrath of God evoked by Israel's disobedience. The Book of Deuteronomy shows Moses exhorting his people as follows: "But if you will not obey the voice of the Lord your God or be careful to do all his commandments . . . Yahweh will cause you to be defeated before your enemies" (Deut. 28:15, 25). The explication of this scheme forms an important part of the Book of Deuteronomy: the aspects of the curse are matched at every point with the blessings of prosperity and victory for obedience (Deut. 28:1-68). The great national disasters as late as the time of Deuteronomy were interpreted as the result of disobedience. This simple explanation of defeat completely overlooked inferior military resources, unwise leadership, or lack of preparedness. A sharply stereotyped view of history thus emerged. It was projected backward in the Deuteronomistic history, which was written in the early period of the Babylonian captivity,[9] so that the complex pattern of success and failure in the preceding 600 years was explained by a simple formula (e.g., Judges 2:11-23).

The moral of this Deuteronomic principle was to be righteous so as to continue in triumph. Israel was required, according to this principle, only to obey God's commandments, and Yahweh would automatically give it "rest" from its enemies. Israel would earn unbroken peace and prosperity, and even enjoy a position of international supremacy. Thus Deuteronomy 28:1 naively asserts: "If you obey the voice of Yahweh your God, being careful to do all his commandments which I command you this day, Yahweh your God will set you high above all the nations of the earth."

The Deuteronomic Principle in American History

The Deuteronomic principle also gave inspiration and a distinctive shape to the American experience. In 1630, John Winthrop told fellow settlers aboard the *Arbella* on the voyage to America that if they obeyed the covenant, God would grant them domestic peace, prosperity, victory over their enemies, and a status superior to all other nations. "Wee shall finde that the God of Israell is among us, when tenn of us shall be able to resist a thousand of our enemies, when hee shall make us a prayse and glory, that men shall say of succeeding plantacions: the Lord make it like that of New England: for we must Consider that wee shall be as a Citty upon a Hill, the eies of all people are uppon us."

But Winthrop warned, in the words of Deuteronomy 30, that if they turned away, they would "surely perish."[10]

This scheme lies at the heart of political sermons throughout American history. In 1777, Nicholas Street preached on the Deuteronomic theme of "The American States Acting Over the Part of the Children of Israel in the Wilderness and Thereby Impeding Their Entrance Into Canaan's Rest." The calamities the colonists were experiencing were due to God's wrath, which was provoked by their sins. Peace would not be restored until they repented. This excerpt from Street's sermon exhibits the Deuteronomic flavor:

> God has a righteous controversy with us in this land; and our iniquities have arrived to that aggravated height, that they have called for these sore calamities that we feel! And the British nation are the rod of God's anger to scourge and chastise us for our sins. . . . Therefore let us be humble, kiss the rod and accept the punishment of our sins . . . that God may be intreated for the land, spare his heritage, and not give it up to a reproach but restore to us our liberties as at the first, and our privileges as at the beginning.[11]

At the conclusion of the American Revolution, Ezra Stiles preached before the Connecticut General Assembly on the theme of "The United States Elevated to Glory and Honour." His text (from Deut. 26:19) led him to claim that "God's American Israel" was being lifted by God "high above all nations." He linked the victorious outcome of the Revolution with American virtue and divine pleasure.[12] Samuel Langdon, in his 1788 election-day sermon before the general court at Concord, New Hampshire, stated the same Deuteronomic theme explicitly. He challenged his hearers to adhere to the principles of the God-given Constitution: "By this you will increase in numbers, wealth, and power, and obtain reputation and dignity among the nations; whereas, the contrary conduct will make you poor, distressed, and contemptible."[13] He exhorted the new American nation: "Rise! Rise to fame among all nations, as a wise and understanding people! Political life and death are set before you; be a free, numerous, well ordered, and happy people! The way has been plainly set before you; if you pursue it, your prosperity is sure; but if not, distress and ruin will overtake you."[14]

These sentiments received popular expression during the War of 1812 in a poem by Francis Scott Key, which quickly became a national favorite. "The Star-spangled Banner" stated the Deuteronomic principle in its third stanza, claiming the inevitable victory for those who trust in God: "Then conquer we must, when our cause it is just, And this be our motto: 'In God is our Trust.'"

The conditions for victory were precisely those of the Book of Deuteronomy: the justice of the cause and the faithfulness of the people. Adverse power factors played no role, and the sentiment overlooked the tragic reverses of history. Even after the Civil War, when such dimensions should have been clearly visible, these Deuteronomic sentiments, rather than the tragic vision of Lincoln, prevailed in the victorious North. The Civil War monument in Des Moines, Iowa, expressed the thought in its essential form: "Right is right, since God is God. And right the day has won." The conviction was that the North won the war not because it was more powerful but because it was on the side of divine rightness.

This mythic belief played a decisive role in the laissez-faire economic system, which became the arena for victory in the post–Civil War period. The conviction was that prosperity marked the reward for virtue, that no one in America would be in poverty unless he or she had done wrong. The famous Brooklyn preacher Henry Ward Beecher stated this clearly: "There may be reasons of poverty which do not involve wrong; but looking comprehensively through city and town and village and country, the general truth will stand, that no man in this land suffers from poverty unless it be more than his fault — unless it be his sin."[15] Beecher expressed this principle in another way in one of his sermons: "Nowhere else does wealth so directly point towards virtue in morality, and spirituality in religion, as in America."[16] The widely quoted sermon by Bishop William Lawrence, "The Relation of Wealth to Morals," states the same Deuteronomic point: "In the long run, it is only to the man of morality that wealth comes. . . . Put ten thousand immoral men to live and work in one fertile valley and ten thousand moral men to live and work in the next valley, and the question is soon answered as to who wins the material wealth. Godliness is in league with riches."[17] The popular Horatio Alger tales, written by a graduate of the Cambridge Divinity School after the Civil War, were adulatory stories about the giants of industry based on precisely the same principle. Success in the competitive economic system was the sign of divine favor, a proof of the rightness of one's motives and methods. As Americans became more and more secular, the motif of divine favor tended to drop aside, but the premise of success as a sign of virtue remained.

Given these adaptations of the Deuteronomic principle, the popular American belief in its own superiority stands forth in mythic clarity. That America is the most prosperous nation on earth is proudly boasted, not because wealth has served to overcome inequities or eliminate human need but because it proves our virtue. The statistics concerning American military and industrial power are proudly displayed in debates concerning the validity of current policies and attitudes; statistical superiority is taken to prove moral superiority. That America has never started or lost a war is a boast that every school child learns. Its appeal obviously is more mythic than historical. It is not based on a balanced appraisal of the causes and the outcome of the War of 1812, the complicity of the nation in provoking the Mexican War and the Indian Wars, the Spanish-American War, the incident in the Gulf of Tonkin, or the secret war waged in Laos. The appeal of the myth is so fundamental that disclosures of complicity in these instances do little to alter popular consciousness. If we believe we have never started a war, this confirms in our minds our virtuous lack of aggressiveness. And if we have never lost, this is clear Deuteronomic proof that "our cause it is just."

The flattering implications of the popular myth that America is "number one in the world" are deeply threatened, however, if the nation should happen to lose or fall behind. Such eventualities hardly threaten the physical survival of the nation. Nor can rebuffs to client regimes, the loss of competitive superiority in some aspect of production, or defeat in some United Nations vote or in the race for gold medals at the Olympics be rationally viewed as mortal threats. But they are psychic threats. Americans fiercely resist and bitterly resent them because they threaten the mythic base of moral superiority.

There can be little argument that the avoidance of such defeat became a primary preoccupation in the Vietnam War. Long before 1968, when the hopes for a clear-cut American victory had been shattered by the Tet offensive, Pentagon analysts frankly admitted in a confidential memo that 70 percent of the U.S. objective in Vietnam was to avoid an embarrassing defeat. Such an assessment can hardly possess the precision of a percentile, but it emphatically betrays a predominantly self-serving intent.[18] It was clearly the primary goal in President Nixon's secret plan for disengagement. As he said on January 24, 1973, in a message announcing the peace agreement, "Throughout the years of negotiations, we have insisted on peace with honor."[19] The content of that "honor," as spelled out in his earlier addresses, was to retrieve our prisoners without admitting defeat, to ensure the preservation of our "allies" in South Vietnam, and to save face during the transition period with some forms of international controls. The package was restated in the peace agreement message: "Now that we have achieved an honorable agreement, let us be proud that America did not settle for a peace that would have betrayed our allies, that would have abandoned our prisoners of war or that would have ended the war for us, but would have continued the war for the 50 million people of Indochina."[20] To force the other side to acquiesce in a face-saving solution to keep such honor intact was the reason for the U.S. bombing and mining in North Vietnam that gradually evoked the revulsion of the civilized world. And if the twenty thousand additional servicemen, not to mention several hundred thousand Vietnamese who were killed during Nixon's first term died for any cause, it was for precisely this kind of "honor." Their deaths were the price of forestalling defeat and thereby salvaging the image of our virtue.

In a penetrating article on the moral consequences of the Vietnam War, Francine du Plessix Gray notes this dominant concern to maintain the image of American innocence. The "cornerstone" of the Nixon-Kissinger strategy, she writes, "was the obscene rationale of the 'decent interval': the United States must choreograph its eventual departure from Vietnam — thousands of lives lost in the process — in such a way that it does not *appear* to abandon the Saigon regime, thus absolving us of guilt in the tragedy. This search for a false and abstract purity has been but a new modulation of our traditional obsession with American innocence. It is based on myths of moral perfection as theologically antiquated as they are symbolically false."[21] The theological implications of such an acceptance of the Deuteronomic principle are thoroughly idolatrous. That victory for one side or the other may reveal the justice and the power of God is a matter that may be glimpsed at times, but only "in a glass darkly," with the eyes of faith. To claim that such justice is unequivocally visible in the victory of any nation is to lose the sense of the transcendent. And to claim it for one's own nation, with the aim of proving one's selflessness, is nothing short of idolatrous. It places the honor of self or nation in the position of ultimate significance. Whenever this occurs, a terrible distortion in perception follows. Having lost its due sense of finite worth, a nation embarks on campaigns to sustain its presumed infinite superiority, using means that are the very antithesis of the virtues it seeks to defend. It refuses to admit these realities because to do so would threaten the graven image of perfect virtue and good intentions.

Since the idolatrous center of such a system is so fragile, it calls for a defense in every theater of competition. The sense of proportion disappears as the nation squanders its energies against specters on every hand. Every battlefield, no matter how dubious, is pronounced holy. And every victory, no matter how bloodily bought, is thought to confirm the justness of the cause. This chain of illusions is particularly taut in a secular era in which a vital sense of transcendence has been lost and the perennial threat of *hubris* has been forgotten. In such an era the Deuteronomic principle can transform the nation into a terrifying Moloch, the idol whose insatiable appetite is for the blood of its own and its enemies' children. It is then that the God of history, whose righteous purposes cannot be thwarted by human pride, calls forth the hammer of adversity to shatter the clay-footed idol.

Mythic Responses to Defeat

When defeat threatens a zealous nation, it is rare that any element of divine justice is discerned. To admit that the hammer blows are deserved is to give up the idolatrous view of one's own virtue, as long as the Deuteronomic principle is intact. So one resorts to mythic solutions to adversity. The first of these is the *betrayal theory*. If defeat has come to a righteous nation, it must be due to evil conspirators. Someone must have betrayed the cause, thus thwarting the natural rhythm in which goodness brings victory and sin brings defeat. All one has to do is find the traitors and eliminate the obstruction in order to assure the victory. The solution is deceptively simple. This is the initial reaction pattern of any nation that believes in the conspiracy theory of evil. One of the most striking examples is the "stab in the back" idea that emerged in Germany in 1918. A Lutheran clergyman was supposedly the first to formulate the conviction that the German armies had been thwarted by traitors in the homeland. Hindenburg's testimony on the responsibility for the outbreak and length of the war in November 1919 placed the blame on civilian leaders who attempted to negotiate peace while the war was still on: "The German Army was stabbed in the back."[22] This line was used to masterful advantage in the Nazi propaganda that destroyed the Weimar Republic.

The betrayal theory emerged on the center stage of American politics the moment the frustration of the Cold War came to the fore. D. W. Brogan cited this reaction in an article titled "The Illusion of American Omnipotence." Since Americans felt that their virtue assured them of victory under any circumstances, they took the frustration after World War II as a sign that betrayal had taken place. The conviction was that "any situation which distresses or endangers the United States can only exist because some Americans have been fools or knaves."[23] The traitors in this case were thought to be communists and their sympathizers within the government itself. These traitors must have been responsible for the Yalta agreements, the Russian domination of Eastern Europe, and the chaotic decline of Nationalist China after 1945.

The political adaptation of the betrayal theory has since been refined, with underlings often carrying out the business of formulating accusations of betrayal. But the basic strategy remains the same. At times of national frustration and defeat, the desire of a zealous public to destroy scapegoats is shrewdly channeled into the political process. The technique is to combine traditional statements about American virtue and invincibility with the suggestion that the elimination of one's opponent will remove the only impediment to America's triumph. This tactic is much more appealing to a morally fastidious public than the old-fashioned form of elimination that a Phinehas, a John Brown, or a Lee Harvey Oswald could provide. Hatred and self-righteousness are channeled into the voting booth rather than into the rifle barrel. The difficulty is that the betrayal theory works much better in the polling booth than in the arena of international conflict. That the majority of the American voters can be induced to vote against an ostensible traitor to the national dream is no proof of the validity of this myth.

The second solution is the Deuteronomic form of *repentance*. Although less primitive than the scapegoat idea, it is as old as American nationalism itself. Its premise is visible from John Winthrop's admonitions down through the latest political sermons: that the sin of the chosen people is the cause of any dilemma it might presently face. As one looks at our political sermons, whether sacred or secular, the curiously reactionary stamp of the Book of Deuteronomy makes itself felt. Repentance is seen as a turning backward to recover former values; and the call to return is accompanied by glowing promises of the elimination of defeat and humiliation. This form of repentance, in contrast to the radical kind of self-examination and sharpened moral responsibility demanded by the great prophets, lends itself nicely to political rhetoric. The promise to restore victory and honor is flattering to the fragile sense of national superiority. And the recovery of spiritual values is placed on so abstract a level that the nation does not have to admit its actual misdeeds. As in Deuteronomy, one confesses cultic sins and spiritual faults in lieu of admitting actual historical transgressions.

This Deuteronomic form of repentance is implicit in the frequent references to "spiritual" factors in political rhetoric. It played a key role in Eisenhower's first inaugural address, which set forth the "laws of spiritual strength that generate and define our material strength."[24] In the face of the frustrations and perils that confronted the nation in 1953, he called for a renewal of faith in the principles of democratic decency as well as "a conscious renewal of faith in our country and in the watchfulness of a Divine Providence."[25] The Deuteronomic rationale of this kind of rhetoric was put very concisely by John Foster Dulles: "The sum of the whole matter is this, that our civilization cannot survive materially unless it be redeemed spiritually."[26] The great material power of America was being frustrated, not because of an atomic stalemate and the rivalry of superpowers, but because America was not adhering to her spiritual principles. If she regained her hold on those principles, she would surely prevail against communism.

The resurgence of religiosity in the 1950s reflected this "spiritual" form of repentance. It was inspired by Eisenhower's "private prayer," which opened his inaugural address, by the White House prayer breakfasts that he initiated, and by the close liaison he developed with leading clergymen such as Billy Graham and Norman Vincent Peale. Declarations of faith, both private and public, were viewed as the forms of repentance that would guarantee victory in the Cold War. In thoroughly Deuteronomic fashion, frequent religious ceremonies were a means whereby God's favor would be assured and the frustration of foreign threats removed. As Eisenhower said in 1953: "The churches of America are citadels of our faith in individual freedom and human dignity. This faith is the living source of all our spiritual strength. And this strength is our matchless armor in our worldwide struggle against the forces of Godless tyranny and oppression."[27] The president's pastor, Edward L. R. Elson, dedicated his sermons on "America's spiritual recovery" to Eisenhower, "who by personal example and public utterance is giving testimony to the reality of America's spiritual foundations."[28]

The oddly "spiritual" form of repentance was what President Nixon called for in his first inaugural address, in a line that is framed in pious living rooms and offices throughout America: "To a crisis of the spirit, we need an answer of the spirit."[29] The content of this answer is essentially that of Nixon's predecessors back to Deuteronomy. The subsequent lines in his inaugural address spelled out the source: "And to find that answer, we need only to look within ourselves. When we listen to the 'better angels of our nature,' we find that they celebrate the simple things, the basic things — such as goodness, decency, love, kindness." The concrete application of this answer a few lines later was "to lower our voices . . . stop shouting at one another" — an obvious criticism of the vociferous protests that had so unsettled the country. The social evils that had provoked them were not to be confronted and overcome; instead, we were to return to the very ideals that had produced them, and the evils presumably would melt away. No change of the national motivations and policies was necessary: "I know America. I know the heart of America is good."

Nixon spelled out the application of this concept to the threatened defeat in Vietnam in his November 3, 1969, speech to the "great silent majority," which had retained the Deuteronomic ideals. He offered Vietnamization as a way to avert defeat and keep all the traditional ideals intact. His exhortation was to return to the great principles and hold to them with tenacity.

> Our greatness as a nation has been our capacity to do what had to be done when we knew our course was right. . . .
>
> I know it may not be fashionable to speak of patriotism or national destiny these days. But I feel it is appropriate to do so on this occasion. . . . The wheel of destiny has turned so that any hope the world has for the survival of peace and freedom will be determined by whether the American

people have the moral stamina and the courage to meet the challenge of free world leadership.

Let historians not record that when America was the most powerful nation in the world we passed on the other side of the road and allowed the last hopes for peace and freedom of millions of people to be suffocated by the forces of totalitarianism. . . .

Let us be united for peace. Let us also be united against defeat. Because let us understand: North Vietnam cannot defeat or humiliate the United States. Only Americans can do that.[30]

Defeat is possible, in short, only if America lacks "the moral stamina and the courage" to hold to the zealous values. Those who protest should repent and become "united" with the silent majority. The solution is internal, a matter of holding the prescribed values and acting on them. External circumstances do not count. That is why the effectiveness of this peculiar form of repentance is pictured in such grandiose terms. The factors hindering "peace and freedom" throughout the world are thought to be entirely subject to the direct application of American resolve. The strength of the country is presumably such that only one question remains: whether the chosen nation will have enough stamina to apply it.

What this appeal overlooked was that the new weapons of "Vietnamization" — a huge air force to support a large army that seemed reluctant to fight — would not suffice to transform a corrupt and dictatorial Saigon regime into a model of democratic justice, capable of attracting popular support. Something much more than American resolve was required, especially when that resolve was guided more by the desire to sustain our own reputation than to advance the cause of representative government. But these fundamental considerations were set aside as the public responded in overwhelming support of this mythic appeal.

While this Deuteronomic form of repentance has potent capacities for manipulating a zealous public, it should never be mistaken for more authentic forms of repentance. It is vastly different from the repentance to which the great prophets called their people. It turns a nation backward to the old idolatries, to the very beliefs and actions that defeat demonstrates to be false. It confirms the overblown view of our virtue. And thus it impedes a realistic appraisal of the evils we have wrought, the actual possibilities of our situation, or the transcendent justice of God. True repentance is not turning backward in time but turning back from one's bondage to time. It consists of accepting the contingencies of history and the ambiguities of its outcome, rejecting the notion that one is ever fully and finally justified by one's acts in history.

So long as a country relies on these zealous solutions to defeat, the reality of its situation remains disguised. But defeat cannot thereby be averted, no matter how attractive these inappropriate forms of power may seem. It is merely postponed a bit and rendered more corrosive in its coming.

The Impact of Defeat on Civil Religion

The corrosion of defeat may be traced in the history of any zealous nation. It is most destructive when the nation does not confront defeat honestly and directly. If leaders explain defeat away, laying the blame on scapegoats or demanding reactionary forms of repentance, it will gradually consume the ideal of a servant nation. It will hollow out even the most precious forms of civil religion. And if circumstances permit, it can provide the atmosphere in which reactionary and self-destructive revivals can occur.

This process is visible in archetypal form with Israel's experience following the Deuteronomic reform of 621 BCE. Soon after King Josiah had inaugurated a nationalistic revival, he was killed in battle. He was attempting to thwart the Egyptian expeditionary force that was moving through Israelite territory to intervene in a power struggle in the Fertile Crescent. The exemplary Yahwist king and his small but holy army anticipated triumph over the wicked Pharaoh and his invaders. Had not Deuteronomy given assurances in such a case? "When you go forth to war against your enemies, and see horses and chariots and an army larger than your own, you shall not be afraid of them; for Yahweh your God is with you . . . to give you the victory" (Deut. 20:1, 4). But Josiah, who was disguised and could not have been picked out by enemy archers, was killed by a stray arrow that seemed to be directed by destiny. Martin Buber noted that this shattering defeat was "a most important incision in Israelite religious history. The question 'Why?' presses upon all hearts. Why has the king, who unlike his predecessors did Yahweh's will in everything, been snatched away in the prime of his life and in the midst of his plans for the realization of God's word, at the hour when he went forth undismayed, trusting in God's word (Deut. 20:1), to fight the superior force?" The theological implications were that the "ready teaching about reward and punishment in the life of individual and community is shaken. This deity is no more to be formulated. . . . He has become an enigma."[31]

Despite the shocking reversal of Josiah's death, Israelite leaders clung ever more fiercely to the zealous dogmas. They deemed past traitors and former sins to be responsible for the defeat.[32] A dozen years later Israel suffered a shattering defeat at the hands of the Babylonians. Within yet another decade the Israelites opened a suicidal war against their overlords, and Jerusalem was leveled. A handful of fanatics later assassinated the Babylonian governor. When Yahweh failed to destroy the Babylonian relief columns, the Israelite remnant fled to Egypt. Jeremiah assured Israel of Babylonian amnesty (Jer. 42:7-22), but the leaders left the "promised land" and the dream of restoring its destiny. With the civil religion discredited by defeat, perceptive and skeptical minds sought solace in nihilism and occultism, such as the worship of the "queen of heaven," a degenerate deity popularized during the dark ages of Assyrian domination (Jer. 44). A fatal decline in moral integrity, public spirit, and common sense ensued, diminishing Israel's capacity to survive. Only a structure thoroughly rotted from within could have crumbled like that.

The irony of the U.S. situation during the final phase of the Vietnam War was that the convulsive efforts to avoid defeat lest the nation's morale be broken led to the sort of inner corrosion that ancient Israel experienced. President Nixon often stated his fear of what defeat in Vietnam would do: "Our allies would lose confidence in America. Far more dangerous, we would lose confidence in ourselves. . . . Inevitable remorse and divisive recrimination would scar our spirit as a people."[33] What the nation little suspected was that the very effort to avert humiliation through massive violence produced the fatal corrosion. American self-confidence was bound to be disappointed, so it was linked to the achievement of incredible results, such as producing a democratic society by taking the reactionary side in a local power struggle or by ensuring peace for the entire world by continuing some of the most destructive bombing raids in history. Even if the United States could have succeeded in such unlikely enterprises, the faith thereby sustained would be an empty mockery of the nation's religious heritage. Its boast of total unselfishness is as far as one can possibly depart from the spirit of true religion, which admits realistically, "No one is good except God alone" (Luke 18:19). Any nation that attempts to sustain such illusions about itself has already become corroded. Its actions will be so rash and destructive that the national virtue thereby affirmed is already a grotesque caricature of the good.

Since no nation can succeed in transcending its finite limitations, this illusory kind of confidence is bound to crumble. As it does, efforts to reconstruct the shattered self-idolatries become more and more frantic — and more and more violent. The idea that such efforts could evoke the "confidence" of allies or encourage trust in democratic "self-determination" elsewhere in the world was preposterous. Only a public that is prepared to face reality, about both its finite virtue and its limited capabilities, can elicit the respect of world opinion. And the finite variety of self-confidence is the only kind that can survive under the pressure of history.

When the national destiny and religious heritage are linked in an effort to shore up weakened self-confidence, the collapse is all the more destructive when it comes. The idealistic aspects of the civil religion were the first to go down with the wreckage. Supporting this idolatrous effort, as numerous clergy have, is preparing the way for the kind of religious and moral skepticism that generations of zealous warfare have produced in Christian Europe. It is to strengthen the forces that seek to replace the definition of national destiny as democratic servanthood with doctrines of pure national self-interest. When the degenerative process is complete, all that is likely to be left is: "Every person must save himself." As the diplomacy of the post-Vietnam War era illustrates, this became the dominant line in U.S. negotiations with Japan, Europe, and Latin America. The country dropped the noble tradition of impartial and fair-minded diplomacy, which received such approbation during the time of the Marshall Plan; but a public deluded by idolatrous visions of being "totally unselfish" did not even mark its passing. A similar dynamic is likely to recur when it becomes clear that the current "war against terrorism" cannot possibly be won by purely military means, no matter how many cities are bombed or nations invaded.

Above all, the sense of national or personal significance is jeopardized as it is tried to the doomed Deuteronomic dogma. If the life of the community and the individual have meaning only in victory, defeat thrusts it into the abyss of meaninglessness. This lies behind the oft-stated argument in the 1970s that, if we were to lose the war, all those who died therein would have done so in vain. In this argument there is no middle ground between an idolatrous significance predicated on victory and the complete lack of any significance whatsoever; there is no basis for a healthy, finite, and resilient sense of meaning. The fact that meaning is always fragmentary, shot through with the tragic stuff of personal and national folly yet somehow visible in the mysterious purposes of divine righteousness — the key thesis of Lincoln's Gettysburg Address and his second inaugural address — is frosted over by zealous dogma. A people nurtured on the Deuteronomic dogma will allow the most atrocious acts to be committed in its name so long as they promise to hold off defeat a while longer. The psychic conviction is that to submit to the blow is to give up the most precious of all possessions — the sense of meaning. But what significance remains when defeat finally is ineluctable? None whatsoever! National and personal nihilism are the results.

Yet no matter how frantically a nation twists and contorts to avoid the pain, the blow of defeat comes ever and again. No nation, including the most powerful on earth, can avoid it indefinitely. Although it may be particularly humiliating to experience the reversal at the hands of a small and less developed nation such as North Vietnam, whose major resources were its wits and its stamina, the proper question is not how to avoid it, but how to respond to it creatively. This question will gain in urgency as the futility of attempting to stamp out terrorism through military action becomes more and more clear in the years to come, when every military campaign produces a new wave of jihadic violence by people willing to sacrifice their lives in order to avoid their own forms of defeat. We shall find that the Deuteronomic logic is as pervasive and compelling in our opponents as it is in ourselves.

Bringing Prophetic Resources to the Experience of Defeat

Perhaps the most promising approach would be to appropriate the tragic yet realistic heritage of our great prophets, writers, and artists. Those who have explored the depths of the human situation, who have experienced the shattering of their dearest idols and the bitterness of defeat, offer us the resources we need. For unlike the situation of victory that leaves the self complacently anchored in its certainties, the defeat in Southeast Asia and the recent destruction of the World Trade Center call the nation to radical transformation. We have to learn not only to live without our former idols but to take modest steps toward the construction of a healthier culture. No one can do this for us; each of must suffer the agony of death and rebirth. But we cannot hope to undergo this alone, enacting the isolated destiny of lonely martyrs while the public remains unchanged. We must undertake the process as a culture.

The essential starting point is to get the message of defeat straight. This requires a break with the idolatrous and morally evasive forms of the Deuteronomic dogma. We see this in the incident in which Jesus was asked to comment on the implications of Pilate's recent massacre of suspected insurrectionists and on the construction accident at the tower of Siloam (Luke 13:1-5).[34] The Deuteronomic message regarding both of these incidents was that the victims must have sinned to deserve their fate and thus that the righteous should continue to applaud the business of killing culprits who offend divine justice. As Eduard Schweizer explains, "Jesus' response rules out the dogma that particular sinfulness leads to particular disaster. . . ."[35] Such explanations would allow the self to retain its assumed innocence and cling to the vicious dogmas that were catapulting the nation of Israel into a catastrophic war with Rome. The larger message was that the Deuteronomic dogmas were being refuted by current history, and that to continue to follow them in the zealot uprisings against Rome would lead to national suicide. To follow Jesus' admonition — "Unless you repent you will all likewise perish" (Luke 13:5) — would be to turn away from the dogmas and their political enactment.[36] It would be to turn toward the kingdom of God, which accepts enemies unconditionally and calls them into the tasks of reconciliation.

This is precisely the call we must hear today — in the wake of September 11, 2001. For the current interpretations of our crisis, with the typical placing of blame and the naive resolve that "we shall defeat terrorism everywhere in the world" and we will "never make a mistake like Vietnam again," simply lock us into the very complacent dogmas that led to defeat in Southeast Asia. They confirm in us the conviction that we are the innocent in a world in which the guilty should be bombed. What is required of us, both as a nation and as individuals, is to repent of these fatuous beliefs. If we refuse to repent, we shall destroy ourselves by acting out the Deuteronomic scenario to the end. That is the clear message of the defeats of the Galilean insurrectionists and of the American crusaders in Vietnam. The message is equally apt for crusading Israelis and Muslim jihadists who seek to avert defeat by ever more terrible acts of destruction. What is required is the sort of fundamental shift that Abraham Lincoln called for in his time: "The dogmas of the quiet past are inadequate to the stormy present. The occasion is piled high with difficulty, and we must rise with the occasion. As our case is new, so we must think anew and act anew. We must disenthrall ourselves, and then we shall save our country."[37]

To "disenthrall ourselves" from Deuteronomic dogmas brings us face to face with our finitude, both national and personal. It is to admit that we have not been innocent lambs in a wicked world, that our violent crusades have sometimes been misguided, and that we do not have sole access to the wisdom about what other nations should do. It offers us access to the pragmatic wisdom of the Bible, whose premise is: "Be not wise in your own eyes; fear Yahweh, and turn away from evil" (Prov. 3:7). To acknowledge this is to follow also the admonition of the Delphic oracle, which underlies so much of Greek philosophy and drama: "Know thyself — that thou art but human."

If we made this discovery for ourselves and our nation, we might also make the deepest meaning of our religious heritage accessible. One of the contributing factors in our culture's blindness to tragedy has been the superficial grasp of the theology of the cross by our dominant Protestant tradition. The Christ event has been interpreted under the rubric of the resurrection as a sign of triumph and immortality. We may perceive that the tragic death of Christ is virtually inexplicable by dropping in on some half-empty Protestant sanctuary to hear the fumbling Good Friday meditations — in contrast to the self-assured mood in the same sanctuary jammed with the Easter morning crowd. This too must change if American Christianity is to lead its followers to confront defeat. What American religious leaders need today is Paul's theology of the cross, with its grasp of the tragedy of life, its forthright acceptance of human weakness, and its bulwarks against human pride. We need to hear the message of a man who lived with defeat throughout his ministry, and who confessed that he had received this answer to his yearning to be released from the discomfiture of his "thorn in the flesh": "The Lord . . . said to me, 'My grace is sufficient for you, for my power is made perfect in weakness': I will all the more gladly boast of my weaknesses, that the power of Christ may rest upon me. For the sake of Christ, then, I am content with weaknesses, insults, hardships, persecutions, and calamities; for when I am weak, then I am strong" (2 Cor. 12:8-10).

Here is a faith that confronts defeat with courage. It provides a proper humility without the self-pity that marks the "humiliation" Americans strive so desperately to avoid in global affairs. It faces squarely the realities of our human situation and lives creatively out of the power of God. We need preachers today who will proclaim such a faith, messengers who will interpret the good news in such a way as to face our humiliation and defeat rather than disguise it with platitudes. We need forthright men and women who will resolve to "preach the gospel" as Paul did in Corinth, but "not with eloquent wisdom, lest the cross of Christ be emptied of its power" (1 Cor. 1:17).

In the last analysis, to admit defeat should be to acknowledge the transcendent justice of God. To admit defeat should mean to have discovered that the justice we sought to accomplish in Vietnam after 1954 and the current effort to rid the world of terrorism cannot be claimed as identical with divine justice — indeed, may have been repudiated by it. For the healthy way to face a defeat of the Deuteronomic dogma is to discard the idolatry while retaining the sense of divine justice that works its mysterious way through history. If we fall prey to the logic of the dogma and continue to identify divine justice with our own success, defeat will shatter our moral sense and thrust us into skepticism or nihilism. We must grasp the prophetic insight that adversity can be understood as the discipline of sonship, and that defeat can sometimes be a sign not of divine rejection but of suffering love (Hos. 11; Heb. 12). Our sense of having been chosen as a nation must be refined and purified in the "furnace of affliction" (Isa. 48:10) before we can begin to take up our rightful task of being a light to the nations and a servant of justice.

These prophetic resources of tragic vision must be adapted into the popular idiom if our culture is to be transformed. From comic books to television programs, we must develop vivid images of realism and courage in the face of defeat. The most powerful models in this regard may lie in the less than triumphal but hopeful messages from African-American gospel music. The more stoic blues tradition, which originated in the oppressive Mississippi Delta, exploring prejudice, unemployment, prison, family stress, and a variety of other human losses, offers powerful images of coping and the spirit of endurance. Recognizing and interpreting such experiences is a far higher calling than affirming the victories of empire. Those who deal in mythic and symbolic forms of communication must take a particular responsibility at this point. Writers and educators whose task is to communicate our cultural legacy have a similar calling, as do parents and youth workers.

Our communities and our organizations must begin to carry out this task, knowing full well that in a democratic society our destiny is shaped as much by our neighbor's outlook as by our own. Our local governments must take up the cultural task of preparing us for life amid defeat. The publicly supported theaters that present the great tragedies are now essential to our survival. The opera houses and recital halls offering the possibility of creative but tragic catharsis are not luxuries we can allow to be reserved for the wealthy, but they must be maturing institutions that our citizens need for weathering the crises that will not disappear. No longer can we allow our children to be educated on the shallow assumption that there is no importance in the past, and that there are no languages and cultures besides our own that are worthy of mastery. For to master the language and artistic heritage of others is to gain a sense of solidarity with mankind — that tragedy-prone, irrational, but noble species to which we Americans must finally discover we belong.

We must, in short, cultivate more consistently a tragic sense of life if we are to cope with tragedy. We must take up the sort of instruction Herman Melville yearned for in his prose supplement to *Battle-Pieces* and *Aspects of the War,* poems published after the Civil War: "Let us pray that the terrible historical tragedy of our time may not have been enacted without instructing our whole beloved country through pity and terror."[38] What this means for contemporary crises is yet to be worked out, but no one can experience the pity and the terror for us. Following the path of those who have experienced humiliation and defeat before us, we must adapt their insights for ourselves. The task is clearly there to be accomplished, but who will take it up?

We need thinkers who will work out the current implications of Hosea's vision that in the defeat of Israel lay both the wrath and the love of God. Bernhard Anderson put it this way: "To us, the 'wrath' and the 'love' of God may seem contradictory, but to Hosea God's love surpasses human understanding. It has both the dark side of judgment and the promise of hope and renewal (see Hosea 11:10-11). Israel would learn, as did the poet Francis Thompson, that her gloom after all was but 'the shadow of His Hand outstretched caressingly.'"[39]

We need novelists and composers who will portray for us in secular terms what Isaiah meant when he sensed Yahweh's word about Israel after its catastrophic defeat: "Behold, I have refined you, but not like silver; I have tried you in the furnace of affliction" (Isa. 48:10). That tragedy can refine, rather than destroy, that it can burn out the impurities of illusion and pride — such profound possibilities must be translated for us into images with which we can identify and into structures conducive to our transformation. We need playwrights and actors who will create for us dramas like that of Job, taking up that poet's courageous stand against the destructive dogmas of his day, and celebrating that moment of dialogue when the Eternal breaks through and speaks to the human being caught on top of his dung heap. It is crucial for our cultural health to experience the creative, though completely secular, impulse that Archibald MacLeish caught in the climax of his play *J.B.*, when the wife places the chair back on its legs and begins the process of putting things back together again. We must discover that to be fully human is to undergo tragedy and move beyond it in faith.

The most powerful means of catharsis is not in the theater, however, nor on the psychiatrist's couch, but in the prophetic interpretation of current experience. Jeremiah was a pioneer in this regard. He saw the defeats of his time as divinely ordained means to bring the nation back to reality. He insisted on the recognition of personal responsibility, not just by the leaders but also by the entire public. For only as the tragedy touches the individual to transform the twisted heart can it produce rebirth rather than annihilation. No evasion of responsibility is possible with an oracle like this:

> Your ways and your doings
>   have brought this upon you.
> This is your doom, and it is bitter;
>   it has reached your very heart. (Jer. 4:18)

We need more interpreters who will take up this forthright style of commentary on our current events. We need more journalists and historians who will hold us to our responsibilities for the coming tragedies as they unfold, and who will do so in such a way that it reaches the center of motivation and action which for Jeremiah was the "heart." We need teachers and parents who will take such diagnosis for themselves, then adapt it for those in their charge. Our current time is one of judgment, of opportunity, and of decision: the judgment may have already fallen on our infatuation with Deuteronomic justice; the opportunity to be transformed by an acceptance of defeat lies open before us; so we must make the decision about which path we shall follow.

The hard, narrow path of realism leads directly through the fields of adversity and the slough of despond, but it may lead toward a peace that better satisfies our own sense of righteousness as well as that of the rest of our fellow citizens on this endangered planet.

15 Crusades against Symbolic Desecration

God requireth not a uniformity of religion to be enacted and enforced in any civil state; which enforced uniformity . . . is the greatest occasion of civil war, ravishing of conscience, persecution of Jesus Christ in his servants, and of the hypocrisy and destruction of millions of souls. . . . An enforced uniformity of religion throughout a nation or civil state, confounds the civil and the religious, denies the principles of Christianity and civility, and that Jesus Christ is come in the flesh.

Roger Williams, *The Bloudy Tenent of Persecution* (1644)[1]

In this way we are reaffirming the transcendence of religious faith in America's heritage and future; in this way we shall constantly strengthen those spiritual weapons which forever will be our country's most powerful resource in peace and war.

President Dwight D. Eisenhower on Flag Day, 1954,
celebrating the addition of the words "under God"
to the Pledge of Allegiance[2]

As we have shown in our narrative of Captain America's battles to redeem the world, God has often been invoked as an ally or commander. Those accepting this divine imperative to destroy the nation's enemies often turn inward to focus on the social unity and discipline required for the redemptive task. Historically, this attention has come to rest on symbols, rituals, affirmations — and the spirit that lies behind them. Roger Williams, a preacher who opposed the Puritan leaders of Massachusetts Bay, was banished from their presence for refusing to accept their theocratic premise and their emphasis on converting or destroying the Native Americans. He believed that civil authorities should not interfere with religious beliefs. Haunted by his vision of "the blood of so many hundred thousand souls of Protestants and Papists, spilt in the wars of present and former ages, for their respective consciences,"[3] Williams resolved to establish the colony of Rhode Island, toward which Quakers, Anabaptists, and others gravitated in search of religious freedom. In the spirit of prophetic realism, Williams also played the role of peacemaker between his colony and the Narragansett Indians, whose language he learned and taught through publication. Samuel Eliot Morison mentions the "monstrous heresy" propagated by Williams: "For aught anyone knew, the Indian religion was equally acceptable to God with Christianity."[4]

In the intervening years since Roger Williams' prophetic dissent, America has seen a flowering of faiths that fulfill his vision of a tolerant pluralism. Catholicism, Judaism, Buddhism, Islam, and a variety of other confessions have joined the Protestant Christianity first brought to these shores by the Puritans. However, an unexpected development that seems to counter the growth of diversity has been the effort to link God and the nation through symbolic sacralization and compulsory ritual. President Eisenhower's quotation at the head of this chapter represents a cardinal moment in this effort to give America the imprint of God's blessing. Coming at a time of great tension in the Cold War, when the U.S. government sought out enemies within the nation, putting "under God" into the Pledge of Allegiance affirmed a difference between the United States and adversary nations who had adopted state-imposed atheism. Two congressmen from Michigan pressed to add "under God" as an expression of "our dependence on God" and our "faith in his support." When their measure succeeded, they marched to the steps of the Capitol on Flag Day, 1954, to utter the new oath.[5]

During this same period (1955), all national currency — both coins and bills — were theologically stamped with the message "In God We Trust." This motto on the money was espoused as the substitute for the national motto *E Pluribus Unum* ("out of many, one"). Thus, in effect, a message of uniform, state-uttered theological affirmation replaced a sentiment of pride in secular diversity.[6] Eisenhower also focused national attention on his own religion in several ways enumerated by Richard Quebedeaux:

He composed a prayer for his inauguration, was baptized and became a member of Washington's National Presbyterian Church, appointed a staff assistant as a liaison on religious matters, declared a National Day of Prayer (required by a law passed in 1952) and appeared regularly at Prayer Breakfasts beginning in 1953.[7]

All these steps in giving America an official religious identity heightened a recurring conflict with the Jehovah's Witnesses, the Mennonites, the Christadelphians, and others who tend to see allegiance to government — expressed by flag or by salute — as an idolatrous act.[8] It was also offensive to secular-minded individuals and groups, such as the American Civil Liberties Union, who opposed the expression of religious sentiment under the aegis of government.

An intermediate step along the way toward granting the flag a sacred status was the 1989 Flag Protection Statute,[9] which fell just short of bestowing holiness on the flag: its language stated an injunction against anyone who "knowingly mutilates, defaces, physically defiles, burns, maintains on the ground, or tramples on any flag of the United States." The most earnest stride toward granting the flag a sacred status is the ongoing effort to pass a constitutional amendment that overrides the First Amendment's protection of the right of free speech. This movement will surely gain additional credibility and momentum as a result of the September 11 attacks, which were followed by a resurgence of flag display and incidents involving perceived failures of enthusiasm or reverence for the flag. On October 12, 2001, Secretary of Education Rod Paige urged all 107,000 public and private elementary and secondary schools to simultaneously utter the Pledge of Allegiance.[10] The New York City Board of Education required that all students begin their classroom day with the Pledge. The Pennsylvania House of Representatives, on a vote of 200 to 1, demanded that all Pennsylvania students recite the Pledge or sing "The Star-Spangled Banner" daily in their classrooms, in which they were required to display the flag.[11] Major General Patrick Brady, in a letter to the *Chicago Sun Times*, articulated the new intensity and rationale with clarity:

> Burning our flag is the most visible sign of hatred of America. And because of a mistake of the Supreme Court, they are allowed to do that. We should take that away from them. In honor of those who have suffered at the hands of those who hate us, it is time to say to flag-burners that we despise your hatred; we will not allow you to freely desecrate the symbol of all that is decent in the world, the symbol of our unity and of the goodness of those who were massacred.[12]

This is only a small sample of the new compulsions involving the flag that were undertaken almost immediately in the wake of the September 11 attacks. In the pages that follow, we analyze this new stage in zealous nationalism and note the parallels in efforts against desecration in other parts of the world.

The Struggle to Prevent Flag Desecration

The attempt to use law as the instrument to bestow holiness on the flag has been a leitmotif in much of American history. Robert Justin Goldstein, the leading American analyst of the flag protection movement (FPM), has shown in his books *Saving Old Glory* and *Flag Burning and Free Speech* that the "iconization" of the flag was not "the result of gradually emerging popular consensus that the flag should be treated as a sacred object." Instead, he insists, this development resulted primarily from "a deliberate, extensive, and prolonged campaign" engineered by various interest groups at work during the period shortly after 1890.[13]

The initial adoption of the stars and stripes as the national flag in 1777 was intended for the practical purpose of identifying U.S. ships at sea. It drew little popular attention. On land the new flag was flown over forts (such as Fort McHenry, the site of Francis Scott Key's inspiration for the lyrics of "The Star-Spangled Banner") and other public buildings. The U.S. Army used regimental banners, rather than the U.S. flag, until 1834. Finally, with the Mexican War of 1846-1848, the flag began to accompany American soldiers into battle. The flag was not flown over public schools before the Civil War, nor was it ever displayed at private homes. It comes as no surprise, then, that there were few instances of the use of the flag for political protest prior to 1861.

With the Confederate attack on Fort Sumter, public sentiment in the North began to turn toward the flag as a beloved symbol. "Barbara Frietchie," a famous poem by John Greenleaf Whittier, sings of the heroism of an elderly (fictional) woman who stood up against Confederate troops in order to protect the flag. During this time adoring language for the flag began to appear in oratory. Edward Everett proclaimed in a speech delivered at a flag-raising ceremony in 1861 that the "flag of the country, always honored, always beloved, is now at once worshipped, I may say, with the passionate homage of this whole people."[14] With this rising reverence for the flag, it also became a target for provocative political dissent. On at least one occasion, an assault on the flag in reoccupied Southern territory brought very serious repercussions. A Confederate protester in New Orleans was convicted of treason and executed for having pulled down and destroyed a Union flag. He at once gained fame as a Confederate martyr.

The rise in the flag's popularity after the Civil War did not immediately spur a move to have the banner legally set apart as a sacred object. There were, as yet, no flag use laws, nor even advisory "flag etiquette" codes. Politicians freely used the flag in their campaigns, as they do today — printing their names, slogans, and portraits on it. Above all, the flag was extensively used — one might say exploited — in connection with advertising, for virtually any kind of product: "chewing gum, whisky barrels, patent medicines, trolley tickets, toilet paper . . . paper used to wrap fruit, cheese, cigars, and ham," to list some of Goldstein's examples.[15] This development, which remains a strong tradition in today's commerce, was the initial focus of the flag protection movement.

The first backers of flag protection were primarily veterans and members of patriotic organizations. As Goldstein shows, their rhetoric was replete with language that formed the basis of the sacralization of the flag: in seeking legislation, they pushed for the use of the word "desecration." Backers of such laws freely referred to the flag as "sacred," to be classed with the cross and the Bible as deserving of special handling. Even the U.S. House Judiciary Committee, responding to the proposal of an 1890 flag protection bill, asserted that the flag "should be held as a thing sacred." Goldstein discovered numerous and explicit theological analogues for the status of the flag prior to the Spanish-American War in 1898. In his *Flag Burning and Free Speech,* he relates that William Warner, commander-in-chief of the Grand Army of the Republic, "told Union veterans in 1889 that schoolchildren's reverence for the flag should be like that of Israelites for the Ark of the Covenant, and an 1895 FPM [Flag Protection Movement] publication declared that 'the stars and stripes are heaven's benediction' and 'its folds are sacred.'"[16]

In 1898, the year of the Spanish-American War, George Kingsbury Miller urged that Old Glory "should be kept as inviolate as was the Holy of Holies in King Solomon's temple"; he felt comfortable in speaking of "those three sacred jewels, the Bible, the Cross and Flag." By 1918, after the U.S. experience in World War I, William Norman Guthrie wrote a pamphlet, *The Religion of Old Glory,* which included ritual instructions for "Worship unto Old Glory."[17] Such sentiments hardly represented minority voices in American history: between 1897 and 1932, all forty-eight states passed some form of flag-protection legislation.[18] However, court decisions, some at the Supreme Court level, prevented these laws of the states from achieving their goal of a legally enforceable sacred status. In the earlier part of the twentieth century, court rulings on flag desecration prosecutions generally failed because the offending uses of the flag were commercial and the laws were seen as violations because they denied "private property rights, had no valid state purpose, or both."[19] In the latter part of the twentieth century, the laws failed in court decisions that upheld the First Amendment rights of religious minorities and political protestors.

The desire to focus the power of the law on political dissidents emerged especially from the nation's experiences on the domestic home front during the Vietnam War. Opponents of the war frequently burned or otherwise abused the American flag as a display of disrespect for the nation's moral authority. It was also galling to Americans, during the Iran hostage crisis in 1979-1981, to see protestors in Teheran burning the flag for the benefit of U.S. television cameras. In 1968, the U.S. Congress overcame traditional Southern resistance to federal flag legislation and passed the first desecration law. At that time, Representative Hale Boggs (D-LA) reiterated the traditional sentiment of the flag-protection movement: he saw "outrageous acts which go beyond protest and violate things which the overwhelming majority of Americans hold sacred."[20] There was no exaggeration in Boggs' description of public opinion then or now, because, as Goldstein reminds us, opinion polls consistently show that more than 70 percent of Americans believe that "flag desecration should be banned, even if it takes a constitutional amendment to do so."[21]

The language of the flag amendment has been standardized for the past few sessions of Congress. The proposed amendment, in its entirety, reads as follows:

> The Congress and the States shall have power to prohibit the physical desecration of the flag of the United States of America.[22]

In its deliberate use of language generally reserved for the holy, the amendment reflects what Chief Justice William Rehnquist has called "the almost mystical reverence" with which many Americans regard the flag. This sacred aura of the flag continues to be invoked in the effort to give a majority of citizens the legislation that reflects their feeling about the flag. The June 1995 debate on the amendment in the U.S. House of Representatives contained rhetoric that was familiar from a century of discussion. Congressman C. W. ("Bill") Young (R-FL) cited the statement of one of his constituents that "alone of all flags, it has the sanctity of revelation." Representative Toby Roth (R-WI) claimed: "There are still some things sacred in America today, and one is our flag."[23]

The theological problem involved in this was most clearly articulated by Congressman Gerald Kleczka (D-WI). He insisted that "our flag, while revered and held in honor, is a secular symbol and thus should not be worshiped. . . . That is why I am perplexed by the use of the word 'desecration' in connection with the flag. The word actually means 'to violate the sanctity of,' a definition with obvious religious undertones." Kleczka cited William Safire's dictum that "in this democracy, nothing political can be consecrated, 'made sacred.' . . . Any attempt to make the nation's flag sacred — to endow this secular symbol with the holiness required for 'desecration' — not only undermines our political freedom but belittles our worship of the Creator. . . . Should we respect the flag? Always. Should we worship the flag? Never. We salute the flag, but we reserve worship for God."[24]

Representative Gerald B. H. Solomon (R-NY), who oversaw the passage of the proposed amendment in the House of Representatives, claimed that the goal was simply "to restore the Constitution to the way it was understood . . . until 1989."[25] In that year the U.S. Supreme Court, in *Texas v. Johnson*, declared that a Texas flag "desecration" statute violated the free speech principles of the First Amendment when applied to the prosecution of a political protester. In the circumstances of the *Texas v. Johnson* case — a protest in Dallas, the site of the 1984 Republican National Convention, against the presidential nomination of Ronald Reagan — the act of burning the flag was "sufficiently imbued with elements of communication" to bring full First Amendment protection into play, so that Texas's flag desecration statute could not constitutionally be invoked. Significantly, the Supreme Court held that there is "no indication — either in the text of the Constitution or in our cases interpreting it — that a separate juridical category exists for the American flag alone" (491 U.S. 406, 417). The *Johnson* decision does not set the flag apart from other concepts and symbols insofar as the First Amendment is involved. In the eyes of the supporters of the amendment, the *Johnson* decision was an aberration, unwarranted by sound First Amendment principles — a question that continues to be hotly contested in legal circles.

Notwithstanding their insistence that the flag amendment is intended simply to restore First Amendment law to its pre-*Johnson* understandings, the sponsors rejected alternative wording offered by Congressman John Bryant (D-TX), which would have avoided religious language. The alternative wording would have permitted Congress and the states to pass laws "to prohibit the burning, trampling, soiling, or rending of the flag."[26] Instead, they deliberately retained the word "desecrate" — with all of its religious nuancing. If the amendment eventually passes in this form, it will, for the first time in the nation's history, deliberately incorporate the language of the sacred into the Constitution.

The Danger of Sanctifying National Symbols

One of the best ways to focus on the underlying theological issues here is to look back at an important case involving Jehovah's Witnesses. Although it involved the compulsory confession of loyalty rather than desecration as such, the case reminds us that ultimate allegiances are involved. In the case of *West Virginia Board of Education v. Barnette* (1943), the Supreme Court faced what is surely the shadow side of the American flag-protection movement. Justice Robert Jackson's eloquent opinion in *Barnette* has provided much of the inspiration (indeed, the language) for subsequent opinions on the flag and the Constitution, including the *Johnson* case. The *Barnette* case involved a challenge to a West Virginia requirement that the recitation of the Pledge of Allegiance become a regular part of the public school day. Regulations issued by the state school board made the salute compulsory for all children; refusal to salute would be "regarded as an act of insubordination," to be "dealt with accordingly." The punishment provided for this insubordination was expulsion, and the expelled child would be considered "unlawfully absent," so that his or her parents or guardians would be liable to prosecution. Penalties for conviction included fines and up to thirty days in jail. The regulations provided no exceptions for persons objecting to the flag salute on religious grounds. A group of Jehovah's Witnesses, believing that the flag salute contravenes God's commandment against graven images in Exodus 20:4-5, brought suit to enjoin enforcement. At that time, children belonging to the sect were already being expelled from school, parents were being prosecuted, and officials were even threatening to send the "offending" children to reformatories for criminally inclined juveniles.

The court stated the issue starkly: "We are dealing with a compulsion of students to declare a belief" (319 U.S. 631); and it held the state requirements to be unconstitutional, primarily on free-speech grounds. Justice Jackson began with a discussion of the function of symbol in the political realm. "Symbolism," he said, "is a primitive but effective way of communicating ideas. The use of an emblem or flag to symbolize some system, idea, institution, or personality, is a short cut from mind to mind" (319 U.S. 632). He examined the problem of coerced acceptance of symbols, pointing to the resistance shown by early Christians against participation in the Roman imperial cult. The following is some of the key language from his opinion:

> Ultimate futility of such attempts to compel coherence is the lesson of every such effort from the Roman drive to stamp out Christianity as a disturber of its pagan unity, the Inquisition, as a means to religious and dy-

nastic unity, the Siberian exiles as a means to Russian unity, down to the fast failing efforts of our present totalitarian regimes. . . . This case is made difficult not because the principles of its decision are obscure but because the flag involved is our own. Nevertheless, we apply the limitations of the Constitution with no fear that freedom to be intellectually and spiritually diverse or even contrary will disintegrate the social organization. . . . [F]reedom to differ is not limited to things that do not matter much. That would be a mere shadow of freedom. The test of its substance is the right to differ as to things that touch the heart of the existing order. If there is any fixed star in our constitutional constellation, it is that no official, high or petty, can prescribe who shall be orthodox in politics, nationalism, religion, or other matters of opinion or force citizens to confess by word or act their faith therein (319 U.S. 641-642).

This is a strong statement against any sort of government-mandated civil creed, and it is quite relevant to a discussion of the wisdom of the flag amendment. It is a high watermark in the American tradition of prophetic realism.

There is, of course, a real distinction between the *Barnette* situation and the matter of abuse to the flag. *Barnette* dealt with an affirmative coercion to salute the flag, whereas later cases dealt with prohibitions. Yet, the theological issue of the sacred is common to them both. As critics of national policy, we fear the insertion of the language of the holy in the Constitution because we suspect that it will augment the tendency to glorify the country. To better understand this, we can review some strands of holiness embedded in the Judaeo-Christian tradition as they relate to the flag issue.

Holiness as a Theological Issue

The biblical concepts of holiness and the sacred center on God. Hymns of praise such as Psalm 99 extol God's holiness; Isaiah 6:3 proclaims, "Holy, holy, holy is the Lord of hosts." Aspects of the created world may derive holiness in light of their special association with God. An example of this kind of derivative holiness is found in Exodus 3:5: there the ground on which Moses stood, before the burning bush signifying God's presence, is defined as "holy ground." God's people are frequently called "holy" — in the sense of having been called and set apart by God for God's purposes. In Deuteronomy 14:2, the people of Israel are solemnly told, "You are a people holy to the Lord your God; it is you the Lord has chosen out of all peoples on earth to be his people, his treasured possession." The Hebrew word for holy, *qadosh*, carries this nuance. In Leviticus 11:44, God says to Israel: "I am the Lord who brought you up from the land of Egypt, to be your God; you shall be holy, for I am holy." The concept of holiness in the Bible also points to the need for holy living among God's people.

In the New Testament, Jesus Christ is recognized as "the Holy One of God" (Mark 1:24). 1 Peter 1:16, echoing the language of Leviticus to the people of Israel, calls the church to holiness. God's people in the New Testament are frequently called the *hagioi*, which is simply the Greek word for "holy ones," and is generally translated as the "saints." By contrast, the concept of holiness is never applied to the Roman state. The apostle Paul instructs Christians to "be subject to the governing authorities" (Rom. 13:1) — but never to worship them. Indeed, the Romans passage continues as follows: "Pay to all their dues . . . respect to whom respect is due, honor to whom honor is due" (Rom. 13:7). This formulation implies a distinction between the ultimate loyalty that is due only to God and the honors due to the government. This is consistent with the frequent biblical denunciations of political figures for committing idolatry. God criticizes all of the kings of the Northern Kingdom of Israel, and most of the kings of the Southern Kingdom of Judah, on this basis, according to 1 and 2 Kings. Such critiques are also visible in the prophetic literature. In this light, to move a national symbol into the realm of the holy risks being not only a violation of the First and Second Commandments but also of the prophetic spirit found in the Bible. To erode the distinction between transcendent deity and secular symbols is to undercut the possibility of prophetic discernment. Dictionary definitions of "the sacred" should remind us about religious issues in elevating the status of a secular symbol: what they share is the notion of consecration to a deity or the granting of religious authority of the ultimate.[27] Clearly, these are not secular notions.

By using the phrase "setting apart" in connection with a lifting of the flag out of the arena of First Amendment protection, we have hinted that, even without the use of the language of the sacred, a flag amendment may carry subtle theological problems. The clear theological problem, though, appears when the term "desecration" is actually inserted into the text of the Constitution with reference to a secular symbol. This amounts to an express determination by the secular state that a particular symbol belongs to the transcendent sphere.[28]

We find the line of reasoning set forth by Sheldon Nahmod particularly significant.[29] He explores sympathetically the real need societies have for patriotic symbols, reflects on the operation of such symbols, and offers a sophisticated analysis of the issues related to sacralizing them. Nahmod is intrigued by the dissenting opinions in *Johnson* (that of Chief Justice Rehnquist, as well as the separate dissent filed by Justice John Paul Stevens), noting that their concern for the symbolic status of the flag takes priority over careful First Amendment analysis. Nevertheless, Nahmod takes their dissent seriously. He analyzes Rehnquist's opinion in the light of Eliade's notion of hierophany (the sacred making itself seen), which is the function of the flag in the newer understanding of American civil religion. Nahmod shows that the veneration of the flag advocated by the dissenting justices "re-creates American history in the same way that the veneration of an Eastern Orthodox icon re-creates the religious experience that it represents."[30] Nahmod further establishes that "under the reasoning of the Johnson dissent government can, without violating freedom of speech, appropriate a particular patriotic symbol and convert it into a sacred one for political purposes."[31] The majority on the Supreme Court declined to take that step. In the end, Nahmod defends the majority's conclusion despite his understanding of the function of political symbols in promoting social coherence: "We have come too far as a nation . . . and should, by this time, be too mature as a political community to punish political heretics by establishing a blasphemy exception to the first amendment."[32] A flag amendment, it seems, would do just that.

Muslim Campaigns against Desecration

In the underlying sentiment of compelling respect for what state power certifies as the holy, the campaign against blasphemy in the United States has striking similarities to campaigns of the Islamic world. The most notable case involved the *fatwa* issued against Salman Rushdie by the Ayatollah Khomeini of Iran. The Rushdie affair involved the most complex interaction of literature, politics, and religion in the twentieth century. We can here sketch but a few features of a case about which entire volumes have been written.

Ahmed Salman Rushdie was born into a Muslim business family in India. After an education in British schools, he stayed on and began to write novels that achieved critical acclaim in the English-speaking world. His novel *The Satanic Verses* (1988) had a contemporary setting but included characters from previous periods of Islamic history. The plot and language of the story were sexually focused and narrated with the inclusion of obscenities familiar in recent fiction. Among the story's elements were rather distinct comic references to Muhammad ("Mahmoud"), the wives of Muhammad, and the composition of the Koran. In one often-cited scene in the novel, a drunken Mahmoud has fallen in the street and is retrieved to the comfortable bed of "the Grandee's wife," who demands that he make love to her.[33] The publisher had been forewarned that the content of the novel would be explosive (it was, in fact, offensive to Christians, Hindus, and Jews — as well as Muslims) but acted on Western principles of free speech in publishing it. Former U.S. President Jimmy Carter, for example, called it "a direct insult to those millions of Muslims whose sacred beliefs have been violated." The English philosopher Michael Dummett, in a letter to Rushdie, said, "We rightly do not extend the principle of free speech to cover incitement to racial hatred or contempt."[34]

An immediate storm of protest against the novel came in the non-English-speaking world. After its publication on September 26, 1988, protests began by October 3, and Rushdie's homeland government of India banned the book on October 6, quickly followed by bans in Bangladesh, Sri Lanka, Sudan, Oman, and South Africa. Ongoing actions by pressure groups sought to have the publisher, Penguin, withdraw the book from circulation.[35] The most inflammatory moments came when people began to die in protests against the book. On February 12, 1989, ten Muslim protestors against the book were killed by police in Islamabad, Pakistan; the following day, five were killed in Kashmir. Then, on February 14, 1989, the Ayatollah Khomeini declared in a radio broadcast that Rushdie had renounced his faith and had earned the death penalty for his blasphemy:

> I inform the proud Muslim people of the world that the author of *The Satanic Verses* book which is against Islam, the Prophet, and the Koran, and those involved in its publication who were aware of its content, are sentenced to death.

He added that anyone who was to die in the cause of killing Rushdie "will be regarded as a martyr and go directly to heaven."[36]

At this point, Rushdie and his wife went into a period of hiding, occasionally surfacing unexpectedly for literary events in defense of artistic freedom. But almost immediately he apologized for his offense to Islam (on February 19, 1989), and somewhat later he took steps to limit further distribution of his book; he also announced his own conversion back to Islam. However, these gestures did not placate the authorities in Iran. The Ayatollah Khomeini stated that Rushdie had not repented sincerely or sufficiently and that "it is incumbent on every Muslim to employ everything he has got, his life and his wealth, to send him to hell."[37] While Rushdie himself survived the *fatwa*, others associated with the enterprise were not so lucky. Numerous booksellers in the United States and other countries were firebombed. The translator of the book, Ettore Capriola, was stabbed to death in Milan by a man demanding Rushdie's address. On July 11, 1991, Professor Hitoshi Igarishi was stabbed to death at Tsukuba University; the Pakistan Association of Japan announced that "the murder was completely, 100 percent connected with the book. . . . Today we have been congratulating each other. Everyone was really happy."[38] Although Khomeini died shortly after issuing the *fatwa,* officials who succeeded him in the Iranian government continued to announce the duty of all Muslims in the world to execute Rushdie, and they added substantial monetary bounties. On one occasion, Iranian newspapers characterized the order to execute Rushdie as "a divine command to stone the devil to death."[39]

For Americans, an especially cautionary aspect of the Rushdie affair — in the context of sacralizing the flag — is the way the spirit of offense and enforcement broke away from anything resembling law. Rushdie was not a citizen of Iran, for example, which raises the question of jurisdiction for Khomeini's deadly *fatwa.* And Iran sought no cooperation from the forces of international law, no doubt understanding that the more liberal West, even if it regarded *Satanic Verses* as deeply offensive, would do nothing at all about its distribution. Even if Iran would have consulted an international legal body, there is no law under which a satirist of religion can be prosecuted. Iran's solution thus became murder — allegedly sanctioned by God — driven by a fury directed at something mortally offensive to its official religion.

Ominous Parallels in the Flag Desecration Campaign

The disturbing parallel to the U.S. advocates of flag sacralization is in part the vagueness of the proposed flag desecration amendment. Without defining "desecration," the text simply says: "The Congress and the States shall have power to prohibit the physical desecration of the flag of the United States of America." The advocates of this amendment, who have hitherto been thwarted by the Supreme Court's interpretation of the First Amendment protections of free speech, may wish to encourage a proliferation of state-based definitions — in hopes that litigation will eventually "find" a definition that would survive review by the Supreme Court. Where the law is not clear, regional jurisdictions have the freedom to define "desecration" as they see fit rather than defining a standard that is clear to a potential offender of the law. Thus a dissenting citizen, sensing the arbitrariness of prosecution, might experience an impulse to "desecrate" for that very reason. A law that encourages the very behavior it seeks to prevent can hardly be seen as an effective tool for cultivating citizenship. General Colin Powell spoke with clear administrative instincts in 1999 when he addressed Sen. Patrick Leahy about the difficulties of implementing such an amendment:

The First Amendment exists to insure that freedom of speech and expression applies not just to that with which we agree or disagree, but also that which we find outrageous. I would not amend that great shield of democracy to hammer a few miscreants. The flag will still be flying proudly long after they have slunk away. Finally, I shudder to think of the legal morass we will create trying to implement the body of law that will emerge from such an amendment.[40]

A law against desecration might function as the most effective of all recruiting tools for "miscreants" who are determined to defy authority in a way that gives the greatest possible offense.

The vagueness of "desecration" also reminds us about the carelessly indeterminate efforts to make America into a more godly republic. Martin E. Marty, the distinguished historian of American religion, wryly comments on the maddening woolliness of thought during the two decades in which the United States strengthened its symbolic identities with the sacred. In his *Under God, Indivisible, 1941-1960,* Marty observes that the National Council of Churches, convened in 1950, displayed a banner with the slogan that would eventually make its way to the Pledge of Allegiance: "This Nation Under God." He comments: "The council leaders could not, however, agree among themselves about what 'nation' and being 'under' meant or, some would say, even about the character and the charter of 'God.'"[41]

Marty's history of this period also enumerates some moral failures of the churches that wanted to cement the identity between nation and God: their opposition to the admission of Jewish refugees, their comfort with racial segregation and the imprisonment of Japanese Americans, their acquiescence in the fire-bombing of civilian populations in Germany and Japan, and their quiet acceptance of the atomic bombings. Standing on the threshold of new sacralizations of this nation, we have little doubt that future historians will look back with a similar sense of irony on the blindness of our post–September 11 patriotic piety.

Another reason to fear the sacralization of the flag lies in its impact on those groups who, like Jehovah's Witnesses, resist patriotic gestures because of their religious beliefs. The Witnesses are a millennial apocalyptic group who perpetually live with a sense that they are in the last moments of history. Like so many groups of that type, they believe that evil people will be destroyed in an Armageddon that will occur in their lifetime and that the chosen will be spared. In their twentieth-century history, they have been known for resisting blood transfusions, refusing military service and the salute of the flag, and aggressive, door-to-door evangelism and street sales of their apocalyptic publication *The Watch Tower.* Their history in America is strewn with court cases involving their perceived failures of citizenship and patriotism. To Americans lacking the millennial perspective, Jehovah's Witnesses seem to be taking a "free ride" — profiting from the sacrifices for freedom that others make on their behalf.

However, the Witnesses have moments when they seem to be the spiritual canaries in a mine tunnel of history that threatens to explode. The most notable instance of this came during Germany's Nazi period. They refused to give the "Heil Hitler" salute, properly seeing it as idolatrous; and they refused to serve in the army, another unforgivable failing under the Nazi regime. Historians do not entirely agree on how many Witnesses (called "Bible Students") were sent to prison, but the lowest number, cited in Barbara Grizzuti Harrison's *Visions of Glory: A History and a Memory of Jehovah's Witnesses,* is 6,000 of the 25,000 Witnesses living in Germany at that time. Several hundred children were taken from their parents, and several hundred — or several thousand, depending on the source — were killed or starved to death in concentration camps.[42] The Nazi authorities were very clear about what they regarded as criminal. The List of Proscribed Sects described them as follows:

> The danger to the state is not to be underestimated, since the members of this sect on the grounds of their unbelievably strong fanaticism are completely hostile to the law and order of the State. Not only do they refuse to use the German greeting ["Heil Hitler"], to participate in National Socialist or State functions, to do military service, but they put out propaganda against joining the army, and attempt, despite prohibition, to distribute their publications.[43]

Adolf Hitler had made the state policy on religion clear: "We will protect the German priest who is the servant of God, we will wipe out the priest who is the political enemy of the German Reich."[44] This logic was used to punish thousands of other priests and pastors who were resistant, skeptical, or otherwise lacking in zeal for the causes of the state. The equation is almost explicit: whatever we do — that is the work of God. There is no independent, uncoerced standard permissible for judging the behavior of the Reich itself, not even in the realm where we should expect it. It is a moment in history that should inspire hesitation in anyone who aspires to sacralize the symbols of the state and its authority.

Biblical Links between Desecration and Zealous Violence

That symbolic desecration is a suitable target for violent crusades whose outcome will have a redemptive force was not invented by the recent Taliban movement or Osama bin Laden. Its peculiar logic has a biblical foundation that has influenced Christianity, Judaism, and Islam. The zealous nationalists throughout Israel's history followed the antidesecration route and produced one catastrophe after the next, all of which could have been avoided. The prophets consistently criticized the people's concentration on symbolic conformity as a means of assuring divine assistance. Yet in Israel's official history, their critique was suppressed, and the matter of symbolic desecration remained dominant. According to Walter Dietrich, the Deuteronomic history of Israel identified the source of national disaster in the inadequate loyalty of its rulers to Israel's laws, "particularly the commandments concerning cultic unity and purity."[45] The classical sin from this Deuteronomic viewpoint was committed by King Jeroboam (786-46 BCE), who established two cultic centers in the Northern Kingdom of Israel so that its citizens would not have to go to the Southern Kingdom's capital of Jerusalem for religious ceremonies:

> So the king took counsel and made two calves of gold. And he said to the people, "You have gone up to Jerusalem long enough. Behold your gods, O Israel, who brought you up out of the land of Egypt." And he set one in Bethel, and the other he put in Dan.... He also made houses on high places and appointed priests from among all the people, who were not of the Levites. . . . He went up to the altar which he had made in Bethel on the fifteenth day of the eighth month, in the month which he had devised of his own heart; and he ordained a feast for the people of Israel, and went up to the altar to burn incense. (1 Kings 12:28-29, 31, 33)

These cultic transgressions, which are presented as cynical expressions of arbitrary royal power, provoked divine wrath that ultimately destroyed the dynasty. The Deuteronomic historian reports that such actions "became sin to the house of Jeroboam, so as to cut it off and to destroy it from the face of the earth" (1 Kings 13:34). In actuality, the historical and archaeological details lead most commentators to depict "the reign of Jeroboam as a period of peace and prosperity and national expansion during a period of Assyria's relative weakness."[46] Nevertheless, the Bible attributes each disaster in the period thereafter to the alleged "sins of Jeroboam." For example, King Jehoahaz (815-802 BCE) "did what was evil in the sight of the Lord, and followed the sins of Jeroboam the son of Nebat, which he made Israel to sin; he did not depart from them. And the anger of the Lord was kindled against Israel, and he gave them continually into the hand of Hazael king of Syria and into the hand of Benhadad the son of Hazael" (2 Kings 13:2-3). As a result of the conflicts with these kingdoms to the north of Israel, which were engaged in futile attempts to build an alliance against the superpower of Assyria, Israel lost considerable territory and military power.[47] But the Deuteronomic historian did not take these factors into account; political reverses and miscalculations were simply the result of desecration.

The historian used the desecration theory to interpret Israel's surrender to Babylon in 597 BCE. King Jehoiachin "did what was evil in the sight of the Lord, according to all that his father had done" (2 Kings 24:9), so he was "deposed by Nebuchadnezzar and deported to Babylon."[48] The sacking of Jerusalem in 586 BCE occurred because King Zedekiah "did what was evil in the sight of the Lord, according to all that Jehoiakim had done. For because of the anger of the Lord it came to the point in Jerusalem and Judah that he cast them out from his presence" (2 Kings 24:19-20). Instead of recognizing this military disaster as a result of miscalculation in revolting against a vastly superior Babylon while counting on help from an unreliable Egypt,[49] and apparently counting on divine assistance, Israel used the theory of desecration to provide a neat but misleading explanation. It implied to future generations that the avoidance of desecration would guarantee political and military success, which is an erroneous and unrealistic religious precept that makes future disasters ever more likely.

The link between desecration and zealous war to establish an era of peace is particularly clear in the books of Daniel and 1 Maccabees, where the famous "abomination of desolation" occurred when King Antiochus Epiphanes turned the rebuilt temple in Jerusalem into a pagan house of worship (167 BCE). The Hebrew expression implies "something filthy or disgusting" and should probably be translated as "appalling sacrilege."[50] In vengeance against the Hellenistic king who "set up the abomination that makes desolate" (Dan. 11:31), divine wrath would see to it that "the decreed end is poured out on the desolator" (Dan. 9:27). The dominion of the Seleucid kings

shall be taken away,
    to be consumed and destroyed to the end.
And the kingdom and the dominion
    and the greatness of the kingdoms under the whole heaven
    shall be given to the people of the saints of the Most High;
their kingdom shall be an everlasting kingdom,
    and all dominions shall serve and obey them. (Dan. 7:26-27)

While the author of Daniel believed that divine agencies would bring this millennial era of peace in which those who avoided desecration would rule the world, the Book of 1 Maccabees presents militant zeal as the proper cure of the "abomination of desolation" (1 Macc. 1:54). Here we find the model of Phinehas, who killed an Israelite man and his non-Israelite wife for their desecration that he thought would provoke divine wrath. When a Jew followed the royal command to sacrifice to a pagan deity in Modein, Matthias Maccabee

> . . . was inflamed with zeal, and his heart quivered with wrath, and his indignation burst forth in judgment so that he ran and killed him on the altar; and at the same time he killed the king's officer who had come to enforce the sacrificing, pulling down the altar, and showed forth his zeal for the Law, just as Phinehas had done in the case of Zimri the son of Salu. (1 Macc. 2:24-26; see also vss. 45-67)

A violent revolution that ended up freeing Israel from the Hellenistic empire followed this event, thus seeming to confirm the promise of Deuteronomy and the vision of Daniel. Thus campaigns against desecration taking the form of holy war seemed to be blessed by the deity. However, this logic turned out to be as flawed as the beliefs that had led to Israel's earlier destruction. During the first century CE, "it was natural" for Jews "to see parallels between their experience of Roman rule and the Maccabean experience of Seleucid rule and for them to regard the courageous stand of the Maccabees as an example and inspiration at times of tension or confrontation with Rome. . . ."[51] That the Zealot Movement, which opened a holy war against Rome in 66-70 CE, sought to eliminate various forms of Gentile sacrilege is clear from its attacks against magicians, sexual libertines, and visual depictions of pagan deities, its forcible circumcision of non-Jewish populations living in Israel, and its violence against those perceived to desecrate the temple.[52] The result of this campaign, contradicting the theological propaganda, was the utter destruction of Jerusalem and the virtual depopulation of Palestine. It seems likely that the warnings in the New Testament to flee from the "abomination of desolation" (Matt. 24:15; Mark 13:14; Luke 21:20) reflect the early church's nonparticipation in this zealous conflict that aimed to rid Israel of desecration once and for all.[53] It is thus a matter of grave concern when campaigns against desecration begin to assume a central role in modern thought.

Christendom has reluctantly learned its lesson in this regard, inspired by dissenters and realists such as Roger Williams throughout the history of the past four hundred years; but the United States now seems intent to forget this humane legacy. The long-term consequences of a flag amendment will add another chapter to *The Bloudy Tenent of Persecution*, even though none of its advocates desire that end. Islam must also learn that honoring the sacred must be left to communities of faith that work through persuasion rather than coercion. The failure of humanity in our foreign policy will now have an additional excuse: lack of zeal for the cult of the state. In particular, any government involvement in campaigns to protect the holy will inevitably prove disastrous — just as it did for ancient Israel — over and over again. To paraphrase the critique found in Amos 5:21, 24, the authentic deity of a global civil religion declares:

> I hate, I despise your flags,
> and take no delight in your patriotic ceremonies. . . .
> But let justice roll down like waters.

16 Prophetic Realism in Response to Jihad

To-day the United States is practically sovereign on this continent and its fiat is law upon the subjects to which it confines its interposition. Why? It is not simply because of pure friendship or good will felt for it. It is not simply by reason of its high character as a civilized state, nor because wisdom and justice and equity are the invariable characteristics of the dealings of the United States. It is because, in addition to all other grounds, its infinite resources, combined with its isolated position, render it master of the situation and practically invulnerable as against any or all other powers.

Richard Olney, U.S. Secretary of State (1895), privately describing
America's ability to secure its preferred outcome in a
Latin American border dispute[1]

The attack on September 11, 2001, struck at the heart of the American sense of safety and predictability, but the shocks were felt around the world. No one can feel secure in the face of suicidal jihad. The dream that Captain America could protect the world, or that some ultimate defensive system will guarantee security, remains a hollow illusion. Richard Olney's quiet confidence about America's "practically invulnerable" mastery of its "situation" can no longer be imagined. History has brought a permanent season for realists, who, in contrast to the mythic expectations promoted in superheroic fantasy, expect the unexpected. Realists never believe that the application of past solutions will bring security. They avoid illusions that the world can be made safe

313

for utopian ideals or that winning one more war will guarantee generations of peace.

Unlike myth-bound zealots, realists are never certain ahead of time that the cause of disorder is demonic, that adversaries are irredeemable or always corrupt enough to have their price, that violence in the hands of a chosen people is always redemptive, or that the defeat of what may seem to be national interests will necessarily be unjust or even disadvantageous in the long run. Thus realists' responses to crises cannot be charted on mythic maps. Prophetic realists experience the creative freedom that derives from a fresh assessment of the evidence and are stimulated by a vision of transcendent justice. Their aim is more modest than that of the zealots: it is not to eliminate the crisis but to advance gradually through it toward the goal, always realizing that it may never be fully reached.

Whereas zealous nationalism and some forms of pessimistic realism are dominated by the past, prophetic realism is marked by the pull of the future. In Lincoln's political ethic, for example, the vision was the gradual approximation of the Declaration of Independence's principle that "all men are created equal." In his debates with Stephen Douglas in 1858, Lincoln insisted that the Founding Fathers were fully aware that equality was not yet a reality and could not quickly be achieved: "They meant to set up a standard maxim for free society, which should be familiar to all, and revered by all; constantly looked to, constantly labored for, and even though never perfectly attained, constantly approximated, and thereby constantly spreading and deepening its influence and augmenting the happiness and value of life to all men of all colors everywhere."[2] It was this recognition that the vision would never be fully achieved that kept Lincoln from becoming a fanatic; yet it was his retention of the vision that kept him from being merely a political opportunist. There are significant voices in our time that call us in the same direction. For example, James Chace has advocated the kind of realism that "sees the world whole," while pointing to the dangers of "an essentially amoral foreign policy." "What we need," he concludes, "is not jingoism but the highest moral courage in order to live with uncertainty."[3]

We must begin, therefore, by sketching out a vision toward which the nation might strive, weaving it out of the warp of traditional American ideals and the woof of Isaiah's dream of government's role in fostering the age of coexistence. It is not an alien vision, though it is vastly different from the one America has recently been following. It lies buried in one-half of our nation's divided heart, obscured by its long fusion with an incompatible, zealous counterpart. And though it can be seen only dimly, we submit it here in the hope that others may go on to grasp it more fully.

Isaiah's Vision for Conflict Resolution

Isaiah composed his oracles concerning the ideal government at the time of King Hezekiah's accession in 715 BCE.[4] Although Isaiah 9:2-7 and 11:1-9 were later interpreted as prophecies of Christ, it is clear that their original purpose was to provide healthy goals for the new regime at a time when government had gone drastically off its track. The fact that the young king did not accept these goals, choosing instead a revival of crusading militarism that led to disaster, serves only to accentuate their power and wisdom. Their content, spanning the centuries, is amazingly close to the healthy traditions of constitutional nationalism in the United States and in other cultures as well:

> The people who walked in darkness have seen a great light;
> those who dwelt in a land of deep darkness, on them has light shined.
> Thou hast multiplied the nation, thou hast increased its joy;
> They rejoice before thee as with joy at the harvest,
>   as men rejoice when they divide the spoil.
> For the yoke of his burden,
>   and the staff for his shoulder,
>   the rod of his oppressor,
>   thou hast broken as on the day of Midian. (Isa. 9:2-4)

This passage links joyous anticipation to a government that takes up the task of liberation. To set people free from the "oppressor" implies the release not only from foreign exploitation but also from social subordination. It is the same vital purpose stated in the Declaration of Independence: the achievement of equality, life, liberty, and the pursuit of happiness. The motif has been characteristic of American nationalism and was clearly stated in the "four freedoms" declaration prior to World War II. But the striking thing is that this task is not to be accomplished by foreign crusades, as in the popular Israelite and American traditions. The prophet explicitly repudiates the militarization of government in the very next lines: "For every boot of the tramping warrior in battle tumult and every garment rolled in blood will be burned as fuel for the fire" (Isa. 9:5). It is not just the enemy boots and tunics that are to be burned, but "every" relic of military glory. This strikes at the heart of the fallacy in our national ideology: that human liberation is achieved through military power in selfless crusades.

The alternative method is stated in the companion oracle depicting the ideal ruler:

> He shall not judge by what his eyes see, or decide by what his ears hear, but with righteousness he shall judge the poor, and decide with equity for the meek of the earth; and he shall smite the earth [or the "bully"][5] with the rod of his mouth, and with the breath of his lips he shall slay the wicked. Righteousness shall be the girdle of his waist, and faithfulness the girdle of his loins. (Isa. 11:3-5)

The "poor" and the "meek" are to be liberated by equity in the courts and by equal access to material advantages. The government has the unique task of providing justice for those who cannot fend entirely for themselves, and this means contending against exploitation not on the battlefield but in the enforcement of law. "Righteousness" in judgment and "equity" before the law are the means by which this must take place. They are the very antithesis of the qualities that zealous nationalism engenders: stereotyping of the poor, illusions about the virtues of the rich, and scorn for due process of law. Impartiality in the sense of not judging by external appearances must be linked with compassion for the oppressed if true liberation is to occur. This method of approximating the goal of equality is worlds apart from government for the sake of wealthy interest groups, with its benign neglect of those who experience partial justice in every sphere because of their color, class background, or level of educational development. This vision needs to be established as a goal of a new world order that reaches beyond individual nations to the peoples who have fallen behind in global competition. Ask the exploited in every land what they desire most "as with joy in the harvest," and the answer will be, "We want the equal chance we have never had."

A Vision of Global Government

The implications of prophetic realism are not just national in scope. The passion for justice includes the poor of other nations as well: the "meek of the *earth*," not just of Israel or of America, not just of the Northern Hemisphere, where prosperity reigns. The ruthless exploitation of lesser nations by the industrial powers of our time is a clear violation of Isaiah's ideal. It creates smoldering resentment and disorder, which cost far more in the long run than would equity itself. Such resentment is a prime ingredient in Muslim jihadism. The essence of impartiality in Isaiah's sense as well as in our own tradition — that "all men are created equal" — is its indivisibility. We are inhabitants of the one "spaceship earth," to use Barbara Ward's expression, and our compassion must transcend national boundaries if we are to survive. To translate this into effective measures, however, requires impartial law with force behind it.

Isaiah was much more realistic on this point than are many modern idealists in his insistence that the judgment of the ruler's "mouth" and "breath" must have the power to "smite" and even to "slay" oppressors. He recognized that law without enforcement loses its majesty and its capacity to coerce by consent. Modern experience with ineffective international resolutions against aggression confirms his wisdom. And it should not be forgotten that the power of government to coerce compliance with law is an essential component of the American constitutional system. What must be clarified is the distinction between the minimal violence controlled by law that acts in behalf of impartial justice and the crusading violence that shatters restraints on behalf of some biased vision. When Isaiah's ideal ruler has to "smite," it is by his words in the courtroom and not by his hand on some foreign battlefield. Neither crusading zeal nor suicidal jihad is consistent with this biblical vision.

The results of such firm justice are depicted in the closing lines of Isaiah's magnificent vision:

> The wolf shall dwell with the lamb,
>   and the leopard shall lie down with the kid,
>   and the calf and the lion and the fatling together,
>   and a little child shall lead them.
> The cow and the bear shall feed,
>   and their young shall lie down together;
>   and the lion shall eat straw like the ox.
> The sucking child shall play over the hole of the asp,
>   and the weaned child shall put his hand on the adder's den.
>
> (Isa. 11:6-8)

In this oracle we see a vision of mutually transforming coexistence between cultures and classes that can be produced by equality under law. Those who lived by exploitation take up the higher pleasures of mutual enjoyment. For justice defuses conflict and allows each one to maintain his or her integrity without aggression. Each is then free to take up the admirable traits of the former enemy. The prophet dares even to envision the lion, the aggressive symbol of his own Judah, adopting the peaceful attributes of the ox. And those who benefit most are the "sucking child" and the "weaned child," who find their playgrounds safe again. The references to snakes imply the reversal of that destructive pride that led from the first mythic enmity between man and the serpent in Genesis 3:14-15 down to the nationalistic pretensions of Isaiah's time and ours.

Late in his ministry, after the terrible Assyrian invasion of 701 BCE had buried his country's preference for other ideals, Isaiah developed the international implications of his vision.[6] This oracle, whose final lines are chiseled in the United Nations Building in New York, gives the origin of a modern hope for world peace:

> All the nations shall flow to it,
>   and many peoples shall come, and say:
> "Come, let us go up to the mountain of Yahweh,
> to the house of the God of Jacob;
> that he may teach us his ways
> and that we may walk in his paths."
> For out of Zion shall go forth the law,
> and the word of Yahweh from Jerusalem.
> He shall judge between the nations,
> and shall decide for many peoples;
> and they shall beat their swords into plowshares,
> and their spears into pruning hooks;
> nation shall not lift up sword against nation,
> neither shall they learn war any more. (Isa. 2:3-4)

The attraction of Zion's law and the prophetic "word of Yahweh," so powerful that they envision the nations as voluntarily bringing their disputes before it, lay in their impartiality. When rightly administered, the law was no respecter of persons. And the Yahwist prophets dared to pronounce judgment even against the behavior of their own nation.[7] These institutions correspond to the judicial and legislative roles in a modern constitutional system. Compliance depends in large measure on public respect, though requisite amounts of coercive power are available. There is a need for such prestigious institutions on the international scale, attracting the adherence of those they serve by the quality of justice they administer. Like the U.S. Constitution, such institutions require no claim of divine origin to evoke such loyalty. It is sufficient that they are guided by impartiality and blessed in that task by suitable ceremonies of a global civil religion. The organic growth of devotion is required to make such institutions stable, but with the communications system now available, such a process may for the first time be feasible within the finite span of our threatened circumstances.

Waning American Support for International Law

The most distressing aspect of the American response to Islamic jihad after September 11 is that the ideals and strategies of prophetic realism have largely disappeared from public awareness.[8] In his book *On the Law of Nations*,[9] Senator Daniel Patrick Moynihan details the role that international law played in early American thought. He shows that the so-called law of nations was "the first principle of the American legal system": it was referred to as "the Laws of Nature and of Nature's God" in the Declaration of Independence and was explicitly mentioned in the American Constitution: "The Congress shall have power . . . to define and punish . . . Offenses against the Law of Nations . . ." (Article I, Section 8). We should also recall that the writers of the Declaration felt that "a decent respect to the opinions of mankind requires that they should declare the causes which impel them to the separation" — an expression of their desire to immediately occupy an honorable place among other nations of the world. The Supreme Court has declared that "international law is part of our law," thus supporting Moynihan's contention that it "is not higher law or better law; it is *existing* law."[10]

American leaders in the early part of the twentieth century worked hard to enshrine these principles in the covenant of the League of Nations and the charter of the United Nations. Although Moynihan does not mention it, generations of theologians and religious leaders also supported institutional embodiments of the law of nations, including many writers in publications such as the *Christian Century* since its establishment in 1900. They were convinced that the impartial administration of international law could resolve conflicts and ultimately rid the world of the scourge of war.

Moynihan details the erosion in the American commitment to the law of nations as a consequence of the stalemated Cold War. However, even after the close of the Cold War, cynicism about the International Court of Justice and the United Nations has remained so pervasive that millions of Americans are no longer aware of the crucial role these ideas have played in their own heritage: "In the annals of forgetfulness there is nothing quite to compare with the fading from the American mind of the idea of the law of nations."[11] The invasions of Grenada ("Operation Urgent Fury" in 1983) and Panama ("Operation Just Cause" in 1989), as well as the mining of harbors in Nicaragua, flatly violated American commitments under international law. Despite the United States' formal commitment to the International Court in 1946, the Reagan administration withdrew from compulsory jurisdiction in 1985, while the harbor mining incident was under review. In the following year, the court declared that the United States violated international law in a variety of ways in connection with Nicaragua, the "first time in the history of the Court that the United States was found in violation of international law in a matter involving the use of force against another nation."[12]

Moynihan expresses proper indignation at this abandonment of long-standing commitments: "In two centuries of national existence no more pusillanimous act was ever contemplated, much less carried forward, by American officials responsible for our relations with international tribunals."[13] The zealous components in our American ideals had triumphed over our commitment to coexistence under law. We see other evidence of this triumph of zeal over realism in the rejection of the jurisdiction of the International Criminal Court in the autumn of 2001 and the abrogation of international agreements such as the ABM and other weapons-related treaties that reduce military competition.

One could add to the "annals of forgetfulness" the crucial role that religion once played in providing foundations for the law of nations. Their modern form arose from the ashes of the Thirty Years War as a repudiation of religious zealotry. The Peace of Westphalia in 1648 enshrined the system of sovereign states whose relations to one another should be governed by widely accepted principles, including provisions for the protection of religious minorities. Not until religious communities in Europe abandoned their zealous demands for religious uniformity could the modern era of international law begin. Since that time, the principles of tolerance and the moral censure of nations who break the peace have been explicitly affirmed by most religious communities. The currently binding expressions of these principles are found in the Geneva Conventions and the charter of the United Nations, which have virtually universal support in the world's religious institutions. Resolutions of the U.N.'s Security Council have not only legal standing but express "the Laws of Nature and of Nature's God," which religious communities have supported in one form or another since 1648. Despite occasional claims that the U.N.'s Universal Declaration of Human Rights is unsuited to Asians, prophetic realists such as Burmese Nobel laureate Aung San Suu Kyi have strenuously contended that "basic human rights are universal."[14]

As we write these words, America seems to waver in its "war on terrorism" between a prophetically realistic commitment to international institutions and its tendency to go its own zealously nationalistic way. Seeking international support for its actions in responding to al Qaeda's network, the U.S. government secured the passage of U.N. Resolution 1368, which affirmed the right of a nation to respond to aggression with acts of self-defense. President George W. Bush declared "war on terrorism" in that spirit. Having initiated combat in Afghanistan and taken captive numerous prisoners — some native Taliban and other foreign al Qaeda fighters — the United States expressed reluctance to grant them the status to which they were entitled as combatants under the terms of the Geneva Convention for prisoners of war. Interrogations bound by its provisions can limit their responses to requests for information to the statement of name, rank, and serial number. Those terms would also mean that they would have to be released when combat in war would be considered terminated.

Responding to criticism from European countries about the indeterminate status of the prisoners and their detention in chain-link cages with tin roofs, Secretary of State Colin Powell advocated that they be treated as POWs, according to the *New York Times.* Secretary of Defense Donald Rumsfeld and President Bush took the position that they are not "lawful combatants" and therefore cannot be POWs. Speaking to the issue during his press conference with Hamid Karzai, Afghanistan's new leader, President Bush expressed his view this way:

> We are not going to call them prisoners of war . . . and the reason why is al Qaeda is not a known military. These are killers. These are terrorists. They know no countries. And the only thing they know about countries is when they find a country that's been weak and they want to occupy it like a parasite.[15]

Consistent with the strategy of denial, the moving of the prisoners to Guantanamo Bay in Cuba had the apparent purpose of preventing them from invoking rights to which they might otherwise be entitled were they on U.S. soil.[16] The U.S. disposition of this matter, where circumstances of status are admittedly ambiguous, may profoundly affect its reputation as a country that can uphold human rights while struggling with adversaries who have behaved ruthlessly in denying those rights to the citizens of Afghanistan. It also raises the dangerous potential for the mistreatment of Americans, both combatants and noncombatants, should they be captured in the coming conflicts against Muslim militancy, which could happen in many countries.

Moreover, it is useful to recall the role of religion in envisioning this kind of impartial institution of justice embodying international law. It can be traced back to Hebrew prophecy beginning with Amos and Hosea: it discerned Yahweh's law as both impartial and international in scope, striking against the arrogant pretensions of any persons and nations who violate human rights in the belief that God is on their side. Divine retribution would strike down haughty lawbreakers, the prophets taught, whether they belonged to Israel or any other nation. This development climaxed in the work of Isaiah, who revised Israel's mission to the nations by transforming the hope of her imperial triumph into a vision of conflict resolution under impartial international law, as we have shown above. The "swords into plowshares" image is carved on the walls and in the sculpture garden of the U.N. building in New York. It thus stands at the center of a globally focused civil religion, supported by American religionists through their advocacy and support of the founding of the United Nations in 1945.

The absence of a significant commitment to the United Nations by the American public is particularly unwarranted in view of its effective response to the events of September 11, 2001. Robert Keohane points to the remarkable support for antiterrorist activities in the United Nations. Resolutions 1368 and 1373 were unanimously voted in by the Security Council, which includes three Muslim nations.[17] In Keohane's words, these resolutions affirmed the "inherent right of individual or collective self-defense," in accordance with Article 51 of the U.N. Charter. In effect, they declared that military action by the United States against "those responsible for the attacks would be lawful." The second resolution required that all member states "deny safe haven to those who finance, plan, support or commit terrorist acts, or provide safe havens." It also calls on all states to cooperate "to prevent and suppress terrorist attacks and take action against perpetrators of such attacks."[18] These resolutions follow the precedent of vigorous resistance against terrorism. Keohane recounts the record of which most Americans seem unaware:

The Resolutions 1368 and 1373 build on two years of United Nations resolutions against terrorism. In 1999 the Security Council called upon all states to fight terrorism and demanded that the Taliban turn over bin Laden to authorities in a country where he had been indicted. In December 2000 it specifically condemned the Taliban's sheltering and training of terrorists, and demanded, under the mandatory provisions of Chapter VII, that it "cease the provision of sanctuary and training for international terrorists." These resolutions, defied by the Taliban, established a record that justified focusing responses to the September 11 attack on that regime and on Osama bin Laden.

If the United Nations did not exist, obtaining such a collective endorsement of the struggle against terrorism would be impossible. Osama bin Laden and his supporters could more easily claim that attacks against them are "crusades" by the hegemonic United States and its clients. . . . If the United Nations Security Council did not exist, it would have to be invented. But it could not be invented at a moment's notice. Without its continuing presence, our struggle against terrorism would be more difficult, and less likely to succeed.[19]

The restoration of confidence and support for this international institution of prophetic realism is particularly appropriate in view of the complex problems that have emerged since September 11.

Recovering America's Constitutional Mission

The United States is uniquely suited by its constitutional heritage to participate in bringing the prophetic vision of a peaceable kingdom to international fruition. We have experienced the gradual transfer of loyalty from township to state to nation. We have demonstrated the feasibility of allowing local agencies of government to administer affairs in certain areas while allowing for national jurisdiction in others. Sealed by the tragedy of the Civil War, the Union is such that it never even occurs now to the leaders of a state to settle their disputes with a neighboring state by unconstitutional means. For example, border disputes caused by changing courses of rivers, which have provoked wars between nations and tribes from time immemorial, are routinely submitted to the courts. This is an immense cultural achievement that demonstrates that when higher tribunals are revered, states no longer "lift up the sword" against each other.

Extending this constitutional legacy into the international arena is the direction toward which Isaiah's vision and America's historic sense of mission beckon us. Even experienced analysts of international relations have viewed such a vision as feasible. Affirming this ideal, George F. Kennan suggested that we aim at the "restructuring of the international community and the development of the full potential of the United Nations." Such problems as the fragmentation of the world, the imbalance of the voting pattern in the United Nations, and the rigidities of national sovereignties "call out for the sort of study of the problem and leadership in attacking it which the United States is outstandingly equipped to give."[20] But before we can hope to succeed at such a mission, we must disentangle ourselves from the distortion of our heritage produced by adherence to zealous myths.

Unlike Isaiah, we cannot hope for the redemptive monarch who will suddenly do justice for the poor and usher in the golden age. No one will do it for us — not a king, nor an all-powerful president, nor even a superhero who rides in from the plains. In the modern world only an informed public can carry out such tasks. We must become the kind of redeemer nation we are called to be, taking up the task of cooperating in world order without illusions and without self-righteousness, not because we are superior, or somehow have a right to lead, but because we are called to be a servant and a light to the world. This is the vision that should brighten the horizon we will never fully reach.

The American sense of mission, scorned by cynics, secular realists, and disappointed idealists alike, needs to be transformed rather than abandoned. Its sense of how the world should be led to peace has been misguided by zealous myths. The absolutizing of our moral impulses, the delusions of the "grand conspiracy," the distortions of popular stereotypes, the mystique of violence, the idolatrous grasp of the Deuteronomic principle, and our crusades against symbolic desecration have distorted our sense of mission and are driving us toward scenarios of mutual destruction. Our calling now is to separate ourselves from that legacy and to enter a long twilight struggle against what is dark within ourselves. It is not our adversaries alone who must change; it is ourselves. But we cannot accomplish this alone. It calls for the transformation of the mythic forms that shape our culture and define the patterns of our politics. It calls for a creative rechanneling of Captain America's impulse to "fight for right" toward a religious commitment that is shaped both by self-critical questioning and a sense of hope about the possibilities for peace. Only when America's realism qualifies its zeal in these ways can it be said, in Melville's words, that it bears "the ark of the liberties of the world . . . to break a new path in the New World that is ours."

Acknowledgments

The themes for this book were born during the 1970s in a period when the authors were just beginning to collaborate on their common interests in religion, ideology, and national politics. An initial publication, *The Captain America Complex: The Dilemmas of Zealous Nationalism* (The Westminster Press, 1973), authored by Robert Jewett, was followed by a slightly altered second edition of 1984 from Bear Publishing of Santa Fe. While this book preserves much from *The Captain America Complex,* all surviving chapters have been rewritten and six entirely new chapters have been added.

In the team authorship for this book, Robert Jewett has provided the elements of biblical history and theological ethics; John Shelton Lawrence has focused on contemporary political history and ideology. The argument as a whole reflects our common interests in heroic mythology and draws upon our earlier joint efforts, *The American Monomyth* (Doubleday, 1977; University Press of America, 1989), and *The Myth of the American Superhero* (Eerdmans, 2002).

Friends, colleagues, and family members have been generous in suggesting resources that advanced our understanding of the issues: special thanks go to Fred Isaac, Heike Goebel, Alex Klibaner, Nancy C. Lawrence, Mark McDermott, Rachel Schiff, and Bernard Timberg.

Libraries contributing to our recent research include the Berkeley Public Library, Garrett-Evangelical Theological Seminary and Northwestern University, the Flora Lamson Hewlett Graduate Theological Union Library at Berkeley, Morningside College, Princeton Theological Seminary, Ruprecht-Karls-University of Heidelberg, and the University of California-Berkeley.

Special thanks are due for Reinder Van Til, our editor at Eerdmans Publishing Company, whose patience, forbearance, constructive suggestions, and careful editing have guided us toward better structure and style throughout the book.

April, 2002   ROBERT JEWETT
                                                     Heidelberg, Germany
                                                   JOHN SHELTON LAWRENCE
                                                     Berkeley, California

Endnotes

A Comment on Sources

Evolving information formats have made full text electronic databases, the Internet, and the World Wide Web important to this book. For post-1980 periodicals, we have relied on the following sources: the Lexis-Nexis Academic Universe database (University of California at Berkeley), the Gale Group collections (the Berkeley, CA Public Library), and the Personal Edition of the Electric Library <http://www.elibrary.com>. While knowing that cited material and URL addresses can be ephemeral, we also make numerous references to Web sites. We indicate our dates of viewing for such references.

Some citations from *The New York Times* and *Time* magazine were affected by the Supreme Court decision in *New York Times* vs. *Tasini*, rendered June 25, 2001. The ruling held that the newspaper had violated the copyrights of freelance writers in re-selling content to electronic full text aggregators such as Lexis-Nexis. The newspaper responded to its legal defeat by purging from electronic archives 115,000 articles written by 27,000 authors between 1980 and 1995. ("Freelance group files suits against *New York Times*," *Reuters Business Report,* July 5, 2001). Other publications who were not litigants chose to follow their example. Temporarily such articles will no longer be available online; they do however remain in paper indexes and collections and in microfilm.

We also mention here the absence of pagination in electronic full source texts. When we cite from such sources we simply indicate the page range for the article in its original print format (or the beginning page along with the number of pages).

Notes to Chapter 1

1. Herman Melville, *White-Jacket; or, The World in a Man-of-War* (Evanston/Chicago: Northwestern University and Newberry Library, 1970), p. 151. *White-Jacket* was first published in 1850.

2. President George Bush, "Address to the Nation on the Situation in Somalia," Dec. 4, 1992 <http://bushlibrary.tamu.edu/papers/1992/92120400.html>, viewed Jan. 15, 2002.

3. Rousseau's concept of "civil religion" was articulated in the American scene by the sociologist Robert N. Bellah as "a genuine apprehension of universal and transcendent religious reality as seen in or, one could almost say, as revealed through the experience of the American people. . . . our nation stands under higher judgment. . . . the American civil religion is not the worship of the American nation but an understanding of the American experience in the light of ultimate and universal reality. . . ." Citations from Bellah, "Civil Religion in America," *Daedalus* (Winter, 1967), reprinted in Russell E. Richie and Donald G. Jones, eds. *American Civil Religion* (New York: Harper, 1974), pp. 33, 39, 40. Richie and Jones identify five different meanings of "civil religion" as employed by various researchers (pp. 14-17). Bellah's more recent studies include *The Broken Covenant: American Civil Religion in Time of Trial* (San Francisco: Harper & Row, 1976); with Phillip E. Hammond, Bellah authored *Varieties of Civil Religion* (San Francisco: Harper & Row, 1980) and with Frederick E. Greenspahn he served as editor of *Uncivil Religion: Interreligious Hostility in America* (New York: Crossroad, 1987). See also Gail Gehrig, *American Civil Religion: An Assessment* (Storrs, CT: Society for the Scientific Study of Religion, 1981). Gehrig, p. 18, defines civil religion as "the religious symbol system which relates the citizen's role and American society's place in space, time, and history to the conditions of ultimate existence and meaning." See the concise summary of the discussion's evolution in Robert Wuthnow, "Civil Religion," in *Encyclopedia of Politics and Religion,* Robert Wuthnow, ed. (London: Routledge, 1998), pp. 153-157.

4. "Bush gives update on war against terrorism," CNN (Oct. 11, 2001) <http://www.cnn.com/2001/US/10/11/gen.bush.transcript>, viewed Nov. 7, 2001.

5. George W. Bush, "National Day of Prayer and Remembrance for the Victims of the Terrorist Attacks on September 11, 2001," spoken to Washington National Cathedral service on Sept. 14, 2001.

6. Citations from Karen De Young, "Bush Lays Down a Marker for 3 'Evil' States," *Washington Post* (Jan. 30, 2002), p. A1. Iraq's official *Al-Iraq* newspaper responded predictably by identifying the U.S. as "the sole evil on Earth" while Iran's religious leader Ayatollah Khameini expressed a sense of achievement in being condemned by "the most hated Satan in the world." See Hadani Ditmars, "An unlikely alliance of 'evil'," *San Francisco Chronicle* (Feb. 1, 2002), p. A18.

7. "Address by President on Lebanon and Grenada," *New York Times* (Oct. 28, 1983), p. A5.

8. George Bush, "Remarks at the Annual Convention of the National Religious Broadcasters," Jan. 28, 1991. <http://bushlibrary.tamu.edu/papers/1991/91012800.html>, viewed Dec. 5, 2001. See also Andrew Rosenthal, "Bush Vows to Tackle Middle East Issues," *New York Times* (Jan. 29, 1991), p. A13.

9. Jim Wallis, "The Two Paths" (Sept. 21, 2001) and "Overcome Evil with Good" (Sept. 28, 2001), posted in the archives at <http://www.sojo.net>, viewed Oct. 5, 2001.

10. The statement of Melville's comes as an author's narrative comment, not the voice of a fictional character. Stanton Garner, *The Civil War World of Herman Melville* (Lawrence: University Press of Kansas, 1993), p. 26, suggests that this passage embodies Melville's own sense of redemptive mission for America.

11. Frederick Merk, *Manifest Destiny and Mission in American History: A Reinterpretation* (New York: Alfred A. Knopf, 1963), p. 261.

12. *Congressional Record* (56th Cong., 1st Session), vol. 33, p. 711.

13. Cited by Ernest Lee Tuveson, *Redeemer Nation: The Idea of America's Millennial Role* (Chicago: University of Chicago Press, 1968), p. 212.

14. Richard Nixon, *Six Crises* (Garden City, NY: Doubleday, 1962), p. 68.

15. Marc Sandalow, "Bush promises to conquer a new kind of enemy," *San Francisco Chronicle* (Sept. 13, 2001), p. A7.

16. The article "Piracy," *Microsoft Encarta® Encyclopedia 99*, provides the following summary of international law: "Piracy is recognized as an offense against the law of nations. It is a crime not against any particular state, but against all humanity. The crime may be punished in the competent tribunal of any country in which the offender may be found, or carried, although the crime may have been committed on board a foreign vessel on the high seas. The essence of piracy is that the pirate has no valid commission from a sovereign state, or from an insurgent or belligerent government engaged in hostilities with a particular state. Pirates are regarded as common enemies of all people. In that nations have an equal interest in their apprehension and punishment, pirates may be lawfully captured on the high seas by the armed vessels of any state and brought within its territorial jurisdiction for trial in its tribunals." The article also explains that "the practice of hijacking ships or airplanes has developed into a new form of piracy."

17. Cited by Arthur Schlesinger, Jr., "The Two Faces of American Foreign Policy," *Chicago Sun-Times* (Oct. 16, 1983), p. 4.

18. *New York Times*, "From Lies to Remedies" (Sept. 7, 1983), p. A22.

19. Ivo H. Daalder and James M. Lindsay, "A War Nasty, Brutish, and Long," *Current History: A Journal of Contemporary World Affairs* (Dec., 2001), p. 408.

20. Ibid.

21. Ibid., p. 409.

22. Thomas L. Friedman, "Crazier than thou: talking turkey to terrorists," *New York Times* (Feb. 13, 2002), p. A29; see also Norman Podhoretz, "How to Win World War IV," *Commentary* (Feb. 2002), pp. 25-29.

23. *Captain America*, vol. 3, no. 16 (April 1999).

24. *Captain America*, vol. 131 (Nov. 1970).

25. See for example, the accounts of intense forms of polarization in the recent past along conventional liberal-conservative lines. Samuel Lubell, "Hidden Crisis in American Politics," *Los Angeles Times* (June 21, 1970), p. F1; Robert Wuthnow, "Divided We Fall: America's Two Civil Religions," *Christian Century* (April 20, 1988), pp. 395-99.

26. As we write these words, we are aware that the Captain America comic book character has been revived in a fine archival quality color poster from Marvel.com. Titled "The Spirit of America," the poster shouts "CAPTAIN AMERICA WANTS YOU!" Marvel de-

clares it "a breathtaking vision celebrating the legend of comics' fighting sentry, from his battle-born WW2 creation through the Cold-War revival to today's turbulent crusade." <http://www.marvel.com/comics/steranko.htm>, viewed April 1, 2002.

Notes to Chapter 2

1. Rahimullah Yusufzai, "Wrath of God," *Time International* (Jan. 11, 1999), p. 16.

2. Evan Thomas and John Barry, "Evil in the Cross Hairs," *Newsweek* (Dec. 24, 2001), p. 18, International Edition.

3. John McCain (R-AZ), "There Is No Substitute for Victory," *Wall Street Journal* (Oct. 26, 2001), p. A14.

4. George Tenet, ABC News, Feb. 2, 1999. Cited in Mark Juergensmeyer, *Terror in the Mind of God: The Global Rise of Religious Violence* (Berkeley: University of California Press, 2000), p. 230.

5. Ann Coulter, "This Is War," *National Review Online* (Sept. 13, 2001), <http://www.nationalreview.com/coulter/0901301.html>, viewed Oct. 19, 2001.

6. Moises Naim, "Collateral Damage," *Foreign Policy* (Nov.-Dec. 2001), p. 108.

7. Diane Marie Amann, "A new international spirit," *The San Francisco Chronicle* (October 12, 2001), p. A23.

8. Jean Bethke Elshtain, "Commentary," *The Dallas Morning News* (Oct. 6, 2001), <http://www.dallasnews.com/religion/488932_jeancol_06rel.html>, viewed Dec. 15, 2001.

9. "U.S. Religious Leaders Suggest Response to Terror," *America* (Oct. 8, 2001), p. 6.

10. "Deny Them Their Victory," <http://www.sojo.net/response>, viewed Dec. 12, 2001. In describing the origins of the document, which acquired nearly 4,000 signatures by early December, 2000, the sponsors explain that it "was developed in consultation with Jewish, Muslim, and Christian clergy, and circulated for signature beginning Sept. 12 by the Rev. Jim Wallis, Call to Renewal and Sojourners; Dr. Robert W. Edgar, National Council of Churches; the Rev. Wesley Granberg-Michaelson, Reformed Church of America; Rabbi David Saperstein, Religious Action Center of Reform Judaism; and Dr. Ron Sider, Evangelicals for Social Action."

11. Here we follow and cite from Robert O. Keohane, "The United Nations: An Essential Instrument Against Terror" (Oct. 1, 2001), <http://www.duke.edu/web/forums/keohane.html>, viewed Jan. 25, 2002.

12. President George Bush (Senior), quoted in Stanley W. Cloud, "Exorcising an Old Demon," *Time* (March 11, 1991), p. 52.

13. See Lawrence Freedman and Ephraim Karsh, *The Gulf Conflict 1990-1991: Diplomacy and War in the New World Order* (Princeton: Princeton University Press, 1993), pp. 408-9.

14. George W. Bush, "Address to a Joint Session of Congress and the American People," Sept. 20, 2001, <http://www.whitehouse.gov/news/releases/2001/09/20010920-8.html>, viewed Sept. 21, 2001.

15. George W. Bush, "President Holds Prime Time News Conference," <http://www.whitehouse.gov/news/releases/2001/10/20011011-7.html>, viewed Oct. 12, 2001.

16. *Newsweek* (Oct. 15, 2001). In a concession to the popular demonic framework, it

placed on the cover a picture from an anti-U.S. rally in Islamabad from September 28, 2001. A boy wearing a turban — of three or four years in age — held a toy automatic assault weapon with his finger on the trigger.

17. Peter Carlson, "The Solitary Vote of Barbara Lee; Congresswoman against Use of Force," *The Washington Post* (Sept. 19, 2001), p. C1.

18. "Q&A on Terrorism," *The Atlanta Journal and Constitution* (Nov. 22, 2001), p. D2.

19. George W. Bush, "Address to a Joint Session of Congress and the American People," Sept. 20, 2001. <http://www.whitehouse.gov/news/releases/2001/09/20010920-8.html>, viewed Sept. 21, 2001.

20. Edward Epstein, "Bush urges military overhaul," *San Francisco Chronicle* (Dec. 12, 2001), p. A19.

21. Alissa Rubin, "Bombing Alters Afghan's Views of U.S." (Nov. 5, 2001), p. A1.

22. "Amerika im Krieg," *Süddeutsche Zeitung* (Sept. 12, 2001), p. 18.

23. Robert Marquand, "Global empathy: will it last?" *Christian Science Monitor* (Sept. 17, 2001), p. 4.

24. According to Karen Armstrong, this meaning emerged late in Islamic history with the Pakistani journalist Abdul Ala Mawdudi (1903-1979). See Armstrong's *The Battle for God* (New York: Ballantine, 2000), pp. 238-9.

25. Bernard Lewis, "The Revolt of Islam," *The New Yorker* (Nov. 19, 2001), pp. 60-61; Erdmute Heller, "Sterben ist wichtiger als Töten," *Süddeutche Zeitung* (*SZ am Wochenende. Feuilleton-Beilage* (Oct. 20-21, 2001), p. 1.

26. Ahmed Rashid, *Taliban: Militant Islam, Oil, and Fundamentalism in Central Asia* (New Haven: Yale University Press, 2000), p. 133.

27. Ibid., p. 134.

28. Peter Arnett, "CNN March 1997 interview with Osama bin Laden," <http://www.cnn.com>, viewed Sept. 27, 2001.

29. Lee Griffith, *The War on Terrorism and the Terror of God* (Grand Rapids: Eerdmans, 2002), p. 276.

30. Nasra Hassan, "An Arsenal of Believers," *The New Yorker* (Nov. 19, 2001), p. 37.

31. Ibid., p. 36.

32. Ibid., p. 38.

33. Griffith, *The War on Terrorism*, p. 18, citing from the Friends Committee on National Legislation, *Washington Newsletter* (May, 1986).

34. See "Amerika im Krieg," *Süddeutsche Zeitung*, p. 18.

35. Jeffrey M. Jones, "Americans Say U.S. and Allies Winning War on Terrorism," The Gallup Organization (Nov. 14, 2001) <http://gallup.com/poll/releases/pr011114.asp>, viewed Dec. 3, 2001.

36. Michael Howard, "Stumbling into War," *Harper's Magazine* (Jan. 2002), pp. 13-14.

37. *Newsweek* (Dec. 24, 2001). Evan Thomas and John Barry, "Evil in the Cross Hairs," pp. 10-20.

38. Howard, "Stumbling into War," p. 15.

39. John F. Burns, "Extremists vow to continue jihad, with or without bin Laden," *San Francisco Chronicle* (Jan. 27, 2002), p. A5.

Notes to Chapter 3

1. Enduring Freedom Picture Cards, advertised at the Topps Company Web site, <http://www.topps.com/enduringfreedom.html>, viewed Dec. 27, 2001.

2. Cited from the *San Francisco Chronicle* (March 19, 1986) in Michael Paul Rogin, *Ronald Reagan the Movie* (Berkeley: University of California Press, 1987), p. 3.

3. See particularly W. Lloyd Warner, "An American Sacred Ceremony," in Russell E. Richie and Donald G. Jones, eds. *American Civil Religion* (New York: Harper, 1974), pp. 89-114; Catherine L. Albanese, "Dominant and Public Center: Reflections on the 'One' Religion of the United States," *South Atlantic Quarterly,* vol. 81 (1982), p. 24.

4. This formulation is derived from a supreme prophetic realist, Reinhold Niebuhr, who wrote *The Democratic Experience: Past and Prospects,* with Paul E. Sigmund (New York: Frederick A. Praeger, 1969); see Ronald H. Stone, *Professor Reinhold Niebuhr: A Mentor to the Twentieth Century* (Louisville: Westminster/John Knox Press, 1992), pp. 212, 245-51.

5. John Shelton Lawrence and Robert Jewett, *The Myth of the American Superhero* (Grand Rapids: Wm. B. Eerdmans Company, 2002).

6. Sean Kelly, *Digital Press CD-Rom* (vol 1, 2/1997); television ads played from the file Atari4.avi.

7. *Star Wars: Galactic Battleground* advertisement, *Computer Gaming World* (Jan. 2002), pp. 5-6.

8. See Lawrence and Jewett, *American Superhero,* pp. 26-27.

9. See ibid., pp. 27, 55-56.

10. See ibid., pp. 31-35.

11. See ibid., pp. 37-41.

12. See ibid., pp. 41-43.

13. Dennis Dooley and Gary Engle, eds. *Superman at Fifty: The Persistence of a Legend* (Cleveland: Octavia Press, 1987), p. 32.

14. Richard O'Brien, *The Golden Age of Comic Books, 1937-1945* (New York: Ballantine, 1977), p. 5.

15. Kevin Smith, "A Superman for All Seasons," *TV Guide* (Dec. 8, 2001), p. 24. This same issue of *TV Guide* includes "The S Files," pp. 16ff., which lists all the serial resurrections of Superman in movie and television formats.

16. *Captain America,* No. 1 in Joe Simon and Jack Kirby, *Captain America: The Classic Years* (New York: Marvel Comics, 1998), n.p.

17. The solicitation appeared in *Captain America,* No. 1.

18. Les Daniels, *Marvel: Five Fabulous Decades of the World's Greatest Comics* (New York: Harry N. Abrahams, 1991), p. 53.

19. *Captain America,* vol. 3, no. 32 (Aug. 2000).

20. *Captain America,* vol. 3, no. 16 (April 1999).

21. This is Michael Chabon's premise in his novel, *The Amazing Adventure of Kavalier and Clay* (New York: Random House, 2000), which models the creators of "The Escapist" superhero comic on the Siegel and Schuster creators of Superman and on Jack Kirby.

22. Episode titled "All Good Things," *The Next Generation,* June 5, 1994.

23. *Ultimate Doom* (Eidos Interactive, 1995).

24. Instruction Manual, *The Ultimate Doom* (Id Software, 1995), p. 1.

25. "The Columbine Tapes," *Time* (Dec. 20, 1999), pp. 40ff.; letters omitted in the original.

26. Jennifer Harper, "New Trading Cards Celebrate Heroes of 'Freedom,'" *Washington Times* (Oct. 31, 2001) <http:washingtontimes.com>, viewed Nov. 15, 2001.

27. This mythical background explains what European observers find astounding, that a president of modest talents like George W. Bush could derive such impressive accolades and poll ratings from a military campaign of such modest scope; see Wolfgang Koydl, "Vom Panoptikum ins Pantheon," *Süddeutsche Zeitung* (Dec. 27, 2001), p. 4: "It is certainly remarkable what a small war can do for a mediocre politician. For that is what Bush is, no more and no less: solid, unspectacular, average. . . . The tributes and high opinion poll ratings . . . are rather an indication of the dubious political understanding of the voters in the second largest democracy in the world. . . ."

28. George Gerbner and Larry Gross, *Trends in Network Drama and Viewer Conception of Social Reality, 1967-1973 (Violence Profile, no. 6*, Annenberg School of Communications, University of Pennsylvania, Dec. 1974), p. 8.

29. Karl Popper, *The Open Society and Its Enemies* (Princeton: Princeton University Press, 1950), pp. 119-20.

30. Ernest Becker, *Angel in Armor: A Post-Freudian Perspective on the Nature of Man* (New York: Braziller, 1969), pp. 111-14; italics in original.

31. Cover caption, "Die Bush Krieger. Amerikas Feldzug gegen das Böse" (The Bush Warriors Campaign Against Evil), *Der Spiegel*, no. 8 (February 18, 2002); the feature article within the magazine carries the title "Die Herren der Welt" (The World Masters), pp. 162ff.

32. Reported in the March 18, 2002 issue of *Der Spiegel*, no. 12, p. 3, and picked up by Spike Harley, "Mr. America," *Sydney Morning Herald* (March 21, 2002), <http://www.smh.com.au/articles/2002/03/21/Spikeharley21.htm>, viewed March 30, 2002.

Notes to Chapter 4

1. For Scripture quotations in this book, the Revised Standard Version has been employed most often. In some instances Jewett provided his own translations or adapted established versions.

2. Frank Moore Cross, Jr., "The Divine Warrior in Israel's Early Cult," in Alexander Altmann, ed. *Biblical Motifs: Origins and Transformations* (Cambridge: Harvard University Press, 1966), pp. 11-30.

3. See Werner H. Schmidt, *Old Testament Introduction*, tr. M. J. O'Connell with D. J. Reimer (New York/Berlin: de Gruyter; Louisville: Westminster/John Knox, 1999, 2nd ed.), p. 13.

4. Thomas B. Dozeman, *God at War: Power in the Exodus Tradition* (New York/Oxford: Oxford University Press, 1996), pp. 3, 23, 27.

5. See the description of "divine war" in Mesopotamia, Anatolia, Syro-Palestine, and Egypt in Sa-Moon Kang, *Divine War in the Old Testament and in the Ancient Near East*, Beiheft zur Zeitschrift für die alttestamentlliche Wissenschaft 177 (Berlin/New York: de Gruyter, 1989), pp. 11-110.

6. Patrick D. Miller, Jr., *The Divine Warrior in Early Israel* (Cambridge: Harvard University Press, 1973), pp. 164-65: ". . . the establishment of Yahweh's kingship and sanctuary and, in part, his creation (Deut. 32:6) grew out of this cosmic, historical, sacral war, whereas elsewhere these elements all resulted from and were associated with the mythological battle of the gods." See also Charles Sherlock, *The God Who Fights: The War Tradition in Holy Scripture*, Rutherford Studies in Contemporary Theology 6 (Lewiston/Queenston/Lampeter: Edwin Mellen Press, 1993), pp. 21-22, and Peter Partner, *God of Battles: Holy Wars of Christianity and Islam* (Princeton: Princeton University Press, 1997), pp. 1-13.

7. See Rudolf Smend, *Yahweh War and Tribal Confederation: Reflections upon Israel's Earliest History*, tr. by M. G. Rogers (Nashville: Abingdon Press, 1970).

8. See George L. Carey, "Biblical-Theological Perspectives on War and Peace," *The Evangelical Quarterly* (April 1985), p. 165.

9. See George Mendenhall, "The Hebrew Conquest of Palestine," *Biblical Archaeology* 25 (1962), pp. 66-87; Norman K. Gottwald, *The Tribes of Yahweh: A Sociology of the Religion of Liberated Israel* (Maryknoll, NY: Orbis Books, 1979); Gottwald, *The Hebrew Bible — A Socio-Literary Introduction* (Philadelphia: Fortress Press, 1985), pp. 284-88; Schmidt, *Old Testament Introduction*, pp. 15-18; Moshe Weinfeld, *The Promise of the Land: The Inheritance of the Land of Canaan by the Israelites* (Berkeley: University of California Press, 1993), pp. 107-20.

10. Kang, *Divine War*, p. 127; see also John A. Wood, *Perspectives on War in the Bible* (Macon, Georgia: Mercer University Press, 1998), pp. 35-76, for the distinction between Israel's active and passive participation in divine war.

11. See Gerhard von Rad, *Der heilige Krieg im alten Israel* (Göttingen: Vandenhoeck & Ruprecht, 1965, 2nd ed.), pp. 26ff.; Millard C. Lind, *Yahweh Is a Warrior: The Theology of Warfare in Ancient Israel* (Scottdale/Kitchener: Herald Press, 1980), pp. 66-89.

12. See Miller, *Divine Warrior*, p. 191; Kang, *Divine War*, p. 202; Sherlock, *God Who Fights*, pp. 117-23.

13. See particularly Norman K. Gottwald, *All the Kingdoms of the Earth: Israelite Prophecy and International Relations in the Ancient Near East* (New York: Harper & Row, 1964), pp. 63-70.

14. Joseph Blenkinsopp, *A History of Prophecy in Israel* (Louisville: Westminster/John Knox, 1996; revised and enlarged ed.), p. 61: "A prominent feature of prophecy during this period is its association with warfare and religious crusades."

15. See Sherlock, *God Who Fights*, 135-44; Winfried Thiel, "Jehu," *Anchor Bible Dictionary* (New York: Doubleday, 1992), vol. 3, pp. 67-72; John Bright, *A History of Israel* (Philadelphia: Westminster Press, 1972), pp 241-52; Gottwald, *The Hebrew Bible*, pp. 344-46; Norman K. Gottwald, *The Politics of Ancient Israel* (Louisville: Westminster/John Knox Press, 2001), p. 214.

16. Gottwald, *The Politics of Ancient Israel*, p. 226.

17. Gottwald, *All the Kingdoms of the Earth*, p. 83.

18. See Schmidt, *Old Testament Introduction*, pp. 22-23.

19. See Bright, *A History of Israel*, pp. 269-74.

20. See Gottwald, *All the Kingdoms of the Earth*, pp. 103-16.

21. See particularly Blenkinsopp, *A History of Prophecy*, pp. 80-82.

22. See Wood, *Perspectives*, pp. 144-45.

23. See Gottwald, *Hebrew Bible*, pp. 356-58.

24. See Schmidt, *Old Testament Introduction*, pp. 198-99.

25. See Patrick D. Miller, Jr., *Sin and Judgment in the Prophets: A Stylistic and Theological Analysis*, Society of Biblical Literature Monograph Series 27 (Chico, CA: Scholars Press, 1982), pp. 22-24.

26. See Blenkinsopp, *A History of Prophecy*, p. 83.

27. See Bright, *A History of Israel*, pp. 270-71; Gottwald, *All the Kingdoms of the Earth*, pp. 119-20.

28. See Gottwald, *All the Kingdoms of the Earth*, pp. 131-32.

29. See Gottwald, *Hebrew Bible*, pp. 358-63; Schmidt, *Old Testament Introduction*, p. 207.

30. Miller, *Sin and Judgment*, p. 20.

31. See Miller, *Sin and Judgment*, pp. 46-48.

32. Bright, *A History of Israel*, pp. 278-83.

33. See Gottwald, *All the Kingdoms of the Earth*, pp. 165-73.

34. See Gottwald, *Hebrew Bible*, pp. 379-80.

35. See Bright, *A History of Israel*, pp. 316-21.

36. Bright, *A History of Israel*, p. 327: "One would have expected the experiences of 598-97 to have left Judah, for the moment at least, chastened and docile. But nothing of the sort! Zedekiah's reign (597-87) saw nothing but continual agitation and sedition till the nation, seemingly bent on destroying itself, finally succeeded in bringing the roof down on its head. Within ten short years the end had come forever."

37. Wood, *Perspectives*, p. 115, cites Gottwald, *Hebrew Bible*, p. 403, for the assessment that Jeremiah favored co-existence with Babylon and resisted the independence party.

38. See especially Jer. 27:9 and 28:1-4, and the discussion of the "nationalistic prophets" in Blenkinsopp, *A History of Prophecy*, p. 143; see also Gottwald, *Hebrew Bible*, pp. 402-04.

39. Miller, *Sin and Judgment*, pp. 66-67.

40. Bright, *A History of Israel*, p. 331, notes that this nationalistic zeal "centered in the affirmation of Yahweh's choice of Zion as his seat, and his immutable promises to the Davidic dynasty of an eternal rule and victory over its foes."

41. Gottwald, *Hebrew Bible*, p. 592, suggests that there may be an intentional contrast between "a collective individualization of the community of saints as 'human' in its bearing, as against the beastly kingdoms headed by kings who are 'animalistic.'"

42. See the surveys in David M. Rhoads, *Israel in Revolution, 6-74 c.e.: A Political History Based on the Writings of Josephus* (Philadelphia: Fortress Press, 1976), pp. 32-46, 97-110; John Riches, *Jesus and the Transformation of Judaism* (London: Darton, Longman & Todd, 1980), pp. 83-86; Sean P. Kealy, *Jesus and Politics* (Collegeville, MN: Liturgical Press, 1990), pp. 27-47.

43. See Martin Hengel, *The Zealots: Investigations into the Jewish Freedom Movement in the Period from Herod I until 70 a.d.*, tr. D. Smith (Edinburgh: T&T Clark, 1989), pp. 245-48, 271-89, 302-12; Rhoads, *Israel in Revolution*, pp. 94-149.

44. That zeal for the law and rage against its alleged detractors was a common element of these various groups is suggested by Torrey Seland, *Establishment Violence in Philo and Luke: A Study of Non-Conformity to the Torah and Jewish Vigilante Reactions*, Biblical

Interpretation Series 15 (Leiden: Brill, 1995), pp. 13-14, 42-74. He analyzes "zealot establishment violence against some specific deviances from the Torah," p. 13, in contrast to revolutionary violence.

45. The literature is immense, and the following treatment follows those who place Jesus within the context of a society about to explode in zealous violence against Rome, as for example in the work of G. B. Caird, *Jesus and the Jewish Nation* (London: Athlone, 1965); Riches, *Jesus;* E. P. Sanders, *Jesus and Judaism* (Philadelphia: Fortress, 1985); Richard A. Horsley, *Jesus and the Spiral of Violence* (San Francisco: Harper & Row, 1987); R. R. Hobbs, *A Time for War: A Study of Warfare in the Old Testament* (Wilmington, Del.: Michael Glazier, 1989), pp. 230-33; David R. Kaylor, *Jesus the Prophet: His Vision of the Kingdom on Earth* (Louisville: Westminster/John Knox Press, 1994); Scot McKnight, *A New Vision for Israel: The Teachings of Jesus in National Context* (Grand Rapids: Eerdmans, 1999); and William R. Herzog III, *Jesus, Justice, and the Reign of God: A Ministry of Liberation* (Louisville: Westminster/John Knox Press, 2000).

46. That Jesus was a "messianic" and "millenarian" prophet as Dale C. Allison has convincingly demonstrated in *Jesus of Nazareth: Millenarian Prophet* (Minneapolis: Fortress Press, 1998) enhances the significance of the alternative he developed to the violent messianism that was dominant during this pre-revolutionary period.

47. Riches, *Jesus,* p. 168.

48. See Jürgen Becker, *Jesus of Nazareth,* tr. J. E. Crouch (New York/Berlin: de Gruyter, 1998), pp. 259-60.

49. See McKnight, *New Vision for Israel,* pp. 11-13, 140-41, following the lead of Caird, *Jesus and the Jewish Nation.*

50. Josephus, *The Jewish War,* VI.5.2-4.

51. That this prediction was borne out by future events in the Jewish-Roman war is rightly emphasized by McKnight, *New Vision for Israel,* pp. 141-42.

52. See Ernest Lee Tuveson, *Redeemer Nation* (Chicago: University of Chicago Press, 1968), pp. 1-51; David E. Smith, "Millenarian Scholarship in America," *American Quarterly,* vol. 17 (1965), pp. 535-49.

53. See Josephine Massyngberde Ford, *Revelation,* The Anchor Bible 38 (Garden City: Doubleday and Company, 1975), pp. 315-25.

54. See Tuveson, *Redeemer Nation,* pp. 197-202.

55. See particularly the metaphor of God's word as "sharper than any two-edged sword" in Heb. 4:12, a writing that has no trace of redemption through violence.

56. Ford, *Revelation,* pp. 101-4, shows how this metaphor fits into the biblical theme of holy war.

Notes to Chapter 5

1. Cited from Ernest Lee Tuveson, *Redeemer Nation* (Chicago: University of Chicago Press, 1968), pp. 105-6.

2. Winthrop S. Hudson, ed. *Nationalism and Religion in America: Concepts of American Identity and Mission* (New York: Harper & Row, 1970), p. 7.

3. John Fiske, *The Beginnings of New England; or, The Puritan Theocracy in Its Relations to Civil and Religious Liberty* (Boston: Houghton & Mifflin, 1889), p. 147.

4. Michael L. Walzer, *The Revolution of the Saints: A Study in the Origins of Radical Politics* (Cambridge: Harvard University Press, 1965), p. 291.

5. Ibid., p. 294.

6. Ibid., p. 295.

7. Ibid., p. 296.

8. Perry Miller, "Preparation for Salvation in Seventeenth-Century New England," in Paul Goodman, ed. *Essays in American Colonial History* (New York: Holt, Rinehart & Winston, 1967), p. 178.

9. Tuveson, *Redeemer Nation,* pp. 97ff.

10. Jonathan Edwards, *History of the Work of Redemption,* cited by Tuveson, *Redeemer Nation,* p. 100.

11. J. F. Maclear, "The Republic and the Millennium," in Elwyn A. Smith, ed. *The Religion of the Republic* (Philadelphia: Fortress Press, 1971), p. 190.

12. Baumgartner, *Longing for the End,* p. 131.

13. Cited from Perry Miller, "From the Covenant to the Revival," *Nature's Nation* (Cambridge: Harvard University Press, 1967), p. 95.

14. Miller, *Nature's Nation,* p. 97.

15. Bernard Bailyn, *The Ideological Origins of the American Revolution* (Cambridge: Harvard University Press, 1967), p. 54.

16. See Ralph Barton Perry, *Puritanism and Democracy* (New York: Vanguard Press, 1944), pp. 147-218; see also Robert Jewett, *Paul the Apostle to America: Cultural Trends and Pauline Scholarship* (Louisville: Westminster/John Knox Press, 1994), ch. 9, "Paul and the Democratic Prospect."

17. Cited from Sidney E. Meade, "The Nation with a Soul of a Church," *Church History,* vol. 36, no. 3 (1967), p. 280.

18. William G. McLoughlin, "Pietism and the American Character," in H. Cohen, ed. *The American Experience: Approaches to the Study of the United States* (Boston: Houghton Mifflin, 1968), pp. 44-45.

19. See Ernest R. Sandeen, ed. *The Bible and Social Reform* (Philadelphia: Fortress, 1982), chs. 3-5.

20. See Sandeen, ed. *Social Reform,* ch. 2.

21. Cited by Albert K. Weinberg, *Manifest Destiny: A Study of Nationalist Expansionism in American History* (Baltimore: Johns Hopkins Press, 1935), p. 127.

22. Weinberg, *Manifest Destiny,* p. 128.

23. Herman Melville, *White-Jacket* (Evanston: Northwestern University, 1970), p. 189.

24. Cited by Harry J. Carman and Harold C. Syrett, *A History of the American People* (New York: Alfred A. Knopf, 1952), vol. 1, p. 550.

25. Hans Kohn, *American Nationalism: An Interpretive Essay* (New York: Macmillan, 1957), pp. 62-63.

26. Cited by Richard D. Mosier, *Making the American Mind: Social and Moral Ideas in the McGuffey Readers* (New York: King's Crown Press, 1947), p. 21.

27. George Bancroft, *History of the United States of America* (1883-1885), vol. 4 (New York: D. Appleton, 1890-91), pp. 12-13.

28. See Harry V. Jaffa, *Crisis of the House Divided: An Interpretation of the Issues in the Lincoln-Douglas Debates* (Garden City, NY: Doubleday, 1959).

29. Cited by Timothy L. Smith, *Revivalism and Social Reform: In Mid-Nineteenth-Century America* (Nashville: Abingdon Press, 1957), p. 183.

30. Aileen S. Kraditor, *Means and Ends in American Abolitionism: Garrison and His Critics on Strategy and Tactics, 1834-50*, 2nd ed. (New York: Pantheon Books, 1969).

31. Tuveson, *Redeemer Nation,* p. 191.

32. Ibid., pp. 192ff.

33. Ibid., pp. 197ff.

34. Cited from Hudson, *Nationalism,* p. 74.

35. John Hope Franklin, *The Militant South: 1800-1861* (Boston: Beacon Press, 1964).

36. Cited by Franklin, *The Militant South,* p. 230.

37. James W. Silver, *Confederate Morale and Church Propaganda,* 2nd ed. (New York: W. W. Norton, 1967), p. 31.

38. Silver, *Confederate Morale,* p. 17.

39. On the strong connections between religion and Southern zeal for their cause, see the recent case study of Richmond by Harry S. Stout and Christopher Grasso, "Religion and Communications: Richmond as a Case Study," in Randall M. Miller, Harry S. Stout and Charles Reagan Wilson, eds. *Religion and the American Civil War* (New York: Oxford University Press, 1998).

40. Cited by Robert Penn Warren, *The Legacy of the Civil War: Meditations on the Centennial* (New York: Random House, Inc., 1961), p. 104.

41. Don E. Fehrenbacher, ed., *Abraham Lincoln: A Documentary Portrait Through His Speeches and Writings* (New York: Signet, 1964), p. 278.

42. Fehrenbacher, *Abraham Lincoln,* p. 279.

43. Thomas Harry Williams, et al., *A History of the United States since 1865,* 3rd ed. (New York: Alfred A. Knopf, 1969), p. 19.

44. Cited from Ralph Korngold's selection of Congressional testimony in *Thaddeus Stevens: A Being Darkly Wise and Rudely Great* (New York: Harcourt, Brace & Co., 1955), p. 305.

45. W. R. Brock, "Radical Ideology and the Weaknesses of Radical Reconstruction," in S. M. Schreiner, ed. *Reconstruction: A Tragic Era?* (New York: Holt, Rinehart & Winston, 1968), p. 94.

46. Cited by William A. Clebsch, *From Sacred to Profane America: The Role of Religion in American History* (New York: Harper & Row, 1968), pp. 195-96.

47. Cited by Tuveson, *Redeemer Nation,* pp. 203-4.

48. Warren, *Legacy,* pp. 59, 69.

49. Maclear, "Republic," p. 206.

50. See Frederick Merk, *Manifest Destiny and Mission in American History* (New York: Vintage, 1963); Walter LeFeber, *The New Empire: An Interpretation of American Expansion, 1860-1898* (Ithaca, NY: Cornell University Press, 1963).

51. Cited by Hudson, *Nationalism,* pp. 112-17.

52. Cited by Maclear, "Republic," p. 211.

53. Cited by Hudson, *Nationalism,* p. 111.

54. *Louisville Courier-Journal,* April 20, 1898; cited in *Annals of America,* vol. 12, p. 196.

55. Cited by Hudson, *Nationalism,* p. 121.

56. Walter Millis, *The Martial Spirit: A Study of Our War with Spain,* 2nd ed. (New York: Viking Press, 1965), p. xiii.

57. James Chace, "American Jingoism," *Harper's* (May, 1976), p. 39.

58. Cited by Hudson, *Nationalism,* p. 119.

59. *Annals of America,* vol. 14, pp. 65-69.

60. Williams et al., *History,* p. 387.

61. *Annals of America,* vol. 14, pp. 65-69.

62. Ibid., pp. 77-82.

63. Ibid., pp. 77-82.

64. Theodore Roosevelt, *The Foes of Our Own Household* (New York: Charles Scribner's Sons, 1926), p. 33.

65. Jess Yoder, "Preaching on Issues of War and Peace, 1915-1965," in DeWitte T. Holland et al., eds. *Preaching in American History: Selected Issues in the American Pulpit* (Nashville: Abingdon Press, 1969), pp. 239-57.

66. Cited by Ray H. Abrams, *Preachers Present Arms: The Role of the American Churches and Clergy in World Wars I and II, with Some Observations on the War in Vietnam,* rev. ed. (Scottdale, PA: Herald Press, 1969), p. 55.

67. Cited by George Parkin Atwater, "Peter Stood and Warmed Himself," *Atlantic Monthly,* vol. 121 (1918), p. 523.

68. Cited by Abrams, *Preachers Present Arms,* p. 117.

69. Kohn, *Nationalism,* p. 209.

70. Williams et al., *History,* p. 569.

71. Harry Scherman, "The Last Best Hope on Earth," *Atlantic Monthly* (Nov., 1941), p. 567.

72. *Annals of America,* vol. 16, pp. 89-90.

73. Ibid., p. 91.

74. Ibid., p. 104.

75. Ibid., p. 107.

76. See William Henry Chamberlin, *America's Second Crusade* (Chicago: Henry Regnery, 1950), pp. 285-310.

77. *Reader's Digest* (May, 1942), p. 49.

78. Cited by Chamberlin, *Crusade,* pp. 236-37.

79. Peter Marshall, "Quicken the Spirit Within You," *Reader's Digest* (Nov., 1942), p. 132.

80. Stanley High, "War Boom in Religion," *The American Magazine* (Nov., 1942), p. 132.

81. Yoder, "Preaching," p. 249.

82. *Christian Advocate* (Jan. 22, 1942), p. 29.

83. James Bryant Conant, *Our Fighting Faith: Five Addresses to College Students* (Cambridge, MA: Harvard University Press, 1942), pp. 21-22.

84. Williams et al., *History,* p. 620.

85. Chamberlin, *Crusade,* p. 342.

86. James Truslow Adams, "Why Are We Americans Different?" *Reader's Digest* (April, 1944), p. 4.

Notes to Chapter 6

1. George F. Kennan, *Memoirs, 1925-1950* (New York: Pantheon Books, 1967), p. 559.

2. Theodore Sorenson, "From the Eye of the Storm: the key moments of the Cuban Missile Crisis — as seen by a man who was in the thick of it," *Washington Monthly* (Nov. 1997), p. 25 (5).

3. See David McCullough, *Truman* (New York: Simon and Schuster, 1992), pp. 487-89. McCullough, p. 488, reports that Truman read advance copy and said that it would do "nothing but good."

4. James P. Warburg, *The United States in a Changing World: An Historical Analysis of American Foreign Policy* (New York: G. P. Putnam's Sons, 1954), p. 416.

5. Cited by McCullough, *Truman*, p. 490.

6. Cited by Eric F. Goldman, *The Crucial Decade: America, 1945-55* (New York: Alfred A. Knopf, 1956), p. 30.

7. Kennan, *Memoirs*, p. 559.

8. George F. Kennan, *Realities of American Foreign Policy*, 2nd ed. (New York: W. W. Norton, 1966), p. 16.

9. Ibid., p. 23.

10. Cited by *Look Magazine* (Aug. 26, 1969), p. 26.

11. Kennan, *Realities*, p. 83.

12. Kennan, *Realities*, p. 118.

13. Fred Inglis, *Cruel Peace: Everyday Life and the Cold War* (New York: Basic Books, 1991), p. 94.

14. Cited by Goldman, *Crucial Decade*, pp. 78-79.

15. Goldman, *Crucial Decade*, pp. 112-13.

16. Richard M. Nixon, *Six Crises* (Garden City, NY: Doubleday, 1962), p. 71.

17. *Annals of America*, vol. 16, p. 436.

18. Ibid., p. 563.

19. Ibid., p. 565.

20. Arthur A. Ekirch, *Ideas, Ideals, and American Diplomacy: A History of Their Growth and Interaction* (New York: Appleton-Century-Crofts, 1966), p. 186.

21. *The Pentagon Papers*, Commentary by Neil Sheehan (New York: Quadrangle Books, 1971), p. 9.

22. Cited by Thomas Harry Williams et al., *History of the United States since 1865*, 3rd ed. (New York: Knopf, 1969), p. 690.

23. Williams et al., *History*, p. 694.

24. Ibid., p. 693.

25. Goldman, *Crucial Decade*, pp. 205f.

26. Douglas MacArthur, *A Soldier Speaks: Public Papers and Speeches*, ed. by Vorin E. Whan, Jr. (New York: Frederick A. Praeger, 1965), pp. 263f.

27. Goldman, *Crucial Decade*, p. 208.

28. Cited by Louis L. Gerson, *John Foster Dulles* (New York: Cooper Square Publishers, 1967), pp. 87f.

29. Ibid., p. 16.

30. John Foster Dulles, "World Brotherhood Through the State," *Vital Speeches,* vol. 12 (1946), p. 744.

31. Cited by R. D. Challener and John Fenton, "Which Way America? Dulles Always Knew," *American Heritage,* vol. 22, June, 1971, p. 87.

32. Gerson, *Dulles,* p. 26.

33. John Foster Dulles, "Collaboration Must Be Practical," *Vital Speeches,* vol. 11 (1945), p. 248.

34. Cited by Deane and David Heller, *John Foster Dulles: Soldier for Peace* (New York: Holt, Rinehart & Winston, 1960), p. 120.

35. Cited by John R. Beal, *John Foster Dulles: A Biography* (New York: Harper & Brothers, 1957), p. 310.

36. John Foster Dulles, "Policy for security and peace," *Foreign Affairs* (April 1954), pp. 358-359 offers just one formulation of the doctrine.

37. Cited by Gerson, *Dulles,* p. 303.

38. Denna Frank Fleming, *The Cold War and Its Origins, 1917-1960* (Garden City, NY: Doubleday & Company, 1961), vol. 2, p. 692.

39. Cited from Townsend Hoopes's *The Devil and John Foster Dulles* by Stephen W. Twing, *Myths, Models, & U.S. Foreign Policy: The Cultural Shaping of Three Cold Warriors* (Boulder, CO: Lynne Rienner Publishers, 1998).

40. Gerson, *Dulles,* p. 175.

41. Ibid., p. 185.

42. Fleming, *Cold War,* vol. 2, p. 694.

43. *Des Moines Register,* July 9, 1971.

44. Cf. George McTurnan Kahin and John W. Lewis, *The United States in Vietnam,* 2d ed. (New York: Dell, 1969); Nina S. Adams and Alfred W. McCoy, eds., *Laos: War and Revolution* (New York: Harper & Row, 1970).

45. Frederick L. Schuman, *The Cold War: Retrospect and Prospect,* 2d ed. (Baton Rouge: Louisiana State University Press, 1967), pp. 88f.

46. See Schuman, *Cold War.*

47. Will Herberg, *Protestant — Catholic — Jew* (1960), cited by Conrad Cherry, *God's New Israel: Religious Interpretations of American Destiny* (Englewood Cliffs: Prentice-Hall, 1970), pp. 16-17.

48. Evelyn Lincoln, *My Twelve Years with John Kennedy* (New York: David McKay, p. 274); cited in Inglis, *Cruel Peace,* p. 151.

49. See the figures in Aleksandr Fursenko and Timothy Naftali, *'One Hell of a Gamble': The Secret History of the Cuban Missile Crisis* (New York: Norton, 1998), pp. 298-99.

50. Ernesto Betancourt, "Kennedy, Khrushchev, and Castro: a participant's view of the Cuban missile crisis," *Society* (July-August 1998), p. 77 (9).

51. Ibid.

52. John F. Kennedy, "Radio and Television Report to the American People on the Berlin Crisis," July 25, 1961.

53. See Stephen G. Rabe, "After the Missiles of October: John F. Kennedy and Cuba, November 1962 to November 1963," *Presidential Studies Quarterly* (Dec., 2000), p. 714. See note 30 for an account of Kennedy's denials and shifting of blame to Cuba itself.

54. Arthur Schlesinger, Jr., *A Thousand Days: John F. Kennedy in the White House* (Boston: Houghton-Mifflin, 1965), p. 841.

55. "A near tragedy of errors; alumni of the Cuban missile crisis review their lessons," *Time* (Feb. 13, 1989), p. 40.

56. Thomas Blanton, "Annals of Blinksmanship," *The Wilson Quarterly* (Summer 1997) <http://www.gwu.edu/~nsarchiv/nsa/cuba_mis-cri/annals.htm>, viewed Dec. 13, 2001.

57. Transcription quoted in Sorenson, "Eye of the Storm," p. 25.

58. Michael H. Hunt, *Lyndon Johnson's War: America's Cold War Crusade in Vietnam, 1945-1968* (New York: Hill and Wang, 1996), p. 76.

59. Johnson's words cited in Hunt, *Lyndon Johnson's War*, p. 81.

60. "Telephone Conversation Between President Johnson and Senator Richard Russell," Washington, May 27, 1964, 10:55 p.m. Source: U.S. Department of State, Office of the Historian, Foreign Relations of the United States 1964-1968, Volume 27, Mainland Southeast Asia; Regional Affairs, Washington, DC, Document No. 52.

61. (New York: Simon & Schuster, 2001); the summary used below is derived from Cal Thomas, "McGovern had it right," *Washington Times* (Nov. 18, 2001) <http://www.washingtontimes.com>, viewed Dec. 20, 2001.

62. Robert F. Kennedy, "Ending the War in Vietnam — Kansas State University, Mar. 18, 1968." Edwin O. Guthman and C. Richard Allen, eds. *RFK: Collected Speeches* (New York: Viking, 1993), pp. 288-298.

63. See Hunt, *Lyndon Johnson's War*, p. 116.

64. James Chace, "American Jingoism," *Harper's* (May, 1976), p. 42.

65. Richard Nixon, "Address to the American People," April 30, 1970. *Public Papers of the Presidents of the United States: Richard Nixon, 1970*, pp. 405-409.

Notes to Chapter 7

1. Cited by John Robert Greene, *The Presidency of Gerald R. Ford* (Lawrence: University Press of Kansas, 1995), p. 150; he uses Kissinger's remark as his chapter title for the *Mayaguez* incident.

2. Cited by Frances FitzGerald, *Way Out There in the Blue: Reagan, Star Wars, and the End of the Cold War* (New York: Simon and Schuster, 2000), p. 39.

3. *Encarta Encyclopedia* (CD-rom), "Prisoners of War, Vietnam."

4. Congressman Young, *Congressional Record*, H4062-3 (May 14, 1975), pp. 14395-96.

5. Congressman Baumann, *Congressional Record*, H4137 (May 15, 1975), p. 14510.

6. Congressman Burke, *Congressional Record*, H3962 (May 13, 1975), p. 14113.

7. Senator Dole, *Congressional Record*, S8347 (May 15, 1975), p. 14561.

8. Gerald Ford, *A Time to Heal: The Autobiography of Gerald R. Ford* (New York: Harper and Row, 1979), p. 280.

9. Ibid., p. 275.

10. Roy Rowan, *The Four Days of Mayaguez* (New York: W. W. Norton, 1975), p. 189.

11. Richard G. Head, *Crisis Resolution: Presidential Decision Making in the Mayaguez and Korean Confrontations* (Boulder, CO: Westview Press, 1978), p. 120.

12. Rowan, *Four Days,* pp. 220-21.

13. Ibid., p. 223.

14. *Congressional Record,* E2550 (May 20, 1975).

15. Head, *Crisis Resolution,* p. 284.

16. John F. Guilmartin, Jr., *A Very Short War: The Mayaguez and the Battle of Koh Tang* (College Station: Texas A&M Press, 1995), p. 150. Another treatment that details executive misjudgement is Ralph Wetterhahn, *The Last Battle: The Mayaguez Incident and the End of the Vietnam War* (New York: Carroll & Graf, 2001); this book includes interviews with Khmer Rouge military who were present at the execution of U.S. Marines stranded on Koh Tang. See also T. A. M. Smith's review, "Left Behind: 'The Last Battle' skewers the U.S. government for the *Mayaguez* Incident," *San Diego Union Tribune* (June 10, 2001), p. Books-5.

17. Patrick Anderson, "Peanut Farmer for President," *New York Times Magazine* (Dec. 14, 1975), p. 15.

18. Martin Schram, *Running for President 1976: The Carter Campaign* (New York: Stein and Day, 1977), p. 26.

19. Ibid., p. 5.

20. See Jody Powell's "White House Statement: The American Hostages in Iran" (November 9, 1979).

21. *Weekly Compilation of Presidential Documents,* "Lyndhurst, New Jersey" (Oct. 15, 1980), vol. 16, no. 42, p. 2265.

22. *Keeping Faith* (New York: Bantam, 1982), p. 4.

23. Don Oberdorfer, "Now That It's Over . . . The Press Needs to Reflect on Its Role," *Washington Journalism Review* (May 1981), pp. 37-38.

24. See the account of Christian Bourguet and the quote in Pierre Salinger, *America Held Hostage* (New York: Doubleday, 1981), pp. 218-19.

25. See, for example, "Flint, Michigan: Remarks and a Question and Answer Session at a Townhall Meeting." *Weekly Compilation of Presidential Documents,* vol. 16, no. 40, p. 1992.

26. A summary of the operation and photographs of the crash site can be seen in Sid Moody, *444 Days: The American Hostage Story* (New York: Rutledge Press, 1981), pp. 112-19.

27. Martin Schram, *The Great American Video Game: Presidential Politics in the Television Age* (New York: William Morrow, 1987), p. 26.

28. James Conaway, "Looking at Reagan," *Atlantic Monthly* (Oct., 1980), pp. 34, 33, 44.

29. Maureen Dowd, "Other Side of 'Gender Gap': Reagan Seen as Man's Man," *New York Times* (Sept. 17, 1984), pp. A1, 14.

30. James David Barber, "Political Illusionism," *New York Times* (April 26, 1984), p. 25.

31. Garry Wills, *Reagan's America,* p. 381.

32. Cited in the Chicago *Tribune* (October 30, 1980).

33. Bruce Bawer, "Ronald Reagan as Indiana Jones," *Newsweek* (Aug. 27, 1984), p. 14.

34. Citation from Fred Reed, "The Star Wars Swindle: Hawking Nuclear Snake Oil," *Harper's Magazine* (May, 1987), pp. 41, 48.

35. James Cracraft, "Let's Agree to Curb 'Star Wars,'" *Chicago Tribune* (October 16, 1986), p. 27.

36. Anthony Lewis, "Reagan's Dream," *New York Times* (Oct. 6, 1986), p. A27.

37. David Broder, "SDI and Reagan: What a Dream; What a Dreamer," *Chicago Tribune* (October 15, 1986), p. 23.

38. See Michael Paul Rogin, *Ronald Reagan the Movie* (Berkeley: University of California Press, 1987), p. 1.

39. Frances FitzGerald, *Way Out There in the Blue,* pp. 485-489.

40. See "Return of U.S. Unilateralism," *San Francisco Chronicle* (Dec. 14, 2001), p. A34.

41. Arthur Schlesinger, Jr., "The Two Faces of American Foreign Policy," *Chicago Sun-Times* (Oct. 16, 1983), p. 4.

42. *Weekly Compilation of Presidential Documents,* "Day of Thanksgiving for the Freed American Hostages" (Jan. 26, 1981), vol. 17, no. 5, p. 47.

43. See "Freed American Hostages, Remarks at White House Ceremony," *Weekly Compilation of Presidential Documents* (Jan. 21, 1981), vol. 17, no. 5, p. 49.

44. *Weekly Compilation of Presidential Documents,* "Trans World Airlines Hijacking Incident" (July 2, 1985), vol. 21, no. 27, p. 869.

45. Mark Mayfield, "Americans Support Grenada Invasion," *USA Today* (Oct. 31, 1983), p. 7A.

46. "Transcript of Address by President on Lebanon and Grenada," *New York Times* (Oct. 28, 1983), p. 5.

47. *New York Times* (Oct. 28, 1983), p. 5.

48. *Weekly Compilation of Presidential Documents,* "Ceremony for Medical Students from Grenada and U.S. Military Personnel" (Nov. 7, 1983), vol. 19, no. 45, p. 1537.

49. This material is adapted from Robert Jewett, "A Chance to Affirm the Law of Nations," *Christian Century* (Nov. 14, 1990), pp. 1054-55.

50. Daniel Patrick Moynihan, *On the Law of Nations* (Cambridge: Harvard University Press, 1990), p. 147.

51. Ibid., p. 144.

52. George C. Wilson, "Navy Missile Downs Iranian Jetliner," *Washington Post* (July 4, 1988), p. A1.

53. R. W. Apple, "Military Errors: The Snafu as History," *New York Times* (July 5, 1988), p. A8.

54. George Bush, "Inaugural Address," Jan. 20, 1989.

55. Lawrence Freedman and Efraim Karsh, *The Gulf Conflict, 1990-1991: Diplomacy and War in the New World Order* (Princeton, NJ: Princeton University Press, 1993), pp. 44-45.

56. See "Iraq's Occupation of Kuwait: Excerpts from Amnesty International's Report," in Micah L. Sifry and Christopher Cerf, eds. *The Gulf War: History, Documents, Opinions* (New York: Times Books, 1991), pp. 157-160.

57. George Bush, "Remarks at the Annual Convention of the National Religious Broadcasters," Jan. 28, 1991. <http://bushlibrary.tamu.edu/papers/1991/91012800.html>, viewed Jan. 13, 2002.

58. Ibid.

59. See Jack R. Van der Slik and Stephen J. Schwark, "Clinton and the New Covenant: Theology Shaping Politics or Old Politics in Religious Garb?" *Journal of Church and State* (Autumn, 1998), p. 873.

60. Van der Slik and Schwark, *Journal of Church and State,* p. 873.

61. Bill Clinton, "First Inaugural Address," January 21, 1993.

62. Thomas B. Edsall, "The Protean President," *The Atlantic Monthly* (May 1996), p. 42 (4).

63. Bill Clinton, "Second Inaugural Address," Jan. 20, 1997.

64. Andrew Sullivan, "Lies That Matter," *The New Republic* (Sept. 14 and 21, 1998); reprinted in Gabriel Fackre, ed. *Judgment Day at the White House* (Grand Rapids, Michigan: Eerdmans Publishing, 1999), p. 174.

65. Cited by William J. Bennett, *The Death of Outrage: Bill Clinton and the Assault on American Ideals* (New York: Free Press, 1998), p. 46. See also David Maraniss, *The Clinton Enigma: A Four-and-a-Half-Minute Speech Reveals This President's Entire Life* (New York: Simon & Schuster, 1998), pp. 70-75; Stanley A. Renshon, *High Hopes: The Clinton Presidency and the Politics of Ambition,* 2nd ed. (New York/London: Routledge, 1998), pp. 71-72, 271-72, 275-76, 297-98, 304.

66. Richard Roeper, "One thing's certain: Clinton is sorry, all right," *The Chicago Sun-Times* (August 18, 1998), p. 4.

67. Maraniss, *Clinton Enigma,* pp. 37-40.

68. Renshon, *High Hopes,* pp. 256-57.

69. Sullivan, "Lies That Matter," in *Judgment Day,* p. 175.

70. See "Calling for the Removal of U.S. Armed Forces Pursuant to the War Powers Act," House Republican Congress *Legislative Digest,* vol. 28, No. 11. Pt II, April 26, 1999, for a summary of the relevant facts about killings in Kosovo and a summary of constitutional issues arising out of the commitment of U.S. forces. The dissident Republicans authored a resolution attempting to force a U.S. withdrawal, losing on a 214-213 vote. They later sought a federal court order to stop the military action. See "Judge Dismisses House Members War Powers Suit against Clinton," CNN.com, June 8, 1999.

71. "Pentagon Report Whitewashes Civilian Deaths in Yugoslavia," *Human Rights Watch* (Feb. 8, 2000), <http://www.hrw.org/press/2000/02/nato208.htm>, viewed Nov. 15, 2001.

72. Steven Lee Myers, "Chinese Embassy Bombing: A Wide Net of Blame," *New York Times* (April 17, 2000), p. A1.

73. Van der Slik and Schwark, "Clinton and the New Covenant," p. 873.

Notes to Chapter 8

1. *Chicago Sun-Times* (Oct. 29, 1983).

2. Jerry Falwell, *Nuclear War and the Second Coming of Christ* (Pamphlet), quoted in Ronnie Dugger, "Does Reagan Expect a Nuclear Armageddon?" *Washington Post Outlook* (April 8, 1984).

3. For fantasies of selective nuclear destruction as God's purifying tool, see Paul Boyer, *Fallout: A Historian Reflects on America's Encounter with Nuclear Weapons* (Columbus: Ohio State University Press, 1998); citations from Falwell and McIntire, pp. 146-147.

4. See Paul Boyer, *When Time Shall Be No More: Prophecy Belief in Modern American Culture* (Cambridge: Belknap/Harvard University Press, 1992), p. 11, on the book phenomenon.

5. From Ronald Reagan's standard "The Speech" (in support of Barry Goldwater's nomination in 1964 and on other occasions) <http://reagan.webteamone.com/speeches/the_speech.html>, viewed Dec. 15, 2001.

6. Donald Wagner, "Reagan and Begin, Bibi and Jerry: the theopolitical alliance of the Likud party with the American Christian 'right,'" *Arab Studies Quarterly* (Sept. 22, 1998), p. 33.

7. Jerry Falwell, *Listen, America!* (New York: Bantam, 1981).

8. Jeffrey L. Sheler and Mike Tharp, "Dark Prophecies," *U.S. News and World Report* (Dec. 15, 1997), p. 62; Lindsey's book was the basis for a film narrated by Orson Welles — *The Late Great Planet Earth*. Dir. Robert Amram. Amram/RCR, 1976.

9. Tyndale House reported sales of more than 39 million copies of *Left Behind* materials, including audiotapes and children's versions; see "Desecration, Left Behind Book #9, Hits Stores October 31, 2001," Press Release from Tyndale House, May 14, 2001; *Desecration* was scheduled for an advance printing of 3 million copies.

10. See Josephine Massyngberde Ford, "Millennium," *The Anchor Bible Dictionary* (New York: Doubleday, 1992), vol. 4, pp. 832-34, for a convenient discussion of classic texts such as 1 Enoch 93; 2 Enoch 32:3-33; 2 Baruch 29–30; 39:3–40:4; 4 Ezra 7, 20; Sibylline Oracles 5:414-30; see also David E. Aune, "Chiliasmus," *Religion in Geschichte und Gegenwart*, Fourth Edition (Tübingen: Mohr Siebeck, 1999), vol. 2. pp. 136-37.

11. See Robert G. Clouse, ed. *The Meaning of the Millennium: Four Views* (Downers Grove, IL: InterVarsity Press, 1977).

12. See Brian E. Daley, "Chiliasm," *Encyclopedia of Early Christianity*, 2nd ed. (New York: Garland, 1997), vol. 1, pp. 238-41; see also his definitive study, *The Hope of the Early Church: Eschatology in the Patristic Age* (Cambridge: Cambridge University Press, 1991); also Christopher E. Hill, *Regnum Caelorum: Patterns of Future Hope in Early Christianity* (Oxford: Oxford University Press, 1992).

13. Nathan O. Hatch, *The Sacred Cause of Liberty* (New Haven: Yale University Press, 1977), chapter 1.

14. Catherine L. Albanese, "Dominant and Public Center: Reflections on the 'One' Religion of the United States," *South Atlantic Quarterly*, vol. 81 (1982), p. 28; article adapted from *America: Religions and Religion* (Belmont: Wadsworth, 1981); see also Boyer, *When Time Shall Be No More*, pp. 225-52.

15. See C. C. Goen, "Jonathan Edwards: A New Departure in Eschatology," *Church History*, vol. 27 (1959), pp. 25-40; Boyer, *When Time Shall Be No More*, pp. 71-72.

16. See Paul S. Boyer, "Chiliasmus. IV, Nordamerika," *Religion in Geschichte und Gegenwart*, 4th ed. (Tübingen: Mohr Siebeck, 1999), vol. 2, p. 139.

17. Boyer, "Chiliasmus. IV, Nordamerika," p. 139.

18. See Boyer, *When Time Shall Be No More*, pp. 81-84.

19. See Stephen D. O'Leary, *Arguing the Apocalypse: A Theory of Millennial Rhetoric* (New York/Oxford: Oxford University Press, 1994), pp. 93-133.

20. Timothy P. Weber, *Living in the Shadow of the Second Coming*, 2nd ed. (Grand Rapids, MI: Zondervan, 1984).

21. The Latin translation of 1 Thessalonians provided the root from which the term "rapture" sprang, whereas the original Greek term did not find its way into English.

22. Boyer, *When Time Shall Be No More*, p. 75, points out that Increase Mather referred to the Rapture in the early colonial period.

23. For orientation to the recent discussion, see James Callahan, *Primitivistic Piety: The Ecclesiology of the Early Plymouth Brethren* (Lanham: Scarecrow, 1996); a nuanced treatment is available in Russell Chandler, *Doomsday: The End of the World — A View through Time* (Ann Arbor: Servant Publications, 1993), pp. 108-09; Paul S. Boyer, "The Growth of Fundamentalist Apocalyptic in the United States," in *The Encyclopedia of Apocalypticism*. Vol. 3. *Apocalypticism in the Modern Period and the Contemporary Age*, Stephen J. Stein, ed. (New York: Continuum, 1998), pp. 149-51.

24. See the discussion of Margaret Macdonald's role in the Darbyite movement, and the discovery of earlier advocates of the rapture doctrine in Dave MacPherson, *The Rapture Plot* (Simpsonville, SC: Millennium III Publishers, 1995); Dave MacPherson, *The Great Rapture Hoax* (Fletcher, NC: New Puritan Library, 1983).

25. See Chandler, *Doomsday*, pp. 106-07; Boyer, *When Time Shall Be No More*, pp. 98, 158, reports that as many as ten million copies of this reference work have been sold since 1909, and that the 1967 edition alone, published by Oxford University Press, had sold 2.5 million copies by 1992.

26. Boyer, "Fundamentalist Apocalyptic," p. 168.

27. See Chandler, *Doomsday*, pp. 324-25; Erling Jorstad assesses the scale and influence of these evangelists in *The New Christian Right 1981–88: Prospects for the Post-Reagan Decade*, Studies in American Religion 25 (Lewiston: Mellen, 1987), pp. 153-69.

28. Wagner, "Reagan and Begin," p. 33.

29. See Boyer, "Fundamentalist Apocalyptic," pp. 164-69.

30. The debate about the place of the Rapture in the end-time sequence has, of course, been a major issue for fundamentalist churches and theologians for many years; see Richard R. Reiter et al., *The Rapture: Pre-, Mid-, or Post-Tribulational?* (Grand Rapids: Academie, 1984); Chandler, *Doomsday*, pp. 223-43.

31. Hal Lindsey, *The Terminal Generation* (Old Tappan, NJ: Fleming H. Revell, 1976); see the restatement of these views in *Planet Earth — 2000 A.D.* (Palos Verde, CA: Western Front, 1994).

32. Boyer, "Fundamentalist Apocalyptic," p. 167; see "Lindsey's Prophetic Timetable," in O'Leary, *Arguing the Apocalypse*, pp. 147-54.

33. See for example, Grant R. Jeffrey, *Messiah: War in the Middle East & the Road to Armageddon* (New York: Bantam, 1992, revised edition), p. 268; in *Armageddon: Appointment with Destiny* (New York: Bantam, 1990), p. 11, he calculates the battle will occur within a generation of from "forty to seventy years" starting with 1948; Roy H. Hicks appears to fit this time frame in *Another Look at the Rapture* (Tulsa: Harrison House, 1982), pp. 15-22. In *The Beginning of the End* (Wheaton: Tyndale, 1991), 194, Tim F. LaHaye claims it is "probable" that the generation beginning in 1948 will see the end times, but in *No Fear of the Storm* (Sisters, OR: Multnomah, 1992), he seems less sure. For a survey of this date setting, see Boyer, *When Time Shall Be No More*, pp. 187-90.

34. See the forceful critiques of Lindsey's scheme, from evangelical perspectives, by Cornelius Vanderwaal, *Hal Lindsey and Biblical Prophecy* (St. Catharines: Paideia Press, 1978; Neerlandia: Inheritance Publications, 1978, 1991); William M. Alnor, *Soothsayers of the Second Advent* (Old Tappan, NJ: Fleming H. Revell, 1989); Gary DeMar, *Last Days Mad-*

ness: The Folly of Trying to Predict When Christ Will Return (Brentwood: Wolgemuth & Hyatt, 1991); reprint under the title, *Last Days Madness: Obsession of the Modern Church* (Atlanta: American Vision, 1994); B. J. Oropeza, *99 Reasons Why No One Knows When Christ Will Return* (Downers Grove: InterVarsity, 1994); William R. Kimball, *The Rapture: A Question of Timing* (Joplin: College Press, 1985); from a Seventh-Day Adventist perspective, Samuele Bacchiocchi, *Hal Lindsey's Prophetic Jigsaw Puzzle* (Berrien Springs: Biblical Perspectives, 1985). A critique of Jehovah's Witness predictions focused in the period of 1979-80 is offered by Carl Olof Johnsson and Wolfgang Herbst, *The "Sign" of the Last Days — When?* (Atlanta: Commentary Press, 1987). In *Selling Fear: Conspiracy Theories and End-Times Paranoia* (Grand Rapids: Baker, 1997), pp. 184-86, Gregory S. Camp makes a case against Lindsey's conspiratorial argument.

35. For instance, see Marvin J. Rosenthal, *The Pre-Wrath Rapture of the Church* (Nashville: Nelson, 1990), and the critique of Rosenthal in Paul S. Karleen, *The Pre-Wrath Rapture of the Church: Is It Biblical?* (Langhorne: BF Press, 1991). Allen Beechick rejects the pretribulation scenario in *The Pretribulation Rapture* (Denver: Accent Books, 1980), following Robert H. Gundry, *The Church and the Tribulation* (Grand Rapids: Zondervan, 1973). Robert Van Kampen presents his own scenario in *The Rapture Question Answered: Plain and Simple* (Grand Rapids: Revell, 1997).

36. Quotation taken from Holger Jensen, "Trouble in paradise: a doomsday prophet wears out her welcome," *Maclean's* (May 7, 1990), p. 33; see also William Allman, "Fatal attraction: why we love doomsday," *U.S. News and World Report* (April 30, 1990), p. 12.

37. Joe Maxwell, "Camping misses end-time deadline," *Christianity Today* (Oct. 24, 1994), p. 84; see also Edmund D. Cohen, "Harold Camping and the stillborn apocalypse," *Free Inquiry* (Winter, 1994), p. 35.

38. See Sharon Linzey Georgianna, *The Moral Majority and Fundamentalism: Plausibility and Dissonance* (Lewiston: Mellen, 1989), pp. 26-29; Clyde Wilcox, *God's Warriors: The Christian Right in Twentieth-Century America* (Baltimore/London: Johns Hopkins University Press, 1992), pp. 95-96, 120-21; Wilcox, p. 132, found while surveying Moral Majority members in Ohio that most of them were in fact persons who had voted in previous elections. David G. Bromley, ed. *New Christian Politics* (Macon: Mercer, 1984); Robert C. Liebman and Robert Wuthnow, eds. *The New Christian Right: Mobilization and Legitimation* (Hawthorne: Aldine, 1983).

39. Jorstad, *New Christian Right*, pp. 17-19; Samuel S. Hill and Dennis E. Owen, *The New Religious Political Right in America* (Nashville: Abingdon, 1982), p. 43; Georgianna, *Moral Majority*, pp. 36-37, overlooks this key apocalyptic motivation in explaining how "fundamentalist sects became involved in politics." See also David Snowball, *Continuity and Change in the Rhetoric of the Moral Majority* (New York: Praeger, 1991), pp. 40-53.

40. For an account of these developments see Snowball, *Moral Majority*, pp. 151-60.

41. Donald Wagner, "Reagan and Begin, Bibi and Jerry: the theopolitical alliance of the Likud party with the American Christian 'right,'" *Arab Studies Quarterly* (Sept. 22, 1998), p. 33.

42. See the chapter on "The War Metaphor" in Snowball, *Moral Majority*, pp. 123-49; also O'Leary, *Arguing the Apocalypse*, pp. 172-93.

43. In his eighth book on this topic, *The Rapture: Truth or Consequences* (Toronto/New York: Bantam, 1983), Hal Lindsey gives no hint of this recalculation, nor indeed that

his earlier dating scheme had failed. Boyer notes, p. 176, in "Fundamentalist Apocalyptic," that in his later work, Lindsey "retreated from specific date setting."

44. See Rob Boston, *The Most Dangerous Man in America? Pat Robertson and the Rise of the Christian Coalition* (Amherst: Prometheus, 1996), p. 145, citing details from Pat Robertson, *The New Millennium* (Dallas: Word, 1990), p. 312 and other locations. Hubert Morken devotes a chapter (pp. 207-24) to Robertson's predictions throughout his career and about the relevance of the 1967 date (p. 222), in *Pat Robertson: Where He Stands* (Old Tappan: Fleming H. Revell, 1988). For a general assessment of Robertson's orientation, see Gerard Thomas Straub, *Salvation for Sale: An Insider's View of Pat Robertson's Ministry* (Buffalo, NY: Prometheus, 1986), and Boyer, "Fundamentalist Apocalyptic," p. 175.

45. See Russell Chandler, "Apocalypse Near?" *Los Angeles Times* (Sept. 30, 1990); N. W. Hutchings and ten other leaders agree that "within a few years, or even months . . . the events associated with the last seven years of the present dispensation will begin to occur," *Why I Still Believe . . . These Are the Last Days* (Oklahoma City: Harthstone, 1993), p. 3.

46. See Chandler, *Doomsday*, pp. 245-58, 275-85; for example, Marvin Moore argues that the fall of Communism in Eastern Europe is a sign that God "is preparing the world, and especially His people, for the final crisis," which will occur within the generation starting in 1975; see *The Crisis of the End Time: Keeping Your Relationship with Jesus in Earth's Darkest Hour* (Boise/Oshawa: Pacific Press Publishing Association, 1992), pp. 159, 43. Almost a million copies of John F. Walvoord's *Armageddon, Oil and the Middle East Crisis* (Grand Rapids: Zondervan, 1990, rev. ed.) were distributed in close proximity to the Persian Gulf conflict in 1991, interpreted as crucial in the end-time schedule. Edgar C. Whisenant sold 4.5 million copies of *On Borrowed Time: The Bible Dates of the 70th Week of Daniel, Armageddon, the Millennium; 88 reasons why the Rapture will be in 1988: the Feast of Trumpets (Rosh-Hash-Ana) September 11-12-13* (Nashville: World Bible Society, 1988), and then followed it up with other books that keep pushing the date toward the year 2000: *And Now the Earth's Destruction by Fire, Nuclear Bomb Fire: In World War III, World War IV and World War V at Armageddon* (Little Rock: by the author, 1994); *The Final Shout: Rapture Report 1989* (Nashville: World Bible Society, 1989); *120 Biblical Reasons for a Pre-Tribulation Rapture* (Little Rock: The Author, 1992). Harold Camping argues for various forms of "Biblical support" for 1994 as "the end of history" in *1994?* (New York: Vantage, 1992), pp. 481-83, 532; Dave Hunt in *How Close Are We?* (Eugene: Harvest House, 1993), p. 316, says that 1996 is the "most popular date at the moment" but refrains from making a specific prediction. Marvin Byers argued for 1996 as the "change of a millennium" with the Rapture occurring in 2000; see *The Final Victory: The Year 2000* (Shippensburg: Treasure House, 1991, 1994, 2nd ed.), pp. 254-57. Steve Terrell expects the millennium to begin in 2003 with the events of the 90's leading up to it, but is reluctant to set a date for the Rapture in *The 90's: The Decade of the Apocalypse: The European Common Market — The End Has Begun* (Plainfield: Bridge Publishing, 1992; 1994, rev. ed.), pp. 203-06; David Webber and Noah Hutchings argued that "events and conditions all around us foretell the soon return of Jesus Christ" in *Is This the Last Century?* (Nashville: Thomas Nelson, 1979), p. 33; speculating on the possible rebuilding of the Jerusalem temple, they suggest, p. 50, that 2001 might be the year for the beginning of the millennium. See also Lester Frank Sumrall, *I Predict 2000 A.D.* (South Bend: LESEA, 1987).

47. Boyer, *When Time Shall Be No More*, p. 339.

48. For example, James McKeever, *The Rapture Book: Victory in the End Times* (Medford: Omega, 1988); Peter and Patti Lalonde, *Left Behind* (Eugene: Harvest House, 1995); Paul McGuire, *From Earthquakes to Global Unity: The End Times Have Begun* (Lafayette: Huntington House, 1996).

49. For example, see Hart Armstrong, *The Last Seven on Earth, and the First Seven in Heaven* (Wichita: Christian Communications, 1994); Mark Finley, *2000 and Beyond* (Boise/Oshawa: Pacific Press Publishing Association, 1996); Jimmy Swaggart, *Armageddon: The Future of Planet Earth* (Baton Rouge: Jimmy Swaggart Ministries, 1987); David Chilton, *The Great Tribulation* (Fort Worth: Dominion, 1987); Hilton Sutton, *Rapture: Get Right or Get Left* (Tulsa: Harrison House, 1991); Charles Caldwell Ryrie, *What You Should Know about the Rapture* (Chicago: Moody Press, 1981); reprinted as *Come Quickly, Lord Jesus: What You Need to Know about the Rapture* (Eugene: Harvest House, 1996).

50. See Timothy A. James, *The Messiah's Return: Delayed?, Fulfilled?, or Double-Fulfillment* (Bradford: Kingdom Publications, 1991).

51. For example, Lewis R. Walton, *Advent! World Events at the End of Time* (Washington/Hagerstown: Review and Herald, 1986); Arnold Valentin Wallenkampf, *The Apparent Delay: What Role Do We Play in the Timing of Jesus' Return?* (Washington/Hagerstown: Review and Herald, 1994).

52. Dana Milbank, "Religious Right Finds Its Center in Oval Office," *Washington Post* (Dec. 24, 2001), p. A2, observes that the Christian Coalition is "declining. . . . Karl Rove, Bush's top political strategist, said that . . . 'We may be seeing to some degree some return to the sidelines of previously involved religious conservatives.'" We suggest that this decline as well as the resignation of Pat Robertson as leader of the Christian Coalition in December of 2001 may reflect the realization that his apocalyptic timetable has failed.

53. Pat Robertson, *America's Dates with Destiny* (Nashville: Nelson, 1986), p. 20; for an objective overview of his form of civil religion, see Stephen O'Leary and M. W. McFarland, "The Political Use of Mythic Discourse: Prophetic Interpretation in Pat Robertson's Presidential Campaign," *Quarterly Journal of Speech* 75 (Nov. 1989), pp. 433-52.

54. Pat Robertson, *The Secret Kingdom*, with Bob Slosser (Nashville: Nelson, 1987), p. 260.

55. Ibid., p. 266.

56. J. G. Church, "Keeping the Faith," *Time* (Aug. 18, 1986), p. 15.

57. Robertson, *Destiny*, p. 90.

58. Ibid., pp. 73-74.

59. Ibid., p. 95.

60. Ibid., p. 284.

61. Robertson, *Secret Kingdom*, pp. 185, 190.

62. Cited in Boyer, *When Time Shall Be No More*, p. 146; see also O'Leary's definitive study, *Arguing the Apocalypse*, pp. 212-24.

63. Pat Robertson, *The New Millennium* (Dallas: Word, 1990) p. 294.

64. See for example, Clifford Hill, "Editorial," *Prophecy Today*, vol. 17.6 (November/December, 2001), p. 7; Howard Phillips, "Lesson of 9/11," *The Christian Statesman*, vol. 144.6 (Nov.-Dec., 2001), p. 8.

65. See Michael Barkun, "Introduction: Understanding Millennialism," in M. Barkun,

ed. *Millennialism and Violence,* Cass Series on Political Violence 2 (London/Portland: Frank Cass & Co. Ltd., 1999), pp. 6-7.

66. Barkun, "Introduction," p. 8, argues that traditional millenarian movements are in recent decades "being supplanted by what might be called *eclectic millenarianism.*"

67. Gershom Gorenberg, *The End of Days: Fundamentalism and the Struggle for the Temple Mount* (New York: Free Press, 2000), p. 174. Gorenberg is senior editor of *Jerusalem Report* and an Associate of the Center for Millennial Studies in Boston.

68. Ibid., p. 167.

69. Ibid., p. 41.

70. Ibid., p. 112.

71. Ibid., p. 118.

72. Ibid., p. 136.

73. Ibid., p. 187.

74. Ibid., p. 189.

75. Ibid., p. 44.

76. Ibid., p. 244.

77. Ibid., p. 235.

78. Ibid., p. 236.

79. Mark Juergensmeyer, *Terror in the Mind of God: The Global Rise of Religious Violence* (Berkeley: University of California Press, 2000), p. 243.

80. J. Christiaan Beker, *Paul's Apocalyptic Gospel* (Philadelphia: Fortress, 1982); see also Robert Jewett, *Paul the Apostle to America* (Louisville: Westminster/John Knox, 1994), pp. 10-12, 24.

81. See Boyer, *Fallout,* p. 15.

82. Frances FitzGerald, *Way Out There in the Blue: Reagan, Star Wars, and the End of the Cold War* (New York: Simon and Schuster, 2000), p. 460.

Notes to Chapter 9

1. Lisa Beyer, "Middle East: killer without shame," *Time International* (April 8, 1996).

2. Cited by Mark Juergensmeyer, *Terror in the Mind of God* (Berkeley: University of California Press, 2000), p. 71; the martyr quoted is Abdullah Azzam; the "smiling boy" was part of the collection of Hamas videotapes gathered by Anne Marie Oliver and Paul Steinberg.

3. Karen Armstrong, *Islam: A Short History* (New York: Modern Library, 2000), p. 6.

4. John L. Esposito, *Islam: The Straight Path* (New York/Oxford: Oxford University Press, 1998), p. 93.

5. Esposito, *Islam,* p. 15.

6. Ibid., p. 116.

7. Esposito, *Islam,* p. 118; Bernard Lewis, "The Revolt of Islam: When did the conflict with the West begin, and how could it end?" *The New Yorker* (Nov. 19, 2001), p. 59, lists the death date of Wahhab as 1787.

8. Tariq Ali, "The Real Muslim Extremists," *New Statesman* (Oct. 1, 2001), p. 30.

9. Stephen Schwartz, *The Spectator* (Oct. 19, 2001), p. 1.

10. Ibid., p. 2.

11. Esposito, *Islam*, p. 119.

12. Ali, "The Real Muslim Extremists," p. 30; see also Stephen Schwartz, *The Spectator* (Oct. 19, 2001), p. 3.

13. Schwartz, *The Spectator*, p. 3.

14. Ahmed Rashid, *Taliban: Militant Islam, Oil and Fundamentalism in Central Asia* (New Haven: Yale University Press, 2000), p. 132.

15. See the discussions of the 11-13th century "Assassin" movement in Lewis, "The Revolt of Islam," p. 61; also Erdmute Heller, "Sterben ist wichtiger als Töten," *SZ am Wochenende. Feuilleton-Beilage der Süddeutschen Zeitung* (Oct. 20-21, 2001), p. 1.

16. Esposito, *Islam*, p. 162.

17. Ibid., p. 166.

18. For an assessment of the grim statistics of poverty and inadequate development of Islamic countries in comparison with the rest of the world, see Lewis, "The Revolt of Islam," pp. 57-58.

19. See Michael Pohly and Khalid Duran, *Osama bin Laden und der internationale Terrorismus* (Munich: Ullstein List Verlag, 2001), p. 21.

20. Ibid., pp. 21-22.

21. Ibid., p. 22.

22. Ibid., p. 24.

23. Quoted in Abdullah Bin Omar, "The Striving Sheikh: ABDULLAH AZZAM," *Nida'ul Islam* (July-Sept. 1996), <http://www.islam.rog.au/articles/14/AZZAM.HTM>, viewed Jan. 20, 2002.

24. See Pohly and Duran, *Terrorismus*, pp. 30-31.

25. See Pohly and Duran, *Terrorismus*, pp. 40-64.

26. Ruel Marc Gerecht, "The Gospel According to Osama Bin Laden," *Atlantic Monthly* (January, 2002), p. 46.

27. Ibid., p. 47.

28. We therefore do not find it necessary to speculate with Ron Rosenbaum in "Degrees of Evil: Some thoughts on Hitler, bin Laden, and the hierarchy of wickedness," *The Atlantic Monthly* (Feb. 2002), p. 68, that both men share "The final malignant twist of wickedness: turning the murder of innocents, turning public tragedy, into private comedy."

29. Cited by Gerecht, "Osama Bin Laden," p. 47.

30. Ibid., p. 48.

31. Ibid., p. 46.

32. Pohly and Duran, *Terrorismus*, pp. 76-77.

33. See Armstrong, *Islam*, pp. 184-87; Esposito, *Islam*, pp. 50-52.

34. Jürgen Todenhöfer, "Ein mit Dollars beladener Esel kommt weiter als jede Armee," *Süddeutsche Zeitung* (Dec. 29-30, 2001), p. 14.

35. Marianne Williamson, *The Healing of America* (New York: Simon & Schuster, 1997), pp. 315-16.

36. Cited by Gershom Gorenberg, *The End of Days* (New York: Basic Books, 2000), p. 43. Gorenberg draws upon the work of the Islamic scholar David Cook, who has traced the history of apocalyptic violence in Islam. An overview of Cook's findings is conveyed in

David Cook, "Islam's Apocalypse" (Interview), *Presence Magazine*, <http://www.christian-ity.com>, viewed Jan. 2002.

37. Heribert Prantl, "Die Gewalt der Frommen," *Süddeutsche Zeitung* (Dec. 29-30, 2001), p. 4.

38. See the U.S. State Department's "Background Notes: Israel, December 1998," released by its Bureau of Near Eastern Affairs from principal conflicts, U.N. resolutions, and treaties that have been central to the conflict. <http://www.state.gov/www/background_notes/israel_1298_bgn.html>, viewed Feb. 5, 2002.

39. Citation from William Whiston, tr., *The Works of Josephus* (Peabody, MA: Hendrickson Publishers, 1987), Book 7, Chapter 9, sections 393 and 398.

40. Susan Hattis Rolef, ed., *Political Dictionary of the State of Israel* (New York: Macmillan, 1987), p. 214.

41. An extensive account of the Masada legend comes from Nachman Ben-Yehuda, *The Masada Myth: Collective Memory and Mythmaking in Israel* (Madison: University of Wisconsin Press, 1995). The Israeli Ministry of Tourism presents an uplifting version of the story at its website, <http://www.us-israel.org/jsource/judaism/masada.html>, viewed Nov. 19, 2001.

42. Cited in Martin Gilbert, *A History of the Twentieth Century*, vol. 3, *1952-1999* (New York: HarperCollins, 1999), p. 366.

43. Ibid., p. 462.

44. All citations in this paragraph are from Herb Keinon, "A victory remembered as a defeat," *Jerusalem Post* (Sept. 25, 1998), p. 15. See also Charles S. Liebman, "The myth of defeat: the memory of the Yom Kippur War in Israeli society," *Middle Eastern Studies* (July, 1993), pp. 399ff., for a well-developed analysis of war and mythology in Israel.

45. Karen Armstrong, *The Battle for God* (New York: Ballantine, 2000), p. 350; citations from Kahane, p. 349; Martin E. Marty and R. Scott Appleby, *The Glory and the Power: The Fundamentalist Challenge to the Modern World* (Boston: Beacon Press, 1992), pp. 103-109, describe divisions within Gush Emunim over the tactics of violence in confronting Arabs.

46. Armstrong, *Battle for God*, p. 286; italics in original.

47. Ehud Sprinzak, *Brother Against Brother: Violence and Extremism in Israeli Politics from Altalena to the Rabin Assassination* (New York: Free Press, 1999), pp. 213-14.

48. Yehuda Etzion's *The Temple Mount*, cited in Sprinzak, *Brother Against Brother*, p. 164.

49. Sprinzak, *Brother Against Brother*, p. 165.

50. Gershom Gorenberg, *The End of Days: Fundamentalism and the Struggle for the Temple Mount* (New York: Free Press, 2000), pp. 203-204.

51. Ibid., p. 204.

52. Ibid., p. 2.

53. Ibid., p. 205.

54. Ibid., p. 207.

55. Allan C. Brownfeld, "Israel and Judaism: Growth of Religious Extremism in Israel Threatens the Peace Process," *Washington Report on Middle East Affairs* (Aug.-Sept., 2000), pp. 72-74.

56. Gorenberg, *The End of Days*, p. 207.

57. Allan Brownfeld describes the vituperation against Rabin in the ultra-Orthodox weekly *HaShavua* ("The Week") that "regularly called Rabin 'a Kapo,' 'an anti-Semite,' 'ruthless,' and 'a pathological liar' [and] . . . published a symposium on the question of whether Rabin deserved to die and the appropriate means of executing him. By the critical summer of 1995 *HaShavua* went so far as to charge that Rabin and Peres "are leading the state and its citizens to annihilation and must be placed before a firing squad." See Allan C. Brownfeld, "Israel and Judaism."

58. Gilbert, *A History*, p. 805.

59. Lisa Beyer, "Middle East: killer without shame," *Time International* (April 8, 1996); see also Heribert Prantl, "Die Gewalt der Frommen," *Süddeutsche Zeitung* (Dec. 29-30, 2001), p. 4.

60. Quoted in Amir Taheri, *Holy Terror: The Inside Story of Islamic Terrorism* (London: Sphere Books, 1987), p. 7.

61. Juergensmeyer, *Terror in the Mind of God*, p. 72.

62. Ibid., p. 76.

63. David Remnick, "Letter from Jerusalem: The Dreamer," *The New Yorker* (Jan. 7, 2002), p. 56; these views were stated in an interview with Remnick.

64. Ehud Sprinzak, "Kahane: The Nightmare That Liberal Ideologues Could Not Imagine," *Los Angeles Times* (Nov. 1, 1990), p. A1.

65. Thorsten Schmitz, "Der neue Glanz des Davidsterns," *Süddeutsche Zeitung* (Nov. 23, 2001), p. 3. See also Moshe Zimmermann, "Die letzte Strophe," *Süddeutsche Zeitung* (Dec. 17, 2001), p. 13, which reports on the united patriotism of secular Zionists and orthodox settlers, turning the conflict between Jews and Arabs into one between Israel and Islam.

66. Alexander Zvielli, "Rebellion, Pride and Death," *The Jerusalem Post* (Aug. 15, 1997), p. 26.

67. The estimate is mentioned in Robert Jay Lifton's *Destroying the World to Save It: Aum Shinrikyo, Apocalyptic Violence, and the New Global Terrorism* (New York: Metropolitan Books, 1999), p. 37.

68. Cited from Shoko Asahara's *Disaster Approaches* in Juergensmeyer, *Terror in the Mind of God*, p. 109.

69. Lifton, *Destroying the World*, p. 41.

70. Ibid., p. 68.

71. Words are those of Ian Reader, a scholar who studied the document; citation contained in Juergensmeyer, *Terror in the Mind of God*, p. 114.

72. Lifton, *Destroying the World*, pp. 87-88.

73. Edward W. Desmond, "Japan: Under arrest — finally two months after the incident, police seize the alleged mastermind of the subway gas attack," *Time* (May 29, 1995), p. 46.

74. Reinhold Niebuhr, *Moral Man and Immoral Society* (New York: Scribners, 1932/1960), p. 99.

75. Reinhold Niebuhr, *Children of Light and the Children of Darkness* (London: Nisbet and Co., 1945), pp. 93-94.

76. Cited from John Saltmarsh, *Smoke in the Temple* (London, 1646), p. 16, by Niebuhr in *Children of Light*, p. 95.

Notes to Chapter 10

1. Leonard Peikoff, "It Is Time to Declare War," September 20, 2001, posted at <http://www.peikoff.com>, viewed Oct. 15, 2001.

2. Norman H. Snaith, "Jealous, zealous," *A Theological Word Book of the Bible*, ed. by Alan Richardson (New York: Macmillan, 1950), p. 115.

3. Johannes Pedersen, *Israel: Its Life and Culture* (London: Oxford University Press, 1926), vols. 3-4, p. 620.

4. Ibid.

5. Albrecht Stumpff, "zelos," etc., in Gerhard Kittel, ed. *Theological Dictionary of the New Testament*, tr. and ed. by Geoffrey W. Bromiley, vol. 2 (Grand Rapids: Wm. B. Eerdmans Publishing Company, 1964), pp. 877ff.

6. Martin Hengel, *The Zealots* (Edinburgh: T&T Clark, 1989), pp. 224-28.

7. John L. Esposito, *Islam: The Straight Path* (New York/Oxford: Oxford University Press, 1998), 3d ed., pp. 93, 166; Karen Armstrong, *Islam: A Short History* (New York: Modern Library, 2000), p. 6, defines jihad as "the effort to live in the way that God intended for human beings." She describes, pp. 168-70, the radicalization of jihad as a form of holy war against non-Islamic influences in modern "fundamentalist ideologues."

8. David Rhoads, "Zealots," *Anchor Bible Dictionary* (New York: Doubleday, 1992), vol. 6, p. 1044.

9. See *The Random House Dictionary of the English Language* (New York: Random House, 1967).

10. Rhoads, "Zealots," p. 1044; while Phinehas was the "prototype of such zeal," other biblical figures such as Simeon, Levi, Elijah, Josiah, and the Maccabees follow this model. For an analysis of the Phinehas episode and its impact on later developments, see Torrey Seland, *Establishment Violence in Philo and Luke* (Leiden: Brill, 1995), pp. 42-67.

11. "The Phineas Priesthood," *The Christian Century* (Sept. 8, 1999), p. 842.

12. See Michael Barkun, *Religion and the Racist Right: The Origins of the Christian Identity Movement* (Chapel Hill: University of North Carolina Press, 1994), p. 115. Connections between Christian Identity and the views shared by Timothy McVeigh have been analyzed in Mark Juergensmeyer, *Terror in the Mind of God: The Global Rise of Religious Violence* (Berkeley: University of California Press, 2000), pp. 30-36. For an appraisal of the religious dimension of McVeigh's "insurrection," see Garry Wills, *A Necessary Evil: A History of American Distrust of Government* (New York: Simon and Schuster, 1999), pp. 204-6.

13. "Cromwell, Oliver," *Encyclopaedia Britannica* (1963 edition), vol. 6, p. 797.

14. Michael L. Walzer, *The Revolution of the Saints* (Cambridge: Harvard University Press, 1965), p. 72.

15. William Styron, *The Confessions of Nat Turner* (New York: Random House, 1967), pp. 306f.

16. Styron, *Nat Turner*, p. 392.

17. Robert Penn Warren, *The Legacy of the Civil War* (New York: Random House, 1961), p. 22.

18. Comer Vann Woodward, *The Burden of Southern History* (Baton Rouge: Louisiana State University Press, 1960), p. 43.

19. Allan Nevins, *The Emergence of Lincoln,* vol. 2, *Prologue to Civil War, 1859-1861* (New York: Charles Scribner's Sons, 1950), p. 9.

20. Ibid., pp. 95f.

21. Thomas J. Meming, "The Trial of John Brown," *American Heritage* (Aug., 1967), p. 100; italics in original.

22. Woodward, *Burden,* p. 55.

23. Ralph Waldo Emerson, *Miscellanies* (Boston, 1884), p. 268.

24. Henry David Thoreau, *Anti-Slavery and Reform Papers* (Montreal: Harvest House, 1963), p. 44.

25. Ibid., p. 64.

26. Ibid., p. 54.

27. Cited by Ken Chowder, "The Father of American Terrorism," *American Heritage* (Feb. 2000), p. 81.

28. Ken Chowder, "The Father of American Terrorism," p. 81.

29. Winthrop S. Hudson, ed., *Nationalism and Religion in America* (New York: Harper & Row, 1970), p. xi.

30. Arnold S. Rice, *The Ku Klux Klan in American Politics* (Washington, DC: Public Affairs Press, 1963), p. 24.

31. Senator John McCain, "No Substitute for Victory," *Wall Street Journal* (Oct 26, 2001).

32. Leonard Peikoff, "It Is Time to Declare War."

33. Cited by Hans Kohn, *American Nationalism* (New York: Macmillan, 1957), p. 185.

34. *Annals of America,* vol. 12, p. 196.

35. *Annals of America,* vol. 14, pp. 77-82.

36. Allen Drury, "Inside the White House," *Look* (Oct. 19, 1971), p. 52.

37. Dee Brown, *Bury My Heart at Wounded Knee: An Indian History of the American West* (New York: Bantam Books, Inc., 1972), p. 31.

38. Colonel Harry G. Summers, Jr., *On Strategy* (Novato, CA: Presidio Press, 1982), takes Clausewitz's theories of war and works out a "lack of will" theory to account for the failure of U.S. military power in Vietnam.

39. Peter Homans, "Puritanism Revisited: An Analysis of the Contemporary Screen-Image Western," *Studies in Public Communication,* vol. 3 (1961), pp. 73-84.

40. The story of My Lai, its investigation, trials, and public response, has been recounted in numerous volumes. One of the most balanced in viewpoints is David L. Anderson, ed. *Facing My Lai: Moving Beyond the Massacre* (Lawrence: University Press of Kansas, 1998).

41. Eric Severeid, "American Militarism: What Is It Doing to *Us?*" *Look* (Aug. 12, 1969), p. 25.

42. Herbert C. Kelman and Lee H. Lawrence, "Violent Man: American Response to the Trial of Lt. William L. Calley," *Psychology Today* (June, 1972), p. 41.

43. Ibid., p. 45.

44. Winfried Thiel, "Jehu," *Anchor Bible Dictionary* (New York: Doubleday, 1992), vol. 3, p. 670.

45. Thiel, "Jehu," pp. 671-72.

46. See ibid., p. 672.

47. Owen C. Whitehouse, "Jehu," *A Dictionary of the Bible*, ed. by James Hastings (New York: Charles Scribner's Sons, 1905), vol. 2, p. 565; see also John Bright, *A History of Israel* (Philadelphia: The Westminster Press, 1959), p. 235.

48. Richard H. Schulz, Jr., *The Secret War Against Hanoi: Kennedy's and Johnson's Use of Spies, Saboteurs, and Covert Warriors in North Vietnam* (New York: HarperCollins, 1999). The book draws upon previously classified files of the Pentagon.

49. *Des Moines Register* (June 14, 1971).

50. Stanley Karnow, *St. Paul Pioneer Press* (Nov. 27, 1970).

51. From the speech by Lyndon B. Johnson, Aug. 29, 1964, at the Johnson Ranch. Cited in *The Pentagon Papers* (New York: Quadrangle, 1971), p. 311.

52. *Pentagon Papers*, p. 310.

53. Stanley Karnow, *St. Paul Pioneer Press* (Nov. 27, 1970).

54. See our discussion above in chapter 6, based upon Michael Beschloss, *Reaching for Glory: The Johnson White House Tapes, 1964-1965* (New York: Simon and Schuster, 2001).

55. *Des Moines Register* (May 2, 1970).

56. *Des Moines Register* (Nov. 8, 1971).

57. Richard Nixon, *Six Crises* (Garden City, NY: Doubleday, 1962), p. 347.

58. *Des Moines Register*, July 17, 1971.

59. See the March 3 and 17, 1972, issues of *National Review*, which are devoted to "Thoughts on Chairman Nixon's Visit" and "Did Nixon Surrender?"

60. *New York Times* (Aug. 1, 1971), p. E11.

61. Warren, *Legacy*, p. 20.

62. Warren, *Legacy*, pp. 22-23.

63. Ibid., p. 74.

64. Christopher Hitchens, *The Trial of Henry Kissinger* (New York/London: Verso, 2001), has taken inspiration from the arrest of Pinochet in Spain and proposed a war crimes trial for Henry Kissinger. He bases his case on recent Freedom of Information disclosures by the CIA in connection with murders and kidnappings in Peru and the United States involving the oversight of Kissinger. For the revelations about Peru, for example, see the government report posted at <http://foia.state.gov/HincheyReport.htm#6>, viewed February 25, 2002.

65. See Gerhard von Rad, *Old Testament Theology*, vol. 1, tr. by D. M. G. Stalker (New York: Harper & Row, Publishers, Inc., 1962), pp. 203-219; Ernst Käsemann, *Jesus Means Freedom*, tr. by Frank Clarke (Philadelphia: Fortress Press, 1970), pp. 31-41; also Robert Jewett, *Christian Tolerance: Paul's Message to the Modern Church* (Philadelphia: Westminster Press, 1982), pp. 68-91.

66. See John Lawrence, "The Moral Attractiveness of Violence," *Journal of Social Philosophy*, Fall, 1970, p. 5.

67. Horace J. Bridges, "The Duty of Hatred," *Atlantic Monthly*, vol. 122 (1918), p. 464.

68. Rollo May, *Love and Will* (New York: W. W. Norton, 1969), pp. 28-33.

69. See H. L. Strack and P. Billerbeck, *Kommentar zum Neuen Testament aus Talmud and Midrasch*, vol. 3, pp. 94f.

70. See Bo Ivar Reicke, *The New Testament Era: The New Testament Era from 500 B.C. to A.D. 200*, tr. by D. E. Green (Philadelphia: Fortress Press, 1968), pp. 127-195; Hugh J.

Schonfield, *The Passover Plot: New Light on the History of Jesus* (New York: Bernard Geis Associates, 1966), pp. 21-32.

71. See William R. Herzog III, *Jesus, Justice, and the Reign of God* (Louisville: Westminster/John Knox, 2000), p. 216: "In a society filled with honor-shame ripostes, it was easy for anger to escalate into name calling ("you fool") with hellish consequences."

72. See Eugen Drewermann, *Das Matthäusevangelium. Erster Teil: Mt 1,1–7,29* (Olten and Freiburg: Walter-Verlag, 1992), pp. 453-54; Hubert Frankenmölle, *Matthäus Kommentar 1* (Düsseldorf: Patmos Verlag, 1994), p. 232.

73. Jürgen Becker, *Jesus of Nazareth,* tr. by J. E. Crouch (New York: de Gruyter, 1998), pp. 254-58, shows how the "enemy" replaces the Jewish neighbor as the context of the love command.

74. See Robert Jewett, *Letter to Pilgrims: A Commentary on the Epistle to the Hebrews* (New York: Pilgrim Press, 1981), pp. 185-240.

Notes to Chapter 11

1. Senator Joseph McCarthy, "The History of George Catlett Marshall — 1951," *The Congressional Record: Proceedings and Debates of the 82nd Congress, First Session, Volume 97, Part 5* (May 28, 1951–June 27, 1951), pp. 6556-6603.

2. "The Ladenese Epistle, Part I," published online at http://washingtonpost.com, which explains its history as follows: "Written in August 1996, it was published in Al Quds Al Arabi, a London-based newspaper that bin Laden has often used to communicate his views. The text presented here was translated by the Committee for the Defense of Legitimate Rights, a pro–bin Laden organization, and posted on the Internet in October 1996." Original spellings and syntax are preserved.

3. Louis J. Halle, *The Cold War as History* (New York: Harper & Row, 1967), p. 414.

4. Petra Steinberger, "Die Wahrheit liegt irgendwo da draußen," *Süddeutsche Zeitung* (Dec. 29-30, 2001), p. 13, argues that conspiratorial thinking is particularly characteristic of the USA and the Middle East. "The best conspiratorial theories flourish these days in America and the Middle East, and are a substantial aspect of social and political discourse." She refers to the study by the American historian, Robert Goldberg, *Enemies Within: The Culture of Conspiracy in Modern America,* which argues that "conspiracy theories nourish the feeling of belonging to a nation in that one thereby discovers the enemies of the American dream."

5. For an analysis of the links between millennialism and conspiracy thinking, see Michael Barkun, "End-Time Paranoia: Conspiracy Thinking at the Millennium's Close," in C. Kleinhenz and F. J. LeMoine, eds. *Fearful Hope: Approaching the New Millennium* (Madison: University of Wisconsin Press, 1999), pp. 171-76.

6. Paul S. Minear, *I Saw a New Earth: An Introduction to the Visions of the Apocalypse* (Washington, DC: Corpus Books, 1968).

7. See Barkun, "End-Time Paranoia," p. 175: the conspiracy theory concerning a "New World Order" makes "Armageddon possible by conjuring up a suitably demonic adversary. . . ."

8. Bernard Bailyn, *The Ideological Origins of the American Revolution* (Cambridge: Harvard University Press, 1967), pp. 158f.

9. Arthur M. Schlesinger, *Nothing Stands Still* (Cambridge: Harvard University Press, 1969), pp. 182-184.

10. David Brion Davis, *The Slave Power Conspiracy and the Paranoid Style* (Baton Rouge: Louisiana State University Press, 1971).

11. Eric Foner, *Free Soil, Free Labor, Free Men: The Ideology of the Republican Party Before the Civil War* (New York: Oxford University Press, 1972).

12. William W. Freehling, "Paranoia and American History," *The New York Review of Books* (Sept. 23, 1971), p. 39.

13. See Robert K. Murray, *Red Scare: A Study in National Hysteria, 1919-1920* (Minneapolis: University of Minnesota Press, 1955).

14. Murray, *Red Scare,* p. 265.

15. Eric F. Goldman, *The Crucial Decade: America, 1945-55* (New York: Knopf, 1956), p. 123.

16. Goldman, *Crucial Decade,* pp. 212f.

17. Richard Harris, "The Annals of Politics," *The New Yorker* (Nov. 22, 1969), p. 113.

18. Harris, "Annals of Politics," p. 171.

19. Billy James Hargis, *Communism, The Total Lie* (Tulsa, OK: Christian Crusade, 1963), p. 7.

20. *Christian Crusade* (Aug., 1963), p. 15.

21. *Christian Crusade* (March, 1966), p. 12.

22. *Weekly Crusader* (Jan. 18, 1963), p. 6.

23. Cited by Peter Schrag, "America's Other Radicals," *Harper's Magazine* (Aug., 1970), p. 38.

24. See Barkun, "End-Time Paranoia," pp. 174-77, for a parallel phenomenon in New World Order conspiracy theories.

25. From Jerry Rubin's *Do It* (1970), quoted in Paul Hollander, *Political Pilgrims: Travels of Western Intellectuals to the Soviet Union, China, and Cuba, 1928-1978* (New York: Harper & Row, 1981), pp. 186-187.

26. Todd Gitlin, *The Sixties: Years of Hope, Days of Rage* (New York: Bantam Books, 1993), p. 397.

27. Quotations from Todd Gitlin, *The Sixties,* p. 399 for Dohrn citation, p. 404 for Rubin.

28. Cited from *The Chronicle of Higher Education* (Oct. 5, 1970), p. 5.

29. Robert A. Goldberg, *The Enemies Within: The Culture of Conspiracy in Modern America* (New Haven: Yale University Press, 2001).

30. Barkun, "End-Time Paranoia," p. 176.

31. Ibid., p. 176.

32. Ibid., p. 177.

33. See Barkun, "End-Time Paranoia," pp. 177-79.

34. George McTurnan Kahin and John W. Lewis, *The United States in Vietnam,* 2d ed. (New York: Dell, 1969), pp. 18, 30.

35. Ibid., p. 31.

36. Hans Morgenthau, "Reflections on the End of the Republic," *The New York Review of Books* (Sept. 24, 1970), p. 39.

37. *Pentagon Papers* (New York: Quadrangle, 1971), p. 6.

38. Ibid., p. 7.

39. Ibid., p. 7.

40. Halle, *Cold War*, p. 317.

41. Lewis H. Lapham, "Military Theology," *Harper's Magazine* (July, 1971), p. 73.

42. Lapham, "Military Theology," p. 84.

43. Cited in *Harper's Magazine* (June, 1969), p. 37.

44. See Jürgen Becker, *Jesus of Nazareth* (New York: de Gruyter, 1998), pp. 62-64.

45. See Robert Jewett, *Jesus Against the Rapture* (Philadelphia: Westminster Press, 1979), pp. 34-50; Wolfgang Wiefel, *Das Evangelium nach Lukas*, Theologischer Handkommentar zum Neuen Testament 3 (Berlin: Evangelische Verlagsanstalt, 1988), pp. 199-200; Susan Garrett, *The Demise of the Devil: Magic and the Demonic in Luke's Writings* (Minneapolis: Fortress, 1989), pp. 51-52.

46. See Josef Ernst, *Das Evangelium nach Lukas* (Regensburg: Friedrich Pustet, 1993), pp. 334-35.

47. Jewett, *Jesus Against the Rapture*, pp. 15-33.

48. See Joachim Jeremias, *The Parables of Jesus*, tr. by S. H. Hooke, rev. ed. (New York: Charles Scribner's Sons, 1963), pp. 224-227.

49. See Robert H. Stein, *An Introduction to the Parables of Jesus* (Philadelphia: Westminster Press, 1981), pp. 144-45.

50. See Dale C. Allison and W. D. Davies, *A Critical and Exegetical Commentary on the Gospel According to Saint Matthew* (Edinburgh: T&T Clark, 1991), vol. 2, p. 414.

Notes to Chapter 12

1. Quoted in John W. Dower, *War Without Mercy: Race and Power in the Pacific War* (New York: Pantheon, 1986), p. 50.

2. Ibid., p. 247.

3. Ibid., pp. 40-41.

4. Ibid., pp. 64-65.

5. Martin Buber, *Good and Evil: Two Interpretations* (New York: Charles Scribner's Sons, 1952), p. 15.

6. Ibid., p. 19.

7. Peter Riede, *Im Netz des Jägers: Studien zur Feindmetaphorik der Individualpsalmen*, Wissenschaftliche Monographien zum Alten und Neuen Testament 85 (Neukirchen-Vluyn: Neukirchener Verlag, 2000).

8. Riede, *Im Netz des Jägers*, p. 129.

9. See John Shelton Lawrence and Robert Jewett, *The Myth of the American Superhero* (Grand Rapids: Eerdmans, 2002).

10. David E. Aune, *Revelation 6–16*, Word Biblical Commentary 52b (Nashville: Thomas Nelson, 1998), pp. 822-23.

11. See Aune, *Revelation 6–16,* pp. 406-10, for a discussion of parallels in the Old Testament and apocalyptic literature to this prayer for vengeance.

12. Josephine Massyngberde Ford, *Revelation,* The Anchor Bible 38 (Garden City, NY: Doubleday, 1975), p. 237, observes that the association between this torture and Jesus as the lamb (Rev. 14:10) "is embarrassing for the Christian."

13. For the historical background of the beastly metaphors applied to enemy countries, see Aune, *Revelation 6–16,* pp. 731-37.

14. See R. H. Charles, *A Critical and Exegetical Commentary on the Revelation of St. John* (New York: Charles Scribner's Sons, 1920), vol. 2, pp. 216ff.

15. Cited by Michael L. Walzer, *Revolution of the Saints* (Cambridge: Harvard University Press, 1965), p. 285.

16. Cited by Hans Kohn, *American Nationalism* (New York: Macmillan, 1957), p. 13.

17. Cited by Harry J. Carman and Harold C. Syrett, *A History of the American People* (New York: Knopf, 1952), vol. 1, p. 502.

18. *The American Magazine* (Aug., 1944), p. 1.

19. George W. Bush, "State of the Union Address," Jan. 20, 2002, <http://www.whitehouse.gov/news/releases/2002/01/20020129-11.html>, viewed Jan. 22, 2002.

20. A. Dale Tussig, "Education, Foreign Policy and the Popeye Syndrome," *Change Magazine* (Oct., 1971), p. 19.

21. Ibid.

22. See Lee Griffith, *The War on Terrorism and the Terror of God* (Grand Rapids: Eerdmans, 2002), pp. 100-101; Michael Barkun, "Introduction: Understanding Millennialism," in M. Barkun, ed., *Millennialism and Violence* (London: Frank Cass, 1999), p. 6: "In their dichotomized view of the world, only two domains exist; that of the pure, which they inhabit, and that of the impure, in which their adversaries dwell."

23. Stephen D. O'Leary, *Arguing the Apocalypse: A Theory of Millennial Rhetoric* (New York/Oxford: Oxford University Press, 1994), p. 190.

24. Cited in O'Leary, *Arguing the Apocalypse,* p. 191.

25. See Francis G. Hutchins, "Moralists Against Managers," *Atlantic* (July, 1969), p. 54.

26. Ann Coulter, "This is war; we should invade their countries," <http://www.nationalreview.com/coulter/coulter091301.shtml>, viewed Sept. 30, 2001.

27. Glenn Schloss and Mark O'Neill, "Cold War Crash Course," *South China Morning Post* (April 6, 2001), p. 15.

28. Schloss, *South China Morning Post,* p. 15.

29. See the account of Henry Chu, "Jiang's U.S.-Built Plane Is Reportedly Bugged," *Los Angeles Times* (Jan. 19, 2002), p. A7.

30. Roland Watson and Oliver August, "Diplomatic Row over U.S. Bugs in Chinese Plane," *Times* (Jan. 21, 2002).

31. *Sioux City Journal* (Nov. 13, 1967).

32. Cited in *I. F. Stone's Weekly* (Mar. 24, 1969).

33. Ibid.

34. Louis J. Halle, *The Cold War as History* (New York: Harper & Row, 1967), p. 209.

35. Cited by R. D. Challener and John Fenton, "Which Way America?" *American Heritage,* vol. 22, June 1971, p. 91.

36. Citations from presidential addresses printed in the *Des Moines Register* on April 22, 1970; May 2, 1970; April 28, 1972; and May 10, 1972.

37. For a discerning analysis of the political impact of dualistic thinking, see Thomas Flanagan, "The Politics of the Millennium," in M. Barkun, ed. *Millennialism and Violence,* Cass Series on Political Violence 2 (London/Portland: Frank Cass & Co. Ltd., 1999), pp. 171-72.

38. See, for example, the list of sabotage operations in Stanley Karnow, *Vietnam: A History* (New York: Viking Press, 1983), pp. 221-22, for Colonel Edward G. Landsdale's collaborations with Major Lucien Conein; activities included fake Vietminh documents, rumors about Chinese communists, contamination of fuel supplies, etc.

39. See *Pentagon Papers* (New York: Quadrangle, 1971), pp. 3, 53-66, 234-306.

40. Roger Warner, *Backfire: The CIA's Secret War in Laos and Its Link to the War in Vietnam* (New York: Simon and Schuster, 1995), p. 294.

41. Warner, *Backfire,* p. 295.

42. The U.S. Department of Census has not, as of this writing, released figures for the 2000 election. For elections back to 1972, the trend line is steadily downward. For the 1996 presidential elections, a mere 32.4% of eligible 18-24-year-olds voted; see Center for Voting and Democracy for trends in declining registration and turnout, <http://www.fairvote.org/turnout/youth_voters.htm>, viewed January 25, 2002.

43. William G. McLoughlin, "Pietism and the American Character," in H. Cohen, ed., *The American Experience* (Boston: Houghton Mifflin, 1968), p. 52.

44. Daniel Goleman, "A Torturer's Mind: Complex View Emerges," *New York Times* (May 14, 1985), pp. 19, 27.

45. Goleman, "A Torturer's Mind," p. 27.

46. Robert F. Drinan, "Anti-terrorism law is filled with dangers," *National Catholic Reporter* (October 26, 2001), p. 15.

47. See for example, details in Rene Sanchez, "Hate Crimes Against Muslims Nationwide Abate," *Washington Post* (Oct. 26, 2001), p. A2; for a New York–focused survey see Jacob H. Fries, "A Nation Challenged: Relations; Complaints of Anti-Arab Bias Crimes Dip, but Concerns Linger," *New York Times* (Dec. 22, 2001), p. B8.

48. Jack Shaheen, *The TV Arab* (Bowling Green, OH: Bowling Green State University Press, 1984), pp. 4-5.

49. Jack Shaheen, *Reel Bad Arabs: How Hollywood Vilifies a People* (Northampton, Mass.: Interlink Publishing, 2001).

50. Shaheen, *The TV Arab,* p. 12.

51. George W. Bush, "Remarks by the President at Signing of the Patriot Act, Anti-Terrorism Legislation" (Oct. 26, 2001) <http://www.whitehouse.gov/news/releases/2001/2011026-5.html>, viewed Nov. 5, 2001.

52. Dershowitz made his case on the CBS program "60 Minutes," January 20, 2002, and has also stated the position in "Want to torture? Get a warrant," *San Francisco Chronicle* (Jan. 22, 2002), p. A19; an overview of a series of calls for torture is contained in Vicki Haddock, "The Unspeakable," *San Francisco Chronicle* (Nov. 18, 2001), p. D1.

53. Cesare Beccaria, *On Crimes and Punishments,* tr. David Young (Indianapolis, IN: Hackett Publishing Co., 1986), p. 32.

54. See Robert Jewett, *Jesus Against the Rapture* (Philadelphia: Westminster, 1979), pp. 60-63, 124-29.

55. See Robert H. Stein, *An Introduction to the Parables of Jesus* (Philadelphia: Westminster, 1981), pp. 75-77.

56. See Josef Ernst, *Das Evangelium nach Lukas* (Regensburg: Friedrich Pustet, 1993), pp. 262-63.

57. See Robert Tannehill, *Luke,* Abingdon New Testament Commentaries (Nashville: Abingdon Press, 1996), p. 183.

58. Goleman, "A Torturer's Mind," p. 27.

59. Ibid.; the book cited is Elena O. Nightingale and Eric Stover, *The Breaking of Bodies and Minds: Torture, Psychiatric Abuse, and the Health Professions* (New York: W. H. Freeman, 1985).

60. See Jewett, *Jesus Against the Rapture,* pp. 124-42.

61. Cf. Oscar Cullmann, *Jesus and the Revolutionaries,* tr. by Gareth Putnam (New York: Harper & Row, 1970), pp. 82f., n. 11.

62. Ibid., p. 83, n. 14.

63. See Jürgen Becker, *Jesus of Nazareth* (New York: de Gruyter, 1998), pp. 252-53.

64. Donald A. Hagner, *Matthew 1–13,* Word Biblical Commentary 33a (Dallas: Word Book, 1993), p. 132: "Kingdom ethics demands not mechanical compliance to rules but a lifestyle governed by the free grace of God."

Notes to Chapter 13

1. St. Augustine, *Confessions.* tr. by R. S. Pine Coffin (Baltimore, MD: Penguin, 1961), book 6, part 8, pp. 122-23; cited by James B. Twitchell, *Preposterous Violence: Fables of Modern Aggression* (New York: Oxford University Press, 1989), p. 6.

2. See Martin Noth, *Exodus: A Commentary,* tr. by J. S. Bowden (Philadelphia: The Westminster Press, 1962), p. 121.

3. Harvey H. Guthrie, Jr., *Israel's Sacred Songs: A Study of Dominant Themes* (New York: Seabury Press, Inc., 1988), p. 130.

4. Johannes Pedersen, *Israel* (London: Oxford University Press, 1926), vols. 3-4, pp. 21-31.

5. A. Kuschke, "Jericho," *Die Religion in Geschichte and Gegenwart,* 3d ed. (Tübingen: J. C. B. Mohr [Paul Siebeck], 1957-1962), vol. 3, col. 591.

6. Edwin M. Good, "Peace in the OT," *The Interpreter's Dictionary of the Bible* (Nashville: Abingdon Press, 1962), vol. 3, p. 704.

7. See Pedersen, *Israel,* vols. 1-2, pp. 311-318; typical statements are Judg. 8:9; 2 Sam. 19:24, 30; 1 Kings 22:27f.; 1 Chron. 22:18; Jer. 43:12; Micah 5:5; Zech. 9:10.

8. Michael L. Walzer, *Revolution of the Saints* (Cambridge: Harvard University Press, 1965), pp. 278f.

9. *Annals of America,* vol. 18, p. 208.

10. Winthrop S. Hudson, ed., *Nationalism and Religion in America* (New York: Harper & Row, 1970), pp. 96-98.

11. John Eliot, *The Christian Commonwealth: or, the Civil Policy and the Rising Kingdom of Jesus Christ* (London, 1659).

12. See Ernest Lee Tuveson, *Redeemer Nation* (Chicago: University of Chicago Press, 1968), p. 105.

13. R. Pierce Beaver, "Missionary Motivation Through Three Centuries," in *Reinterpretation in American Church History*, ed. by Jerald C. Brauer (Chicago: The University of Chicago Press, 1968), p. 121.

14. Cited in Beaver, "Missionary Motivation," pp. 137f.

15. Hudson, *Nationalism*, p. 115.

16. Hans Kohn, *American Nationalism* (New York: Macmillan, 1957), p. 183.

17. Langdon B. Gilkey, *Shantung Compound: The Story of Men and Women Under Pressure* (New York: Harper & Row, 1966), pp. 181f.

18. Cited by Roy Harvey Pearce, *The Savages of America: A Study of the Indian and the Idea of Civilization* (Baltimore: Johns Hopkins Press, 1965; rev. ed.), p. 23.

19. Robert F. Berkhofer, *Salvation and the Savage: An Analysis of Protestant Missions and American Indian Response, 1787-1882* (Lexington: University of Kentucky Press, 1965), p. 15.

20. Ray A. Billington and James B. Hedges, *Westward Expansion: A History of the American Frontier* (New York: Macmillan, 1949), p. 572.

21. Tuveson, *Redeemer Nation*, pp. 191, 196.

22. Ibid., pp. 203f.

23. Michael A. Bellesiles, *Arming America: The Origins of a National Gun Culture* (New York: Vintage Books, 2000), p. 429.

24. Ibid., p. 379.

25. Ibid., p. 430.

26. Albert K. Weinberg, *Manifest Destiny* (Baltimore: John Hopkins University Press, 1935), p. 285.

27. Walter Millis, *Martial Spirit*, 2nd ed. (New York: Viking, 1965), p. 38.

28. Cited by William Fulbright, "Violence in the American Character," *Annals of America*, vol. 18, p. 209.

29. Franklin Delano Roosevelt, "The Spirit of Man Has Awakened," *Think Magazine's Diary of the U.S. Participation in World War II*, ed. by E. F. Hacket (New York, 1946), p. 320.

30. Harry S. Truman, "I Call upon All Americans," ibid., p. 337.

31. Francis Vivian Drake, "Bomb Germany — and Save a Million American Lives," *Reader's Digest* (July, 1943), pp. 89-92.

32. See H. Bruce Franklin, *War Stars: The Superweapon and the American Imagination* (New York: Oxford University Press, 1988) for a history of America's fascination with technology as a means of responding to even the most complex of social and political issues.

33. John Ford, "The Morality of Obliteration Bombing," *Theological Studies* (1944), pp. 261-309.

34. Louis J. Halle, *The Cold War as History* (New York: Harper & Row, 1967), p. 92.

35. "Radio Report to the American People on the Potsdam Conference, August 9, 1945," *Public Papers of the Presidents, Harry S. Truman*, April 12 to December 31, 1945. Washington, D.C.: U.S. Government Printing Office, pp. 212-213.

36. Sidney J. Slomich, "The Myths and Mores of Nuclear Weaponry," *San Francisco Sunday Examiner and Chronicle* (July 28, 1968), p. 19.

37. According to the Center for Defense Information, the proposed U.S. military budget for 2003 — at the $396 billion level, is "six times larger than that of Russia, the second largest spender." Moreover, "it is more than 26 times as large as the combined spending of the seven nations traditionally identified by the Pentagon as our most likely adversaries (Cuba, Iran, Iraq, Libya, North Korea, Sudan and Korea)." Overall, "the budget exceeds that of the next 25 nations combined." Christopher Hellman, "The Pentagon's Fiscal Year 2003 Budget Request: More of Everything," *The Defense Monitor* (Feb., 2002), p. 4.

38. See the articles by Seumas Milne, "The innocent dead in a coward's war," *The Guardian* (Dec. 20, 2001), and Robert Jensen and Rahul Mahajan, "We can't just forget about dead Afghan civilians," *Houston Chronicle* (Dec. 20, 2001), Section: Viewpoints, Outlook, both of which evaluate the statistical work of Prof. Marc Herold of the University of New Hampshire, who released his finding that at least 3,767 civilians had died in the first two months of the war.

39. Heribert Prantl, "Infinite Punishment," *Süddeutsche Zeitung* (Sept. 18, 2001); reprinted in translation, *World Press Review* (Dec., 2001), p. 10.

40. Jürgen Todenhöfer, "Ein mit Dollars beladener Esel kommt weiter als jede Armee," *Süddeutsche Zeitung* (Dec. 29-30, 2001), p. 14.

41. "U.S. Misled by Afghans? Bombs Kill 65 in Convoy," *International Herald Tribune* (December 22-23, 2000), p. 3.

42. See James Luther Mays, *Hosea: A Commentary* (Philadelphia: Westminster Press, 1969), p. 147.

43. The slight change in style between verse 13a and verse 13b may indicate two separate oracles were joined here by later editors, but both appear to be genuine, and the substantial congruence in thought makes it feasible to consider them together. See Mays, *Hosea*, p. 148.

44. Mays, *Hosea*, pp. 90f.

45. See H. Wheeler Robinson, "Hosea," *The Abingdon Bible Commentary*, ed. by F. C. Eiselen et al. (Nashville: Abingdon Press, 1929), p. 759.

46. See Mays, *Hosea*, p. 28.

47. See Bellesiles, *Arming America*, pp. 434-40, for an account of the popularization of murder that followed the Civil War, with its drastic increase in the availability of guns that were perceived as agents of redemption. Details of Bellesiles' documentation on gun ownership have been seriously challenged by some critics, but we suspect that his account of emerging ideological trends in the public and the associated criminal behavior remains valid.

48. Mays, *Hosea*, p. 64.

49. Ibid., p. 65.

50. Ibid., p. 80.

51. George F. Kennan, *Memoirs: 1925-1950* (New York: Little, Brown & Co., 1967), p. 365.

52. Donald McDonald, "Militarism in America," *The Center Magazine*, vol. 3, no. 1 (1970), p. 29.

53. See Mays, *Hosea*, p. 160.

54. Ibid., p. 161.

55. Estimating the scale of civilian losses in the Indochinese wars has always been contentious, not least because the U.S. wished to minimize negative publicity. The lowest numbers for civilians killed in Vietnam alone are 365,000, consisting of 300,000 in the South and 65,000 in the North. Colonel Harry Summers, Jr. cites these numbers in his *Vietnam War Almanac* (New York: Facts on File, 1985), p. 112, with the comment that "the totals will probably never be known." See also Guenter Lewy, *America in Vietnam* (New York: Oxford University Press, 1978), who uses identical totals and provides a careful discussion of difficulties in compiling totals. A much larger assessment, which includes casualties as well as deaths, comes from Ngo Vinh Long, "Vietnamese Perspectives," in Stanley Kutler, ed. *Encyclopedia of the Vietnam War* (New York: Scribner's, 1996): "The war in Vietnam primarily — and most heavily — affected the Vietnamese people, north and south. . . . According to conservative estimates, about 4 million Vietnamese on all sides were killed, wounded, or missing during the 1965-1975 period alone. The Pentagon's final estimate of civilian casualties for the South, a nation of about 18 million in 1972, was as high as 1,225,000 for the period between 1965 and 1972. A U.S. Senate subcommittee report estimated 1,350,000 civilian casualties, including 415,000 killed, for the same period. "Enemy soldiers" killed were at least 850,000, according to both estimates. A substantial number of these "enemy soldiers," however, were civilians whom the U.S. military defined as "enemy" because they were within free-fire zones, areas controlled by the National Liberation Front (NLF). Estimates of casualties suffered by the Republic of Vietnam Armed Forces ran from 300,000 to 500,000. During the "post-war" of 1973-1975, another half a million Vietnamese were killed and wounded — 340,000 of them were civilians — according to the U.S. and South Vietnamese estimates" (p. 591). To this must be added the casualties of Laos and Cambodia, as well as the cratered and toxic landscapes, the orphans, the disabled, the prostitutes, etc.

56. Spencer Tucker, ed., *Encyclopedia of the Vietnam War: A Political, Social and Military History* (Santa Barbara, CA: ABC/Clio, 1998), pp. 589-90.

57. Mark Moyar, *Phoenix and the Birds of Prey: The CIA's Secret Campaign to Destroy the Viet Cong* (Annapolis: Naval Institute Press, 1997), pp. 231-32.

58. Richard Wasserstrom, "The Laws of War," *The Monist*, vol. 106 (Jan., 1972), p. 12.

59. *Des Moines Register* (Feb. 8, 1968).

60. James D. Smart, "Hosea," *The Interpreter's Dictionary of the Bible*, vol. 2, p. 652.

61. See Robert Jewett, *Jesus Against the Rapture* (Philadelphia: Westminster, 1979), pp. 122-42.

Notes to Chapter 14

1. Richard Nixon, "Address to the American People," April 30, 1970. *Public Papers of the Presidents of the United States: Richard Nixon, 1970*, pp. 405-409.

2. Dana Milbank, "Religious Right Finds Its Center in Oval Office," *Washington Post* (Dec. 24, 2001), p. A2.

3. D. W. Brogan, "Americans: 'Short Distance' Crusaders," *Des Moines Register* (Oct. 29, 1967).

4. David L. Larson, "Objectivity, Propaganda, and the Puritan Ethic," in *The Puritan Ethic in United States Foreign Policy,* David L. Larson, ed. (New York: D. Van Nostrand Company, Inc., 1966), p. 23; italics in original.

5. See Gerhard von Rad, *Der heilige Krieg im alten Israel,* 2nd ed. (Göttingen: Vandenhoeck & Ruprecht, 1965), pp. 7-9, for a complete list.

6. Johannes Pedersen, *Israel* (London: Oxford University Press, 1926), vols. 3-4, p. 15.

7. See von Rad, *Der heilige Krieg,* p. 31.

8. See Robert H. Pfeiffer, *Introduction to the Old Testament,* rev. ed. (New York: Harper & Brothers, 1948), p. 186.

9. See Steven L. McKinzie, "Deuteronomistic History," *Anchor Bible Dictionary,* Vol. 2 (1992), pp. 160-68.

10. Cited in Conrad Cherry, ed. *God's New Israel: Religious Interpretations of American Destiny* (Englewood Cliffs: Prentice-Hall, 1971), p. 43.

11. Ibid., p. 81.

12. Ibid., p. 83.

13. Ibid., p. 98.

14. Ibid., p. 100.

15. Cited by Henry F. May, *Protestant Churches and Industrial America* (New York: Harper & Row, 1967), p. 69.

16. Cherry, *God's New Israel,* p. 239.

17. Cherry, *God's New Israel,* p. 246.

18. From *Pentagon Papers,* noted by David Halberstam, *The Best and the Brightest* (New York: Random House, 1972), p. 515.

19. *International Herald Tribune* (Jan. 25, 1973).

20. *International Herald Tribune* (Jan. 25, 1973).

21. Francine du Plessix Gray, "The Moral Consequences: Landlords in Eden," *Saturday Review of the Society* (Dec., 1972), p. 78.

22. Andreas Dorpalen, *Hindenburg and the Weimar Republic* (Princeton: Princeton University Press, 1964), p. 51.

23. D. W. Brogan, "The Illusion of American Omnipotence," *Harper's Magazine* (Dec. 1952), pp. 21-28.

24. Dwight D. Eisenhower, *Peace with Justice: Selected Addresses* (New York: Columbia University Press, 1961), p. 32.

25. Eisenhower, *Peace with Justice,* p. 28.

26. Deane and David Heller, *John Foster Dulles* (New York: Holt, Rinehart & Winston, 1960), p. 239.

27. Edward L. R. Elson, *America's Spiritual Recovery* (Grand Rapids, MI: Fleming H. Revell Company, 1954), p. 135.

28. Elson, *America's Spiritual Recovery,* Dedication.

29. Richard M. Nixon, *Setting the Course: The First Year: Major Policy Statements by President Richard Nixon, with commentaries by Richard Wilson* (New York: Funk & Wagnalls Company, 1970), pp. 5-7.

30. Ibid., pp. 28-30.

31. Martin Buber, *The Prophetic Faith,* tr. by Carlyle Witton Davies (New York: The Macmillan Company, 1949), pp. 170f.

32. See 2 Chron. 35:1-19 for the account of the elaborate Passover Josiah staged just prior to his demise; for the official, Deuteronomic explanation for Josiah's defeat, see 2 Kings 23:26f.

33. Nixon's speech of Nov. 3, 1969, in *Setting the Course*, p. 28.

34. S. MacLean Gilmour, "The Gospel of Luke," *Interpreter's Bible* (Nashville: Abingdon Press, 1951-1957), vol. 8, p. 239; William Barclay, *The Gospel of Luke*, 2d ed. (Philadelphia: The Westminster Press, 1956), p. 177.

35. Eduard Schweizer, *The Good News According to Luke*, tr. D. E. Green (Atlanta: John Knox Press, 1973), p. 219; see also Wolfgang Wiefel, *Das Evangelium nach Lukas* (Berlin: Evangelische Verlagsanstalt, 1988), p. 253; Josef Ernst, *Das Evangelium nach Lukas*, (Regensburg: Friedrich Pustet, 1993), p. 312.

36. See Ernst, *Lukas*, p. 312.

37. Second Annual Message to Congress, Dec. 1, 1882, cited from *Abraham Lincoln, Speeches and Writings*, ed. by R. P. Basler (New York: World Publishing Co., 1946), p. 688.

38. Cited by Robert Penn Warren, *Legacy of the Civil War* (New York: Random House, 1961), p. 107.

39. Bernhard W. Anderson, *Understanding the Old Testament* (Engelwood Cliffs, NJ: Prentice-Hall, Inc., 1957), p. 248.

Notes to Chapter 15

1. Henry Steele Commager, ed. *Living Ideas in America* (New York: Harper, 1951), p. 500.

2. Eisenhower statement from U.S. Government Info/Resources Web site, "Pledge of Allegiance," <http://usgovinfo.about.com/blpledge.htm>, viewed Jan. 15, 2002. The discussion of the flag issues in this chapter is adapted from Robert Jewett and Constance Collora, "Our flag should be honored, not held as sacred," *The United Methodist Reporter* (September 2, 1995), and "Guest Editorial: On Turning the Flag into a Sacred Object," *The Journal of Church and State* (Autumn, 1995), pp. 741-52.

3. Commager, *Living Ideas*, p. 499.

4. See Samuel Eliot Morison, *The Oxford History of the American People* (New York: Oxford University Press, 1965), p. 68.

5. Details from Martin E. Marty, *Modern American Religion*, vol. 3, *Under God, Indivisible, 1941-1960* (Chicago: University of Chicago Press, 1996), p. 301. Marty provides an extensive account of the anti-communist political and religious rhetoric that foreshadowed this moment of flag sacralization, pp. 298-301.

6. For details on these sacralizations, see Deane William Ferm, "Religious Thought Since World War II," Charles H. Lippey and Peter W. Williams, eds. *Encyclopedia of American Religious Experience: Studies of Traditions and Movements* (New York: Charles Scribner's Sons, 1988), vol. 2, p. 1159; see also Donald G. Jones, "Civic and Public Religion," vol. 3, p. 1405.

7. Richard Quebedeaux, "Conservative and Charismatic Developments of the Later Twentieth Century," in Lippey and Williams, *Encyclopedia*, vol. 2, p. 963.

8. See Jerry Bergman, "The modern religious objection to flag salute in America: a

history and evaluation," *Journal of Church and State* (Spring 1997), pp. 215-236, for a review of the theological stances of dissenting churches and the resulting persecutions.

9. 1989 Flag Protection Statute (18 U.S.C. 700, 1996). It passed by margins of a 91-9 vote in the Senate and a 380-38 vote in the House.

10. "Pledge of Allegiance goes national today," *Atlanta Constitution* (Oct. 12, 2001), p. E7.

11. "God makes a comeback in the classroom," *Washington Times* (Oct. 20, 2001).

12. Maj. Gen. Patrick Brady, "Letters," *Chicago Sun-Times* (Oct. 30, 2001), p. 30.

13. Robert Justin Goldstein, *Saving Old Glory* (Boulder, CO: Westview, 1995), pp. 1-2.

14. Goldstein, *Saving Old Glory,* p. 6.

15. Robert Justin Goldstein, *Flag Burning and Free Speech* (Lawrence, KS: University Press of Kansas, 2000), pp. 6-7.

16. Ibid., pp. 14-15.

17. Ibid., p. 14.

18. Ibid., p. 20.

19. Ibid., p. 30.

20. Ibid., p. 22.

21. Ibid., p. xv.

22. This was the language of House Resolution 36 and Senate Resolution 7 during the 107th Congress of 2001.

23. Young citation at *Congressional Record* (June 28, 1995) H 6435; Roth at H 6442.

24. Representative Kleczka, *Congressional Record,* H 6435.

25. Representative Solomon, *Congressional Record,* H 6404.

26. Representative Bryant, *Congressional Record,* H 6436.

27. See, for example, the *Oxford Latin Dictionary:* "consecrated to a deity, hallowed" and "to confer with sacred authority."

28. There are significant scholarly resources that could be of help to the religious community in evaluating of this issue. Rudolf Otto's classic, *The Idea of the Holy,* and the work of Mircea Eliade, such as *The Sacred and the Profane: The Nature of Religion,* are possible scholarly starting points. It is interesting to note that legal scholar Sheldon Nahmod drew on the work of both Otto and Eliade in his law review article on "The Sacred Flag and the First Amendment," *Indiana Law Journal* 66 (1991). A few articles have appeared in religious periodicals that deal with the theological dimensions of the flag issue. James E. Wood, Jr. reviewed the legal status of the flag in a strongly cautionary editorial published in the *Journal of Church and State,* in which he warned that "to make sacred a nation's flag is idolatry" ("Making a Nation's Flag a Sacred Symbol," Aug. 1989, pp. 375-380). Harvard Law Professor Mary Ann Glendon, writing in *First Things,* described the impact of the flag issue on the civil religion ("Reflections on the Flag-Burning Case," March 1990, pp. 11-13). Also in *First Things,* William Johnson Everett warned that the flag amendment would insert an element of coercion in the American civil religion and erode the "transcendence in terms of which governments themselves must be judged" ("The Flag Amendment Is a Religious Issue," Dec. 1990, p. 8). Reversing his earlier position, James M. Wall now opposes the word "desecration" in the amendment "Flag-burning revisited," *The Christian Century* [July 19-26, 1995], p. 699).

29. Nahmod, "The Sacred Flag," pp. 511ff.

30. Nahmod, "The Sacred Flag," p. 535.

31. Ibid., p. 533.

32. Ibid., p. 548.

33. Salman Rushdie, *The Satanic Verses* (New York: Viking, 1988), p. 120.

34. Carter statement in M. M. Ahsan and A. R. Kidwai, eds. *Sacrifice versus Civility: Muslim Perspective on the Satanic Verses Affair* (Leicester, UK: The Islamic Foundation, 1991), p. 90; Dummett statement appears on p. 99.

35. The chronology of protests can be found in several books, among them M. M. Ahsan and A. R. Kidwai, eds., *Sacrifice versus Civility*, pp. 9-24; see also Carmel Bedford, *Fiction, Fact and the Fatwa: 2,000 Days of Censorship* (Article 19, The International Center Against Censorship, 1994), passim.

36. Bedford, *Fact, Fiction, and the Fatwa*, p. 1.

37. Ibid., p. 5.

38. Both cases of murder listed in Bedford, *Fact, Fiction, and the Fatwa*, p. 66.

39. Bedford, *Fact, Fiction, and the Fatwa*, p. 84.

40. Letter from Gen. Colin Powell to Sen. Patrick Leahy, May 18, 1999. Posted by American Society of Newspaper Editors, <http://www.asne.org/ideas/flagpowell.htm>, viewed Jan. 5, 2002.

41. Marty, *Under God, Indivisible, 1941-1960*, p. 273.

42. Barbara Grizzuti Harrison, *Visions of Glory: A History and a Memory of Jehovah's Witnesses* (New York: Simon and Schuster, 1978), p. 283.

43. Cited in ibid., p. 284.

44. Cited in ibid., p. 291.

45. Walter Dietrich, "Deuteronomistisches Geschichtswerk," *Religion in Geschichte und Gegenwart*, 4th ed. (Tübingen: Mohr Siebeck, 1999), vol. 2, p. 691; see also G. N. Knoppers, *Two Nations Under God*, Harvard Semitic Monographs 52-53 (Cambridge: Harvard University Press, 1993-94).

46. Keith W. Whitelam, "Jeroboam," *Anchor Bible Dictionary* (New York: Doubleday, 1992), vol. 3, p. 746.

47. See T. R. Hobbs, "Jehoahaz," *Anchor Bible Dictionary* (New York: Doubleday, 1992), vol. 3, p. 659.

48. John M. Berredge, "Jehoiachin," *Anchor Bible Dictionary* (New York: Doubleday, 1992), vol. 3, p. 662.

49. See Robert Althann, "Zedekiah," *Anchor Bible Dictionary* (New York: Doubleday, 1992), vol. 6, pp. 1069-70.

50. David Wenham, "Abomination of Desolation," *Anchor Bible Dictionary* (New York: Doubleday, 1992), vol. 1, p. 29.

51. Ibid., p. 30.

52. Martin Hengel, *The Zealots* (Edinburgh: T&T Clark, 1989), section 4D.

53. For an account of scholarly debate on these texts, see David Wenham, "Abomination of Desolation," *Anchor Bible Dictionary* (New York: Doubleday, 1992), vol. 1, pp. 29-31; also David Wenham, *The Rediscovery of Jesus' Eschatological Discourse* (Sheffield: Sheffield Academic Press, 1984).

Notes to Chapter 16

1. Letter of Instruction to American Ambassador T. F. Bayard in London from Secretary of State Richard Olney, 20 July, 1895 in Thomas G. Paterson, ed. *Major Problems in American Foreign Policy,* Vol. 1, *To 1914* (Lexington, Mass.: D. C. Heath, 1989), pp. 350-353.

2. Speech at Springfield, Illinois, 1857, cited by Harry V. Jaffa, *Crisis of the House Divided* (Garden City, NY: Doubleday, 1959), p. 316.

3. James Chace, "American Jingoism," *Harper's* (May, 1976), p. 44.

4. See R. B. Y. Scott, "Isaiah," *The Interpreter's Bible,* (Nashville: Abingdon, 1951-57), vol. 5, pp. 232, 249.

5. Ibid., p. 249.

6. Ibid., p. 180.

7. See Norman K. Gottwald, *All the Kingdoms of the Earth: Israelite Prophecy and International Relations in the Ancient Near East* (New York: Harper & Row, 1964), p. 202.

8. Even Lee Griffith's excellent book, *The War on Terrorism and the Terror of God* (Grand Rapids: Eerdmans, 2002), recommends hope in non-violence (pp. 277-78) but overlooks the prophetic vision of lawful conflict resolution that is the essential framework for any successful campaign of love.

9. Daniel Patrick Moynihan, *On the Law of Nations* (Cambridge: Harvard University Press, 1990).

10. Ibid., p. 19.

11. Ibid. p. 99.

12. Ibid, p. 147.

13. Ibid., p. 144.

14. Hwang Yawnghwe, speaking for Aung San Suu Kyi in a consultation at the University of Virginia, in Jeffrey Hopkins, ed. *The Art of Peace: Nobel Peace Laureates Discuss Human Rights, Conflict and Reconciliation* (Ithaca: Snow Lion Publications, 2000), p. 151.

15. "Remarks by the President and Chairman of the Afghan Interim Authority Hamid Karzai, The Rose Garden," White House Press Release, Jan. 28, 2002.

16. Katharine O. Seelye, "Powell splits from Bush over status of prisoners," *San Francisco Chronicle* (Jan. 27, 2002), pp. A1, 20; the article originally appeared in the *New York Times.*

17. Robert O. Keohane, "The United Nations: An Essential Instrument against Terror" (Oct. 1, 2001), <http://www.duke.edu/web/forums/keohane.html>, viewed Jan. 25, 2002.

18. Ibid.

19. Ibid.

20. George F. Kennan, "After the Cold War: American Foreign Policy in the 1970s," *Foreign Affairs,* vol. 51 (Oct., 1972), p. 227.

Index of Names and Subjects

Index of Ancient Texts